Richard and Cosima Wagner

Richard and Cosima Wagner

Biography of a Marriage

by

Geoffrey Skelton

BOSTON
HOUGHTON MIFFLIN COMPANY
1982

Library of Congress Cataloging in Publication Data

Skelton, Geoffrey.
Richard and Cosima Wagner.

Bibliography: p.
Includes index.
1. Wagner, Richard, 1813-1883. 2. Composers—
Germany—Biography. 3. Wagner, Cosima, 1837-1930.
I. Title.

ML410.W1S43	782.1'092'2 [B]	82-1000
ISBN 0-395-31836-X		AACR2

Printed in the United States of America

V 10 9 8 7 6 5 4 3 2 1

Contents

List of Illustrations

Following page 240

Villa d'Angri, Naples

Malwida von Meysenbug

Paul Joukowsky

Auguste Renoir's portrait of Wagner, painted in Palermo in 1882 (*reproduced by permission of Musées Nationaux, Paris*)

King Ludwig II of Bavaria

Carl Friedrich Glasenapp, Hans von Wolzogen and Heinrich von Stein

Hermann Levi

Count Arthur Gobineau

Wagner with family and friends outside the *salon* in Wahnfried: Blandine, Heinrich von Stein, Cosima, Daniela, Wagner, Siegfried, Isolde, Eva, Paul Joukowsky

All illustrations, unless otherwise stated, are reproduced by permission of the Richard-Wagner-Gedenkstätte and the Nationalarchiv Richard Wagner Stiftung in Bayreuth.

Introduction

The recent publication in full of Richard Wagner's *Brown Book* and of Cosima Wagner's *Diaries* has provided an opportunity to take a fresh look at one of the most significant relationships in musical history. Neither the *Brown Book* nor the *Diaries* were entirely unknown previously, for both Wagner's and Cosima's official biographers (Carl Friedrich Glasenapp and Richard Graf Du Moulin Eckart respectively) were given the privilege of seeing them long before publication. However, in the nature of things they made only selective use of them. In addition, Wagner's and Cosima's daughter Eva took it on herself to block out in both manuscripts certain passages which she thought unsuitable for public consumption. These passages have now been restored. If they add little or nothing to our factual knowledge, they do at least enable us to form a clearer picture of the human implications. And in this connection the recent discovery and publication of a few letters exchanged between Wagner and Cosima – presumably the only ones that escaped burning on her instructions – have also been of significance.

Besides taking advantage of the new material, I have aimed in this book to provide an account of Wagner (during at least one section of his life) that is neither sycophantic in the earlier manner nor censorious in the style of some later biographers, preferring to let the protagonists speak wherever possible for themselves. At this distance of time I feel it should be possible to abandon the tone of moral outrage and try instead to look on the facts of his life with understanding. For that reason I have paid rather more attention than is usual to his articles and essays, as well as to his letters, for they are often as revealing about his character and outlook as any of his deeds.

A small amount of newly published material concerning King Ludwig II of Bavaria and Judith Gautier has enabled me to see their relationships with Wagner and Cosima in a somewhat clearer light, and Cosima's own entries in her diaries reveal much about those other important figures in their lives – her father, Franz Liszt, and her first husband, Hans von Bülow – that substantially alters the picture as it previously appeared. Much that is tantalising about the latter still remains, though I have found in various publications, now out of print, documents which, brought together, help to provide better explanations of the break-up of Cosima's first marriage than the superficial assertion that "Wagner stole his best friend's wife".

My own researches in the Wahnfried archives in Bayreuth have produced a few new items of varying importance which I have incorporated in my book. For permission to use these, and for his kind help in general, I am much indebted to the director of the archives, Dr Manfred Eger. The published books and articles of which I have made use in writing my book are listed in the bibliography at the back, and to the authors, editors, publishers and copyright holders of these I here express my gratitude. The translations from German and French texts are mainiy my own.

GEOFFREY SKELTON

Richard and Cosima Wagner

CHAPTER I

OCTOBER 1853 – NOVEMBER 1863:

The Beginnings

"I SEE IN my mind once more my parting from Hans, my stay in Augsburg with the two girls, embarking on the ship, the stars, which Loldi noticed, the single light illuminating the dense black night in my heart as I watched over the children in the ship and gazed rigidly and numbly into the unveiled countenance of my destiny. That night was the womb of all my blessings, annihilating all pretence – a holy night, awesome in its acknowledgement of original sin, the silent prophet of love's redeeming power!"

With these words, written in her diary ten years later, Cosima described her feelings on 16 November 1868 when, at the age of thirty, she left her husband Hans von Bülow and joined Richard Wagner at Tribschen, his house beside the Lake of Lucerne in Switzerland. From that time until Wagner's death in 1883 they were never separated for more than a few days.

Cosima's decision was no impulsive one. Her two younger daughters, Isolde (Loldi) and Eva, whom she took with her to Tribschen, were Wagner's children, and, at the time of her flight from Munich, she was already pregnant with his third child. Her marriage to Hans von Bülow had been little more than nominal for at least four years, and the chief aim in maintaining it had been to keep the support, financial and artistic, of the young king of Bavaria, Ludwig II, Bülow's sponsor as well as Wagner's. There was bound, however, to come a moment when the pretence would have to be dropped, and it would certainly have come much earlier but for the idealism and innocence of the young king, who refused to listen to the gossip which was current in Munich almost from the very beginning of Wagner's association with that city.

Officially, when Cosima left Munich with her two younger daughters, she had gone to Versailles to visit her stepsister Claire Charnacé, and her two elder daughters, Daniela and Blandine, remained in Munich with Bülow, their father. For the first months of her life in Tribschen she did not leave the house at all, since nobody was supposed to know that she was there. Even Bülow, who did know, was apparently unaware that she was expecting another child. It was the birth of this child, Siegfried, on

6 June 1869, that put an end to the last lingering doubts. Bülow consented to a divorce, and on 25 August 1870, in the Protestant church in Lucerne, Cosima von Bülow, the daughter of Franz Liszt, became Cosima Wagner.

Without this marriage the world would possibly never have seen the final products of Wagner's genius which emerged in its course: the completion of *Der Ring des Nibelungen*, the building of the festival theatre in Bayreuth, the composition of *Parsifal*. Cosima's contribution was far more than that of providing Wagner with a settled family existence in which to pursue his work, though that in itself was an important factor; she was also his active assistant in all his undertakings. What she had attempted to do for Bülow in the early years of their marriage, economising in her housekeeping in order to help finance his concerts, writing in secret the libretto for an opera he wished to compose on the subject of Merlin and presenting it to him as a surprise Christmas present – such things she did for Wagner too. But the reaction was different. Bülow had feelings of inferiority towards his wife: he felt her to be intellectually above him and possessed of a will far stronger than his own. His sense of inadequacy towards her sometimes expressed itself in savage sarcasm, which she found deeply wounding.

Wagner had no inhibitions of this kind. He acknowledged no intellectual superiors and accepted Cosima's deference as no more than his right. And, because of this, he found no difficulty in being generous. His frequent words of praise and of love, each one gratefully recorded in her diary, gave her the feeling of being needed and enabled her to repress, almost ecstatically, the stirrings of self-will inside her. If she had the urge to dominate, it was not over her husband, but in his service. The spirit of self-sacrifice was very strong in her, and in this she was the true daughter of Franz Liszt, whose willingness to give his help to fellow musicians, from the humblest young pianist to composers of the stature of Berlioz and Wagner, is legendary. And it might be seen as the desire to help that first attracted Cosima to Hans von Bülow.

The second of Liszt's three children by his mistress, the French countess Marie d'Agoult, she was born on Christmas Day 1837, and brought up in Paris with her sister Blandine and brother Daniel by their widowed grandmother, Anna Liszt. Liszt himself, after his final break with Marie d'Agoult in 1844, travelled around Europe giving piano recitals, and his children seldom saw him. Even after his decision in 1847 to abandon his pianistic career and to settle down in Weimar as court musical director with his new mistress, the Polish-born Princess Carolyne von Sayn-Wittgenstein, his children saw little of him. Princess Carolyne was more concerned with promoting Liszt's career as a composer than with making a home for him and his family.

And so they remained in Paris, first with their homely grandmother, then – in order to improve their social graces – with Princess Carolyne's former Russian governess, the aged Madame Patersi de Fossombroni, who was sent to Paris especially to look after the two girls together with her sister, Madame Saint-Mars, who already lived there. It was part of the duties of these two strict but not unkind ladies to ensure that the children were kept at a distance from their mother, who, now enjoying a considerable reputation as a writer under the pseudonym of Daniel Stern, lived close by in the Champs Elysées.

The effect on Blandine, Cosima and Daniel of knowing themselves to be the children of two celebrities, neither of whom showed much desire for their company, was profound. Deprived of normal parental affection, they formed strong emotional attachments with each other, seeing themselves as creatures apart, as indeed they were, for they appear to have had no friends of any significance to them. Even their grandmother, after the arrival of Madame Patersi, was kept away from them as much as possible. When eventually their mother began to show some interest in them, Liszt became alarmed. Encouraged by Princess Carolyne, he decided in 1855 to remove them from Paris, but not to his own home in Weimar. Instead, he put Blandine and Cosima in the charge of a friend, Franziska von Bülow, who, recently divorced from her husband, was living in some penury in Berlin with her son Hans, a former pupil of Liszt, and her daughter Isa. Daniel, at boarding school in Paris, was allowed to continue his studies there, but he spent his holidays in Weimar with his father or in Berlin with his sisters.

The emotional disturbances of this upheaval affected them all, and the ugliest aspects of it are seen in the parents' letters to their children. "You will be eating the bread of a strange woman," Marie d'Agoult wrote to Blandine on 15 August 1855, "who is not your father's wife and will never become so." This was apparently a reference to Princess Carolyne. "I would sooner see you earning your own living or begging than this final humiliation," she continued.

Liszt, on hearing of this letter, retaliated with one no less inconsiderate of his children's feelings: "From your birth to this day your mother has never troubled herself in the slightest about the bread you eat, the place you live in, etc. Although she has always enjoyed a considerable income, she has nevertheless thought it right to reserve this entirely for her own personal comforts, and for the past nineteen years to leave to me exclusively the task of providing for all your needs and paying for your education." Princess Carolyne also complained that she was being made to feel like a stranger. Anna Liszt alone showed some regard for the children's susceptibilities when she wrote to her son on 3 September 1855: "But, my dear child, think what it means, giving these children into the care of a fourth person, in a strange country where they know nobody. This is certainly not a matter of indifference to them, and I fear, if this happens, that one or the other of them will fall ill. . . . They are good children and must be treated with love, for they have very sensitive hearts. . . . Think again, I beg you.''

Liszt, though he loved his mother, was not in the habit of listening to her. Blandine and Cosima, then aged nineteen and seventeen respectively, were sent to live with Frau von Bülow, and her son Hans, at Liszt's request, took on the task of giving them piano lessons.

Bülow was twenty-five years old, and he earned a modest existence teaching the piano at the Stern Conservatory in Berlin. Occasionally he conducted concerts there, devoting his attention mainly to the music of Wagner and Liszt, both regarded in Berlin as dangerous modernists. At a concert on 19 October 1855 he was hissed after conducting Wagner's *Tannhäuser* Overture, and was so affected by the experience that he fainted in his dressing-room. Cosima, who had been present, suggested to his mother that they should wait up until he returned home, in order to console him, but Frau von Bülow saw no reason for any such gesture. When Bülow reached home at two in the morning, he found Cosima awaiting him alone.

This little act of sympathy led eventually to his request to Liszt, in November 1855, for permission to woo his daughter. It was not a question of mutual physical attraction but, on her side, a desire to find a recipient for that loving urge to help which had so far in her life been disdained. On Bülow's side there was certainly gratitude for the kind of sympathy he was not accustomed to receive, on an emotional level, from his somewhat domineering mother, but also doubt whether he was worthy to receive it. He wrote to Jessie Laussot on 13 June 1856, after he had become unofficially engaged to Cosima, about Liszt's two daughters: ''These wonderful girls have every right to their name – full of talent, wit and life, they are interesting personalities such as I seldom meet. A man other than myself would be happy to be with them. I am inhibited by their obvious superiority, and the impossibility of making myself sufficiently interesting to them prevents me from enjoying the pleasure of their company as much as I should like. There you have a confession whose frankness you will appreciate. For a young man it is not flattering, but utterly true.''

He had already shown something of the same diffidence in a letter that he wrote on 20 April 1856 to Liszt, whose first reaction to Bülow's interest in Cosima was to treat the matter lightly, owing to his daughter's tender age: ''Will you be kind enough to accept without a disbelieving smile my admission that it is due only to a certain inborn shyness, a certain difficulty in expressing myself that has often been my downfall, that I have not spoken to you before of my love for your daughter Cosima. What I feel for her is more than love; the thought of becoming even closer to you, whom I regard as the main author and motive force of my present and future existence, constitutes all the happiness I expect on this earth. For me Cosima Liszt transcends all other women, not only because she bears your name, but also because she so resembles you, because she is in so many ways the exact mirror of your personality. And, since she permits me to love her, I do not have to regard my adoration as an illusion, nor my request for her hand as a fantasy which, once expressed, must cause you, so to speak, to pass to the next item on the agenda." He then went on to talk of his "insignificance", his "common" birth, his lack of financial security, as reasons why he should not push his claims too easily, as well as consideration for Cosima herself. "Was it not my duty to wait, to give your daughter sufficient time to consider whether her feelings towards me were based on real and genuine sympathy and not due to impulse? Could her preference for me not have been conditioned by the solitariness of her life and the few acquaintances she has made? I can with a good conscience assure you that, after the first favourable acceptance of my advances, I made no effort to bind her to me; I have done nothing at all to raise myself in her estimation; the respect which I owed to her as your daughter enabled her to look on me with complete freedom and, if disappointed in me, to take back her word. Six months have passed, and it appears that your daughter has retained her feelings towards me. I thus feel more entitled than I did previously – that is to say, if you can recognise any entitlement – to ask you for your consent for me to look on Cosima as my fiancée. I swear to you that, however much I feel bound to her by my love, I should never hesitate to sacrifice myself to her happiness and release her, were she to realise that she had made a mistake in regard to me. Her will, even indeed her whim, shall be sacred to me."

As a result of this letter Liszt gave his consent to the engagement, though he insisted that it should last a year at least. To Frau von Bülow, who was not pleased by her son's choice, Liszt commented that Hans could certainly make a more advantageous match. But opposition to the marriage was never urgent enough – nor were the feelings of the young couple themselves – to prevent its taking place. Cosima described her own state of mind in a letter written much later (28 March 1881) to her daughter Daniela: "When, nearly twenty-six years ago your father, after an acquaintance of six weeks, declared his love, there arose a whole host of difficulties and, besides those imparted to me, doubts which could not be revealed to a girl of only seventeen. I spent two years in this most curious state, the engagement revealed to nobody. And how we came to be married I do not to this day really know. But one thing I do know:

that I never asked even for an explanation. I was glad to be loved, and, as to the rest – I gave it no thought."

The marriage took place on 18 August 1857 at the Hedwigskirche in Berlin, a Roman Catholic church, for Cosima had been brought up strictly in the Catholic faith. Bülow was a Protestant, though no very devout one, and he had no objection to a Catholic wedding, nor to their children being brought up as Roman Catholics.

His first act after the wedding was to take his nineteen-year-old bride to visit Richard Wagner in Zurich.

In later years Wagner was fond of telling Cosima that they should have eloped at the time of her visit to Zurich, before her marriage to Bülow had had a chance to settle down. But he himself had been like Tristan, unsure of his own mind, and she had been "that silly goose, Isolde".

However, this was only playful daydreaming. At the time of Bülow's visit in August, Wagner hardly knew Cosima as a person. Their first meeting had been in Paris on 10 October 1853, when Liszt took him to see his three children, but that was an occasion which meant more to the children than to their visitor. Wagner's interest at this time was purely in Bülow, whose musical sponsor he had been even before Liszt, having encouraged him to defy his parents and abandon his legal studies to become a musician, and helping him even more practically by securing him an engagement as conductor in St Gallen in 1850. Bülow had confided to him the difficulties in the way of his marriage, and Wagner was sympathetic, having, as he told him in a letter dated 1 April 1857, "very pleasant memories" of Cosima. In the same letter he looked forward to seeing him in the summer. By then he would be living in the Asyl, a little cottage placed at his disposal by a wealthy German industrialist, Otto Wesendonck, and working on *Siegfried*. "If you come to visit me, I promise you will be with me in paradise as long as you stay. I much want to make music with you: you must play me my new things, otherwise they will remain quite strange to me."

During that visit to the Asyl, Cosima met the two women who were most important to Wagner at that time. These were his wife Minna and Mathilde Wesendonck, the wife of his benefactor. Music from *Siegfried* was played and, asked for her opinion, she remained tongue-tied and relapsed into tears. Her attitude towards Wagner himself was one of reserve, which may initially have been due to his lack of outward polish. Wagner, then forty-four years old, could conduct himself acceptably in polite society when he wished to, but among his intimate friends he was apt to express himself directly and, in moments of excitement, to make no attempt to conceal his middle-class Saxon origins. He himself suspected this may have been the cause, and he wrote to Bülow on

18 January 1858: "My wholly inconsiderate familiarity towards people I like has only too often led to my causing offence: I can only hope the disapproval of your dear young wife will not be long-lasting."

Wagner wrote this letter from Paris, where he had gone for a few weeks to escape his domestic difficulties in Zurich, arising out of the growing hostility between Minna and Mathilde Wesendonck. In Paris he met Cosima's sister Blandine and her husband Emile Ollivier, a French lawyer who later became an important political figure. Blandine had risked her father's displeasure by returning to Paris, thus depriving Cosima, in the months of her engagement to Bülow, of a very desirable confidante. Blandine's marriage followed shortly after Cosima's, in October 1857.

Probably it was the contrast between Blandine's cordiality and the hostility he still detected in Cosima – he came back to that in a letter written in Paris on 10 February 1858 to Bülow, to whom he had now entrusted the task of making the piano score of *Tristan und Isolde* – that led him to write to her direct on his return to Zurich. This letter, which has only very recently come to light, reveals his difficulties in finding the right tone towards her. There is no trace in it of the ease and impulsiveness of his normal letter-writing style:

"Today, in contrast to my usual wretched days, I am having a truly miserable day, which has the advantage of preventing me from seizing on my medicine, my work. Instead, I shall see whether I cannot improve my position by paying off my debts, and relieve my gloomy mood by the knowledge that the man of sadness has made some amends to the lady of gladness. No, do not hesitate to show me your dislike; I do not let it upset me: my wretchedness assures me that nobody can really dislike me, unless he is mistaken about me – and that tickles my sense of humour and in consequence provides me with the only joy of which I am capable. I have the feeling that the high spirits I showed when you were both here did perhaps to a certain extent lead you astray; otherwise there is much I should find it difficult to explain. That was a very curious time! In the mornings I put my misery into verse, and the rest of the day I spent laughing at it with you. But all the same, it was a boundless relief to me to be able to do so, and it was only because I had you dear young people with me that I found it possible. And this gave me the only true happiness of which I am at present capable. And when in the evenings Hans played me to rest, and you listened so magnificently, it meant the end of a golden day. – Now in the mornings I am putting my misery to music: but I have nobody now with whom I can laugh at it – this is not possible with my dear good wife. Thus I remain stuck in it all day long, and in the evenings my own music stays silent: I cannot even beguile myself with the sound of it for a while. And so my days bring me nothing but misery, and that does not raise my spirits, though it can happen that a miraculous power transforms my misery into indescribable bliss; when that happens, I feel so unutterably happy and exalted that I am filled with unbelievable pride, and how wretched the world then looks in comparison with me! Such transports must, however, be atoned for, and my misery then overwhelms me again like a flood. So things will not be as they should be until you come with Hans to visit me again."

Cosima's response to this letter has not been preserved; she herself destroyed all her letters to Wagner (with one or two exceptions to be mentioned later), so that it is impossible to quote any direct evidence of her feelings towards him at this time. Bülow described it, in a letter to Wagner after the second visit to Zurich, as awe: "In your presence her usual talkativeness tends to dry up, her open and expansive nature to withdraw. . . . She still fears that you must think her childish and too insignificant to love and understand you, whereas in fact she is one of the few people who could do just that."

This second visit to Zurich, which lasted from 21 July to 16 August 1858, did nothing outwardly to bring Wagner closer to Cosima, since it coincided with a major crisis in his own life. On 7 April, Minna had intercepted and read a long letter from Wagner to Mathilde which she took to be evidence of a sinful relationship. Her jealous rage led to fearful scenes for Wagner and great embarrassment for Mathilde, who objected to seeing her perhaps purely soulful relationship with Wagner brought down to the level of an ordinary affair. Wagner sought to escape from his difficult situation by inviting a succession of friends to stay, including the singers Joseph Tichatschek and Albert Niemann and the pianist Karl Klindworth. Soon after their arrival, Bülow wrote on 24 June to Richard Pohl, a friend of both himself and Wagner, reporting that the atmosphere at the Asyl was "sultry and thunderladen". Wagner, he said, had become much more difficult to converse with, "though his basically noble nature has not suffered". He added that, if it had not been for the presence in Zurich of his mother-in-law, Countess d'Agoult, to whom he had become greatly attached, he would have left at once.

Cosima did leave, though only for the purpose of accompanying her mother to Geneva, and she returned to Zurich with another of Wagner's young protégés, Karl Ritter, a friend of Bülow's. Between them there occurred in Geneva a strange episode to which Cosima never referred, and our knowledge of it is due entirely to the diary which Wagner wrote for Mathilde Wesendonck after his departure for Venice. During his journey there Karl Ritter, who accompanied him, told Wagner that he and Cosima had come close to committing suicide together. "In a sudden frightful outburst Cosima asked him to kill her; he in return offered to die with her, but this she utterly rejected. After they had taken a trip on the lake together, Cosima with the intention of drowning herself, Karl of following her example, she abandoned her resolve, since she could not dissuade Karl from his desire to die with her. And so it was all left in an obscure emotional balance; they parted with an agreement to tell each other in three weeks' time what their mutual outlook, feelings and later resolutions were." It appears that Cosima did indeed write to Ritter three weeks later, expressing her sorrow and shame, thanking him for his kind protection and begging him to forget the incident.

Cosima's grounds for seeking to end her life are not easy to guess at: certainly they had nothing to do with any personal feelings between herself and Ritter. Perhaps the thunderladen atmosphere of the Asyl, to which she was now returning, had aroused in her thoughts of the difficulty of human relationships, which may have included her own with Bülow; perhaps also the musical work in which they were at the time immersed, *Tristan und Isolde*, with its message of a perfect union attainable only in death, might have had something to do with it. But, whether this was indeed the moment at which Cosima became conscious of her love for Wagner and felt a sense of her own inadequacy and insignificance in his eyes, he himself failed to recognise it. He may have wondered why, when a few days later he left for Venice, Cosima should have fallen on her knees and in tears kissed his hands, but his own account of the incident in Geneva gives no hint that he saw it as in any way connected with himself. For Wagner, Cosima remained a "wild" and impulsive child, and certainly not a woman who, however much he might have denied it in later years, could disturb his emotional attachment to Mathilde Wesendonck.

He valued her intelligence sufficiently, however, to suggest that she should undertake the translation of *Tannhäuser* into French for the Paris production of 1861. In a newly-discovered letter from Paris, dated 19 September 1859, he wrote to her: "You both profess to love me, and to wish to help me wherever you can. And so I ask you, my dear child, to get down straight away to producing a translation of *Tannh.* on your own account. . . . You and Hans together should be able to produce the best."

His request was certainly not mere indulgence – his sense of professionalism was far too rigid for that. Cosima possessed all the necessary qualifications. She had now become a regular contributor to a Parisian magazine, *La Revue Germanique*, and for this she wrote articles on political subjects, and also translated a number of German works into French. Since she had been brought up in Paris, her main language was French, and in fact French was the language in which she and Bülow preferred to converse and correspond, for he too, though of purely

German origin, spoke it as easily as his native language. Cosima's German, though fluent, always remained slightly defective.

She began a translation of *Tannhäuser*, but did not complete it. She excused herself on the grounds that she found the task beyond her, but the true reason was her concern over her brother Daniel. He had been studying in Vienna and, when he came to stay with Cosima and Bülow in Berlin in August 1859, his health was already broken. During the next few months Cosima was fully occupied looking after him as his condition steadily deteriorated. On 13 December he died, at the age of twenty. To both Cosima and Bülow it was a time of all-absorbing grief.

Between the years 1858 and 1861 Wagner's contacts with Cosima were purely by correspondence, and in this (little of which still exists) one can assume that Cosima was usually acting as her husband's agent rather than in her own person. Of all his young protégés – and there was a long list of them, fulfilling the role during his first marriage of the sons he never had – Bülow was the one Wagner respected most. He admired him as a conductor, as a pianist and even as a composer, discerning in him a singleness of devotion towards art fully equal to his own. When in 1859 he settled in Paris – and at the same time attempted once again to repair his marriage with Minna – he invited Bülow there to help him organise and conduct concerts to earn his living. During the ensuing months, which culminated in the disastrous production of the revised *Tannhäuser* in March 1861, Bülow journeyed frequently from Berlin to join him, but Cosima stayed at home.

When she and Wagner next met, in Bad Reichenhall in August 1861, Cosima was the mother of a ten-month-old daughter, Daniela, but in his eyes she was still a "wild child". In his autobiography, written years later, Wagner claimed, on taking leave of Cosima at Reichenhall, to have received from her "a somewhat timid questioning glance". One must of course be wary of taking words written in the light of after-events too literally, and particularly in this case, when *My Life (Mein Leben)* was dictated to Cosima. It was in fact only in the following year that their relationship showed anything like an approach to a true understanding, though even now only on a light-hearted, unspoken basis. In the summer of 1862 Bülow and Cosima came to stay with Wagner in Biebrich, a village on the Rhine where he had settled down to write the music of *Die Meistersinger von Nürnberg*. After a final attempt to live peaceably with his wife Minna, he had now decided on a definite separation, and had embarked on his long-drawn-out affair with Mathilde Maier, the daughter of a lawyer in the neighbouring town of Mainz.

Just as, responding to some creative need in him, he had cast Mathilde Wesendonck and himself in the roles of doomed lovers when writing *Die*

Walküre and *Tristan und Isolde*, now Mathilde Maier was called upon to be the respectable small-town Eva to his humorously resigned Hans Sachs. Part of her attraction was her unattainability in the face of bourgeois convention. At the time of Cosima's visit he wrote to Mathilde: "You are so many-sided, and always so sure and so genuine, that there is no part of you I would wish to take away from you in order to delight in it as my own. So you will remain entirely mine even if I am never allowed to possess you: and thus for me you are the ultimate source of noble enlightenment."

At the time of the visit to Biebrich, Bülow was in a depressed and nervous state, a condition not unusual with him, owing to his habit of driving himself so hard in his work that his physical strength broke under the strain. The proximity of Wagner served this time only to feed his feelings of inferiority. "With Wagner as a neighbour," he wrote to a friend, "everything else shrinks so wretchedly, seems so childish, so utterly empty." Surrounded by the sounds of *Die Meistersinger*, he could not bear to read the proofs of his own songs. "I have lost all sense of my own identity and with it my joy in life. What use can one make of a helpless piety?"

It was towards the end of this visit, during an expedition to Frankfurt, that the little event occurred which Wagner described in *My Life*, after noting that he had detected in Cosima a melting of her reserve towards him: "Everything was still wrapped in silence and mystery, but the feeling inside me that she belonged to me assumed such certainty that it drove me in a moment of eccentricity to a display of rash high spirits. Once, when accompanying Cosima across an open square in Frankfurt to her hotel, I espied an empty wheelbarrow standing there, and on the spur of the moment I invited her to sit in it, so that I might wheel her to her hotel; she was instantly ready to comply, whereas I, astonished in turn by this, lost the courage to carry out my mad design. Bülow, who was following us, had seen the incident; Cosima explained very guilelessly to him what had been in our minds, and unfortunately I was unable to conclude that his high spirits matched ours, for he chided his wife for her temerity."

This slight incident was for Wagner something in the nature of a turning-point. Always pleased by any show of spontaneous impulse, he suddenly detected in Cosima a woman who, unlike any other he had known, might be prepared to join happily and without question in anything he demanded of her. It had not been so with his wife Minna, who could never forgive him for abandoning a respectable career in Dresden for his political ideals and spending his time writing musical works that nobody could produce; nor with Mathilde Wesendonck, who was holding tight to her respectable marriage; nor with his current love,

Mathilde Maier. As for Cosima, the event also had its special significance. Recording, years later, another instance in which she complied with one of Wagner's impulses, she wrote in her diary on 1 November 1878: "The wheelbarrow has become for me the celestial Wain, in which he bears me on and on towards our spiritual home."

Their next meeting was in Leipzig on 1 November 1862, at a concert at which Wagner conducted the first performance of the overture to *Die Meistersinger von Nürnberg*. Bülow and Cosima travelled there especially for the concert, she in mourning for her sister Blandine, who had died on 11 September shortly after giving birth to a son. From Vienna, Wagner wrote to Bülow on 22 November: "Oh, children, when I saw you both again in Leipzig, my heart leapt! Without a doubt, I love you both very much! Heavens, to be intimate, to belong to one another – that is the only way, but, oh, how difficult it is! The heart is not enough by itself: one must be skilful as well! Profound and intimate greetings to you both."

For Cosima, pregnant with her second child, this was the period of greatest isolation. She wrote to a friend, Alfred Meissner, soon after Blandine's death: "The unusual position in which our birth placed us forged a bond between the three of us which is beyond the capacity of most brothers and sisters to visualise, and which I now trail behind me like a heavy and burdensome chain. I shall never again love anyone as I loved these two, and I often have the feeling of being uprooted, since I am always seeking in my heart for these two beings who were so young, so rare, so truly sacred, so utterly my own, and I feel nothing but emptiness."

Bülow had proved incapable, even while Daniel and Blandine were still alive, of taking first place in her affections. The arrival of his mother, who came shortly after Blandine's death to share his home following the marriage of her daughter Isa, made things no easier for him. His relations with his domineering mother were always uncomfortable: he was by no means compliant, but his attempts to resist her placed a great strain on his nerves and led in addition to feelings of remorse. Cosima's relations with Frau von Bülow were calm on the surface, but underneath a silent battle was raging. The bleakness of her life at this period can be seen in her account of the birth of her second daughter, Blandine, on 20 March 1863. She recalled it in her diary on 19 March 1869:

"At this hour of the evening six years ago I was feeling very unwell; unwell and at the same time wretched. How wearily and gloomily I brought my baby into the world, without any assistance, how indifferently did the father greet it! Only Richard, far away, was concerned about me, and I did not know it. How dreary, how empty, how inwardly disturbed was my life at that time! How could I ever thank R. enough for what his love has done for me? At that time I was feeling so wretched that I told nobody that my labour pains had come, and that the baby was already there when they summoned the midwife. My mother-in-law was living in the house, Hans was at home, there were servants in plenty, and I was walking up and down in the *salon* all by myself, wriggling like a worm and whimpering; a cry I could not suppress woke the household and they carried me to my bed, where Boni [Blandine] then crept out. In every home a coming child is a time of joy, but I hardly dared tell Hans that I was pregnant, so unfriendly was his reaction, as if his comfort were being disturbed. I have never told anyone about this before; now I am writing it down – not to complain about Hans (he had many worries on his mind, and he did not know what pleases and what hurts a woman, for I had always kept silent), but because I cannot think without shuddering of that night in Berlin, which serves to make utterly clear to me the subsequent course of my destiny."

At the time of Blandine's birth Wagner was in St Petersburg, and the only existing evidence that he was thinking of Cosima is contained in a letter to Bülow dated 18 March 1863, asking the bare question: "Father yet?" Having run out of money in Biebrich, he had been obliged to abandon the composition of *Die Meistersinger* and go in search of conducting engagements. He set up his main residence in Vienna, where rehearsals for the long-planned first production of *Tristan und Isolde* had at last been resumed. He took with him a young actress, Friederike Meyer, whom he had met in Frankfurt.

Wagner's affair with Friederike was emotionally the least complicated of his relationships. "She is not very pretty," his friend Peter Cornelius wrote in his diary on 20 November 1862, "but she has a face full of lively expression. . . . If he has to have a liaison of this kind, he seems to have chosen quite well." In other words, Friederike was his mistress, but from a tactical point of view an unwise choice, for she was the sister of Luise Dustmann, the singer who was rehearsing the role of Isolde in Vienna, and Frau Dustmann disapproved strongly of her sister's behaviour, which gave rise to a great deal of gossip. There was more than one reason why the Viennese production of *Tristan und Isolde* never came to fruition – among them the inability to find a suitable Tristan and Luise Dustmann's indifferent health – but Wagner's relationship with Friederike certainly played a part, since it cost him the sympathies of those most likely to have been of help to him. The loss of anticipated royalties left him no alternative but to seek more conducting engagements, and in the following year his time was filled with travelling and conducting, in Vienna, Prague and, between February and April, in St Petersburg and Moscow. Friederike returned to Frankfurt.

After settling down at last in a rented villa in the Viennese suburb of Penzing, Wagner wrote to Bülow on 22 June 1863: "Well, I should be solitary now: and indeed I have already tried to do a little work. But I cannot with a good conscience say that I am well. I feel with increasing force that I need some pleasant female company around me; it is not enough just to refuse to admit to being lonely. But where to find it without stealing it? My unhappy Friederike M. would willingly join me: but what an abyss of renewed difficulties and worries that would cause! Hesitant and apprehensive over each new contact, I have up till now denied myself even the acquisition of a dog. At all costs I need tranquillity, and so there is nothing I can do but ward off! – You have no idea what emotional torments *this* still causes me with regard to my wife. She writes to me very seldom, but, when now and again a letter does come, I always feel I have been hit by a disaster. Every contact, however slight, tells me how frivolously foolish I am not to break with her entirely, but always to leave an opening through which hope can come and go to torment the poor woman. I have now reached this stage, but still I am assailed by a thousand anxious and torturing forebodings. God, what wretched creatures we mortals are with all our over-sensitive feelings!"

In his desire for female company Wagner turned again to Mathilde Maier, with whom he had been corresponding copiously and warmly ever since leaving Biebrich. He had even discussed with her the possibility of settling down in Mainz in order to be near her, and, as he explained in a letter dated 5 May 1863, it was only his desire for a period of quiet in his life that made him decide, when the villa in Penzing was offered him, to remain in Vienna. But he threw out a hint: "I have a few nice guest rooms for the summer; my treasure will come often with her Mama or cousin to visit me." According to his account in *My Life*, this proposal caused some consternation in Mathilde's family, and he was tactfully advised by one of her friends that, if he would first divorce his wife, he would find the rest easy enough to arrange. Wagner was resolutely set against dissolving his marriage with Minna. "I withdrew my invitation," he wrote in *My Life*, "ascribing it to impulse, and tried to calm ruffled feelings as well as I could." His letter of 11 May to Mathilde was, however, anything but placatory: "God knows how far your family's bourgeois bigotry extends. . . . Oh, dear, how pitiful you all are – too pitiful for words! *Something* ought to be ventured when one is dealing with a Wagner!"

This setback seemed in no way to affect his feelings for Mathilde herself. "Ah, child," he wrote in the same letter the following day, "I am now fifty years old! At that age love knows only one wish – that of the Flying Dutchman: a rest after storms. But, you being what you are, I do not abandon the hope of achieving it with you in some form or other."

With Cosima, beyond paying her and Bülow a visit in Berlin on his departure for and return from Russia, he had little to do, though he never neglected to send greetings to her in his letters to Bülow.

Extravagant living soon used up all Wagner's money and he was obliged to resort to borrowing. The occasional concert in Budapest, Prague and Karlsruhe could not stave off for long the financial catastrophe towards which he was heading. An attempt to make progress with *Die Meistersinger* was abandoned after orchestrating a few bars of the first act. He wrote to Mathilde Maier from Budapest on 20 July 1863: "The saddest thing of all is that my work no longer gives me pleasure. I am simply not in the mood for such light-hearted music. Altogether I find music more and more burdensome: through it I fall victim to the main bedevilment of my life: what does music mean to people? Just amusement, sensual titillation! It would be better for me to give it all up, and just confine myself to writing poetry."

A conducting engagement at Löwenberg, to which he travelled from Mainz after spending a day and a night with Mathilde and her family, brought him on 28 November 1863 to Berlin. There he visited Bülow and Cosima. "Hans was particularly anxious that I should attend a concert which he was to conduct that evening, and this led me to stay on overnight," he wrote in *My Life*. "We talked, as light-heartedly as we could manage on a day of cold, raw and overcast weather, of my wretched financial position. . . . Since Bülow had preparations to make for his concert, I drove once more along the promenade in a fine carriage, alone with Cosima. This time our joking gave way to silence: we looked speechlessly into each other's eyes and, in an urgent desire for truth between us, felt constrained to acknowledge our mutual unhappiness, for which there was no need of words. With tears and sobs we sealed our vow to live for each other alone. It brought us great relief. A feeling of deep comfort gave us the ease to listen to the concert with our minds at rest."

For Cosima this meeting represented the moment of decision, and in later years she celebrated its anniversary with little gifts to Wagner. For him, however, the moment of decision had not yet arrived.

CHAPTER II

DECEMBER 1863 – NOVEMBER 1864:

Mariafeld and Starnberg

IN LÖWENBERG, WHERE a friend of Liszt's, Prince Hohenzollern-Hechingen, maintained a private orchestra, Wagner discovered a former acquaintance among the invited guests. Henriette von Bissing was the sister of Eliza Wille, at whose house in Mariafeld he had met her during his years in Zurich. Recently widowed, she was in possession of a large fortune, and, after hearing from Wagner of the financial difficulties that prevented him from settling down to his composing work, she offered to provide him with sufficient money to allow him to remain in Vienna, free of conducting engagements, and complete *Die Meistersinger*. So great was her interest in him that she followed him from Löwenberg to Breslau, where he conducted a concert on 7 December. However, Frau von Bissing's sudden infatuation with Wagner aroused great opposition among her family, and, after his return to Vienna, she withdrew her promise to help him. The reason for this, he recorded in *My Life*, he eventually learned from Frau Wille. "And if I do save Wagner," Frau Bissing had told her sister, "it will still be only Mathilde Wesendonck he loves."

Henriette von Bissing may occupy a very small place in Wagner's love life, but it is evident that their short relationship was not entirely devoid of emotional currents on his side as well. He must surely still have been thinking of her when he wrote in his *Annals* (his reminders for use in his autobiography) in April 1864: "Idea of divorce from Minna and going out after a wealthy marriage."

Now irretrievably in debt, he was obliged to leave Vienna in order to escape his creditors. An appeal to Otto Wesendonck to grant him hospitality in Zurich having been abruptly refused, he next appealed to François Wille, and in fact arrived in Mariafeld on 26 March 1864 without allowing time for a reply. He found Eliza Wille alone there with her two sons, her husband François being on a visit to Constantinople. From there Wagner wrote at once to Peter Cornelius in Vienna: "Frau Wille seems destined to become the agent of my destiny: she is loyal and pure as gold, a friend through thick and thin. She is also the closest and most sympathetic friend of Frau Wesendonck – as well as of her own sister, Frau von Bissing. These three, I now see, love me equally: but in Frau v.B.'s case jealousy (I rather suspected it!) so gained the upper hand that it is only now – after this discovery – that I begin to understand the reason for her behaviour towards me. Frau Wille, on the other hand . . . now understands me completely and appreciates that what I need is just a pleasant tranquillity and no upsetting relationships."

In her own reminiscences Eliza Wille recorded that, at his request, she left him to look after himself, keeping visitors away and providing him (with the help of Mathilde Wesendonck) with enough pocket money to satisfy his local creditors. Sometimes, she noted, he appeared dejected, and he went for frequent walks by himself, but now and again his humour revived, and he was attentive to her and her sons, spending many hours talking about his past life.

He had reason enough for dejection. The severity of this crisis in his life was at least as great as that of 1849, when his revolutionary activities in Dresden obliged him to flee to Switzerland and begin a new life in Zurich. Now he was fifteen years older, the *Ring* and *Die Meistersinger* unfinished and *Tristan und Isolde*, five years after its completion, still unperformed. In 1863 he had published the text of the *Ring*, and in his introduction he had called on "a prince or a group of dedicated people" to provide him with the means of completing and producing his work. His appeal had brought no response at all. "My condition is a very curious one," he wrote to Cornelius on 8 April. "It rests on a very delicate balance: one push, and that is the end, leaving nothing more to be got from me, not a thing. What I need is a *light*: a *human being* must emerge *now* to give me energetic help – then I shall find the strength to repay that help: otherwise not – I feel sure of that."

Frau Wille's efforts to comfort him did not always meet with success. She wrote in her reminiscences: "Wagner said to me: 'How can you talk of the future, when all my manuscripts are locked away in the cupboard? Who is to stage the work which I alone, and nobody else, can bring into existence with the aid of friendly spirits, in such a way that the whole world can say: so it is, that is how the composer saw and wanted his work to be?' He walked up and down the room in agitation. Coming suddenly to a standstill in front of me, he said: 'I am built in a different way, I have excitable nerves, I need beauty, brilliance and light! I cannot spend my life in a miserable organist's post like your beloved Bach. Is it so very reprehensible of me to feel that I deserve the little bit of luxury I enjoy? I who provide pleasure for the world and all its thousands of people?'"

On 10 April he sent a brief note to Cosima, asking her to tell Bülow to write to him immediately on his return from St Petersburg, where he was fulfilling a conducting engagement. "I need the advice and loyal help of all those who care for me, to make and carry out decisions which must if possible restore my ailing life to the extent that I shall be able to produce a few things still. . . . Here I have not peace, but merely a refuge. I cannot even begin to think of work: this says it all."

His letters to Mathilde Maier, more chastened than those from Vienna, show that he still had very tender feelings for her: why else should he have gone out of his way, in mentioning Eliza Wille and her hospitality, to describe her in two of his letters as "very ugly"? In his letter of 5 April he said that he had come to Mariafeld in some hope of being able to complete *Die Meistersinger* there. "Now, however, I have fallen ill again, and have been unable for two days to leave my room. The clouds above the lake and the mountains are as grey and impenetrable as my own future. My future! Something might be said about that, especially since I must now force myself to regard all hope as sinful. I am often being urged to get a divorce and to marry a wealthy woman. That sounds sensible enough, particularly when one thinks of it as a true '*mariage de raison*'. But to me it seems rather as it would be if *you* were to have the bright idea of suddenly marrying a rich man in order to help me. Yes, it is easy to say such things; but it is hardly worth talking about."

His suggestion to Mathilde was that she and her mother should move to a larger house containing a room for him, for which he would pay rent. "This room in your house would be a real possession for the rest of my days, come what may, and the enjoyment of it would belong to my most cherished delights and consolations."

Mathilde (whose letters to Wagner have not been preserved) appears to have been ready, though reluctantly, to respond to this suggestion, but in his next letter on 14 April Wagner withdrew it, telling her that it had only been an idea arising out of the thought that, if he were faced with the choice of remaining in Switzerland or living in Mathilde's home, he would prefer the latter. In the event, he told her, difficulties had arisen which made it unlikely that he would remain in Switzerland, and these were "connected with the family in Zurich you know about, and I can no longer put up with such things".

The "family in Zurich" was Mathilde Wesendonck's, and it was true that she was resisting all attempts to revive their former relationship. Yet the immediate cause of Wagner's departure from Switzerland was the return of François Wille, who made it clear that he was not prepared to house his wife's guest indefinitely. Eliza Wille wrote in her reminiscences: "When Wagner came on me alone in the evening, he approached and addressed me with an earnest solemnity: 'My friend, you do not realise the extent of my sufferings, nor the depths of misery which lie before me.' His words startled me. As I looked at him, I do not know what it was that suddenly came over me and filled me with a curious confidence. 'No,' I said, 'it is not a depth of misery that lies before you. Something is going to happen. What? I do not know. But it will be something good, different from what you imagine. Be patient, and it will lead you to happiness!'"

This piece of feminine intuition earned Eliza Wille the title of prophetess from Wagner, for only a few days after he left Mariafeld for Stuttgart, with vague hopes of interesting the conductor there – Karl Eckert, a friend from his Vienna days – in a production of *Tristan und Isolde*, an emissary of the new King of Bavaria, Ludwig II, tracked him down and handed him a ring and a photograph of the king. This emissary, Franz von Pfistermeister, also conveyed a verbal message from the king which, according to August Röckel, ran: "As this stone glows, so does the desire burn in him to meet the author and composer of *Lohengrin*."

Two days later, on 4 May 1864, Wagner found himself in Munich standing before the handsome young monarch, who offered him a yearly income, a house, freedom to write and produce his works as he thought fit, and an immediate sum of money sufficient to pay off the most pressing of his debts in Vienna.

Wagner wrote to Eliza Wille that same day: "Unfortunately he is so beautiful, so spiritual, so full of soul and splendour, that I fear his life must dissolve like a divine and evanescent dream in this vulgar world. He loves me with all the intensity and ardour of first love: he knows everything about me and my works and understands me like my own soul." After describing the king's proposals, he went on: "I shall be relieved of all want, I am to have whatever I need – all I have to do is stay at his side. What do you say to this? – What can you say? – Is it not extraordinary? – Can it be anything but a dream? – Imagine how moved I am! My happiness is so great that I feel utterly shattered by it. You can have no idea of the magic of his eyes: may he only continue to live! It is an almost incredible miracle!"

The young king was equally moved by their first meeting. He wrote to his cousin Sophie: "If you could have seen how ashamed his gratitude made me feel when I gave him my hand with the assurance that I would see to it that his great *Ring* work would not only be completed, but be produced in accordance with his desires. He bowed low over my hand and seemed to be moved by what seemed to me so natural, for he remained a long while in that position without saying a word. I felt as if we had exchanged roles. I stooped down to him and pressed him to my heart, with the feeling of speaking to myself a formal oath: to remain loyal to him all my life."

Wagner wrote to Mathilde Maier on the following day from the Hotel Bavière in Munich, telling her that his meeting with the king had been "one great, unending love scene". He enclosed a letter to him from the king which had arrived that day; in it the king confirmed what had been promised at their meeting, and he added: "Unknown to you, my friend, you have been the *only source of joy* to me since the tenderest years of my youth: you spoke to my heart as no other has ever done, you are my best teacher and tutor."

Ludwig was born on 25 August 1845, the year in which (as both he and Wagner loved to recall) *Tannhäuser* was first staged, and his father ascended the Bavarian throne in 1848 as Maximilian II. Ludwig's childhood was not a happy one, for neither his father nor his Prussian mother demonstrated much affection for their two children; his younger brother Otto was virtually his only companion in a life dominated by governesses and tutors. King Maximilian was interested both in literature and architecture, but not in music, while Queen Marie had no intellectual interests at all. Ludwig was fifteen years old when he saw his first opera. It was *Lohengrin*. "Bad as the production was," he wrote to Wagner later, "I was able to appreciate the essence of this divine work: in that performance was sown the seed of our love and friendship till death; the spark, which soon developed into a mighty flame for our sacred ideals, was at that time ignited within me." According to his contemporary biographer, Gottfried von Böhm, the young prince had wept tears of ecstasy in the opera house and immediately set about learning the text of *Lohengrin* and Wagner's other music dramas by heart. He thought out ideas of his own for costumes and scenery to illustrate the legend of the Holy Grail and persuaded his art tutor to draw them for him. He also started to read Wagner's prose works, including the theoretical *Das Kunstwerk der Zukunft* (*The Artwork of the Future*). When in 1863 Wagner published the text of the *Ring*, Ludwig vowed on reading it that, when the time arrived, he would be the prince who would respond to Wagner's appeal for help in staging the work. His opportunity soon came, for on 10 March 1864 King Maximilian died, and Ludwig became King of Bavaria at the age of eighteen.

The news of the turn in Wagner's fortunes was not conveyed to Bülow and Cosima until 11 May. In a short note from Vienna, where he had gone to settle his affairs, Wagner simply announced that "the prince of my foreword to *Der Ring des Nibelungen* has been found: divine, gloriously handsome, an ideal realised". He followed that the next day with a longer letter: "My happiness, and my power, are now so great that my only concern is not to earn the reproach of abusing them. Hence also my caution, as far as good deeds are concerned, to demand nothing, but simply to accept. The excitement caused, and the envy, are

so great that we have felt obliged publicly to present the yearly salary the
king has voluntarily granted me as extremely small. Keep to *this* figure
yourself towards the world and my supporters, but I can tell you that I
am being generously provided for in every way, and so can use all my
subsidiary earnings wholly to pay off my debts."

The salary granted Wagner was in fact 4,000 florins yearly, not by any
means a lavish sum, but it was supplemented by a house free of rent and
extra payments from the king's private purse whenever required.
Wagner, having paid off his debts in Vienna, returned from there to the
house provided for him, the Haus Pellet on Lake Starnberg, some fifteen
miles south of Munich. With him he brought the couple who had been
his servants in Penzing, Franz and Anna Mrazek, their three-month-old
child and an elderly pointer named Pohl which had attached itself to
him there. His house lay close to Berg, a small royal lodge that Ludwig
preferred to the Residenz in Munich, and Wagner paid daily visits to him
there.

"I am not inviting you both to come and stay with me for any length of
time this year," he wrote to Bülow on 18 May, "since I have now got to
the stage when I shy away, not only from excitement, but from stimula-
tion as well. Next year I shall, I hope, have reached the stage of
suggesting to you both a plan for spending a pleasant summer together.
But it would be splendid if you yourself could at some time spare me a
week; I must even ask you, if you can manage it, to help me in the task of
giving my wonderful young king some idea of my *Ring* music. I have
already mentioned you to him, and he is looking forward to it. This
really is the finest of my conquests: not a speck, not a wisp of cloud in the
sky; the pure, deep, complete devotion of a pupil to his master. There is
no other pupil who is so completely my *own* as this one. It is quite incredible! You would have to hear this splendid youth, to see him and to
sense him. 'Parzival.' He is reported to be firm, strict and very conscien-
tious in affairs of state: he stands entirely by himself, influenced by
nobody, and everyone regards him as a true king in the full sense of the
word."

This impression of the young monarch was fully shared by his
Bavarian compatriots, who were captivated by his youth, his tall and
handsome appearance and his undoubted intelligence. But a suspicion
of possible flaws in his character was expressed by his new minister of
justice, Edouard von Bomhard, in a diary entry written after his first visit
to the king in his Alpine palace at Hohenschwangau later that year: "The
young man of nineteen years, full of the charm of youthful beauty,
nobility of expression and form, with his thick and luxuriant brown
hair, his truly splendid eyes so full of intelligence and feeling, dressed in
a formal black suit with decorations on his chest, received me graciously

and, with the words, 'First you must look at my view,' opened the window and showed me the beautiful surroundings, the mountains close behind and the two lakes nestling picturesquely in the valley. With me he went through the principal duties of the minister of justice, obviously well prepared beforehand by the head of his cabinet, for he showed a surprising grasp of the subject. . . . I very soon began to notice that at times, when his eyes and his whole being seemed to denote graciousness and benevolence, he would suddenly draw himself up and, gazing around with an earnest, even severe expression, would assume a sombre appearance completely in contrast with his gracious, youthful looks. I found myself thinking: if there are two natures developing within this young man, as appearances seemed to suggest at our first meeting, God grant that the good side win."

Wagner, in the intoxication of his first months in Bavaria, detected no flaws in Ludwig. "I am now reading my texts to him," he wrote to Mathilde Maier on 18 May. "When anything seems unclear to him, he asks eagerly for an explanation, with intensity and splendid powers of comprehension. His response is often very moving: his beautiful face expresses profound sorrow and great joy, according to how I direct his feelings. Only one thing makes him sad: when he detects in me some doubt whether all my artistic intentions can ever really be carried out. He wants my ideal to be realised, and to achieve that intends to renounce all pastimes, so as to preserve all his means intact for my purposes. There is only one thing that would make him really unhappy – if I were to pretend to be, or appear different to what I am. He is divine! If I am Wotan, then he is my Siegfried."

However, the king could not in the nature of things give Wagner the companionship for which he always craved. Though he had little liking for social gatherings, Wagner always loved to have a few intimate friends around him. So far he had none in Munich, as he became painfully aware when he found himself spending his fifty-first birthday alone in the large villa at Starnberg with the king's cabinet secretary Pfistermeister and his two servants. Bülow, already invited to join him, made the excuse of a forthcoming engagement in Karlsruhe; Peter Cornelius, working on a new opera in Vienna, was unwilling to break off. Wagner's feelings of loneliness were still further aggravated by the news that Mathilde Wesendonck had refused to accept the letter which he had written to her and entrusted to Eliza Wille on leaving Mariafeld. He wrote to Frau Wille on 26 May complaining of what he called "the conceited belief of the Philistine soul in its 'practical wisdom'. When a feminine soul so forgets all the instincts of love as to judge, pity and reprove the object of her love from the standpoint of this conventional philistinism, it is more than one can accept. Fate has already punished me for having spoilt and pampered my own wife through my excessive indulgence, to such an extent that she finally lost all ability to be fair towards me. The consequence of that can be seen.

"I do not wish to take on myself the blame for delivering our friend from her constrictions by a similar indulgence, resulting in a similar estrangement from me; I should have the feeling of trifling with her were I not to make her aware, while there is still time, of the injustice she does me and has often done me before. I return her childish note herewith: no one, my dear friend, is better able than you are to show her, when the opportunity arises, that the miserable afflictions I have suffered have made me neither evil nor *wicked*, and the childish exhortation to me to be good is therefore senseless. My last letter, if she had not rejected it, would have taught her better and more correctly what I am: it was a *final* letter, a sacred letter. And that it remains, in spite of the good fortune which has now so suddenly befallen me, for it concerned my innermost being, which happiness cannot alter, and whoever understood it would also have realised that I already bore that same happiness within me. Let her then strive to discover me again: she had me once and understood me; that she could lose and misunderstand me, that I can – acknowledge, but not excuse. Let her atone for it! – for she means too much to me for me to trifle with her. . . . Shall I ever be able to dispense entirely with the 'feminine'? I tell myself with a deep sigh that I almost wish I could!''

His next attempt to relieve his loneliness, after another attempt to coax Cornelius to Starnberg had failed, was addressed to Bülow. In the most tempting terms he invited Bülow "with wife, children and servants", to join him at Starnberg for the whole of the summer, where they would be given a complete floor of his house to themselves. "So, my dear Hans, no dismal thoughts, I implore you! No doubts about this and that. Any anxieties you may have I am in a position to dispose of. Trust me! – We shall not disturb each other in the least. Everything is self-contained. When we feel the need to be alone, we need not see each other all day. But we shall have each other if we want. Ah, how much I stand in need of a noble, pleasant contact such as this with people who are dear to me! And how much I look forward to your children! There is a three-month-old baby in the house already: I do not notice it, but I am pleased all the same. Truly, good people, it is only you I lack to complete my happiness."

What reply Bülow made to this appeal cannot be known, since all the letters he wrote to Wagner between 1 May 1861 and 5 December 1867 were destroyed. But among the letters from Wagner to Cosima that have recently come to light is one dated a week later, 16 June 1864, which begins: "I returned here yesterday to find a letter from Hans which shows me that the poor man is in a very bad state – just as I always feared it would happen some day as a result of the unnatural over-exertion of his powers." He then went on to describe in detail his regret at having never been able to help Bülow's career in any material way. His hesitation in summoning him to his side now that his own fortunes had changed had been due to a fear of raising false hopes, but now that he was convinced of the genuineness of King Ludwig's regard for him, he felt confident that the move to Munich would be to Bülow's benefit, and he asked Cosima's aid in making clear to her husband, at her own discretion, what he was now able to offer:

"Repeatedly during the past I have been told of Hans's efforts to free himself of the job of giving lessons: he himself told me, regretfully, of vain efforts to find a conducting post, if only temporary (as in Schwerin), though that is a dismal prospect these days. . . . And Hans even told me once of his plan to retire to Gotha, where living is particularly cheap, and with the help of your small allowance and occasional tours to manage well enough to be able to give up lessons entirely. Now I hear the latest news from Berlin, of his quarrel with Stern and his throwing up his post with him; and on top of that the feelings of torment that such situations give rise to. – And at the same time I see what my dear young king is lacking: his education did not include music, he knows only my works, but nothing at all by Beethoven or virtually any other music. He longs to make this deficiency good, but he cannot start taking lessons in playing himself. It must all be conveyed to him on the lines of intelligent conversation. I cannot play things to him, but how divinely and quite uniquely Hans could! I suggested it to him, and now he is agog for refreshment from this source. The king's cabinet secretary Pfistermeister, the true basis for the solidity of my relationship, is urging me to get hold of Hans. All it now needs, I know, is a few pleasant hours between us three, the king, Hans and myself, and the situation will solve itself, without need of any further words from me – that means, according to my feelings and knowledge of the conditions here, quite simply that Hans will stay on as pianist to the king at a salary of about 1,500 florins, *at the very least*. . . . Hans, if he wishes, can make his concert tours, will give hardly *any* lessons more, need trouble himself with nothing, can work in comfort, and – I shall have you *both*! This is all so simple and so easy to achieve. . . .

"As far as you and your children are concerned, my dear Cosima, you must base your decision solely on your doctor's advice: if he agrees, do not let yourselves be deterred by any other considerations from the summer holiday I am offering you. I assure you that here you will all be completely undisturbed and will also not disturb me in the least: we do not need to see each other for days on end – even weeks, if you like – so large is my house and so well supplied with servants and all other necessities. Now I have nothing more to say! Is it enough?" He ended his letter with a postscript: "We have here a lovely cowshed with forty splendid Swiss cows. What milk for the children!!!"

All this time Wagner had been corresponding with Mathilde Maier, and his letter to her of 22 June was no less urgent than that to Cosima, from whom he was still awaiting a definite reply. "Dear child, I am driving myself to death and can find no rest," he wrote to Mathilde. "I must have somebody to take over the running of my house. I cannot avoid giving you a shock and shaking you once again out of your tranquillity with the question: Will you come to me and run my house for me?"

In her reply Mathilde apparently told him that her mother would certainly not approve of his suggestion, but he gained the impression that she herself would not be unwilling. So on 25 June he wrote down a long letter to Mathilde's mother, in which he explained the impossibility of his living with his wife and his reluctance to divorce her, owing to the effect such a shock would have on her in the precarious state of her health. What he now required, he said, was a female person who would above all take over the running of his house and also be close enough to him in education and character to satisfy his intellectual needs. What he was seeking was a woman who could satisfy these needs, in which sensuality should have no place. And the woman he considered ideal for this position was her daughter Mathilde. Would she give her consent to this arrangement? "Or, in order that I might venture to put this question, would you require further and more definite assurances from me? Should I assure you that Mathilde would be looked after well and respectfully in my home, and protected from any scandal emphatically and energetically? Or should it be possible, without giving rise to a suspicion of impious desires, to consider the prospect of my wife's death, and in this event the prospect of my asking you for your daughter's hand?"

This letter Wagner sent, not to Mathilde's mother, but to Mathilde herself, leaving it to her discretion to pass it on. The outcome was an agitated letter from Mathilde, in which she must have asked Wagner if he were trying to destroy her family, for his reply, dated 29 June, began: "Oh, my dear child, in no circumstances do I want that! I can and will bear anything in the world rather than a renewal of storms of emotion and battles which I see would ensue, were you to give my letter to your good mother! Yes, all right, I am an egoist – I want peace, tranquillity and gentle cherishing – and I renounce everything, everything that can be gained only with trouble and strife and suppressed grief. I must and I shall seek help without upsetting you." Apologising for having written his letter, he begged her not to show it to her mother. "I made a mistake.

For the moment there can be no question of a change in the position between us. It hardly befits me after this to ask you once again to calm yourself, but it is all I can do. My languishing life is wretched and highly unsatisfactory; but it would be quite awful, and utterly unbearable if I were suddenly to become involved again in an emotional turmoil for which I no longer have the strength, and which would rob me of my peace for ever." The letter ended with consoling assurances that Mathilde need not worry about him: friends were coming to stay, and work and impending performances would perhaps help to keep him from any acts of rashness. "Farewell, look after yourself and continue loving me, in spite of everything!"

The friends who were coming to stay were the Bülows, and on the very day he wrote his letter to Mathilde, Cosima arrived at Starnberg, accompanied only by her two little daughters and a nurserymaid. Bülow was still detained in Berlin.

The story of the next few weeks cannot be related with any degree of factual certainty, and for very obvious reasons, for it is the period in which Wagner's and Cosima's love for each other found its physical consummation, resulting in the birth of their first child, Isolde, on 10 April 1865. Which of them took the initiative can only be surmised. Wagner's passionate letters to Mathilde Maier, written at the very time he was inviting Bülow and Cosima to join him at Starnberg, hardly suggest that he was thinking of Cosima in the light of a mistress. His letter to her of 16 June could of course have been just a cunning lover's ruse to deceive Bülow and bring Cosima and himself together. But, if this were so, would Wagner have chosen the moment of her impending arrival to implore Mathilde to come to him too?

It seems right to conclude that, when Cosima arrived in Starnberg, Wagner had no idea that she was prepared to be more than the platonic friend of old. Her readiness to become his mistress in addition must have swept aside all those fears of "emotional turmoil" of which he had written to Mathilde – and with them all Mathilde's claims on him. These had possibly always been tenuous. She was for him the symbol of a calm and contented domestic life, which was in his case an unfulfillable dream. Mathilde was an intelligent woman, but she was conventional. In fact, her basic similarity, in terms of character, to Wagner's wife Minna is striking: Minna had by all accounts, Wagner's as well as his friends', run his household very efficiently, both in the early times of penury and later, in more comfortable circumstances, in Dresden. It was her failure to understand the strength of her husband's artistic ideals, his inability to compromise with the world and settle for a life of comfortable mediocrity, that led to bitterness and recrimination and finally to the break-up of their marriage.

To find Wagner wooing another woman of the same stamp, and one to all appearances even more conventional in sexual matters than Minna had been, might seem surprising, until one reflects that it was these very qualities which attracted him to Minna in the first place. They might therefore have reflected a need within him which even the experience of Minna could not obliterate – a dream of a quiet and comfortable home life that would enable him to pursue his artistic aims undisturbed. Wagner had no taste for the Bohemian life, of which he had had experience enough both in his childhood (his stepfather Ludwig Geyer, his eldest brother Albert and three of his five sisters had been singers or actors) and during his early career as a conductor. He may have enjoyed the company of unconventional people for short periods of his own choosing, but the desire in him for a solid and respectable background was always very strong. All the women he had encountered in his life had offered him either the one or the other, but only Cosima had the capacity – or the vision – to satisfy him in both.

However, this was not to happen at once. Karl and Käthi Eckert came from Stuttgart to spend a week at Starnberg before Bülow arrived on 7 July, and another friend, Karl Klindworth, came from London to join them shortly after. At some time during this period Cosima and Wagner must have reached an understanding, since his letter to Mathilde Maier, dated 19 July, quite clearly reflected his uneasiness in regard to her: "For you to come to me under the only possible conditions *now* prevailing would have the completely opposite effect to the one I longed for: it would be a source of indescribable and now quite unbearable emotional torment for me; and from this no amount of tender loving silence and secrecy on your side would be able to protect me. And so, my dear one, be kind and accept my sincere request for pardon. I ought to have spared you this final torment: that I could not do so, and that my bitterness again overwhelmed me, is and has been punishment enough for the over-hastiness, inconsiderate as it certainly was, with which I again so suddenly took you by storm. Forgive me. . . . Let me know soon, I urgently beg you, that we have returned to the former paths we abandoned."

Owing to the king's absence it was only at the end of July that Wagner was able to introduce Bülow, and, since duty kept Ludwig in Munich, they had to travel to the city for the musical sessions. Though the desired object was achieved, and the king offered Bülow an engagement at two thousand florins a year (more than four times his salary in Berlin) as his pianist, the daily journey by boat and train proved a great strain on

Bülow's already fragile health. Within a few days he was confined to his bed with rheumatic fever, his arms and legs temporarily paralysed.

That his severe illness might have had basically psychosomatic causes seems feasible. Bülow was a man of great nervous tension, and later on in his life, at times of personal distress, he suffered illnesses with similar paralytic effects. It is quite possible that he may have been told at some time during his stay in Starnberg of the change in his marriage from exclusive possession to something in the nature of a *ménage à trois*. "I wanted to try combining my former existence with my new life," Cosima wrote in her diary on 8 January 1869. "I believed in the possibility of fusing together all the diverging feelings – abuse and insults proved to me that I was being a fool." She attached no date to her decision, which could have been made much later, but her conduct in the following weeks suggests that it may indeed have been made during the weeks in Starnberg.

Bülow was expected in Karlsruhe in the middle of August for the annual meeting of the *Tonkünstlerverein*, at which Liszt would be present. At the same time Wagner had been invited to Hohenschwangau for the king's birthday celebrations, during which he planned to perform his *Huldigungsmarsch*, written in July for the occasion. When the time came for his departure, Bülow's illness was at its height, and there could be no question of his going to Karlsruhe. Instead, he was transferred to the Hotel de Bavière in Munich, where he could receive medical attention unobtainable in the country, while Cosima, who might have been expected to remain close to her husband during his illness, went off to Karlsruhe alone. "Hans to Munich: ill and raging in hotel," Wagner wrote in his *Annals*.

Bülow's rage might of course have been due simply to vexation with his illness, or to resentment at being left alone in the hotel. If he had been entirely oblivious of the relationship between Cosima and Wagner, there would indeed seem to be no other grounds for dissatisfaction, since by now he knew that all he needed to do to free himself from his dreary teaching duties in Berlin was to accept King Ludwig's offer. On 29 September, after his recovery from his illness and his return to Berlin, he wrote to his close friend, the composer Joachim Raff: "In many ways the call to Munich is a salvation. I do not conceal from myself the difficulties and unpleasantnesses that might await me there. But I have no hankering at all for a bed of roses, only for a possible field of activity, and one less sterile and sterilising than the one I have here." This was indeed a sceptical appraisal of his prospects in Munich, but it does not suggest any positive repugnance towards the job itself.

It seems evident that Cosima went to Karlsruhe with the intention of confiding in her father about the difficult position in which she now found herself. Perhaps she did not yet know for certain that she was pregnant with Wagner's child, but two entries in Wagner's *Brown Book* (of which more later) make it clear that Liszt learned of his association with Cosima in the summer of 1864. She returned from Karlsruhe, Wagner wrote, "sleepless, restless, weak, frail, miserable, lacerated". From Karlsruhe Liszt wrote to Princess Wittgenstein in Rome: "Cosima is showing very good sense in this situation and will set things to rights. She will possibly go back tomorrow to take care of her husband. For I am very worried about Hans, who wishes to return to Berlin, though meanwhile the king has in the friendliest possible way offered him a yearly salary of two thousand florins."

Cosima did not leave the following day, but remained in Karlsruhe until the end of the *Tonkünstlerverein* meeting, then returned to Munich together with her father. Liszt, whose relations with Wagner were at this time rather cool, told Princess Wittgenstein in a letter that he had at first been reluctant to visit the place in which Wagner had now found his "glorious fortune", but, having been assured by Cosima that Wagner was at Hohenschwangau, he felt he could visit Bülow in his hotel without running the risk of a meeting. However, Wagner returned to Munich unexpectedly, and they met at Bülow's bedside. It may have been an entirely fortuitous encounter, or it may equally well have been planned: obviously, if it had been Liszt's intention to discuss with Bülow what should be done about Cosima's "infatuation", Wagner's presence at the bedside would have proved an inhibiting factor. However, there is no evidence to support the suspicion of a collusion between Wagner and Cosima to prevent the discussion.

The basic cause of the present coolness between Wagner and Liszt was Wagner's dislike of Princess Wittgenstein, who in his view had a stifling influence on Liszt. In consequence, they had tended in recent years to keep out of each other's way. Yet when they did meet, the personal affection between them invariably, if briefly, reasserted itself. That had happened in August 1861 in Weimar, and now it happened again in Munich, for Liszt, who had come there expecting and hoping to avoid Wagner, immediately on meeting him accepted an invitation to spend a day and a night at Starnberg.

There they went together through the first act of *Die Meistersinger*, the only part so far completed, and Liszt was predictably enchanted by it. He wrote to Princess Wittgenstein the day after his visit that what had happened to Wagner bordered on a miracle: "Solomon was wrong when he said there was nothing new under the sun. I am fully convinced of that since yesterday evening – after Wagner showed me some of the king's letters to him. Basically nothing between us can have been changed by all this. The good fortune which has at last come on him whom I have now dubbed 'the Glorious' will possibly soften some of the rough edges of his character."

On 3 September Liszt returned to Weimar, Bülow and Cosima to Berlin. Wagner, alone again, complained to Eliza Wille on 9 September that he felt as if he were living in "a bewitched castle". But he nevertheless began at last to feel within him a revival of the creative impulse which had so long been dormant. He wrote to Bülow on 23 September: "I am feeling dizzy and have need of all the recklessness and energy of my character, for – seriously – I am now getting down to the completion of the *Nibelungen*: this work is the only one which at present appeals to me. If anything is to come of it, I must delay no longer. If after this I am still alive, I shall console myself with *Die Meistersinger*: at present I am too tense to occupy my mind with Beckmesser and Pogner."

On 27 September he began work on the orchestration of the first act of *Siegfried*, which he had so far completed up to the end of the first scene.* But, while engaged on what for him was only work of a more or less mechanical nature, he was already beginning to think of the un-written third act. A week later, on 30 September, he wrote again to Bülow: "I am wonderfully in the mood for the third act of *Siegfried*, par-ticularly for the first scene with Wotan: what a prelude that is to be! Short, but – accentuated."

This second letter was chiefly devoted to personal matters, to the house in Munich (Briennerstrasse 21) into which he was preparing to move and to an apartment in a house nearby which he thought suitable for Bülow and his family. He seems to have been in no doubt that they would be returning to Munich. He expressed his pleasure that Liszt had been staying with them in Berlin: "I shall no doubt continue to be annoyed with him up to the day of my death, though for one reason only – that I cannot have him for my own. Why, oh, why can he not decide to belong to us entirely?" There follows then, clearly in reply to some remark by Bülow about Cosima's indifferent health, a passage which has since proved a puzzle to successive biographers: "I am worried too about Cosima's indisposition. Everything in connection with her is extraordinary and unusual: what she requires is freedom in its noblest sense. She is childlike and deep – the dictates of her character will always and inevitably lead her to sublime heights. And nobody can help her, except she herself. She belongs to a special world order which we must learn, from her, to understand. In future days you will have a greater measure of leisure and personal freedom to pay attention to this and

---

* *Siegfried* was composed up to the end of the second act in the years 1856/57, and then laid aside in "orchestral sketch" form, i.e. the music written on three or four staves with indications of the final scoring. The full orchestral score of Act I, Scene 1, had also been completed before Wagner put the work aside to compose *Tristan und Isolde*.

find your noble place at her side. That too provides me with some consolation."

These remarks must indeed have mystified Bülow if at that time he knew nothing of the true relationship between Cosima and Wagner. But, if Cosima had by then told him of her decision to divide her attentions equally between him and Wagner, he would have found them clear enough. His situation was an appalling one: both his deep devotion to Wagner and the opportunities opened to his career were powerful incentives to accept the post he had been offered in Munich, yet, in doing so, he must have been aware that he was consenting to yield up a part of his wife.

He was alone in Berlin when Wagner's letter arrived. Cosima had left to accompany her father on a trip to Löwenberg, Eisenach and Paris – in itself a sign that all was not well between her and Bülow at this time. Liszt's sympathies were entirely with his son-in-law, and there can be no doubt that he did his utmost to persuade his daughter to give up what, in his worldly-wise way, he saw as just a passing infatuation for Wagner. Yet in the end it was Liszt who persuaded Bülow to take the risk and accept the post in Munich. "There is no more point in delay," he wrote from Rome on 21 October 1864. "A complex task, laborious duties, will devolve on you. You will meet them satisfactorily. Through them your external career will gain in magnitude and your *inner self* will rise to its natural heights. My prayers and my deepest affection will be yours always."

Bülow, it seems, was still hesitant about committing himself, but his subsequent letter to Wagner must at least have hinted at acceptance, for Wagner replied on 11 November from his new home in the Briennerstrasse, to which he had moved on 15 October: "You write so finely and so encouragingly that you make me feel really glad. I now have everything I could possibly wish for, all so pleasant and friendly – except that I lack – people, a few nice, thoroughly congenial people who belong to me entirely. These cannot be entirely new people: they must have grown with me to be part of my life. So come, and complete what happiness is available to me on this earth!"

It needed yet another letter from Liszt finally to persuade Bülow to accept his fate. Liszt wrote from Rome on 12 November: "For many years you have given me so much cause to love you, to recognise your worth and be proud of you, that I beg you to dispose at once of the only annoyance that occasionally disturbs our usual affectionate relationship. This annoyance arises from your injustice towards yourself and a certain strange lack of confidence in your own superiority, so marked and well-attested as it otherwise is. Fair and generous to the point of heroism as you are to everyone else, you persist in ascribing imaginary faults and errors to yourself. I wish I could persuade you to drop this habit . . . and discover a way of sharing my feelings about the real value of your heart and character, your intelligence and your talent. Do try to leave all those headaches and rheumatic pains behind you in Berlin, together with your old furniture – and let us make a new start in Munich.''

On 20 November Bülow and Cosima arrived in Munich with their two daughters and took up residence in an apartment in the Luitpoldstrasse, close to Wagner's home.

CHAPTER III

DECEMBER 1864 – DECEMBER 1865:

Munich and the Brown Book

THE EMPHASIS PLACED on personal relationships in the first two chapters, to the virtual exclusion of artistic matters, has been due mainly to the desire to trace in detail the development of the relationship between Wagner and Cosima and to establish the background against which it came to maturity. That stage was reached in the summer of 1864 in Starnberg, when their marriage can be said to have begun, though its legal confirmation was still six years away. The first artistic fruits of their love for each other were those serene and tender musical themes, initially intended for a quartet or a symphony, which were later incorporated into the love scene between Brünnhilde and Siegfried in the third act of *Siegfried* and, even more felicitously, in the *Siegfried Idyll*. The verbal expression was a poem entitled "An Dich" ("To Thee"), which Wagner wrote on 1 October 1864, shortly after Cosima had left Starnberg to return with Bülow to Berlin, a tender love poem in which Wagner compared himself to a setting sun and Cosima to the evening star, Venus, whose glow banished approaching night and promised him a new day.

What might, in contrast, be described as "work" was restricted during the weeks in Starnberg to the *Huldigungsmarsch*, the first performance of which, abandoned at Hohenschwangau owing to the presence there of King Ludwig's disapproving mother, took place in the courtyard of the Munich Residenz on 5 October; and an essay entitled "Über Staat und Religion" ("On State and Religion"). This was a response to Ludwig's wish to know to what extent, if at all, Wagner had changed his views on human society since defining them so forcefully in those works of his Zurich years, which had proved such an inspiration to Ludwig in his earliest youth. In his essay, written in July, Wagner admitted that in those previous works he had in reality been thinking only of his art, "that art which was for me a matter of such seriousness that I was concerned only in seeking and demanding a justifiable basis for it in the realms of life, the state and, finally, religion".

His mistake, he went on to say, was in taking his art too seriously and life too lightly. The world's main need was stability, and this was

achieved by organisation into states, "in which the tendency of the individual is naturally to obtain as much security for himself as is possible
with the least possible personal sacrifice". It was this egotistical attitude
which made it imperative that no *single* party should rule the state, and
the guarantee against such imbalance was the monarch, whose task it
was to represent justness and mercy. Only the monarch, through the
"superhuman" nature of his position, was able to make the ordinary
citizen conscious of the fact that humanity bore within itself an infinitely
deeper and more comprehensive need than could be satisfied by the
state alone. And it was the task of religion to lead mankind to a realisation of its proper worth.

Arguing his way through the relative merits of dogma and faith,
Wagner asserted that true religion existed "only in the profoundest and
most sacred inner depths of the individual, where no quarrel between
rationalists and supernaturalists, between church and state has ever
penetrated; for it is the very nature of true religion that, away from the
deceptive daylight of the world, it shines in the night of the deepest
depths of the human consciousness with a light entirely different from
that of the world's sun, and perceivable only from these depths". And he
came to the conclusion that only through practical example could such
perceptions be conveyed to others: the true agents of salvation were not
"power-hungry priests", but saints and martyrs.

And what, Wagner finally asked, was the function of art in all this?
Here he introduced that element of human consciousness which he
called *Wahn* (a word for which there is no adequate English translation):
it was analogous, he explained, to that instinct in bees and ants which
caused them to work together for the good of a whole that individually
they could not grasp. In human beings this underlying instinct found its
unconscious expression in patriotism – a dangerous emotion, since it
could give rise to injustice and violence towards other states. The dis-
advantage of the state, he concluded, was that it concentrated too
exclusively on the material aspects of life, of religion, that it ignored these
in favour of a future reward in heaven. The duty of art was to examine
and illuminate life through presenting it to an uncomprehending world
in the form of a deliberate and conscious pretence.

This essay has been worth summarising at some length, since it reveals
much of Wagner's basic outlook. The stress he placed on the monarch's
role clearly owed something to the fact that the essay was addressed to
King Ludwig, but there is no reason to believe that he was being insincere in advocating a monarchical system: he did genuinely believe in
it, and throughout his life it was not the system he attacked, but the
princes who so woefully failed to live up to the ideal he ascribed to them.
For Ludwig, however, it was perilous advice. In him the idea of the

monarch as a being appointed by God to his solitary mission was already strong, and the words of his revered master could only serve to increase still further his belief in the divine right of kings – a belief that in the end led to his tragic downfall.

Wagner's first weeks in the Briennerstrasse, whatever promise of happiness they may have contained, were shadowed by apprehension and depression. The reason was partly physical: haemorrhoids (for which he had to undergo a slight operation), boils and chills plagued him from October 1864 onwards. Another difficulty arose through the visit of Mathilde Maier and her mother, who had seen an erroneous newspaper report that he was seriously ill with typhoid fever. They arrived just as he was moving into the Briennerstrasse, and he entertained them as well as he could. During Mathilde's visit Cosima also arrived in Munich to make arrangements for the move of her own family. After both had departed, Wagner wrote to Mathilde on 7 November, apologising for his nervy state during her visit: "Forgive me if I seemed hard; basically my bitterness was directed only against myself. In six months' time . . . when I shall have resumed my artistic activity both outwardly and inwardly – how lovable you will find me then!"

The first of his works that Wagner staged in Munich for the king's benefit was *Der Fliegende Holländer*, which had not been seen there before. He himself conducted the first two performances on 4 and 8 December. These were followed on 11 December by a concert consisting mainly of extracts from his uncompleted or unperformed works: the Prelude and "Pogner's Address" from *Die Meistersinger*, the Prelude and "Liebestod" from *Tristan und Isolde*, Siegmund's "Spring Song", the "Ride of the Valkyries" and Wotan's "Farewell" from *Die Walküre*, and the "Forging Songs" from *Siegfried*. Ludwig, who attended the final rehearsal on 10 December, wrote ecstatically on the following morning: "It becomes ever clearer to me that I am not in a position to reward you according to your deserts; all I do for you, all I can undertake on your behalf, amounts only to a grateful stammering. A mortal spirit cannot aspire to the level of a divine one; but it can love and honour; you are and will eternally remain my only love . . . I am like a spark, filled with longing to merge into the radiance of your sun, to bask in its beams and to leave this earth when it no longer shines."

Wagner had begun a letter to the King at the same time, expressing the fear that he might have strained the king's patience too far by making him witness all the rigours of rehearsal. The king's letter, which arrived before he had completed his, brought an immediate change of tone: "Oh, faint-hearted creature that I am!! So, even in my love for him, the only one, he must continue to fill me with courage! Without him I am nothing. I need him even to teach me for the first time what it is to love. . . . Oh, my King, you are divine!"

Such highflown phrases, common between Wagner and the king in the first two years after their meeting and always liable to break out again when some musical event moved them, have led to the surmise that there may have been a homosexual element in their feelings for each other. Ludwig was indeed a homosexual, though it must be doubtful whether at that time this was fully recognised, even by Ludwig himself – he was, after all, only nineteen years old. Wagner, whose heterosexual interests need no emphasis, professed to understand homosexuality, but to have a personal distaste for it. The relationship was rather that of father and son, the young king representing for Wagner the son he had never had, Wagner for Ludwig the father he had not found in the cold and remote King Maximilian.

"If this very extraordinary and far-reaching venture comes to nothing," Wagner wrote to Mathilde Maier on 17 December, "there will be only my age, my loneliness and my depression to blame. In the will of my friend everything is already complete and mature." Ludwig had by now decided on the erection of a special theatre in Munich for the production of Wagner's works, and he had given Wagner permission to entrust his friend, the architect Gottfried Semper, with the preparation of plans; he was also eager to reform the existing school of music to train musicians in accordance with Wagner's ideas.

If the king underestimated the practical difficulties of bringing all these plans to fruition, Wagner himself did not. He was aware that the existing staff at the Munich Court Theatre, including the artistic director, Wilhelm Schmitt, and the highly conservative conductor, Franz Lachner, did not look kindly on this royal favourite who by his very presence threatened their jobs, and among the singers there were few whom he considered adequate for the model performances of his works he planned to stage. Guest singers would have to be brought in – an added source of jealousy against the outsider and the "foreigners" he had already imported or was about to import: Bülow from Berlin, Semper from Zurich, and (to work in the reformed music school) both Cornelius from Vienna and the singing teacher Friedrich Schmitt from Leipzig. And it was certainly a matter for concern that the man Ludwig appointed Prime Minister of Bavaria at this time, Ludwig von der Pfordten, had been a minister in Saxony and had vivid memories of the part Wagner had played in the Dresden uprising of 1849.

At the moment, however, there were no open signs of trouble. Bülow, still in poor health on his return to Munich in November, was sufficiently restored to take part in a concert in Munich on Christmas Day, when he played the solo part, with Lachner conducting, of Beethoven's

"Emperor" Concerto in the presence of the king. He was given a very friendly reception. The next of Wagner's friends to arrive was Peter Cornelius, who in his impecunious state found the king's offer of one thousand florins annually for no very clearly defined duties impossible to resist. His first opera, *Der Barbier von Bagdad*, had been a sensational failure in Weimar in 1858; since then it had not been performed anywhere. Anxious to restore his fortunes as a composer with a new opera, *Le Cid*, Cornelius was reluctant to resume the intimate kind of friendship he had had with Wagner in the Vienna years. He could not compose in Wagner's vicinity, he told his brother Carl in a letter dated 26 November 1864: "He consumes me." However, the composition of *Le Cid* being now virtually complete and Wagner holding out the prospect of a production in Munich, his resistance broke down, and he arrived there on 30 December.

Two days later, on 1 January 1865, he wrote in his diary: "I paid a visit to the Bülows. Hans was indisposed, his condition a cause for concern. Both are noble and refined people, but heaven knows how things stand between them, how they live together – I shall get a glimpse of that as time goes on. I had a very animated conversation with Cosima; she is a person with whom one finds oneself at once immersed in soul-searching subjects." To Heinrich Porges, a mutual friend who was soon himself to join the little band of supporters in Munich, he wrote on 8 January: "The Bülows are very nice and friendly. We have already formed a sort of parental clique against Wagner. Recently I was discussing with Hans in all seriousness whether we ought to provide him with a peri or not." He noted in his diary that he found Wagner much changed from the man whose life he had shared in Vienna: he was irritable, withdrawn and domineering.

The first shadow to appear between Wagner and the king occurred in the early days of February, when in an unguarded moment Wagner referred to him, in an interview with Pfistermeister, as *"mein Junge"* ("my boy"). The king's cabinet secretary, no friend now to Wagner in any case, was so incensed by this lack of respect that he at once reported it to the king. When on the following day, 6 February, Wagner went to the Residenz to see Ludwig, he was denied admittance. The rumours that he had fallen into disgrace gave Wagner's enemies the signal to launch an attack on him, and on 19 February an anonymous article appeared in the *Augsburger Allgemeine Zeitung*, denouncing him for living extravagantly at the king's expense. Wagner replied three days later with a dignified statement: it was his own affair, he declared, how he spent his money, fairly earned in the king's service. Ludwig very soon forgave him his indiscreet remark and, though considering it expedient to avoid personal meetings for the time being, assured him of his undying loyalty. ("Love can achieve everything: we shall triumph!")

"Why in a place where I have sought only rest and leisure to work undisturbed," Wagner wrote to Frau Wille on 26 February, "have I become involved in a responsibility which lays the salvation of a divinely gifted human being, perhaps even the welfare of a state, in my hands? . . . He lacks the person he really needs." This, he wrote, was what really disturbed him, not the intrigues.

Relieved for the time being from his visits to the king, he concentrated on his production of *Tristan und Isolde*, now at last to be brought to the stage, six years after its completion. He introduced his chosen Tristan, Ludwig Schnorr von Carolsfeld, to Munich on 3 March in a performance of *Tannhäuser*, coaching him the day before in a role which Schnorr had already sung many times, but which, he wrote to his mother, he now saw he had never fully understood. Wagner was greatly impressed by Schnorr's quickness of response. His performance would, he assured Ludwig, make up for the deficiencies in the rest of the production, a standard repertory performance, conducted by Lachner, of the original Dresden version.

Being unwilling to entrust Lachner with the conducting of *Tristan und Isolde*, Wagner wrote a tactful letter to the king on 12 March, pointing out that the opera house's musical director could not be expected to take a subordinate position to himself as producer, and thus it would be more expedient to give the conductor's task to Bülow, if the king would provide the necessary authority. To this Ludwig at once assented, and Bülow was given the official title of "court conductor for special services".

Rehearsals began on 10 March in the little rococo Residenztheater adjoining the much larger opera house. From Dresden Wagner brought in, beside Schnorr and his wife Malvina, his old friend Anton Mitterwurzer (Wolfram in the first production of *Tannhäuser* in 1845) to sing the role of Kurwenal. He offered the part of King Marke to Johann Nepomuk Beck, a singer he had admired in Vienna, but it went eventually to Zottmayer of Hanover, a singer whom Bülow described as "weak in the head, but strong in the lungs". The remaining singers were members of the Munich company, and scenery and costumes were prepared by the resident designers, Angelo Quaglio and Franz Seitz respectively.

Wagner was under no illusions about the difficulties of producing this work of his in which, as he later told Cosima, "he had felt the urge to run himself to a standstill musically", in contrast to all his previous works, in which the music was often subordinated to dramatic considerations. Its small cast and lack of bold visual effects suited the intimate little Residenztheater to perfection, and Wagner pleaded with the king to be allowed to stage it there rather than in the large house.

He wrote on 20 April: "Everything depends solely on the portrayal of the purely human aspects. The action throughout is of a delicate, inward nature: here every quiver of a facial expression, every blinking of an eye must make its effect." Ludwig gave his consent ("HE wishes it, that is enough for me!"), but, as rehearsals progressed, acoustical difficulties caused Wagner to change his mind, and he wrote to Ludwig on 1 May: "The substantial, sensual sound of the orchestra, which no device can dampen, and against which all our efforts at interpretation struggle in vain, force me to return with my cherished singers from this small but noisy room to the large theatre. Here – in the large theatre – I am subject to the two drawbacks I wanted so much to avoid: the excessive distance between actor and onlooker (for the expressive gestures) and the disturbing effects of a large audience, which for the first performances I should have liked to have been smaller and more selective. These I must now sacrifice in the interests of musical clarity. Oh, for my invisible, sunken – transfigured orchestra in the theatre of the future!"

In the city the rehearsals were being watched with curiosity, not unmixed with malice. The news of the king's intention to build a grandiose new theatre for Wagner's works had got around, and there was a growing feeling of apprehension about the likely cost to the citizens themselves of the king's infatuation with his favourite composer. The newspapers, always in search of ways to discredit Wagner and his disciples, were provided with a splendid opportunity by Bülow, who during rehearsals requested that the orchestra should be enlarged for the *Tristan* performances. When told that this would mean the loss of thirty seats in the stalls, he replied: "Well, what do thirty *Schweinehunde* more or less matter?" The ensuing scandal was not fully assuaged by Bülow's public apology, in which he asserted that his derogatory remark, spoken in ignorance of the fact that members of the press were within hearing, had been directed, not at the Munich public in general, but solely at Wagner's enemies. Apart from this, he declared, the word "*Schweinehund*" (probably best translated by "cur") was not considered particularly abusive in the northern part of Germany from which he came. If the first performance of *Tristan und Isolde* had taken place on 15 May as planned, only a week after Bülow made his indiscreet remark, there would certainly have been a demonstration against him. But at the last moment Malvina von Schnorr, whose progress as Isolde had advanced so strikingly that Wagner himself was describing her to the king as a worthy successor to the famous Wilhelmine Schröder-Devrient, became indisposed, and the opening was postponed until 10 June.

Anger having died down by this time, there were no demonstrations, but the newspapers continued to be hostile, *Der Volksbote* commenting sourly that all the applause with which the work was received was due to "an immense *claque*, following blatant manoeuvres such as Munich has never before witnessed". In fact there was no *claque* in the usual meaning of the word, but it is true that the audience was "selective" in that it included a large contingent of Wagner's supporters from outside the city, all of whom had been encouraged to apply for tickets.

The king's reaction to *Tristan und Isolde* was ecstatic to the point of incoherence. He wrote to Wagner immediately after the performance: "What rapture! – *Perfect*. Overwhelmed by delight! – . . . To drown . . . sink down – unconscious – highest bliss. – *Divine* work!" And Wagner's reply, written just before the second performance on 13 June, was equally euphoric. "I say quite boldly: beside *our Tristan*, as it will again sound and resound today, there is nothing comparable in kind to be set. And this was – your beginning! . . . What is success, what is failure? To be, to be what is needed – that is everything!"

Three performances of *Tristan und Isolde* had been scheduled. Ludwig had intended to see them all, but the prospect of having to share his royal box with King Otto of Greece on 19 June made him decide to miss the third performance and to apply to King Johann of Saxony for permission to retain the Schnorrs and Mitterwurzer a few days longer. The fourth and last performance took place on 1 July. Schnorr remained in Munich to sing, on 12 July, at a private concert for the king, some of the music from the *Ring* and *Die Meistersinger*, and he also sang Erik in a performance of *Der Fliegende Holländer*. Returning to Dresden, he fell ill with rheumatic fever, and on 21 July he died, at the age of only twenty-nine.

In his "Reminiscences of Schnorr von Carolsfeld", written three years after the singer's death, Wagner provided a vivid description of the man in whom so many of his hopes had rested and whose premature death was a blow from which he never fully recovered. He remarked on his preliminary alarm over Schnorr's corpulence when he first saw him in 1862, singing Lohengrin at Karlsruhe, but the power of his acting and the beauty of his "full, pliant and brilliant" voice soon overcame his concern at the physical drawbacks. What most impressed him about Schnorr was his complete intellectual grasp of the role he was playing and his ability to interpret even so complicated a psychological state as Tristan's in the third act in such a way that he commanded complete attention: "The orchestra disappeared entirely, or – to put it more correctly – seemed to be contained within his portrayal."

Schnorr, he said in this article, was to have been at the centre of the new school of music in Munich. He would have given up his career as an opera singer and become a teacher of dramatic art in Wagner's sense of the word, singing only in special productions. But the superb quality of the singer's Tristan made Wagner apprehensive of proceeding too quickly, and led to his decision not to allow further performances of

Tristan und Isolde for the time being. "With this production, as with the work itself, there had occurred a too powerful, almost desperate step into the new territories which had still to be conquered. Gulfs and abysses still yawned, and these had first to be carefully filled up."

Because of this sense of the revolutionary nature of his *Tristan und Isolde*, Wagner kept a much tighter control over its performances than with any other work of his, with the later exception of *Parsifal*. Part of his reluctance to see it staged was undoubtedly due to its associations with the unforgettable Schnorr, but it owed something also to his feeling, frequently recorded in Cosima's diary, that the work demanded too much of the audience, and he talked of making cuts in it, particularly in the second act, and of thinning down the orchestration, which he felt was at times too heavy. However, he never did so.

On 10 April 1865, the day on which the first orchestral rehearsal of *Tristan und Isolde* took place, Cosima gave birth to her third daughter, who was given the name of Isolde. Wagner regarded her as his child, but in the eyes of the law she belonged to Hans von Bülow. And not only in the eyes of the law: Bülow himself continued obstinately throughout his life to claim Isolde as the child of his loins, and he even provided her with a share in his estate, a mark of recognition withheld from Cosima's two remaining children, Eva and Siegfried, though both of them were born while legally she was still Bülow's wife. This, together with remarks concerning Isolde made during his lifetime, suggests that his claim to be her father was based, not on social convention, but on genuine belief.

This is one of the factors that make it impossible to establish with complete certainty the extent of Bülow's knowledge of the relationship between Cosima and Wagner at that time. It is clearly possible that he did not know until later that it was an adulterous relationship, but in that case Isolde's birth must be accepted as proof that he himself was living a normal sexual life with Cosima at the time her relations with Wagner first became intimate. Wagner was no less convinced that Isolde was his child. At the end of the composition sketch of *Götterdämmerung* he wrote: "Thus accomplished and concluded on the day on which seven years ago my Loldchen was born, 10 April 1872," and for her birthday in 1880 he wrote a little poem: "Fifteen years ago you were born: / The whole world pricked up its ears; / Others wanted *Tristan und Isolde* − / But all I wished for and wanted / Was a little daughter: Isolde! / May she now live a thousand years, / And *Tristan und Isolde* also!" Cosima herself kept silent on the subject, and many years later she allowed Isolde to take her to court in an effort to establish, on behalf of her own son, that she was Wagner's child: Isolde lost her case (in 1914). The conclusion seems inescapable that Cosima herself was not entirely sure.

Both she and Bülow spent a great deal of their time in Wagner's house in the Briennerstrasse, where, in addition to the Mrazeks, Wagner now had a housekeeper. Verena Weidmann, known as Vreneli, had first come to his notice while he was working in 1859 on the third act of *Tristan und Isolde* in Lucerne; she was a chambermaid at the Schweizerhof, the hotel in which he was living, and she impressed him with her devoted attention. A child of the people, full of good sense, Vreneli had no intellectual pretensions, and Wagner treated her, from the time she joined him in September 1864, as a privileged higher servant. She repaid him with unfailing loyalty, remaining in his service until 1872.

Cosima's self-assumed duties in the Briennerstrasse were secretarial rather than domestic. King Ludwig had expressed a wish to read all of Wagner's writings, and Wagner gave Cosima the task of recovering the manuscripts from the widely scattered places in which they lay, so that copies could be made for the king. Mathilde Wesendonck, pained to receive from Cosima a request for the many papers in her possession, wrote to Wagner on 13 January saying that she was unwilling to part with anything except at his direct request. Wagner was careful in his reply to conceal from Mathilde, Cosima's real status in his household. He put the whole blame for the request on the king: "Everything that I have ever committed to paper must be gathered together from hidden files everywhere. He knows that he should not involve me overmuch in this work, and he always craftily turns to acquaintances. That is what he has done here."

Mathilde Wesendonck was not the only of his former friends to resent the manner in which Cosima began to interpose herself between them and Wagner. Cornelius in particular soon turned from an intimate companion into a jealous and suspicious adversary. He was understandably absent from Munich during the preparations for *Tristan und Isolde*, since his *Le Cid* was being rehearsed in Weimar at the same time. But after the launching of *Le Cid* on 21 May he remained in Weimar, thereby missing the performances of *Tristan und Isolde*, and it became evident that a battle of wills was in progress. Wagner was annoyed by his absence, and in his letters made bitter remarks which only strengthened Cornelius's resolve to keep his distance. Finally Bülow intervened. "Speak out," he wrote to Cornelius on 4 July. "Make use of me if you find it embarrassing to tell W. direct what is on your mind. I shall act entirely in accordance with your wishes, either with diplomatic discretion or with a sergeant-major-like gruffness. . . . I know that at the bottom of your heart you dislike me. I have no romance left in me, very little love, considerably more hatred and a terrible amount of scorn and disillusion. But I wonder if there is anybody who, having gone through all I have gone through and not succumbed, would not likewise have turned into a Bonaparte." This letter, and probably the hint it contained that Bülow would do his best to have *Le Cid* staged in Munich (a hope that came to nothing), succeeded in persuading Cornelius to make his peace with Wagner, and he returned to Munich to resume his duties at the music school. On 10 August he wrote to his future wife: "With Bülow's wife I am in disgrace for the rest of eternity, I'm sure of that." And basically this was true. Though on the surface their relations remained amicable, Cosima found it impossible to forgive anybody whose loyalty towards Wagner was not as steadfast and self-sacrificing as her own.

She knew that Wagner, for all his demandingness, was deeply devoted to his friends, and in their occasional rebellions against him she detected an egotism equal to his own, but one which, measured by achievements, was considerably less justified. Cornelius had caused Wagner genuine pain through his absence from the *Tristan* performances, and she made it her duty to shield him from such emotional disturbances as far as she was able. It seemed to his friends – not only Cornelius, but also to Semper and to another close friend in Vienna, the young pianist Karl Tausig – that they could no longer gain access to Wagner except with Cosima's consent, or at least in her presence. "The Delphic oracle", Tausig called her.

With the king Cosima as yet had nothing to do, and she was scarcely mentioned by Wagner in their correspondence, except as Bülow's wife and one of the trusted circle of friends on whom their artistic hopes rested. But in his letter to Ludwig of 21–22 July Wagner gave the king a hint of her true significance to him: "What was I engaged in when your letter arrived yesterday? – To save you from guessing, I shall tell you: I was dictating my biography! Friend Cosima never ceases reminding me of our king's wish. Now the most favourable hours of the day are being filled by my relating my story truthfully to my friend, who carefully writes it all down. She is amazed how flowingly it all proceeds, as if I were reading it out of a book. . . . We have decided to continue the dictation up to my union with you, my magnificent friend, and from then on Cosima is to continue the biography alone, and one day, it is to be hoped, complete it."

The first page of Wagner's autobiography *Mein Leben* (*My Life*) bears the inscription "Munich, 17 July 1865" and the intertwined initials "W, R, C", presumably standing for "Wagner, Richard, Cosima". Forty pages were written down before work was put aside. An entry in the margin of the last page reveals why: "Broken off through Schnorr's death (21 July '65)."

Even without that, work would have been interrupted. A new motive had been added to Liszt's determination to do all in his power to save

Bülow's marriage, for he had recently taken orders as a minor canon, which gave him some, though not all, of the powers of a Roman Catholic priest. An an abbé it was impossible for him to condone among his family any behaviour that might look like immorality. It was neither thoughtlessness nor sentimentality that had led him to take orders, he wrote to Bülow on 25 April: "It might be described rather as a consequence of than an alteration in my life, at any rate in the way it has developed in recent years."

The refusal of the Vatican to recognise Princess Carolyne's divorce in Russia from Prince Nicholas Sayn-Wittgenstein had prevented Liszt from marrying her in 1861, and since then they had lived apart, she in the Via del Babuino in Rome, he dividing his time between Weimar, where he had an apartment in the grounds of the ducal palace, and Rome, where he lived in rooms in the Villa d'Este. His lifestyle had become increasingly modest. Though he still taught at Weimar, he demanded no fees from his piano pupils, nor did he accept payment for the concerts he still gave occasionally in places of his own choosing. Travelling everywhere by train, second-class, with a single manservant, he did indeed appear to have turned his back on all the vain pleasures of the world. In March 1864 Princess Carolyne's husband died, and the once desired union could have taken place, for as an abbé Liszt was still permitted to marry. However, neither showed any eagerness: she was by now immersed in literary activities, writing a huge work on the interior causes of the exterior weakness of the Church, while he concerned himself mainly with composition, most of it of a religious kind. Yet the deep bond between them persisted, despite all separations, for the rest of his life. Nothing – neither her jealousies nor her growing eccentricities as she laboured in her room in the Via del Babuino, stuffy from the smoke of her cigars, on the book which he found unreadable – could weaken his devotion. When he was away from Rome he wrote to her constantly, even about the embarrassments that the occasional love affairs in which he was still likely to become involved caused him. He might, while away from her, sometimes sigh about his yoke, and she, when he was in Rome, might seem to outsiders to treat him with little respect, but the ties remained insoluble.

At this stage Liszt did not recognise in the love between Cosima and Wagner anything akin to the bond between himself and Princess Wittgenstein. In order to cure his daughter of her "infatuation", he invited her and Bülow to attend the first performance in Budapest of his new oratorio, *Die heilige Elisabeth*, on 15 August, then to join him in a prolonged tour of Hungary. It was decided (by whom is not clear) that Wagner should not correspond with Cosima during this separation. She wrote frequently to him, but he kept to the agreement – at any rate to outward appearances. In fact, he did write to her.

He did so in his *Brown Book* (in German *Das braune Buch*). Cosima had made him a present of a large notebook covered in brown leather, its bronze bindings, fitted with a lock, adorned with twelve stones of green malachite. They decided that in this notebook Wagner would write his replies to her letters, and she would read them on her return. The *Brown Book* begins with some twenty-six letters addressed to Cosima between 8 August and 13 September. Although passages from these letters have been published before, it was not until 1975 that the *Brown Book* was published as a whole, revealing for the first time material which Cosima's daughter Eva had attempted in later years to conceal by sticking pages together or by blotting out whole sentences.

Following Cosima's departure for Budapest, Wagner went off to one of King Ludwig's Alpine hunting lodges on the Hochkopf, a mountain to the south of Munich. Accompanied only by his servant Franz Mrazek and his dog Pohl, he planned to do some work on the orchestration of *Siegfried*, but very little was done. At first he was exhilarated by the isolation and beauty of his surroundings and wrote merrily to Cosima of an expedition he made in his nightshirt by moonlight in a vain search for water, for the king's lodge turned out to be very primitive. He ended his letter with a confident declaration: "I love you with an ultimate love" – this incidentally one of the sentences Eva Chamberlain felt obliged to blot out. But two days later he caught a feverish cold, the weather turned bad and he began to feel lonely. "We must not part again, do you hear? – That's one thing, and if we stay together for ever we shall see what happens about the rest," he wrote on 14 August.

His depression, which his reading of Victor Hugo's *Les Misérables* did nothing to alleviate, led on 15 August to an outburst, following the arrival of two letters from Cosima in which she told him that, on a visit to Vienna, Bülow had prevented her from going to see the house in which Wagner had lived: "What madness! And that fool Hans who wouldn't let you go to Penzing and showed you the shops of Vienna instead! Can one believe it? Can one believe it? And this, if you please, is my only friend! – Ah, foolish hearts! Blind eyes!! – But how beautiful, how beautiful you are, my wife! – Yes, you are mine, and only *you* have any right to *me*. No one else has any knowledge of me. Oh, heavens, how long shall we have to go on tormenting ourselves in this existence? And yet – what am I saying? Was it not in this existence that we found each other?"

Cosima, writing her letters from Hungary with no means of gauging Wagner's present mood, occasionally said the wrong thing. In one letter she appears to have shown jealousy of Mathilde Maier, who had been in Munich for the *Tristan* performances, and this brought a reproach, only half humorous in tone. But his main resentment was directed towards Liszt. "What a nasty letter you wrote me yesterday!" he wrote on 18 August. "What you are actually saying to me is nothing else but that you have been wrong to love me so much, and as a result to treat your father so badly, he being the only one who really loves you. That is nice! And this you find quite easy to say, especially when you are away from me and with your father!" In the struggle to win Cosima for himself Wagner saw Liszt as his main adversary. It was, however, less Liszt himself he feared – rather his daughter's devotion to him. Wagner could never feel sure of Cosima while she was in her father's company.

In his depressed state he found himself taking stock of his present situation in Munich, and he came to the conclusion that it was in danger of falling apart through over-hastiness. In March he had written for the king a lengthy account of the paths to be pursued in setting up his music school, and Semper had submitted his plans for the erection of the special Wagner theatre. Two plans had been prepared, one for a grandiose building on the banks of the river Isar, to be approached by a wide new road through the outskirts of the inner city, the other for a temporary theatre to be erected inside the Glaspalast, an existing building on the lines of London's Crystal Palace. Wagner was in favour of the latter, not only because it could be built more quickly, but also because it would enable him to test at less cost the effectiveness of his revolutionary constructional ideas, which he had already worked out with Semper during the years in Zurich. Ludwig preferred the monumental building, but the public outcry against the enormous expense of it, and Wagner's argument that he would be able to see the *Ring* sooner in the more modest building, brought him round to the temporary theatre. Now a letter from him to Wagner on the Hochkopf, dated 14 August, showed that he was again shifting his ground: "In September Semper will arrive in Munich, select the site and immediately come here to discuss the matter personally with me. In my mind's eye I already see the majestic building standing in front of me; thousands are making a pilgrimage from near and far for the national festival; what sounds are setting my inner being trembling with bliss? I hear the waters of the Rhine flowing past. . . ."

In his very lengthy reply, written on 20 August, Wagner sought to curb the king's enthusiasm, urging the necessity for himself of a period of tranquillity in which he could complete *Siegfried* and *Götterdämmerung*: "My health, my spirits, all my energies will be restored to me only when I am once again wholly absorbed in this one element to which I belong, the element for which I am organised and destined. It is because I have been isolated so long from this element that I have become miserable, indisposed and moribund." There would be no time to stage model performances of his existing works, hence no hurry to complete the special theatre.

The seeds of the music school were already planted, he went on to say: in Schmitt he had a singing teacher in whom he had every confidence, but it would take a year at least to produce singers of the required standard, and then they would be only singers. Who could take on Schnorr's task of turning them into fine actors? This, only time would reveal, but in the meantime it would be a good idea to engage Schnorr's wife Malvina, and he suggested that Ludwig might take her on as a singer in his private employ at 1,500 florins a year, with a similar salary as a teacher at the school, and special payments for every appearance she should make on stage. As for the director of the school, there was only one choice: Bülow. "Fate has placed him in my path. Were I to die today, Hans Bülow would be the only man to whom I could entrust my works. Indeed, when I at last reach the point of making my will, I shall state quite explicitly that he alone is authorised to perform my works. Bülow has all the attributes of a very great artist, and in addition abilities of a kind I myself do not possess. He lacks only one thing: imaginative productivity. But, if he were to possess that, he would be lost to me, and that is why – because of what he does *not* have – he is so indispensable to me. I do not need to praise him: his quite incomparable achievement as conductor of *Tristan* filled everybody with amazement. Beside myself there is no one who could conduct like that. His fame as a practising musician is surpassed only by Liszt: otherwise nobody is his equal."

And finally, in this very long and persuasive letter, Wagner brought in Cosima: "To secure my works for yourself and the world by making their performance possible – this only you can do. . . . You shall be the guiding star for the small band of chosen spirits to whose love Fate has entrusted me and my works. A high-minded, profoundly noble feminine spirit is interwoven in this circle. If you should ever feel the need for true and profound enlightenment about anything regarding me that you do not understand, address yourself to this rare being, who will reveal it all to you as clearly as the Norns in their reflecting pool."

After writing his letter to the king, Wagner decided to return to Munich. In the evening, after all his possessions had been packed, he took his *Brown Book* and wrote a reply to Cosima's last letter, which contained news of Budapest and Liszt's new oratorio: "It told me that you still love me. That pleased me most of all. But why can I simply not take heart any more? Now that I have abandoned hope, shall love alone remain to me, and even faith, faith in myself, vanish? You love me, I still believe that. But am I not flattering myself? I no longer know any joy.

Maybe I never knew it. I feel as if all I have ever known is ecstasy, power-ful, violent – but fleeting."

Where, he asked, was he to find salvation and a return of his con-fidence in himself? "In love? – Yes, my soul, in my love for *you*, my wife. Certainly that will work – I know it. You can still entice my work from my soul. But, oh, give me the peace for it! Stay with me, do not leave again. Tell poor Hans openly that without you I cannot manage any longer. Oh, heavens, if only you could be my wife in the world's eyes! This constant coming and going, coming back, having to go off again, letting you be at the disposal of others – it is dreadful! Peace, peace! You, my poorest one, are being destroyed for me by it. Instead of smiles and happy hand-waves, always these convulsions, these dreams, these frights, these apparitions! – Oh, heavens, who really knows the person at his side? What do even our dearest friends know of us? If it does not come to them from the stars, like Parzival, no one discovers from within who the other is. And so I fear we shall after all be destroyed: we are wearing each other out. Should one break out against it? Break with – ? What would that achieve? – Madness! Could peace, nice cheerful smiles reward us? Alas, it would only bring us sighs." But at the end he wrote and underlined the words: "*You are still my wife!*"

Wagner returned to Munich on 21 August, declining Ludwig's invita-tion to join him at Hohenschwangau for his twentieth birthday on 25 August. Instead, he sent his birthday gift: the original orchestral score of *Das Rheingold*, which he had persuaded Otto Wesendonck to return to him for that purpose. Cosima also sent the king a personal gift at Wagner's suggestion: a cushion on which she embroidered the Flying Dutchman's ship, Tannhäuser's sprouting staff, Lohengrin's swan, Siegfried's sword and Tristan's bowl. In his letter of thanks, Ludwig agreed to all Wagner's proposals for Bülow and Malvina Schnorr. "Now we, your friends, must continue working sturdily and hard, while our beloved, divine friend lives withdrawn from the world, in order to spend all his time dreaming in his blissful realms, creating. . . . But I must set about my work slowly and cautiously – I have to! Do not lose heart, however: your will shall be done!"

Replying gratefully to this letter on 29 August, Wagner wrote: "What I have in mind to do, and what only I and nobody else can ever bring about, is tremendous: you will see it in my *Parzival* sketch." He had begun work on this on 27 August, the subject, which had been in his mind for many years, perhaps recalled by the reference, already quoted, that he made to it in his letter to Cosima in the *Brown Book*. It certainly struck him as significant that the king should have asked independently for news of it at the very time it rose to the surface in his own thoughts. "How strange – the king is asking longingly about Parzival!" he wrote slantingly across a whole page of the *Brown Book* on 26 August, and on the next page he began his detailed synopsis, some seven thousand words long, which closely reflects the work as it finally, years later, came to be written. Basing himself on the epic poem of the medieval German poet Wolfram von Eschenbach, Wagner had already, in 1857, worked out a sketch (now lost) for its dramatic shape. Now, while still retaining the names as they appear in Wolfram's poem (Parzival, Anfortas, etc.), he adapted it and added to it in his usual manner of dealing with legends, introducing an important new character of his own invention, Gurnemanz (Gurnemans in the synopsis). The work took him four days, and at the end of it he scribbled across the page of his *Brown Book*: "Well, that was help in need!"

The meaning of that is clear from his entry in the *Brown Book* the following day (31 August). It started with a quotation from *Tristan und Isolde* – "The ship – do you not see it yet?" – and continued: "As long as I sat working at *Parzival*, fantasy was a great help: whenever the red curtain over the door moved, my heart trembled: she will emerge from behind it! – Now the imaginary tension is dissolved – once again reality, complete and naked, has to be dealt with!" He felt that in her accounts of her journeyings Cosima showed no understanding for his sufferings, and he bitterly recalled her failure to appreciate that his reluctance to attend Schnorr's funeral in the previous month had been due to his unwillingness to be separated from her. He had in the end travelled to Dresden without her: "The separation from *her* made me more miserable than my grief for my lost friend. . . . And she? – I came back, and had to count the days until it should please another to allow her to come to me. She goes off, not to a solemn funeral – no! She lets herself be led about, here, there and everywhere – and when all has been decided, she will perhaps return. Dear wife, I know this causes you suffering, but that you are quite unable to imagine my suffering does tell me that a man's love is deeper than a woman's."

The entry on the following day (1 September) was even bitterer, so much so that Eva Chamberlain sought to suppress it entirely by sticking the pages together – no doubt primarily on account of the savage attack on Liszt: "I shall finally come to hate my friend utterly. Already I no longer believe in his love. He has never loved. He who loves may mourn, and enters into no special relationship with Almighty God. The man of piety does not love: all he cares about is domination. I know what I am saying. I loathe all this Catholic rubbish to the very depths of my soul: whoever seeks refuge in it must certainly have a lot to repent. . . . Your father is repugnant to me, and in the times when I could tolerate him, there was more Christianity in my blind indulgence than in all his sanctimoniousness."

There were more angry entries in the *Brown Book* on the following days, and hard things were said about the festival theatre and its architect Semper, who came to visit him: "I cannot and will not see anybody, not even the dearest and most intelligent; when Cos is not there, everything that happens in her absence is a torture to me. How I hate this projected theatre – yes, and how childish the king seems for insisting on this project so passionately! Now I have Semper and am supposed to deal with him, to discuss the senseless project!"

At last, on 13 September, Cosima and Bülow returned to Munich, after an absence of five weeks. Far from having extinguished the love between her and Wagner, the separation had seemingly only fanned it, and Cosima, who doubtless now read the *Brown Book* and saw the extent of Wagner's dependence on her, was soon once more corresponding with officials on his behalf, writing to friends in his name and copying out his early writings for the king. Most of her time was spent with him in the Briennerstrasse.

Cornelius, who had borne the brunt of Wagner's moodiness during the days preceding Cosima's return, noted with dismay that her influence was undiminished, and in a letter to his future wife, written on 9 October, gave a sour account of an evening at which he and Heinrich Porges had been present: "Yesterday Wagner said with great pathos, admittedly under the influence of wine: 'I have only *one* friend, and that is Bülow.' Porges and I were sitting there, and I suppose we ought to have felt greatly insulted. Still, it is probably better if we do not exert ourselves overmuch to appear as bosom friends. Cosima, on the other hand, was beside herself that he had not said: 'I have only *one* friend, and that is Liszt.' She squabbled with him all evening and contradicted him in everything."

Wagner did not use the period of leisure he had insisted upon to resume work on the *Ring*. Instead, he embarked on a series of observations in diary form on a wide variety of subjects, beginning with the press and the need he felt for a newspaper of his own to represent his artistic ideals, passing via history, statecraft and religion to a consideration of what constituted the true German spirit, which he identified with Luther, Bach, Kant, Mozart, Goethe, Beethoven and Schiller.

His observations were addressed to the king and were prompted, he told Mathilde Maier in his letter of 22 September, by his desire to improve Ludwig's education, and as a substitute for the personal talks they were no longer able to enjoy. He continued with this diary until 27 September, when he put an end to it, possibly because it had come to his knowledge that in his enthusiasm Ludwig was having passages copied and circulated to his ministers for action. With their hostility towards him already at a high pitch, he clearly realised – or, as an entry in the

Brown Book on 24 October suggests, was persuaded by Cosima – that it would be wise at the moment to stop expressing his views on worldly matters.

In order to allow Wagner to get on with his work undisturbed, Ludwig had raised his pension to eight thousand florins yearly, arranged for the house in the Briennerstrasse to be bought and put at his disposal rent-free, and granted him a sum of 40,000 florins as a capital payment. When, on 19 October, he received word that this money was ready for collection, Wagner was reluctant to go to the treasury office himself, fearing that the citizens of Munich might seize the opportunity to demonstrate once more against what they saw as his exploitation of their king. Cosima volunteered to go in his place, and set off with her daughter Daniela and the nursemaid. At the treasury office she found huge piles of silver coins waiting for collection, and the treasury officials answered her protests with assertions that no banknotes were available. She sent the nursemaid to order two cabs, and into these she herself helped to load the coins, in full view of passers-by. Describing the incident to Ludwig in a letter dated 1 January 1866, she spoke lightly of her great naïveté. Wagner, she said, was downright appalled. "He thanked me and all but reproached me. Then he admitted my courage and said it lay like a weight on his conscience that my friendship with him had put me in such a position. I smiled and said that it was all over now."

In this humiliating incident Wagner saw the direct hand of Pfistermeister, and indeed it was true that the cabinet secretary had tried to dissuade Ludwig from giving Wagner extra sums of money on top of his allowance. From that moment Wagner counted Pfistermeister among his most implacable enemies, and he lost no opportunity of denigrating him to the king.

It was now clear that, if his ideas were to be realised in Munich, he would have to take them in hand himself. On 23 October, under cover of paying a visit to his dentist, he went off to Vienna to talk to Julius Fröbel, a friend who worked there as an assistant on the journal *Der Botschafter*. Fröbel, he felt, would be the right man to edit the newspaper he hoped, with the king's support, to establish in Munich.

There, for his communications with Cosima, he again made use of his *Brown Book*, and his words revealed more confidence in her love for him than he had felt on the Hochkopf. She, on the other hand, still lacked confidence in him. Before leaving Munich he had received from Eliza Wille a letter, enclosing another to her from Mathilde Wesendonck. In this Mathilde stated her views on that letter from Wagner which she had once refused to accept. Wagner made the mistake of showing these two letters to Cosima. From his entries in the *Brown Book* it is clear that

Cosima was suspicious of Wagner's motives in showing her the correspondence and his projected reply to Frau Wille. Since he apologised for his thoughtlessness, the quarrel was of little account in the end. However, his reply to Frau Wille, which was never sent and is thus preserved in the Wahnfried archives, is worth quoting as a demonstration of the completeness with which Cosima had ousted Mathilde Wesendonck from his heart. Mathilde's letter, he declared, "could have been more natural, less ornate; but only the power of real love could give it the beauty it lacks. Our friend always displayed a dubious tendency towards glossing over her own weaknesses or – in the vulgar phrase – whitewashing herself. A frank and loving 'Forgive me, I have sinned' never crosses the lips of a weak person. Good luck to her, happy woman!" What Mathilde had in fact said must unfortunately remain unknown, for her letter appears to have been destroyed.

Having arranged with Fröbel to come to Munich when the time was ripe to launch the newspaper, Wagner returned home on 28 October, but a fortnight later, on 11 November, left Munich again to spend a few days with Ludwig at Hohenschwangau. The invitation could be seen as something of a demonstration on the king's part, for his grandfather, the deposed King Ludwig I, had just warned him of the dangers he was incurring through his infatuation with Wagner. "No one will ever separate us," he wrote to Wagner on 2 November. "I defy the false light of day: it shall never have any effect on me!"

There were many things to be discussed between them – the projected newspaper, Semper's theatre, the politicians and officials who were constantly placing obstacles in their way – and together they roamed the countryside that was so dear to Ludwig. "Here it was," he wrote to Cosima during Wagner's visit, "that while still a boy I strode rejoicing through wood and meadow, bearing his image in heart and mind. On the reflecting surface of the Alpsee I read *Der Ring des Nibelungen*. And now to see this yearned-for being at my side, to be allowed to spend the whole day with him – what undeserved happiness for me!" On their outings they were accompanied only by Ludwig's close friend and adjutant, Prince Paul of Thurn and Taxis, a young man for whom Wagner had a great liking, and in the evening music was played by the royal band, mainly pieces by Wagner, many of which he conducted himself. He also read the first pages of his autobiography to the king, and he wrote in his *Brown Book* on 13 November: "Parzival listened with immense seriousness, and time and again broke out into splendid laughter. Truly I have only just begun to realise all the nobility and fineness of his love. . . . He exceeds everything imaginable. He is myself in a handsome, youthful rebirth: entirely me, and only himself to the extent that he is handsome and powerful."

He left Hohenschwangau on 18 November in the highest of spirits, as his entry in the *Brown Book* that day shows: "This is a bad diary, is it not, Cos – nothing at all to be found in it? Oh, my Cosima! I am coming to you today! I could be happy here only because I knew my beautiful and wonderful wife to be there! Cosima, Ludwig, how fine you are! United with you both, how powerful, how fine am I! Pray for poor Hans! Greetings, greetings, my wife! I am redeemed – I am happy!"

His happiness was swiftly shattered. In his efforts to persuade the king to replace his officials with others more in sympathy with their aims, he concentrated first of all on Pfistermeister and the secretary of the royal treasury, Julius von Hofmann, known to himself and the king by the nicknames of Mime and Fafner respectively. In telling Ludwig, as he did in his letter of 27 November, that Pfistermeister felt himself to be more powerful than the king, he chose the surest means of convincing Ludwig of the need for action. However, though swift to recognise a need, Ludwig tended to be slow in doing anything about it – a weakness in his character that Wagner had perhaps not yet fully identified. He vowed to overcome the "treacherous Mime and Fafner", but he had not done so when Wagner approached him with an even more radical suggestion: that he should dismiss the head of his government, von der Pfordten, as well, and invite a liberal minister, Max von Neumayr, to form a new cabinet in his place. The fact that the king had dismissed Neumayr only a few weeks previously, when as minister of the interior he had failed to quell an anti-government demonstration in Munich, did not seem to Wagner a drawback. It would be a proof of the king's justness, he said, to recognise and make good his "mistake".

At this point Ludwig came back to reality. He had had good reasons for dismissing Neumayr, he wrote to Wagner on 27 November: "How illogical it would be for me to charge the same man, with whom (I repeat) I have *every reason for dissatisfaction*, with the forming of a cabinet! Pfistermeister is an insignificant and unimaginative person, no doubt about that; I shall not leave him in the cabinet much longer, but to dismiss him and the other members of the cabinet now does not seem to me to be indicated; the time has not yet come."

It could hardly be expected that exchanges of this kind between Wagner and the king could remain undetected, and the article which appeared in the Munich newspaper *Der Volksbote* on 26 November was undoubtedly inspired by the ministers and officials Wagner was seeking to undermine. The article not only revived the old reproach of Wagner's extravagance, but voiced the suspicion that he and his friends were interested in securing money and power for themselves rather than in introducing the democratic ideas they professed to hold.

Whether the anonymous article which appeared three days later in another newspaper, the Munich *Neueste Nachrichten*, was written by Wagner himself, by Cosima (in whose handwriting a draft exists) or by one of their friends cannot be established for certain, but it was approved by Wagner. Referring to the recent signs of unrest in the city, the anonymous author declared: "All this is nothing but a game being played in the interests of personal advantage of the meanest sort, and it can in addition be traced back to an extremely small number of individuals. I dare maintain that, with the removal of two or three persons who enjoy not the slightest respect among the Bavarian people, the king and the Bavarian people can be relieved at a single stroke from these annoying disturbances."

This was the handle for which von der Pfordten had been waiting. He wrote to the king on 1 December, telling him in forceful language that the time had come for him to choose between the love and veneration of his loyal people and the friendship of Richard Wagner. "This man who dares to maintain that loyal members of the cabinet enjoy not the slightest respect among the Bavarian people is himself, it would be truer to say, despised by all those sections of the people among whom the throne must and can find its support; despised not because of his democratic outlook, which even the democrats deny he has, but because of his ingratitude and treachery towards sponsors and friends, his presumptuous and dissolute boastfulness and extravagance, the shameless way in which he plunders the undeserved graciousness of Your Majesty."

Confronted by von der Pfordten's threat to resign, taking the whole cabinet with him; by the representations of his mother and other members of the royal family; and by rumours of public demonstrations which might even endanger Wagner's life, the king gave in, though he still hesitated for a while. "Oh, my dear friend, 'great was the torment of the last few days'," he wrote to Wagner on 3 December from Hohenschwangau. "That article in the *Neueste Nachrichten* contributed not a little to embitter the end of my stay here. Doubtless it was written by one of your friends, who hoped to do you a service by it; but unfortunately it has harmed rather than helped you." On 6 December he sent his second cabinet secretary, Johann von Lutz, to the house in the Briennerstrasse to tell Wagner that he must leave Munich as soon as possible "for a few months". He wrote to him on the following day: "Believe me, I had to do it. . . . I know you feel with me, can fully appreciate my profound suffering; I could not do otherwise, be convinced of that; *never* doubt the loyalty of your best friend. It will not be for ever."

In his reply Wagner made no reproaches, unless one is hinted at in the opening sentence: "You are surely under no illusions concerning the length of my banishment." He asked to be allowed a few days to settle his affairs and then to leave Munich unobserved.

Bülow was away on a concert tour when Lutz came to Wagner's house with the king's order. Cosima was there, and the news came as such a shock to her that she almost fainted. Her main fears were for Wagner's safety, and during the three following days and nights she remained constantly at his side as he packed his bags in the Briennerstrasse.

On 10 December, at five o'clock in the morning, he left Munich by train for Bern, accompanied by his servant Franz and his dog Pohl. Only three people were there to see him off: Cornelius, Porges and Cosima.

CHAPTER IV

DECEMBER 1865 – FEBRUARY 1867:

Tribschen and Die Meistersinger

IN ITS NEAR-ILLEGIBILITY Wagner's letter to August Röckel, written in Bern on 12 December 1865, revealed his agitation over the sudden change in his fortunes. "Am I still hopeful? Alas, I am in despair! It is too, too hard, and I fear all hope of help from any prince has vanished for ever. . . . How I shall salvage the final task of my life I can scarcely think." But he was also concerned for the king, having heard on his journey rumours that Ludwig himself was in danger. "How things stand with my finances I am at the moment not clear. As long as they do not actually put an end to the king, it will be all right, for I do not doubt his loyalty: but – his prudence!" And he urged Röckel, his former musical assistant and fellow-revolutionary in Dresden, now working in Munich as a political journalist, to spread the story around that he had left Munich of his own volition, as a means of diverting anger from the king.

He himself set about presenting his departure in this light. From Vevey on the Lake of Geneva, where he went after two days in Bern, he wrote on 17 December to Mathilde Maier, telling her that, though he had pretended to be angered by his banishment, it had really come as a relief to him. "Soon I hope to be able really to work, which I should never, never have been able to do in Munich. I had already told the king that: he knew of my wish to leave. However, they conjured up a fog for his benefit, pretending that I was in great danger, and that a dreadful revolution, directed straight at me, was about to break out. The poor man believed that the only means of protecting me was to send me away, and he has since been sending me heartbreaking letters. That is the position."

To Ludwig himself he wrote on 20 December a comforting letter, saying it would be wise if he were to keep out of the way for a considerable while: "People must stop believing I am still in this world. . . . Let us drop everything, the school and heaven knows what else, for which we need other people. We have no people now. Time will tell, and one day it will come about. . . . Continue to think of me kindly, and never doubt my faith in you."

Ludwig's official position was not, as Wagner had at first imagined, in any danger, but the blow to his personal feelings had been great, and the main task of consoling him fell to Cosima and Bülow, who had now returned to Munich from his concert tour. Ludwig wrote to her in pitiful terms, constantly assuring her that he could not have acted otherwise than he had done, and begging her not to condemn him. Her assurances, reinforced by the gift at Christmas – doubtless with Wagner's approval – of the original score of his first opera, *Die Feen*, did not calm him, and he wrote to her on 2 January 1866 that he was thinking of abdication, even of suicide: "I wish to go to him, if I can be of any help to him in distant lands (oh, tell me please!), yes, to him, otherwise – to die – yes – to die. Do not shudder at the thought, do not do that! To live for him and with him – without him life must lose all its value and content for me – so away, away. . . . Ah, how consoling it is to know there is one being, one among millions, to whom I can pour out my heart! I yearn for a letter from you."

Cosima replied the following day, writing, as she told him, with tears in her eyes: "You are everything to us – everything to our friend, whose saviour you were. May Your Majesty never lose your joy and pride in your noble deed – it was the first link of a wonderful chain; what is happening here now is nothing, nothing, nothing. It may keep our friend away some time longer, but all the more joyful and peaceful will be his eventual return." She consoled him with the prospect of a meeting with Wagner in the spring – if not in Munich, then somewhere else – and she and Bülow, in a further effort to restore his spirits, made him a present of the handwritten third draft of the text of *Der Junge Siegfried*, Wagner's first version of *Siegfried*, which he had given to Bülow years earlier. The king's gratitude was touchingly humble: "Oh, your gift, I hardly dare accept it. I can fully appreciate how much this priceless jewel meant to your dear husband."

Wagner moved into La Campagne aux Artichauts, a large villa outside Geneva, on 28 December, and there he was joined by his housekeeper Vreneli and Franz's wife Anna with her young family. He was not wholly satisfied with the house, complaining to Cosima that it was cold and draughty and shabbily furnished. Once settled in, he returned to the attack on Ludwig's ministers and officials, in particular Pfistermeister. In his letter to the king of 8 January 1866 he commented regretfully on Ludwig's apparent inability to see who his enemies were. They had used him, Wagner, as a convenient means of diverting attention from their own treachery, and would do so again were he to return. He advised the king to remain calm and to concentrate on strengthening his own position by quietly observing and then acting with prudence. "While I am *creating* here, you must be *ruling* there, being utterly and completely the king that by the grace of God you are." He ended with a few words of hope: "And should you call on me to visit you, in some lonely, quiet, unobserved place, a hint is enough, and I shall come, however far away I may be – that as a matter of course. In May 1867 we shall stage *Die Meistersinger von Nürnberg* in Nuremberg, then – back to work: *Siegfried, Götterdämmerung*."

Free now to concentrate on his work, secure in the knowledge that the king would continue to pay his yearly allowance, his thoughts turned, not to *Siegfried*, the second act of which he had completed in full score in Munich a week before he left, but to his other uncompleted work, which he had abandoned in Biebrich, two and a half years earlier, towards the end of the first act. He resumed work on *Die Meistersinger* on 12 January.

The knowledge that Wagner now felt able to resume composition in Switzerland did nothing to cure Ludwig's depression. "Is it so utterly impossible for him to find the tranquillity he longs for here?" he wrote to Cosima. The thought had also occurred to Wagner himself. Anxious over the effect his letter might have on the king, he followed it on 12 January with a telegram, in which he hinted that the separation need be no more than "fairly long". On the same day he wrote to Cosima, saying that, if he felt he could really be of help to the king, he would have to sacrifice his tranquillity and return. "But, alas, that is not really to be thought of, as you must certainly realise. So you must resign yourself. I think I shall try Toulon, Arles or Avignon."

His impulse to put an even greater distance between himself and Munich by moving to France was certainly influenced by his fears that he might be unable to withstand his own longing to return – though on Cosima's account rather than Ludwig's. She sought to detain him with a telegram announcing her own impending visit to Geneva, but he was not to be shifted. At the bottom of a piece of musical manuscript paper containing an excerpt from the first act of *Die Meistersinger* (a passage he had just composed) he wrote to her on 20 January: "The news of your intention to visit me tomorrow affected me terribly. For God's sake, my love, no half-measures now! We have suffered enough not to torture ourselves all over again. In a month's time – God willing – reunited in peace, no more *talk*, nothing more of *Munich*. . . . Let me seek our nest of peace! Nothing else – no words."

He left Geneva on 22 January for Lyon. It had been Cosima, he wrote that night in his *Brown Book*, who had once suggested this "refuge" to him, but he found it unattractive: "These childish, monstrous cities," he wrote, "like a thousand-voice Italian opera *unisono*! Not a sign of life!" Toulon, to which he journeyed the following day, pleased him no better and he went on to Marseilles. There, on the evening of 25 January, he received, forwarded from Geneva, a telegram from Anton Pusinelli, his friend and doctor in Dresden: "Your wife died last night."

Wagner's last meeting with Minna had been in November 1862, when he visited her in Dresden following his concert appearance in Leipzig, and very few letters had passed between them since. But in the years following their final separation, he had striven conscientiously to provide her with the means of living in comfort, and indeed his borrowings from moneylenders in Vienna that had led him into disaster were in part due to the necessity he felt to maintain her allowance. Minna herself, only shortly before her sudden death from a heart attack, had replied to a newspaper report of her husband's neglect of her with a firm denial that she was living in any need.

Wagner sent a telegram to Pusinelli asking him to arrange the funeral, and followed this on 26 January with a letter, in which he explained that, since Pusinelli's telegram had been forwarded from Geneva without a date, he could not know exactly when his wife had died. A sore finger which required treatment would keep him in Marseilles a few more days. "I had already had the feeling, and told a few of my friends," he went on, "that after all the shocks and worries that have so long beset me – and in recent times with increasing intensity – that I could expect the next news of misfortune either to annihilate me completely or to leave me all but unaffected. After a difficult night I can only describe my condition up till this morning as one of complete stupor, in which I sit numbly brooding – brooding, without knowing what I was trying to work out."

He returned to Les Artichauts three days later, and the following day wrote a letter to Cosima, telling her that his main feeling was one of overwhelming tiredness: "I still have this house for the next two months. For two months nobody has the right to throw me out: this happy thought gives me the feeling that all life is mine! Give way with me to this deeply consoling assurance! From Marseilles I at once sent instructions to Dresden to give my wife the respects and honours she would have received if she had died happily beside the husband she had made happy. I am so absentminded that today I put a bandage around a healthy finger instead of the sore one, and only hours later was made aware by the pain of my mistake. A curious aberration."

A more straightforward attack on his emotions was the death during his absence of his old dog Pohl. His landlord had buried the body in the vegetable garden of Les Artichauts. Wagner had it exhumed and re-interred beneath a tree behind the house, wrapped in the carpet on which the dog had always lain and enclosed in a wooden coffin. Over the grave he placed a marble tablet inscribed: "To his Pohl, R.W."

Then he returned to his work on *Die Meistersinger*. "His walks without his faithful dog became too boring," Vreneli recalled in the reminiscences she later wrote down for Cosima. "He wanted another companion. Then he was offered the big Newfoundland Russ, whose faithful eyes at once won his favour. The dog was bought, and from then on one never saw him without Russ and a whip he never used." Vreneli modestly omitted to mention in her account that Russ was purchased for him by her out of her own savings.

All the time Wagner had been absent in France Ludwig persisted in his appeals to him to return to Munich, and began eventually to show impatience with his steady refusals. "He judges things without understanding definitely and exactly the conditions of which he speaks," the king wrote to Cosima. "In many ways he reminds me of Tasso, who also tended to imagine an artificial, hostile web of treachery hanging threateningly over his head. In some respects, I admit, the dear one may be right, but not in all, not in all."

Wagner, having failed to find in France a suitable "nest of peace", and now with at least one of the barriers to his union with Cosima removed, at last showed signs of weakening. On 3 February he wrote to the king declaring that his position in Munich had hitherto been too vulnerable, too obviously dependent on the king's favour; if he were now to return, it could only be on three conditions: that he should at once be granted Bavarian nationality, that the house in the Briennerstrasse should be made over to him outright, and that his allowance should be assured by royal decree for the rest of his life. It was the first condition that proved insurmountable: Ludwig's ministers took the view that as a Bavarian citizen Wagner would interfere in political matters even more than he had done previously, and they were unwilling to grant it.

That prospect cut off, Wagner decided to remain in Switzerland, but to choose a spot close enough to Munich to allow Cosima to travel back and forth without difficulty. For this arrangement they had a convincing excuse: Wagner's desire to continue work on his autobiography. With Bülow's approval she joined him in Geneva for this purpose on 8 March, bringing Daniela with her, and Wagner resumed the dictation of *My Life* to her on the following day. At the same time he worked on the orchestration of the first act of *Die Meistersinger*, the orchestral sketch of which he had completed on 21 February. He finished the full score of that act on 23 March, and a week later they set off together on a search for his new home.

They visited Lausanne, Bern and Interlaken, but found nothing suitable. Then, on 30 March, as they were crossing the lake, the Vierwaldstättersee, on their way to Lucerne, they caught sight of a house standing on a tongue of land jutting out into the water: Tribschen. It did not, however, immediately strike them as the house they had been looking for, and on the following day, after spending the night in Lucerne, they separated, she returning to Munich, he to Geneva. After their vain search, the king's suggestion to Cosima that Wagner might spend the summer at his hunting lodge at Riss, near Garmisch, struck her as a miracle. But Wagner found himself thinking increasingly of the house on the Vierwaldstättersee. In a series of letters and telegrams under the pseudonyms "Will" (Wagner) and "Vorstel" (Cosima) – names taken from the title of Schopenhauer's book *Die Welt als Wille und Vorstellung* – she pleaded for acceptance of the king's suggestion and he argued in favour of Tribschen. He put an end to the discussion by returning to Lucerne on 4 April and signing an agreement with the owner, Colonel Am Rhyn, and on 15 April he moved into Tribschen, his home for the next seven years.

A square villa, three storeys high, Tribschen was (and still is, for it is now a Wagner museum) a plain building, standing on a raised embankment in grounds running down to the lakeside. What beauty it possessed it owed mainly to its superb position, with splendid, undisturbed views of the surrounding mountains, dominated by the two peaks of the Rigi and Mount Pilatus. It was the tongue of land on which it stood that induced Wagner to associate the name "Tribschen" with the German verb *treiben* (to drive), or more precisely its past participle form *trieb*, the equivalent of the English word "drift". He believed – without any authority beyond his own imagination – that the tongue of land had been formed by currents in the lake, and he changed the name of the house into Triebschen.*

Two days after moving in, Wagner wrote to Cosima: "Today, Tuesday, lovely morning – market day – boat after boat from Ury, Schwyz and Unterwalden on their way to Lucerne market. A delicious sight, quite indescribably beautiful – against this background, on this delightfully smooth lake surface, every boat woven around with a gleaming circle of silver. A morning such as this is not too dearly won at the price of a difficult month of winter. Now I understand my choice and the winter I am approaching: Walther has already celebrated it in song, '*Am stillen Herd zur Winterszeit, wenn Hof und Haus mir eingeschneit*' ['By silent hearth in wintertime, when house and yard are covered in snow']. Then I shall remember this spring morning, and how I shall love the winter here! Truthfulness, absolute truthfulness, that must be our dogma, and to this bond, to this belief I can admit only one person more: Parzival. And so let him be our guardian angel. Once again, let nobody disturb us here, let our holy peace prevail. These are the last

* This is the form in which it appears in the letters of Wagner and his friends, and consequently in many books about him. However, in the years before Wagner lived there – and in its origins the house dates back to the seventeenth century – and after he left it, the name was (and still is) spelt Tribschen. Thus this will be the form adopted in this book, except in quotations.

years of a difficult, tormented life that will here reach its goal, be given its crown."

Bülow was included in the bond. On 8 April Wagner wrote to him, offering him the ground and second floors of Tribschen for himself and his family. He himself would occupy the first floor. "Hans, you will do what I ask? Surely you will, for you know that I love you and that – apart from my giddy, though wonderful relationship with this young king – nothing, nothing keeps me on this earth but you and your family."

Bülow's response to this urgent plea was to despatch Cosima with all three daughters to Tribschen, where they arrived on 11 May. He himself remained in Munich, where he was busy conducting concerts.

Both Cosima and Ludwig were disappointed by Wagner's refusal of the king's offer of his hunting lodge at Riss. However, they accepted it philosophically. "Yes, you are right," Ludwig wrote to her on 7 April, "we should leave him in peace to seek his own path; he will surely find the right way."

The king was in any case at this time facing – or ought to have been facing – difficulties of his own, and ones of a far more urgent nature. Bismarck's expansionist policies had brought Prussia to the brink of war with Austria, the other great power in the prevailing loose confederation of German states known as the *Deutscher Bund*. Inevitably Bavaria would be drawn into this war, but whether on the side of Prussia or Austria had still to be decided. The Austrian ambassador, Count Blome, reported to Vienna: "The young king continues to lead his indolent life and sees virtually nobody except the pianist Bülow. He says: 'I do not want a war,' and takes no further interest in the matter."

Ludwig's reluctance to talk about war was due less to indolence than to a genuine horror of violence. But the Austrian ambassador's remark was typical of the kind of contempt with which statesmen were now beginning to regard this young monarch who was so reluctant to perform the state duties expected of him. Ludwig was not prepared in May to open Parliament, though Pfistermeister, still his cabinet secretary, sought to persuade him of the vital importance of this gesture in the present political atmosphere. Pfistermeister wrote to the king's physician (von Gietl) on 15 May in some anxiety, telling him that Ludwig was talking of giving up the throne on grounds of mental illness: "It is possible, in view of the great repulsion the king feels against performing this celebration in particular, that my obstinate persuasions, and my reference to the hostility the omission of a personal appearance would surely cause at this time, had an irritating and disturbing effect on him. In the hours in which he was alone, he worked himself into a mood of increasing vexation and even came to the bitter conclusion that he is having to make personal sacrifices and at the same time is still not allowed to have Herr R. Wagner at his side, for heaven knows how long. This then brought him on to the idea that it would be better for him to abdicate in favour of Prince Otto his brother, who is after all now of age, and to go to Wagner in Switzerland, rather than to dwell in sorrow on the throne."

Pfistermeister passed on to Gietl the king's instructions that his doctor should start spreading the news of his abdication, adding that he was confident Gietl would do no such thing; but he begged for advice on how to set about calming Ludwig down. He concluded: "After negotiating with me for an hour and a half over such matters, he rode off at three in the afternoon via Seeshaupt to the island for dinner, and then at once returned, as a few times before during the past few days, in a heavy shower of rain. That will certainly cool him off, but it is not very good for his health."

Ludwig's thoughts of abdication had already been conveyed to Wagner. In the early hours of 15 May, before his interview with his cabinet secretary, Ludwig despatched a telegram to Tribschen: "Ever increasing yearning for the dear one. The horizon grows ever darker, the glare of day's peaceful sun an indescribable torture. I beg my friend for prompt answer to following questions: if it is my dear one's will and wish, I shall gladly renounce the crown and empty glory and come to him, never to leave his side again. And when he is seated at his mysterious loom creating his blessed works, let it be my concern to shield him from the world which robs him of peace and tranquillity; for I must say it again: to be separated from him and *alone* is something I can no longer bear. To be united with him and living at his side, withdrawn from earthly existence, is the only way of preserving myself from despair and death. This is not the result of a fleeting angry impulse, but horrible, excruciating truth. I longingly await your reply. Ludwig."

Appalled by the king's action in entrusting such a message to the public telegraph system, Wagner replied the same day, urging Ludwig to have patience for a further six months. He framed his reply in the form of an appeal, stressing the importance of the king's position to himself personally and to their common cause. He begged him to turn his attention to state affairs, to remain in his Munich residence and show himself to the people. "If you love me in the way I long for you to do, listen to me when I implore you to open Parliament yourself on 22 May. You chose my birthday for this important and fateful ceremony: make your precious gift complete – go yourself to Munich and open the Landtag in person! I shall bless you on this day, more fervently than ever, if you grant me this wish."

Wagner was a better psychologist than the king's ministers: Ludwig spoke no more for the moment of abdication. But he could not bring himself to sacrifice Wagner's birthday to the Landtag. Instead, he sent Paul von Taxis to prepare the way, then slipped out of Berg and travelled secretly by train to Lucerne. On the afternoon of 22 May he presented himself on the doorstep of Tribschen, to the unbounded surprise of Wagner and Cosima. There he stayed two nights, and on the morning of 24 May left with Paul von Taxis to return to Munich. From the railway station at Zurich he sent Wagner a telegram: "Deeply moved at parting. Steeled by blissful time spent together, firmly resolved to tear out weeds by their roots. Proud and confident of victory."

The news of Ludwig's secret visit to Tribschen soon became known in Munich. In consequence there were no cheers for him when on 27 May he drove through the streets on his way to open the Landtag, and in the chamber itself his reception was "ice-cold", as he told Cosima in a telegram sent off from Starnberg that afternoon: "Press appalling. Does my friend think I am beset by a moment of vexation or remorse? Oh, no. Unshakeably firm in contemplation of great goal. Happy and blessed through those blissful hours."

During his visit to Tribschen Wagner repeated his advice to Ludwig to show himself as much as possible to the people in an effort to win their support against their enemies, and to keep silent about Richard Wagner. But within a very few days he found it necessary to retract the latter request. Now that he was out of Munich, the newspapers set about his "accomplices" (as the *Neuer Bayerischer Kurier* called them) who were still living there – in particular "the carrier pigeon Madame Dr Hanns de Bülow". The *Volksbote* was even more virulent: "It is not even a year since the well-known 'Madame Hans de Bülow' collected 40,000 florins from the royal treasury in those two famous cabs for her 'friend' (or what else?)," it wrote on 31 May. "But what are 40,000 florins? 'Madame Hans' can now start looking for cabs once again, for the day before yesterday writs were issued against this same Richard Wagner for the recovery of debts amounting to no less than 26,000 florins, as the *Volksbote* learns on completely reliable authority. At the moment this same 'Madame Hans' . . . is with her 'friend' (or what else?) in Lucerne, and she was also there during the royal visit."

For Bülow, still in Munich, this public attack on his wife and by implication on himself was more than he could stand. He issued a challenge to the editor of the *Volksbote* (it was not taken up) and asked the king to accept his resignation from his posts in Munich. Wagner, to whom Bülow appealed for advice and support, wrote to Ludwig on 6 June: "A man who, putting his trust in my star and yielding to my eager persuasions, gave up the prospect of an extremely influential and advantageous position in Berlin after years of patient waiting in order to accept your royal invitation to Munich, now sees himself obliged by a public treatment unparalleled in the grubby history of German court life . . . to leave, with all apparent signs of disgrace, a place and an activity in which in any other country his spotless integrity and his un-exampled artistic achievements would have earned him high recogni-tion. His noble wife, who with dedicated sympathy and self-sacrifice stood consolingly by the side of the friend of her father, her husband's mentor, the highly regarded protégé of the king she holds in such fervent esteem – she, as a reward for the love a kind monarch has shown to his persecuted friend, is dragged publicly through the mire and bespattered by a shame which would soil even the angel of innocence himself. . . . To you, my king and my dear friend, I address in this moment of need the single wish that you should break your silence, at least in this single instance: write a letter expressing your satisfaction with my friend Hans von Bülow and at the same time your royal in-dignation over the disgraceful treatment accorded him and his wife by some newspapers in Munich, the city of your residence, and allow the recipient to publish it.''

Cosima, who had hurried to Munich to confer with Bülow on how to counter this new attack, made her own plea to the king. She wrote on 7 June: "I have three children, to whom I owe the duty of transmitting the honourable name of their father free of stain; for the sake of these children, so that they will not one day revile the love I bear to our friend, I beg you, my exalted friend, to write that letter."

Since one of these three children was almost certainly Wagner's and the fourth with which she was at that time pregnant was undoubtedly his, Cosima's appeal was just as lacking in scruple as Wagner's own, for both of them were making use of the king's innocence to protect themselves from a disclosure of what was indeed the truth. Wagner in his letter of 9 June went even further in the matter of deceiving the king. In this he explained at length the circumstances in which Cosima had collected his 40,000 florins in the previous October, and in December had spent four nights at his house immediately following the news of his banishment. In injured tones he told the king what their enemies had made of these two events: "Today they are being talked about thus: the wife of my loyal friend B. is my —— [Wagner's omission]. She slept four nights in my house, and got herself paid for her caresses with the sacks of gold she enticed from the royal treasury. Friend B. made no objection, and on top of that helped himself to the gratuity he extracted from the court orchestra. Thus it is. Such things happen to the friends of the King of Bavaria in his royal seat, Munich."

Ludwig accepted all these protestations in good faith. With his letter of 6 June Wagner had sent him the draft of a letter he might write in Bülow's support. This spoke of the pain the libellous newspaper attacks on Bülow's honour had caused him, the king, and continued: "Since I have become familiar with your selfless and honourable behaviour and, like the musical public of Munich, also with your incomparable artistic achievements – and since I have furthermore been in a position to gain particular knowledge of the noble and generous character of your respected wife, who with the most sympathetic concern has stood solicitously at the side of her father's friend, her husband's mentor – there is no other way for me but to investigate the inexplicable aspects of these criminal public libels and, having achieved a clear picture of these disgraceful activities, to ensure that the evildoers are brought to justice with unsparing severity." All this and more Ludwig had copied out with only minor alterations, and at the end he added in his own handwriting: "A thousand cordial greetings from a loyal friend to the dear occupants of homely Triebschen. I remain, my dear Herr von Bülow, ever your devoted Ludwig."

Between the writing of this letter on 11 June and its publication in the Munich *Neueste Nachrichten* on 20 June, war broke out between Prussia and Austria, and Bavaria was involved on Austria's side. That at so momentous a time Ludwig should be seen devoting his attention to such relatively petty matters did nothing to improve his reputation with either public or politicians; nor did his decision to shut himself away on an island in the Starnberg lake, the Roseninsel, with only Paul von Taxis and his favourite groom for company. The Austrian ambassador reported to Vienna: "For three days neither his ministers nor his cabinet secretaries have been able to see him. A boat carries the papers requiring signature back and forth. . . . And that at a time when it is a question of war or peace."

Ludwig and Paul von Taxis occupied themselves on the Roseninsel reading the text of *Die Meistersinger* and the synopsis of *Parzival*. This was no more gratifying to Wagner than it was to Count Blome, for at the beginning of June he had written down for Ludwig's benefit a "political programme" to counter the effects of the impending war. Briefly, this called on Bavaria to summon a meeting of the remaining German states in order to discuss the formation of a confederation in which each state, while retaining its independence, would be pledged to the defence of the whole. It was in effect the idea of a third German entity to match the individual power of Prussia and Austria. At the head of this new body Ludwig, as monarch of the largest uncommitted German state, should stand.

Ludwig took no notice at all of this suggestion, and Wagner expressed his disappointment in his letter of 18 June, four days after the outbreak of war: "With bleeding heart I have to acknowledge what is now written on the German flag: 'For Austria or for Prussia'. Yet fourteen days ago

Fate offered the chance, now perhaps gone for ever, for the German princes to conclude that closer permanent federation which might have been the truly 'German' federation, one before which the two treaty-breaking powers would have been obliged to appear as before a judge. . . . Where are we now? Where is our Germany? Alas, I meant to keep silent, and to leave you happily dreaming on the Roseninsel, dreaming of all that lies deep in the heart of the universal spirit, high above all this misery." Now, he went on, he saw another way in which Ludwig might perhaps fulfil his destiny: by placing himself at the head of his troops. "Arise! Arise! Fate is calling you! It desires you to leave this bog which is your residence – and go out into your country. Journey through Bavaria, console our Germany. . . . At the head of your army you are mighty against all the miserable worms in your dismal palace! There you will also conquer me again."

This idea did seize Ludwig's imagination, and he set off, accompanied by Paul von Taxis, to review his troops, now pledged to the Austrian cause. Unfortunately he could not see them all, he told Wagner in his letter of 2 July, for he was held up in Munich by urgent business, and by the time he arrived some of the army had already crossed the Bavarian border, but nevertheless he was greeted with lusty cheers. He and Paul von Taxis, he added, were now back on the Roseninsel, "where yesterday we celebrated in blissful memory the anniversary of the final *Tristan* performance."

Through all these personal and political crises Wagner had been working steadily on the second act of *Die Meistersinger*, which he began on 15 May. In Munich feeling was still running high against Bülow, and he thought it best to stand by his resignation and leave the city for a while. He joined his family at Tribschen on 14 June. Besides the controversy caused by the king's letter there was another complicating factor: Bülow was by nationality Prussian, and it was soon being rumoured in Munich that he was an enemy spy. In a letter to his friend Joachim Raff from Tribschen Bülow claimed to be unaffected by all these events: "I now see things as less tragic than they actually are. The only really disturbing aspect is the very considerable financial loss the Munich episode has caused in my life. But the decision to renounce it is a positive gain. I am weary of music, weary of the future, but particularly weary of the present: I mean to put limits on myself, become obscure (that will go quicker than with fame) and continue life as unobtrusively as possible under another sky. *Voilà.*"

On 3 July Prussia defeated Austria at the battle of Sadowa, and a week later Bavaria was defeated at a battle near Kissingen, thus putting an end to the war. Wagner wrote a consoling letter to Ludwig, deploring "the loss of my last hope of a great and noble fatherland worthy of my artistic ideals", and pointing to *Die Meistersinger*, with its sturdy German character, as a means of achieving it still, at least in spirit. He then turned to the subject of Bülow, asking the king to regard his resignation as withdrawn, but to grant him leave until such time as it would be expedient for him to return to Munich.

Ludwig replied on 18 July, giving his assent, but it was clear that his main thoughts were at the moment elsewhere. "God grant that Bavaria's independence can be preserved!" he wrote. "If not, if we lose our identity abroad when we come beneath the hegemony of Prussia, then I go – I have no wish to be a shadow king without power." Three days later he wrote to Cosima asking her to inform Wagner of his resolve to lay down the crown and join him in Switzerland: "He must be merciful, not ask me to bear any longer these torments of hell!"

Once again Wagner strove to put new courage into him by reminding him that the achievement of their mutual ideals demanded that they should both stick to their posts: "*Die Meistersinger* has become our friend in need," he wrote on 24 July. "It points to Nuremberg, where it belongs and where it shall first be presented to the world. What a stroke of Fate! Nuremberg, the old, the real seat of German art, of German originality and splendour, the mighty old imperial city, well-preserved like a noble jewel – awakened to new life through the hard work of its cheerful, vigorous, enlightened and liberal people under the protection of the Bavarian crown! There, my beloved friend, I had hoped to summon you in the coming year, to be enthusiastically greeted by a populace, reinforced by friends of my art from all Germany, which would have felt happy and honoured to be permitted to welcome us within its walls. . . . There, and there alone, must the whole of Germany be made to see what our 'model performances' mean. . . . This was my quietly benevolent plan, which would preserve for Bavaria the king on whom the hopes of all of noble mind among the people are set. But now you lose patience: my Walther wishes to quit the field in despair. Shall I, like Sachs, tell myself: 'Take care, this must not be'? That I do not dare, but cordially and in friendship I describe to you my plan. If you can find the strength to carry out this plan as king – how splendid that would be! What it would cost you would be – patience until next spring."

"Wonderfully strengthened, feel hero's courage within, will hold out," Ludwig replied by telegram on 26 July. He signed it "Walther".

The assumption that it was during these eventful weeks that Bülow first became aware of the true relationship between Wagner and Cosima has been effectively demolished by Ernest Newman in his biography of the composer. The story that Bülow came on the truth when he inadvertently opened a letter from Wagner to Cosima the previous May

Above: Tribschen on the
Lake of Lucerne, and
Mount Pilatus

Right: Richard Wagner
during the Tribschen years

Below: Friedrich Nietzsche

Left:
King Ludwig II
of Bavaria at
age of eighteen

Right: Cosima in the
first years of her
marriage to Hans von
Bülow

Above left: Franz Liszt

Above right:
Marie d'Agoult

Left: Hans von Bülow
during the 1860s

Cosima's children: Isolde and Blandine (standing),
Eva, Siegfried and Daniela (seated)

was based, as Newman showed, on a fanciful interpretation of a remark made by Peter Cornelius in a letter to his future wife. However, though there can be no doubt that Bülow already knew much, the letter he wrote to Raff from Tribschen on 26 August shows that something occurred there to cause him even greater distress. "You can have no idea of what has been going on," he wrote. "I should scarcely be capable of making clear to you verbally, let alone in a letter, the dreadful, unbelievable thing that has struck me." Since he had written to Raff only a fortnight earlier (on 12 August) about his difficulties in Munich, it is clear that he was here referring to something else. "If the correct formulation of a problem can be regarded as halfway to its solution," he went on, "so too can the clear definition of a shameful situation go halfway towards liberating one from it. It is true, however, that in the present case the most shameful aspect was the terrible confusion, the difficulty of bringing the others involved to a proper realisation of it, that is to say, to a calm state of pessimistic despair. Since February 1865 I had not been in the slightest doubt about the 'utter rottenness' of things, though to what lengths they would turn out to extend was something I never permitted myself to dream, or rather to suffer nightmares about. Forgive me, I am again speaking in riddles, and those 'considerations' which I have from the very start wished to the devil I am still unable today to send to the devil. So – later . . ."

This was the closest Bülow ever came to confiding his personal troubles to any of his friends, at any rate in the published sources. Raff was probably his most intimate friend, a fellow pupil of Liszt whom he had known since his boyhood and who, though eight years older than himself, he could look on as an equal rather than a master, as both Liszt and Wagner were. And he must here have been referring to something he had discovered in the fortnight between his two letters to Raff. Was it perhaps that his wife was pregnant again? If he still believed (and the possibility cannot be discounted) that Cosima's previous child, Isolde, was his, then the new pregnancy must have revealed to him beyond all doubt that his wife's relationship with Wagner was an adulterous one. If, on the other hand, he knew of and had accepted that situation already, there must have been something in the attitude of Wagner and Cosima regarding the coming child that deeply offended him.

Whatever was decided between them at that time about their mutual relationship, they were agreed that, as far as the outside world was concerned, the fiction of a valid marriage between Bülow and Cosima must still be maintained. Bülow decided to start a new life in Basel teaching and giving concerts, and he told his friends (including Raff) that his wife and children would join him there if and as soon as he established himself. Basel was close enough to Tribschen to enable Cosima to move

frequently and unobtrusively between Wagner and Bülow. It was also –
and this was the explanation Cosima gave to the king – close enough to
Bavaria to enable Bülow to go there whenever Ludwig felt the wish for
some private music-making.

While she and Bülow were in Munich winding up their domestic
arrangements, Wagner remained in Tribschen working on the second
act of *Die Meistersinger*. On 5 September, one day before completing the
composition sketch, he wrote to the king: "I feel desperately that I *must*
finish this work before I die. Of the *Nibelungen* I have completed enough
to give the world some idea of what it is about. As for *Parzival*, the sound
of it is sufficiently reflected for understanding friends in both *Lohengrin*
and *Tristan*. But *Die Meistersinger* is entirely new: nobody can know at all
how it is going to be. In it I smile in deepest scorn on my stupid enemies,
I rescue all that is good and noble from the common herd, I build on
ruins a new world of German splendour. And it all sings – sings tenderly,
merrily, cheekily, comically – but sings!"

He began work on the third act on 2 October, by which time Bülow
was settled in Basel and Cosima back at Tribschen. The arrival on 30
October of a 23-year-old musician from Vienna, engaged on the
recommendation of Heinrich Esser, conductor of the court opera there,
caused Cosima some preliminary apprehension. Wagner required
someone to copy the score of *Die Meistersinger* as it was completed, and
Cosima wrote to the king hoping that the young man would behave
"quietly and modestly" and not disturb their tranquil household. His
name was Hans Richter, and he had declined a conducting post for the
privilege of working close to Wagner, of whom at the beginning he
naturally enough stood in some awe. However, he noted in his diary that
Wagner was "extraordinarily nice" to him, "and keeps urging me to
make my stay here as pleasant as possible". Though at first he was given
into Vreneli's care (Cosima's doing, presumably), he rapidly endeared
himself to the children with his games and his horn-playing and was
promoted to the family table.

Cosima's anxious efforts to keep Wagner undisturbed while he was
working were thwarted when, on 10 November, Malvina Schnorr came
to visit him at Tribschen. She brought with her one of her pupils, Isidore
von Reutter, and the purpose of their visit was to inform Wagner of
important dreams this young woman had experienced. In them the
departed spirit of Ludwig Schnorr had appeared and informed Isidore
that she was to marry King Ludwig, Wagner acting as go-between. It was
also hinted that Malvina herself should marry Wagner. He and Cosima
came to the conclusion that Isidore was an adventuress and Malvina her
innocent dupe, and they took energetic steps to separate them, beginning with an order forbidding Isidore to enter the house again. Cosima,

who since Malvina's arrival in Munich in March had cultivated close ties of friendship with her, took on herself the task of persuading her of the error of her ways. She succeeded only in arousing her enmity, and on 12 November Malvina left Tribschen vowing to expose Cosima's true relationship with Wagner, both to Bülow and to the king. Since Malvina, now enjoying a pension from the king as a *Kammersängerin* (as the direct result of Wagner's own efforts on her behalf), was in a position to create an embarrassing situation, Wagner attempted to forestall her by himself telling the king in his letter of 22 November about Isidore's designs (though he did not mention her name) and Malvina's gullibility. The first he attributed to a possible trick inspired by his enemies, the second to Malvina's eccentricity and – possibly – incipient madness.

Cosima, too, thought it prudent to play the matter down as far as possible. She wrote to Ludwig on 25 November: "I was so utterly grateful to Frau v. Schnorr for having brought to life our friend's Isolde that I took her completely to my heart and gave no thought at all to various things which she might or might not understand. Our friend did the same, and, as long as there was no interference, everything was in order. Now, however, there has arisen a confusion in which presumption, importunity and heaven knows what else join hands to create an unbearable situation. . . . Our friend has now resumed his work, which the spooky tales made impossible except on one single day during the whole week. Beckmesser is raging against Sachs: '*O Schuster voller Ränke*' ['Oh, cobbler full of scheming'] – I had to laugh out loud when he yesterday played to me the beginning of the furious outburst."

These efforts to minimise the effects of Malvina's threatened denunciation achieved their aim. When Ludwig received her letter in the middle of December on his return from a tour of his kingdom, he sent it on to Cosima with the remark: "A strange mixture of clarity and error, of truth and fiction."

Following the Malvina episode, Wagner was able to work uninterruptedly on the third act of *Die Meistersinger*, but progress was slowed by certain compositional problems. For the opening stanzas of the "Prize Song" he had had both words and melody written down as early as 1862, but, when he reached that point in composition, he was dissatisfied with both. The melody which we now know came to him, as he noted on the first written version of it, on 28 September, but, since it did not fit the original words, he took the very unusual step of writing down the music in his composition sketch and leaving a blank space for the words. For the aftersong he now decided to use his love motive, which had already appeared in the overture and at various points throughout the first two acts, adapting it rhythmically to match the preceding stanzas. On 24 December the words for the whole new version at last came to him. Cosima sent a copy of it to Ludwig on 31 December as a New Year's greeting. "When he played it to me on Christmas Eve," she wrote, "I burst into tears of joy."

Yet the problem was not yet finally solved. Wagner's instinct told him that he would have to find a different way of presenting the "Prize Song" in the second scene of the third act, since a mere repetition of it would be liable to fall flat dramatically. It took him a considerable time to find the solution, which entailed modifications of both music and words. The final dramatic problem concerned the work's ending. While composing the music Wagner decided that the curtain should descend with Walther's winning of Eva: his subsequent rejection of the mastersingers and Sachs's defence of them might, he felt, seem an anti-climax. Cosima reported to the king: "I made such an unhappy face, and argued too that Walther's *will ohne Meister selig sein* ['I prefer happiness without the masters'] was so much in character, that he began to think again." The problem kept him busy throughout the night, she added, and he finally solved it by inserting some additional words and music to Sachs's final address. This passage, the sketch of which bears the date 28 January 1867, consists of those famous words beginning "*Habt acht, uns dräuen üble Streich'!*" ("Take heed, we are threatened by evid deeds!") which in later times have been brought up as evidence of Wagner's aggressive nationalism – an ironic fate, in view of the fact that they were inserted only as an afterthought, against his own dramatic instincts, in response to Cosima's pleas!

The only shadow over Tribschen as *Die Meistersinger* neared completion came from Bülow. Frustrated by his solitary life in Basel, where musical activities were few and modest, he began to think seriously of a return to Munich. He came to Tribschen to spend Christmas with his family, and Wagner was appalled, as he told Ludwig in his letter of 2 January, by the state of his health. "His appearance is unrecognisable, in the grip of a fever which returns daily and against which no medicine is of any avail." Cosima too, he added, was having sleepless nights on his account. He begged Ludwig to do something to restore Bülow's confidence: "Appoint him immediately as your conductor, give him the decoration he so richly deserves. . . . Then summon him to carry out the plan for the music school . . . put in his hands the reorganisation of your court orchestra, as well as the musical supervision in your court theatre."

Ludwig responded by giving Bülow an appointment as "court conductor extraordinary", with the task of making preparations for the production of *Die Meistersinger* in the coming summer.

Wagner completed his composition sketch on 7 February. Ten days later, on 17 February, Cosima gave birth at Tribschen to her fourth daughter. She was named Eva after the heroine of *Die Meistersinger*, and, as Cosima lay in labour, Wagner played melodies from his new work on the piano in the room below to soothe her. Bülow came from Basel to see Cosima on the day of Eva's birth and, according to Marie von Bülow, his second wife, basing her account on "a reliable source", he said to her amid tears: "I forgive you." "What is needed is not forgiveness," Cosima is reported to have replied, "but understanding."

CHAPTER V

The Second Munich Attempt

IN THE FINAL months of 1866 Wagner had the satisfaction of seeing his two main political adversaries in Munich removed from office. In October Max von Neumayr took Pfistermeister's place as cabinet secretary, though he lasted only two months before giving way to Johann von Lutz. In December Pfordten resigned: his successor as prime minister was a liberal, Prince Chlodwig von Hohenlohe-Schillingsfürst. In January 1867 Ludwig himself won the favour of his people by announcing his engagement to his cousin Sophie Charlotte, a daughter of Duke Maximilian of Bavaria and sister of Empress Elisabeth of Austria. Now it suddenly seemed that all the plans that had gone into abeyance on Wagner's banishment – the theatre, the music school, the newspaper – had once again become practical possibilities.

Encouraged by the king, Semper had continued to work on his plans for the theatre, and on 1 January 1867, at his invitation, Wagner went to Zurich with Cosima and Bülow to inspect the plaster model Semper had made of it. The sight kindled his interest in the theatre, which had hitherto been so tepid that he had not even troubled to give Semper his address since leaving Munich a year ago. He wrote to the king the following day: "It is a miracle: my idea, my suggestions and stipulations have been completely grasped by Semper's genius and . . . carried out in so novel and practical a way that the noble simplicity of the conception must meet with the admiration of every connoisseur."

Nevertheless, he was by no means pleased when Semper took his model to Munich later in January and showed it to the king, who at once decided to begin building the theatre. "If I were to think only of my own peace and security," Wagner wrote to Semper at the beginning of February, "I should feel bound to advise the king against building the theatre now, for everything to do with it that can be presented in an odious light will – as I do not need to tell you – be placed entirely to my account, while the whole credit will go to you."

It was the same fear of re-arousing hostility against himself that prompted Wagner to warn Röckel against talking so indiscreetly about his own political ambitions. "Unless you make things impossible with utterly childish wilfulness," he wrote to Röckel on 5 February, "you can now look forward to a uniquely advantageous and useful position that will serve the general interest as well as your own personal ones. If in Hoh[enlohe] and the King of B. you espy 'enemies of the people' and similar demons, then that will be the end of everything."

There was caution too on the other side. The king sent his new court secretary, Lorenz Düfflipp, to Tribschen at the end of January to discuss the erection of the theatre, Bülow's recall to Munich and the basis of Wagner's own return. Under conditions of great secrecy Hohenlohe sent his personal physician, Dr Oskar Schanzenbach, to interview Wagner at the beginning of February and to report back confidentially to him on his political attitude.

Ludwig's engagement to Duchess Sophie Charlotte was closely bound up with his feelings for Wagner. During the miserable months of their separation, Ludwig had paid frequent visits to his cousin, whom he had known from childhood, and she consoled him by singing excerpts from the roles of Senta, Elisabeth and Elsa. But when Sophie's mother, Duchess Ludovika, noting their meetings, demanded to know his intentions, he admitted that he felt no urge to marry her. Her mother's prompt ban on further meetings moved him to change his mind, and he consented to an official engagement. But a letter written by him at this time to an unknown correspondent, quoted by Alfred Freiherr von Mensi-Klarbach, revealed the nature of his feelings towards her: "Console her and put her mind completely at rest, and tell her you believe my affection will turn into love. Should the marriage come about, she will, however, have to accept my condition that my promise to remain true to her will be cancelled by the death of the beloved person who means everything to me." That person was Richard Wagner, on whose death, as Ludwig had already declared to Sophie, he had vowed to take his own life.

To Cosima, who had written warmly congratulating him on his engagement, Ludwig replied: "This year must be the year of our salvation. It has begun so well, it will bring us closer to our goal, and soon the splendid work, begun with so much torment, will be crowned with success." He conveyed Sophie's greetings, which she reinforced a few days later with a personal letter to Wagner. "With the awakening of spring you must return and put an end to the painful separation," she wrote.

Düfflipp visited Bülow in Basel after seeing Wagner at Tribschen and invited him in the king's name to return to Munich at Easter as court conductor and head of the new music school. Bülow, after asking for time to consider, wrote declining the offer, to Wagner's great consternation. His reluctance to return to Munich was ostensibly connected with previous public attacks on his honour, but in his letter of 20 February to the king Wagner hinted that there was more behind it than that: "He has for too long been deprived of the great influence of his wife, which always helped to clear his mind and enlighten him. It so happened that a great misfortune overtook your loyal subjects – that is something that cannot be denied – and it is saying not a little to wonder whether we shall recover from it." He mentioned Eva's birth in his letter, but did not divulge what part this had played in the "misfortune" to which he alluded.

Wagner completed the orchestral sketch of *Die Meistersinger* on 5 March, and four days later arrived in Munich. He saw Ludwig on 10 March, their first meeting since the king's birthday visit to Tribschen, and among the subjects they discussed was *Die Meistersinger*, the first performance of which, they decided, should form part of Ludwig's wedding celebrations in the summer. The prospect of conducting it had begun to weaken Bülow's resolve, and Wagner was able to tell the king that Bülow would be joining him in a few days' time in Munich to reconsider his earlier decision.

Wagner paid a visit to Prince Hohenlohe, whom he was meeting for the first time, and on 17 March he had another meeting with Ludwig, only his second in a period of over a week. In view of all Ludwig's professed yearnings in the past months, his inaccessibility struck Wagner as strange, and he was inclined to believe, as he admitted to the king later, that his officials were deliberately keeping them apart. Ludwig's family was also frowning on the reconciliation. For Wagner's meeting with Sophie on 16 March at the home of her eldest brother, Duke Ludwig, elaborate precautions were taken to make it look – if discovered at all – like a chance encounter. Wagner was pleased with the king's bride. "A loving, rapturously loving woman, beautiful and gracious, delightful, youthful, like a breath of spring!" he wrote to Ludwig immediately after their meeting.

Even before visiting Munich Wagner had declared that he would not be persuaded to settle there again permanently, and the cool reception he experienced from Ludwig's officials confirmed his resolve to remain in Switzerland. On the other hand Bülow, who joined him there on 13 March, did consent to return in April as court conductor and director of the music school, and to supervise new productions of *Lohengrin* and the revised *Tannhäuser*. He agreed to establish a permanent home, in which rooms would be set aside for Wagner to use on his occasional visits to Munich. They left Munich together on 18 March and parted at Augsburg, Wagner returning to Tribschen and to Cosima, Bülow to Basel. Four days later, on 22 March, Wagner began work on the full score of the second act of *Die Meistersinger*.

It soon became evident on what personal terms Bülow had consented to return to Munich: that Cosima should go with him and resume her place as his wife. She joined him in Basel on 16 April, leaving Isolde and Eva at Tribschen with Wagner (Daniela and Blandine were at the time visiting their grandmother in Berlin). From Olten, a railway station along the route, she sent Wagner a telegram containing a quotation from Ernst von Feuchtersleben's poem "Es ist bestimmt in Gottes Rat": "It is decreed in God's great plan / That what he loves must every man / Once part from" – words which signified for Wagner, as Cosima noted later in her diary (31 July 1879) "sounds like those outside the portals of a monastery, and even more: complete renunciation, mortification." He that same evening wrote down a few desolate words in his *Brown Book*: "In my whole life I do not think I have ever been as sad as I am now!! How easily that is said, and how unspeakable it is. . . . Today she departed. What this parting said! What help in seeing each other again? The parting remains. It is wretched!"

It had been decided that Bülow and Cosima should resume their married life for a trial period of one year. During this year Wagner and Cosima would continue to see each other, in Munich and in Tribschen, but in effect it was a return to the situation of their previous year in Munich – a difficult one then, but much more difficult now, after the months they had been together at Tribschen, living to all intents and purposes as man and wife. "It is lonely here now," Wagner wrote on 25 April to Mathilde Maier from Tribschen. "The younger children, Isolde and Eva, are still here. It is a novel and highly pleasant experience for me to concern myself with these young lives. . . . My whole life is work. I have my daily quota. If I do not achieve it, I feel ill." Hans Richter was still there with him, copying out pages of the score as Wagner completed them, as well as Vreneli, who earlier in the year had married the porter at the Schweizerhof Hotel, Jakob Stocker. He too was now a member of the household staff.

The king had invited Wagner to spend his birthday with him at Berg, but he felt great reluctance to uproot himself again, and he wrote to Ludwig on 15 May begging to be excused, pleading illness and an urgent desire to complete the score of *Die Meistersinger* in time for its production in October, the time now fixed for the royal wedding. Ludwig, however, insisted on his presence, and Cosima warned him by telegram that he would be wise to comply. He left Tribschen on 21 May in no good mood, and joined Cosima and Bülow in Munich in their apartment at Arcostrasse 11. His birthday was celebrated with Cosima on the following day in the Villa Prestele, the house on the Starnberg lake which Ludwig had put at his disposal, and in the afternoon he visited Ludwig at Berg.

During the fortnight he spent at the villa Ludwig was absent most of the time, making private excursions of his own. Wagner therefore transferred his attention to the Munich opera house, where Bülow was preparing the new production of *Lohengrin*. To demonstrate to Ludwig what true Wagnerian singing was, Wagner had invited Joseph Tichatschek, his original Rienzi and Tannhäuser in Dresden, to sing the title role, though now, at the age of sixty, his operatic career was all but over. "His Holy Grail narration has amazed and touched us all," Wagner wrote to the king on 6 June after a rehearsal. "This noble simplicity, this incisive portrait, borne on the shining, golden foundation of an incomparably clear and noble voice, has moved and inspired us all like a miracle from the great old days. Believe with me – forget all prejudices, and with me you will receive the finest reward."

Wagner had failed to take into account Ludwig's basic unmusicality and his romantic attitude to *Lohengrin* in particular. The sight of the elderly Tichatschek at the dress rehearsal on 11 June so appalled the king that he immediately sent Düfflipp to Wagner and Bülow with orders that the role must be given to some other singer for the first performance. Wagner, offended as much by the way the rebuff was inflicted as by the rebuff itself, wrote to the king on the following day from Starnberg: "I fear, my gracious friend, that your gaze, this time too sharp, has destroyed much that has been laboriously built up; and the only wish that now remains to me is that, with eyes as keen as those which wrecked this illusion, you should now look in other directions in order in particular to preserve your friend, who now feels his presence in the vicinity to which you so kindly summoned him as an embarrassment and a growing humiliation." The only course open to him, he concluded, was to return to his own Montsalvat, Tribschen. He waited a few days longer in the hope of a summons from the king, then, when it did not come, left Munich on 15 June.

Ludwig, equally upset, took refuge in his lodge on the Hochkopf. From there he wrote to Wagner on 21 June: "I feel that, if you had known how terrible is the punishment you have inflicted on me (the harsh punishment of separation), you would hardly have resolved on this step. But I shall not tire my friend with lamentations, will not complain; I kiss the hand that struck me. . . . I forbear from writing anything about the *Lohengrin* performance: you know what this divine work means and will always mean to me; I cannot possibly describe it; but the fact that it had to be this sublime work in particular which was this time the cause of so much pain for me, is something I shall never forget. You are the only physician capable of healing this wound."

Wagner was in no mood to do so. In his reply of 25 June he firmly repeated his intention of remaining at Tribschen, visiting Munich as rarely as possible, but he ended on a more conciliatory note: "I shall write to you often and at length, if this is what you would like: never, I swear it, shall this splendid and noble bond of love and friendship be dissolved between us!"

Ludwig seized eagerly on this assurance and ignored the complaints, and an outward reconciliation was achieved. But the quarrel left its mark behind: Wagner now knew that in Ludwig he no longer had a monarch whom he could command as he wished—Tichatschek's dismissal and his replacement by Heinrich Vogl, a singer for whom Wagner had no regard at all, was a humiliation which never ceased to rankle. Ludwig, on the other hand, gained the knowledge that he could follow his own inclinations as he chose, confident that Wagner, though he might complain, would not break off relations with him entirely.

He finished the final score of the second act of *Die Meistersinger* on 22 June and started on the third act four days later. Until its completion on 24 October he did not stir from Tribschen, and, as part of Ludwig's punishment for his behaviour over *Lohengrin*, he refused to attend the first performance of *Tannhäuser*, which took place on 1 August. Ludwig, being in court mourning for a deceased uncle (King Otto of Greece), missed it also, but a private performance was given for him two days later. It was the first time the revised version had been staged since its disastrous launching in Paris in March 1861, and its production had been regarded in advance, by Wagner as well as by the king, as a very important occasion. Yet—no doubt in retaliation for Wagner's gesture in absenting himself—Ludwig wrote him not a single word about it.

Bülow and his family came to Tribschen during August, but it was significant that they all came separately. Bülow arrived on 5 August, Daniela and Isolde on 6 August. Bülow left for St Moritz on 7 August, and on 11 August Cosima arrived at Tribschen with Blandine. Eva had of course been at Tribschen with Wagner all the time. Bülow's short visit was chiefly concerned with discussions of the preparations for *Die Meistersinger*, but Wagner's letter to him, written on 10 September, while Cosima was still at Tribschen, shows that their personal problems were foremost in their minds:

"Your concern for Beckmesser's lute touches me greatly, but everything in connection with you touches and moves me . . . right up to these sad times in which we have to face in painful earnest what the nature of our relationship is to be. The Munich arrangement was based on an alleviation of our distress through art—what divided us should hold us together, what we sacrificed should serve to enrich us. So often was I deeply and inwardly moved by you when we were borne on the heights of our mutual task: then, to you too, everything was clear and understandable. Now this agreement has been taken from us. What enthusiasm alone revealed to us like a flash of lightning must now be consciously regarded in a calm, clear light, what is necessary and inescapable must be incorporated in a sensible act of will.

"What are you saying to me when you continually address me as 'honoured master'? How often have I appealed to your heart! Are you now saying that the friend sacrifices himself to the 'master'? True, it is only as 'master' that I can lay claim to the sacrifice: am I to continue to produce, or have I come to an end? That is the decision hanging over my head. To enable my creative work to continue I too have already made great sacrifices, sacrifices of deepest friendship. Now, inexorably, the finger points: only through a friend's sacrifice can the means to continue be assured. Do you believe in friendship? Love of the master!

"And if this is how, alas, it must be, then do not hesitate to have Beckmesser's lute constructed. Many thanks for taking care of this – it reminds me of my duty. If only I could bring you some real joy!"

On 14 September Cosima left Tribschen with her three elder daughters to rejoin Bülow in Munich, and once again Wagner was left alone with Eva. On 30 September he wrote again to Bülow after studying his youthful tone poem *Nirwana*, revised the previous year: "You strangest of mortals! How hard it will be for you to make anything of yourself! And yet I feel so clearly how close to me you are, and how much I depend on you. If only you could understand your destiny! If you were to succumb, it would only be because your heart, like your mind, inclined towards too radiant a model. In your youthful work, now revised, I see unmistakable signs of these excessive spiritual strivings; I can think of nothing to set beside this piece in any respect; a youthful work such as this marks you out for mastery of the highest conceivable kind; it is an utterance of such novelty and daemonic clarity that it makes one shudder to have to recognise it as a youthful work. There is too much here, and that is disquieting. And, Hans, it is exactly the same with your heart: Fate demands from it that largeness and fineness which alone can match the significance of the inner artistic spirit with which it endowed you. Do not fail in your tremendous duties: acknowledge them, recognise them in the gaze of your friend, look them proudly and courageously in the face and – provided you obey them – you must without fail develop into a model of extraordinary nobility. My good Hans, it is worth it! All it needs now is caution and prudent care. Your success can and will come from inside yourself. It demands nothing more of you than to live up to what is inside you – and this is something incomparably rare and fine."

Though Wagner genuinely admired Bülow's *Nirwana*, and bestowed on it higher praise than he was wont to find for the works of any other of his younger contemporaries, it is evident that he was using it in this letter as a peg on which to hang his view of Bülow's role in his own destiny. It was a plea to him to accept the place he occupied in it: subsidiary, but not necessarily ignoble.

Liszt was also at Tribschen from 9 to 10 October. He had been in Munich since 20 September and had attended performances of both *Tannhäuser* and *Lohengrin*. In his *Annals* Wagner recorded simply: "Liszt's visit: feared, but pleasurable." What he feared was another attempt to persuade him to relinquish his claims on Cosima, and this was duly made, but without much conviction, for in reply to Wagner's question for what he should live if not for Cosima, Liszt could only point weakly to a portrait of King Ludwig. What was pleasurable was their joint immersion in *Die Meistersinger*, with which – as always with his music – Wagner captured all his sympathies. He wrote to the king following Liszt's departure: "We discovered old times again, lovelier than before. He is a dear, great, unique person!" Though he did not yet mention it to the king, he had formed a plan for bringing Liszt closer to his side by putting him in charge of church music in the new music school, which had been officially inaugurated on 1 October. However, Liszt eventually declined the invitation.

King Ludwig was also struggling with emotional problems. On 11 October it was officially announced that his engagement to Sophie was at an end. He wrote to Cosima: "You can imagine how terrible it was for me to see the wedding day coming closer and closer and to realise that this bond could never bring happiness either to her or to me. . . . What would have happened to all our plans if this unpropitious marriage had been sealed, if my inner suffering, my grief and sorrow had reduced me to despair – where would I have found the energy and enthusiasm for our ideals?" In his letter to Wagner of 19 October Ludwig described his engagement as a nightmare: he had been momentarily dazzled by Sophie's charm and grace, "which are more outside than inside". The expenses of the cancelled marriage, he went on to say, had been so great that he would now have to put off the construction of the festival theatre until the following year.

In his reply of 25 October Wagner congratulated Ludwig on his courage in recognising his mistake, and he took the opportunity – in the hope no doubt that his experience with Sophie had made the young man wiser and maturer – to hint cautiously at his and Cosima's own secret, which must inevitably come into the open one day. Referring to his autobiography, he wrote: "You will learn about my life; and that of our friend [Cosima] will also reveal to you great suffering, arising from mistakes whose consequences cannot be overcome by a noble heart on its own. Oh, how much of life is then uselessly wasted! And so – it was a dream: may it be a warning to you."

By breaking his engagement Ludwig had again forfeited the regard of his people, whose sympathies were all on Sophie's side. Wagner implored Ludwig to set about regaining their respect by firm and forthright acts and more frequent public appearances. He might begin, he suggested, by getting rid of such outdated and useless theatre lackeys as Lachner and Schmitt, and by giving Bülow the support he deserved. And he should offer official appointments to Liszt and Semper, both of them geniuses with an international reputation. He ended his letter: "Yesterday I wrote the final note in my new score. The glorious deed is done. It will carry us to divine fame. I was very, very exhausted, but also very, very proud. Your love shines within me. So now – the flag is hoisted."

This call to action aroused from Ludwig only a feeble response. He did, on 21 November, get rid of Schmitt, replacing him as director of the court opera with Baron Karl von Perfall, though even then he lacked conviction: "He is admittedly incompetent," he wrote to Wagner, "but at least he will not dare to disobey his instructions." Lachner, who had tactfully been sent on holiday while Bülow was bringing out the new productions of *Lohengrin* and *Tannhäuser*, was not finally disposed of until January of the following year, and then he was only given leave of absence, not definitely replaced. As for the public appearances, these became if anything rarer than before.

Beside the music school, at which Cornelius and Porges were now teaching, the most positive sign of development, from Wagner's point of view, was the establishment of a newspaper to propagate his ideas. The first issue of the *Süddeutsche Presse*, which had been provided by Hohenlohe with a state subsidy, appeared on 1 October, edited by Fröbel and with Porges in charge of its art pages. Wagner, though he had vowed to keep away from political utterances, had throughout the summer been corresponding at length with Fröbel about the newspaper's political outlook, which was to be patriotic but independent of parties. Under the heading of *German Art and German Politics* he began a series of anonymous articles which were basically an elaboration of the diary he had written for Ludwig's private consumption in 1865. The first article appeared in the opening number, and thereafter they were published weekly. Ludwig wrote to Wagner on 21 November: "Whoever is not delighted by the magic of the language and converted by the profundity of the intellect they reveal – such a person does not, by God, deserve to live." And in his reply of 30 November Wagner wrote: "I am expecting much from the impression my disclosures may make, particularly on the better people engaged in the theatre itself; perhaps it is with them that our main hope lies. The venerable court and state officials will of course be the last, and that makes me sad for your sake, for that, alas, is the world with which you have to do."

It was some of these officials who, after the appearance of Wagner's thirteenth article, descended on the editorial offices of the *Süddeutsche Presse* on 19 December and, in the king's name, forbade the publication of the remaining two articles. Reading that thirteenth article today, one may find it difficult to see in Wagner's not very savage attack on bureaucracy anything to warrant such drastic action. The real reasons behind the ban remain obscure, but the action was taken with the king's approval, and his complete change of face seems to have had less to do with the content of the articles than with his personal disenchantment with Wagner and his associates. This was set in motion by the reappearance in Munich of Malvina von Schnorr, determined to try once again to get her revenge on Wagner and Cosima for their treatment of her in the matter of Isidore Reutter. Wagner attempted to forestall her in his letter of 30 November to the king, describing her as an embittered woman, and demanding that she should be ordered to apologise to Cosima for her libels; furthermore, since she was no longer employable by him, he suggested her pension from the king might be reduced.

His letter annoyed Ludwig, who sent it to Düfflipp with a note attached: "The eternal wrangles and complaints on the part of Wagner, Porges, Fröbel and the rest of them have become thoroughly repugnant to me. . . . The thread of my patience is at last beginning to break." Düfflipp's subsequent report on a meeting with Fröbel, which the king received on 13 December, contained some disturbing revelations that strained his patience still further, among them a hint, allegedly dropped by Fröbel, that the true author of the articles in the *Süddeutsche Presse* was not Wagner, but Cosima. "I cannot believe my eyes," Ludwig wrote to Düfflipp in reply. "This refined and intellectual Frau v. Bülow devoting herself to scribbling for the press, writing these unholy articles! I should never have thought the cultivated Cosima capable of such pranks!" And he went on: "But I am even more amazed that you believe there is something fishy in the matter between Wagner, Fr. v. Bülow and Fr. v. Schnorr. If that sorry rumour, which I could never make up my mind to believe, should turn out to be true after all, if adultery should really be involved – then beware!"

Cosima believed, or professed to believe, that Fröbel had himself instigated the ban on Wagner's articles in order to save his own skin, being under the impression that Wagner was in disgrace with the king. Her relations with Fröbel had by now developed into open hostility, and on

27 December he denounced her to Ludwig as a political intriguer. Wagner, who had come to Munich to spend Christmas with the Bülow family, was present when Düfflipp arrived later that day with a message from the king. It contained a warning to Cosima that she should cease meddling in public affairs. Wagner went next day to see Ludwig, with whom he spent two and a half hours. What was said at that interview is nowhere recorded, but after it Wagner wrote in his *Annals*: "Reconciliation and apology to C." And indeed that same evening the king wrote to Cosima: "After a long, long time bliss has once more entered my soul, for this evening I spent a sublime and blessed hour with my loyally beloved friend. Alas, it passed all too swiftly. One thing I implore you, my dear friend: forget your last conversation with Düfflipp, please consider everything he told you as unsaid, I gladly take it all back; it was a passing cloud, which must not be allowed to obscure our sun."

Cosima sought to gain her revenge on Fröbel by asking the king to order him, through Prince Hohenlohe, to print the two articles which (according to her) he had suppressed. Fröbel, she explained, would of course refuse to do so, having committed himself too strongly against them, and thus a plausible excuse would be found to get rid of him entirely. However, by this time Ludwig had had enough. He returned the unpublished articles, copies of which she sent with her letter, adding only a brief comment that he had "read them with lively interest". That was the end of the matter. Fröbel continued to run the newspaper until 1873.

Another member of Wagner's circle was also causing problems at this same time. Following the king's decision to postpone the construction of the theatre, Wagner urged that, as compensation for all his work on it, Semper should be offered an official position in Munich. Ludwig agreed to appoint him "senior architect and intendant of all buildings included in the king's civil list". However, in spite of verbal promises, Semper found himself waiting in vain for an official summons, and finally he decided to treat the whole project as abandoned, and submitted to the treasury office in Munich a claim for 37,305 florins, representing the expenses he had accrued in designing the theatre. That was in March 1868, and this time it was not only the king who was annoyed, but Wagner, who saw Semper's action as a lack of confidence in himself. Semper did eventually get his money (though not until January 1869), but it was at the cost of a rift between him and Wagner that took years to heal.

The abandonment of the theatre project meant little to Wagner, who had always felt that Munich was not the right place for it, and had supported the idea more out of deference to Ludwig than from any inner conviction of his own. But it was one more proof that his second attempt to establish himself in Munich would be as unsuccessful as his first. Bülow was of the same opinion, and he bitterly regretted having allowed himself to be persuaded into returning. For this he blamed Wagner and Cosima, and he spared neither his reproaches.

However, for the time being all personal recriminations were as far as possible set aside as, at the beginning of 1868, preparations for the production of *Die Meistersinger* gathered momentum. At this stage Wagner was content to leave most of the practical work to Bülow and to Richter, who in December had taken up his new position as coach for soloists and chorus at the Munich opera. He himself returned on 8 February to Tribschen, where he occupied himself writing an introduction for the publication of *German Art and German Politics* in book form, and enjoying the company of his daughter Eva, whose first birthday on 17 February he celebrated by playing melodies from *Die Meistersinger* to her. "At each noticeable turn in the melody she bends her neck over her legs to watch my fingers," he wrote to Cosima, "then she smiles, laughs, listens very carefully and looks pleased again."

Ludwig, with whom he had not been in contact since their meeting at Christmas, wrote to him at Tribschen on 9 March pleading for news. Though they had apparently been reconciled as a result of that meeting, Wagner found it difficult to forgive him for the part he had played in the suppression of his articles. "Why do you now disturb my silence and awaken in me the old intoxicating strains of hope?" he wrote on 12 March. The king's reply to that, written on 16 March, expressed contrition, but he defended himself with some spirit: "Oh, my dear friend, if only I could convince you of the true state of things! I know these wretched newspapers, through which you have learnt all these damnable lies and slanders about me; woe to me, if I had allowed myself on an earlier occasion to be led astray by what I learned about you!" To Wagner's reproach that he had so far failed to take advantage of his position as king to further their ideals he responded: "You say it would have been so easy for me, I had everything within my power, but I did not choose to act. That is true, and I do not deny it. But I know that the power is still mine, and the victory too. Death, where is thy sting? If I hid myself behind clouds, I am still what I always was, not as miserable, as bereft of power as it might seem. . . . For I clearly recognise the great task and will carry it out loyally and conscientiously, believe you me."

Wagner returned to Munich on 17 March to join in the preparations for *Die Meistersinger*. The failure to find a suitable tenor for the role of Walther von Stolzing, which Wagner resolutely refused to give to Vogl, meant that a production in spring would no longer be possible, but by the time of his return to Tribschen on 22 April singers had been found for most of the main roles, including Franz Betz from Vienna as Hans

Sachs; Mathilde Mallinger, a member of the Munich company, as Eva; and as the apprentice David, Karl (or Max, as he is sometimes called) Schlosser, from Augsburg – a hitherto unsuccessful singer whom, Cosima tells us in her diary, Wagner discovered working in a bakery. For Walther a likely candidate had been found in Franz Nachbaur, and Richter was despatched to Darmstadt to do some preliminary work with him. To supervise the staging Wagner brought in Reinhart Hallwachs from Stuttgart. While Hallwachs and Bülow were conducting rehearsals, the Munich designers Quaglio, Jank and Döll prepared the sets and Franz Seitz the costumes.

Wagner meanwhile occupied himself at Tribschen with literary work: a foreword for a second edition of *Opera and Drama*, which he wrote in the form of an open letter to Constantin Frantz, a German political writer of federalist views who had visited him at Tribschen in 1866; and his reminiscences of Ludwig Schnorr von Carolsfeld. He made some notes in connection with *Die Sieger*, his projected music drama on a Buddhist theme, but musically all that came to be written down was a sketch in the *Brown Book* entitled "*Romeo und Julie*", a sombre theme which appears to have had some connection with Ludwig Schnorr.

Cosima and the children joined him at Tribschen on 12 May, but it was an unrewarding visit. "Great confusion of feelings," Wagner wrote in his *Annals*, "always new difficulties." Cosima and he returned separately to Munich a week later, and he celebrated his birthday with King Ludwig on the Roseninsel, from which they made an excursion across the Starnberg lake in a steamer named *Tristan*. "It was one of those days," the king wrote to him afterwards, "on which one feels freed for ever from the world and its sorrows."

Wagner remained in Munich to supervise the rehearsals of *Die Meistersinger* and reported to Ludwig his complete satisfaction with their progress. His entries in his *Annals* suggest, however, that personal relationships were not always cordial: "Piano rehearsals: heavy, oppressive feeling from Hans's deep hostility and estrangement. Management uncooperative throughout . . . Perfall's anxiety-chicanery . . . June: orchestral rehearsals: serious trouble with H. – Perfall intriguing wherever possible. Apparent rebellion in orchestra . . . Dress rehearsal: again annoyance over – everything."

Nevertheless, he was pleased with the final result, full of praise for his singers (who had been joined by Gustav Hölzel of Vienna as Beckmesser), for the stage decorators, and for Hallwachs and Richter. He begged Ludwig in his letter on 17 June to reward the latter with a position worthy of his skills (a request Ludwig fulfilled by appointing Richter court musical director on 10 September).

The first performance on 21 June was attended by the usual gathering of friends and relations, among them Jessie Laussot and Mathilde Maier, the most notable absentee being Liszt. Wagner, who had planned to watch the performance secretly from Cosima's box, was sent for by the king in the middle of the Prelude and, much to Cosima's disappointment, was obliged to remain with him in the royal box until the end. More than that, he was invited by Ludwig to take his bow after the second and third acts from there, a departure from protocol which shocked the orthodox profoundly. It was a wonder, the *Kemptener Zeitung* commented on the following day, that the theatre roof did not fall in.

Though the press reviews of *Die Meistersinger* were mostly unfavourable (Hanslick called it "an interesting case of musical deviation or sickness"), there was no doubt of its success with the public. In Munich, it was given six further performances before the theatre closed at the end of July for the summer holidays, and other theatres eagerly sought permission to stage it. Wagner, conscious of a potentially valuable source of income, yielded to the persuasions of his publisher Schott and withdrew his objections against cuts being made in his work at theatres outside Munich. It was an uncharacteristic concession, but he was practical enough to realise that in *Die Meistersinger* he had created a work with a genuine popular appeal, his first indeed since *Lohengrin*, a full eighteen years earlier. In deciding, however, to launch it on the wider career denied to either *Tristan* or the *Ring*, he felt it of vital importance that his Munich production should be beyond reproach, in order to act as a model, and on 25 June he wrote to Bülow, pointing out a few weaknesses that required attention: "The main missing element is that indispensable discretion, that conscious restraint of volume (particularly in the symphonic accompaniment of the musical dialogue on the stage). The important thing here is, while making every figure as clear as possible, always to avoid any violent accentuation, and to keep the volume generally in a correct relationship. In general the orchestral players need to be reminded of this."

As regards the singers, whom he praised (especially Betz and Nachbaur), he stressed the importance of ironing out all uncertainties before these degenerated into a habit. "Our valuable friends and mastersinger colleagues are now familiar enough with my basic principles: they know their task is to present, through complete truthfulness of dramatic understanding and interpretation, not operatic roles, but real and clearly recognisable dramatic characters, convincing down to the smallest detail. In what manner it is the music that alone makes such characterisation possible – that must remain the secret of the initiated; as far as the actors are concerned, it will be enough if they stop being conventional 'opera singers'."

Wagner returned to Tribschen on 24 June and there, with only Cosima's children for company, he fell into a post-production melancholy. "Gloomy depressed mood," he wrote in his *Annals*. "Great clarity dawning as to my condition and the state of things. Profoundest lack of spirits for movement of any kind: reason for total incapacity of will seen in fate of relationship with Cos. and Hans. Everything futile; complete failure of Munich attempts. Thought imperative never to return there. . . . Surrender to most wretched fate seems inevitable: really foreseen by Cos. since our last year's separation: believing in nothing, she consequently could not help doubting me."

On 12 July Cosima, still in Munich, received a letter from the king: "Two years ago I felt it my duty as a loyal friend to tell you about that letter from Frau v. Schnorr in which she had the temerity to utter slanders of the most disgraceful kind against you and your friend. Equally, as a loyal friend I now feel unable to conceal from you what I have just learnt from a thoroughly reliable source: that a man who up till now was always regarded by Wagner as a loyal and upright friend has been uttering the same base slanders about you and your friend. This man is Röckel. . . . I beg you to beware of this person and also to warn our friend against him."

Cosima sent the king's letter to Wagner. Since the information had come from him, Wagner wrote to Ludwig on 16 July from Tribschen, it had had "a very shattering effect on her great and free soul. She asks me humbly to lay her farewells at your feet and to request you to release her from the obligation of replying to you." As for himself, Wagner went on, he saw it as a slander against his old friend Röckel, in whose baseness he would, failing the most incontrovertible proofs, find it impossible to believe. Cosima, he declared, felt it impossible that she should now return to Munich. "The question will then arise whether the artistic conditions in Munich will take a sufficiently hopeful course to persuade Bülow to prolong his stay there in such difficult circumstances; if not, there will be nothing for him but to rely on your magnanimity graciously to relieve him of his post."

In spite of his assurances of faith in the integrity of Röckel, who vigorously denied having spread the tales of which he was accused, Wagner put an end to their friendship – an act which might seem illogical when viewed in the light of an entry in Cosima's diary on 9 December 1880: "In the morning we went through former times of separation: 'We would not have stayed alive much longer,' he [Wagner] says, 'and that is why I seized on Röckel's misdeed as if it were a salvation.'" This suggests that Wagner, though he did believe Röckel to have been guilty, was secretly grateful to him for at last bringing matters to a head.

However, Cosima was not so easily persuaded that the need for sub-terfuge was now past and the time for her to leave Bülow had come. Though by now she was quite sure of her desires, she was still reluctant to take the final step, above all out of consideration for her children. Wagner's insistence that in no circumstances would he be prepared to return to Munich revealed the extent of the dilemma. She joined him and the children at Tribschen on 22 July, and they resumed work on *My Life*. The dominating theme remained, however. In his *Brown Book* Wagner wrote down on 19 and 22 August a few brief notes for a play on the subject of Martin Luther's marriage to the nun Katharina von Bora which seem to have some connection with his own situation.

More significant, because more direct, is the entry in the *Brown Book* immediately following these notes on Luther's dilemma, also dated 22 August. Here, in somewhat tortuous phrases, Wagner seems laboriously to have been working his way towards the implications of a love between two persons that is mutual and unegotistical. "Two beings who truly love," he began, "have only one single faith – their consciousness of being loved." Love being a state in which feelings are at their most sensitive, any jarring note arising from irritability or indisposition can have a devastating effect: even a slight reproach can put one's whole feeling of being loved in doubt. Love is indivisible, and what in any other state would be a partial disappointment seems to lovers to destroy the whole relationship. Yet, human frailty being what it is, such moments of dis-harmony are bound to occur. What can be done to counteract their effect? The lover must adopt the outlook of the Christian, "who has learnt to keep himself in balance by means of his faith in the inexhaust-ible forbearance of the Redeemer". If he is assailed by recurring thoughts of a deep-lying hostility in the loved one towards him, he should seek the reason for these thoughts in his own doubts of being loved, and nowhere else; he should not see it as evidence of a faltering of love itself in the other person. He should examine himself and realise that the doubts which are causing him to falter are having the very same effect on the loved one, and for the very same reasons – yet he knows his own love is ardent and ineradicable. Perhaps in this way he might indeed come to recognise clearly the nature of love, something he had pre-viously felt only as the pleasure of being loved. By acknowledging this, he might find the means of combating the doubts by which his faith has been beset – by remembering that, "whatever comes to you from the person you love, you will be loved in exactly the same measure as you yourself love".

While Wagner and Cosima were struggling with their emotional difficulties in Tribschen, Bülow was similarly occupied in Wiesbaden, where he stayed with Raff for three weeks between 22 August and 9

September. According to Cosima's biographer, Richard Graf Du Moulin Eckart, he spent some of his time there in pistol practice, having resolved to challenge Wagner to a duel, but he was brought back to reality by Raff, who told him: "You cannot exchange shots with the master." Some doubt must be thrown on this story, since at the time it was said to have occurred Bülow was already back in Munich. However, it can surely be assumed that, with Cosima's departure for Tribschen on 22 July, Bülow was aware that the moment of crisis was at hand.

Wagner and Cosima set out for Italy on 14 September, accompanied only by Jakob Stocker, Vreneli's husband. They went first to the Borromean Islands, then to Genoa and Milan, where they occupied themselves visiting picture galleries: "Much joy. Cos. full of life," he wrote in his *Annals*. On 28 September they visited Cosima's birthplace on Lake Como, and on the following day were back in Switzerland. In Bellinzona they learned of the violent catastrophe that had struck the canton of Ticino, where whole villages were being destroyed by floods and landslides. It was one of the worst disasters ever to ravage Switzerland, and to Cosima, as she later recalled in her diary, it seemed like a judgment of God upon her as, out of consideration for Jakob, they struggled to reach Tribschen in time for Vreneli's confinement.

Part of the journey had to be accomplished on foot in raging thunderstorms, wading through mud or at times, where bridges had been swept away, through swollen streams. "I have never met a pluckier woman," Jakob told his wife afterwards (she passed on his tribute in a letter to Cosima dated 24 December 1886). "She went with us through all those terrible exertions without a word of complaint." They arrived back in Tribschen on 6 October to find that Vreneli's son had already been born. "I shall never forget the day of your return," Vreneli wrote in her letter to Cosima. "I could see how much you had suffered, and I saw then that even greater sufferings lay ahead of you. . . . However, you have an iron constitution."

Having already informed Bülow in a letter from Faido of her decision to leave him, Cosima returned to Munich on 14 October with her four daughters to complete the final arrangements. Wagner accompanied them as far as Augsburg, then returned to Tribschen, from where he wrote to the king, at last telling him, though in very veiled terms, the true state of affairs. He described the perilous journey with Cosima through Ticino, and declared that he had thought his last days had come. "On the edge of destruction, life once more revealed itself to us, lit by long flashes of lightning, in all its terrible earnestness. No further deception was possible. To look death in the face means to recognise the whole truth: to rescue what is eternal in it means to turn one's back on all deceit. Our friend returned to Munich two days ago with her children to settle her affairs and with all dignity to put her unalterable decisions into effect. . . . There is nothing for me to do but stand by her: may you, my kind and noble friend, place yourself loyally at my side." Four days later, his first letter to the king not yet sent, he wrote a second: "I fear Bülow will soon be left very isolated, and he will be needing protection against indignities. This protection I confidently request from you, my noble friend, and shall be happy if Bülow gains the strength through artistic activity to hold up his head: may he not be deprived of this final salvation by being left to the mercies of jealous enemies!"

What happened in Munich between Cosima and Bülow can only be pieced together from isolated scraps of evidence. According to Wagner's letter of 24 August 1869 to Marie Muchanoff, she asked Bülow for a divorce, but he, for the sake of the children, still hesitated. She, believing that it would be easier to get a divorce if she became a Protestant, wrote to Wagner of her intention of going to Rome, presumably to consult with her father before taking this step. Fearing the outcome of Liszt's influence over his daughter, he conceived the desperate plan of despatching Cosima's stepsister, Claire Charnacé, to Munich in an attempt to dissuade her from going to Rome. Cosima, who had left her home in the Arcostrasse to stay with Wagner's old servants, the Mrazeks, responded to the news of Claire's impending arrival with an angry telegram on 27 October: "Wilful interference making life unbearable. Painful bitterness over this playing about with a weary being's peace of mind." Another telegram followed later the same day: "For me Claire's arrival the most disagreeable event, refusal of Rome journey the saddest." Wagner wrote in his *Annals*: "Great depression: decide to make trip, calling at Arcostrasse. C. calmer." He left for Munich on 1 November and saw Cosima in her temporary home, where she had Eva with her. They evidently decided that there was nothing he could do in Munich, and on 2 November he went to Leipzig to stay with his sister Ottilie Brockhaus and her family. From there he wrote on 4 November to the king, requesting an audience: "(Family?)", he wrote in his *Annals*, which leaves it unclear what exactly he wished from Ludwig on this occasion. On 5 November he telegraphed to Cosima: "Friendly here, but useless. Much conversation strenuous. Am inclined, if agreed, to return to Tr. soon. Great longing for news. Mood good and confident." Cosima replied on the same day: "Wrote yesterday. Return agreed. Decisions impossible at present. Request patience and notification of departure." Wagner's telegram of 8 November read: "Received and answered. Touched, but unmoved. Purest clarity of will. Expecting no interview. Travelling Monday evening direct, home Tuesday evening. Loyallest greetings and blessings." Receiving news from Düfflipp that the king was too busy to see him, Wagner left Leipzig on 10 November to return to Switzerland. From Augsburg he telegraphed Cosima that he would be there till evening. Cosima replied: "Children coming to visit on five o'clock train. Please meet. Greetings from their mother."

Why Cosima chose to send Daniela, Blandine and Isolde with their nursemaid Hermine to Augsburg, some fifty miles from Munich, remains unexplained. Possibly she entrusted a letter to Wagner to Hermine, who was in on the secret, and the children were despatched with her to avoid suspicion. On 11 November, after putting the children on the train to Munich, he went on to Tribschen, where on 15 November he received a telegram from Cosima: "Not writing for reasons of caution. Leaving tomorrow. Will telegraph again. In good health, cheerful." On the afternoon of 16 November she left Munich with Isolde and Eva, bound for Tribschen, which they reached late that same night.

CHAPTER VI

Resumption of the Ring

SINCE THE PUBLICATION of Cosima's voluminous diaries, which she began to write on 1 January 1869, the biographer has for the last fourteen years of Wagner's life a complete record of his daily activities, so that he can at least be reasonably sure of his facts. All the same, the diaries must be approached with a certain degree of scepticism. Cosima wrote them avowedly for the benefit of her children, and thus she strove always to present Wagner in the best possible light, and to conceal from them aspects of his character and behaviour which may at times have caused her sorrow. If, in the process of writing down something like one million words over a period of fourteen years, she did occasionally forget the children and permit herself that kind of self-communion more typical of the diary form, it was invariably in order to castigate, not Wagner, but herself. Whenever they were at variance, she was always ready to conclude that he was right and she wrong. Part of this process may have been subconscious – the effort of a woman who has made sacrifices and endured scandal to persuade herself that she had not done so in vain. But it owed much also to her deep and intuitive understanding of Wagner's character. In the ordinary affairs of life, as in his art, he had to dominate, and to him love and loyalty meant a complete subjugation to his will. Those who were willing to submit to him did not, unless they wished to, become mere slaves. They were repaid with kindness and sympathy, and this was Wagner's way of expressing his gratitude, for behind the urge to dominate was a constant desire for reassurance. There were some in his life, including Minna and later Nietzsche, who found his demands on their unquestioning loyalty unbearably oppressive, and their relationships ended in a complete and mutually bitter rupture. Others, like Peter Cornelius for instance, had the feeling, after attempting to assert their independence, that they had lost more than they had gained, and capitulated. "I am quite determined to stick to him steadfastly," he wrote to his future wife on 3 February 1867, "to go with him through thick and thin, partisan to the last ditch. When I see how others, like Bülow, Liszt, Berlioz, Tausig, Damrosch, treat me, ignore me, forget me, and how he, the moment I show him even a hint of my heart, is always ready to give me his full friendship, then I tell myself that it is Fate that has brought us together."

By nature Cosima was anything but a slave, and in the long years of her widowhood she displayed a will just as indomitable as Wagner's own. Her diaries show that she had to struggle to overcome her self-will, but it was not done in a spirit of cold calculation for tactical advantage. Believing absolutely both in him and in his work, she understood that he functioned best when he could confront what he saw as a hostile world from the security of a small, loyal and loving family circle. Once having made the decision to provide him with this security, she gave herself entirely to the task of maintaining it.

For the first few weeks after her arrival Cosima's presence at Tribschen remained a closely guarded secret. Only Bülow, who informed his friends that she had gone with her two youngest daughters to visit her stepsister Claire in Versailles, knew where she really was. During this time Wagner and she continued with the dictation of *My Life*. He was also engaged in making a fair copy of the second act of *Siegfried* and preparing his pamphlet *Judaism in Music* for republication. On this latter activity Cosima looked with some apprehension, feeling that it might draw unwelcome attention to them at a time when they least required it.

She was fully conscious of the enormity of the step she had taken. She now also knew herself to be pregnant again, and it was this knowledge, as much as the realisation of the suffering a capitulation would cause Wagner, that prevented her in the first weeks from returning to Munich. Having left Daniela and Blandine there out of feelings of compassion for Bülow, she now felt guilty at having abandoned them, and the absence of any news of them plunged her into a misery that made her cling even more desperately to Wagner. "It is for me downright agony to be separated from him, even for a single instant," she wrote in her diary on 11 January 1869. "No letter from the children. Hans keeps silent, my father must now be in Germany; how alien everything to do with the world has now become to me! And I know that nobody in it has ever loved me."

Wagner, too, was anxious about the effect that his admission of his true relations with Cosima might have on the king. Alive to his new responsibilities as a family man, he had written on 23 November 1868 to Düfflipp, requesting an advance of 10,000 florins to invest in a pension fund, the loan to be paid off by deducting 2,000 florins annually from his allowance of 8,000 florins. Düfflipp indicated in his reply that, in view of the king's present mood towards him and towards Semper's demands for payment for the plans of the abandoned theatre, the matter might be difficult to arrange. Wagner's Christmas presents to Ludwig – the original score of *Rienzi* and a *de luxe* copy of the piano arrangement of

Die Meistersinger – were sent in the hope of softening him. He followed this on 29 December with a letter to Ludwig declaring that his present tranquil life at Tribschen was to the benefit of everybody: "Everything here is now working like clockwork, and indeed the time set aside for work is so generous that I scarcely find time even for reading and for the walks so necessary to my health. I am in regular correspondence with Bülow about the theatre and the school." He had, he declared, felt such an urge to begin at once on *Parzival* that he had had to fight a battle with himself in the interests of *Siegfried* and *Götterdämmerung*: however, they had now been "saved". With his letter he enclosed one from Cosima to the king, pretending that he had just received it for forwarding; it contained assurances of gratitude and steadfast loyalty just as effusive as Wagner's own.

They had to wait until 10 February before receiving Ludwig's reply, which was reassuring. His silence, he said, had been due to the pressure of work, and he hoped neither Wagner nor Cosima would have seen it as a cooling of his friendship. He had now begun to take pleasure in the royal duties he had previously found so hateful. However, such dreary occupations had to be balanced by delights, he remarked, and in the summer he intended to have *Tristan und Isolde* performed, also *Das Rheingold*: "Do what you can, my dearest friend, to make this production possible, I *implore* you."

Ludwig's announcement of his intention to have *Das Rheingold* staged in Munich cannot be accurately described as a bombshell. Wagner himself might be held responsible for having put the idea into his mind, when a year previously – on 5 February 1868 – he wrote to Düfflipp about Perfall's plans for improving the stage of the court theatre. Following its reconstruction, he told Düfflipp, "it would not be impossible, in case the king should wish it, to mount a temporary production of the separate parts of the *Ring*, perhaps in successive years." And his reply to the king on 24 February gave no sign that he actively disapproved of Ludwig's intention: "Through . . . all the . . . kindnesses you have shown me, you have undeniably gained the complete right to dispose over my works and their performance in any way you think fit." He told Ludwig that he would be unable to take an active part in the production himself, but he would be prepared to instruct Hallwachs and all others concerned in the correct manner of presenting the work. "Another point is the condition under which the performance of the separate parts of my *Nibelungen* may be presented to the *public*. My wishes regarding this I shall permit myself to make known to you in detail at the proper time. And so, fairest master, make your commands. I shall only help – never hinder!"

Legally of course Ludwig was entitled to do as he pleased, for in October 1864 Wagner had sold all the rights in the *Ring* to him.

However, in proposing to take the initiative with its production, he knew he was entering dangerous territory. That the mild initial response delighted him may be deduced from the fact that on receipt of it Wagner's request for a loan of 10,000 florins to invest in a pension was promptly granted.

On 23 February, the day before writing his letter to the king, Wagner completed the full score of the second act of *Siegfried*. "This work of construction has additionally served to enable me, by constant application to it, to immerse myself again entirely in the spirit of my work and to familiarise myself with it to such an extent that I can now continue with it as if I had never been interrupted," he said in his letter. He was now at last about to start on the third act, which he described as "the centre of the great cosmic tragedy. . . . Since the days of my return to Munich from that wonderful week in Hohenschwangau, when so many anxious questions about our future had to be discussed, I conceived the theme that has been pursuing me ever since – the one that greets us at the very start of this act and proclaims the god's resolve, his last question, his final will. Fear has so far held me back from writing down things that have often struck me like lightning during my lonely walks through wind and weather. But the proud joy of the pair united until death also found its musical tones in these times."

He began work on the composition sketch of the third act on 1 March. "May Heaven bless him!" Cosima wrote in her diary on that day. "Richard says jokingly at lunch that, if he ever completes the *Nibelungen*, I shall deserve an order *pour le mérite*. It is difficult to combine bringing up children with an artistic life, but I am determined to succeed."

A personal letter to Cosima from the king, received in March, showed that she too had been forgiven, and thus she was able to emerge from her hiding and go beyond the grounds of Tribschen, which she had not left since her arrival. A chance meeting with their landlord, Colonel Am Rhyn, had in any case betrayed her presence there, and the secret could not have been maintained much longer. She pretended, in her reply to the king's letter as to all others, that she had just come to Tribschen on her return from Versailles. In fact, the restored freedom of movement made little difference to her life, for neither Wagner nor she had cultivated any friendships in Lucerne, and, beyond calling on their landlord's wife and their neighbours, Count Hugo and Countess Caroline von Waldbott-Bassenheim, she continued her secluded existence. The most important result of her acknowledged presence at Tribschen was that Bülow at last consented to allow Daniela and Blandine to visit her there. On 8 April she went joyfully to Zurich to collect them.

Although no definite decision had yet been made, it was tacitly assumed by Bülow, Wagner and Cosima that the elder children would remain with their mother. On the day of their departure from Munich Bülow wrote to Wagner: "I found the parting from them painful. Seldom as I saw them, they have become tremendously dear to me, because their original sterling character remains so steadfast. Their mother will, I think, be satisfied with them, and I do not in the least begrudge her her pleasure."

During these days Wagner's new edition of *Judaism in Music* was published in Leipzig by J. J. Weber. Why, at a time when *Die Meistersinger* was restoring his popularity, he should have chosen to reissue this essay, which had lost him much support on its first appearance in 1850, he explained in a new foreword. This was cast in the form of a letter to Marie Muchanoff, who, he said, had recently expressed to him her wonder that a composer whose works enjoyed so much admiration should invariably be treated with so much hostility by the press. To answer her question, he reminded her that *Judaism in Music* had originally been published under a pseudonym, K. Freigedank, and the reason for that had been his desire that his ideas about the Jewish influence on German culture should be read objectively, and not seen as the view of a composer "envious of the success of others". However, the device had worked against him. It soon became known who the author was, and in revenge the Jewish-dominated press united to suppress all mention of *Judaism in Music*. By reissuing it under his own name, he now threw the matter open to debate, though he realised that the power of the Jews in the fields of music and the press had increased in the meantime, perhaps past remedying. If, however, there was a genuine process of assimilation going on, then the reprint of an essay that pointed out the difficulties of this problem might help towards resolving them.

As Cosima had feared, the reappearance of *Judaism in Music* caused a stir, above all among the Jews themselves, and there was a demonstration against it in the theatre at Mannheim during a performance of *Die Meistersinger*. Some newspapers were hostile, but others were friendly in tone, and these included some Roman Catholic publications – an ironical outcome in view of Wagner's set belief that Germany's cultural backwardness was the work of what he called the "three J's": Jews, Jesuits and journalists. Bülow, writing to Liszt on 13 March, remarked that "Wagner's famous brochure" was causing revolts in Vienna, and added: "All the better." There were some individuals who expressed their disapproval to the author, but it cannot be claimed that in Wagner's lifetime the essay was regarded with anything like the disgust it aroused in post-Hitler years. He was by no means alone in his antipathy towards the Jews. Cosima was as anti-Semitic as he was, and even the cosmopolitan Marie Muchanoff (who as Madame Kalergis had long been one of Wagner's wealthy patrons) wrote to her daughter that she felt very honoured by the dedication of the book to her, and she agreed wholeheartedly with everything Wagner said about Mendelssohn and Meyerbeer. "If Wagner had attacked the persecuted Jews," she added, "I should not have approved, but I love outspokenness towards the powerful and the triumphant."

By now Wagner had begun to have misgivings about the production of *Das Rheingold* in Munich, and he wrote to Ludwig on 22 March, pleading that the performance should be confined to an audience of guests invited personally by the king. His request brought no response and on 4 April Cosima noted: "The projected production . . . distresses him deeply, the means are not at hand, and now things will be forced, his great work cut to pieces – it is a great shame, and I am in deadly fear that dealing with it, even if only from here, will completely rob him of his will to continue his work. – He looks bad and his whole nature is changed." However, after discussing the production with Richter, who was to conduct it, and then with Hallwachs and the stage machinist Friedrich Carl Brandt, all of whom visited him in Tribschen in early April, he put the matter temporarily out of his mind and resumed work on *Siegfried*.

Beside her anxieties about Wagner, Cosima had much else to worry her, and happiness was not fully restored by the arrival of her two elder daughters. To her continual feelings of remorse towards Bülow, who was still, with what she described as his "typical indecision", holding out in Munich, though neither conducting nor giving much attention to the music school, was added anxiety about her mother in Paris. She, so Claire informed her, had suffered a mental breakdown, and her life was in danger. And at Tribschen itself there were differences between her and Wagner concerning the approaching confinement. He wished it to take place at home, she wanted it to be "far away from here and in secret, for the sake of the elder children". Such diverging attitudes led to silly little squabbles; but peace could always be restored when he played to her the music he was writing for *Siegfried*. "He is delighted," she wrote on 19 May, "that several themes which date from the 'Starnberg days' and which we had jokingly earmarked for quartets and symphonies have now found their niche ('*Ewig war ich, ewig bin ich*'). Great surge of joy at this coming together of life and art."

It was a slightly earlier passage from *Siegfried* that Friedrich Nietzsche heard when he stood outside Tribschen during a Whitsun excursion to Lucerne in May, "an excruciating discord repeated again and again" which he later identified as belonging to Brünnhilde's words, "*Verwundet hat mich, der mich geweckt*." Nietzsche, a deep admirer of Wagner's music since becoming acquainted with the piano score of

Tristan und Isolde at the age of sixteen, had met Wagner on 8 November of the previous year at the home of Hermann and Ottilie Brockhaus, and they had found a common bond in their veneration for Schopenhauer. Wagner had then invited the young man to visit him at Tribschen when he happened to be in the neighbourhood. In the following February Nietzsche, still only twenty-four years of age, was appointed professor of classical philology at the University of Basel. His visit to Lucerne at Whitsun in the company of friends was primarily in the interests of sightseeing, and he was by no means sure, when he eventually plucked up courage to present his card at Tribschen, that Wagner would remember him. Wagner did, and on the following morning, 17 May, Nietzsche paid his first call. Cosima, meeting him for the first time, was as much captivated by him as Wagner was, and on 20 May she wrote inviting him to come to Tribschen for Wagner's birthday. Nietzsche was unable to free himself from his duties, but he wrote a letter to Wagner, in which he declared that it was given only to a few people to appreciate the significance of a genius during his lifetime: "I make bold to count myself among these 'select few', since realising how incapable the world at large is of comprehending your personality, or of feeling the deeply ethical current by which your life, your writings and your music are permeated – in short, of sensing an atmosphere of that serious and more spiritual outlook upon life of which we poor Germans have been robbed overnight, as it were, by every conceivable sort of political misery, philosophical nonsense and aggressive Judaism. It is to you and Schopenhauer that I owe my ability of holding fast to the vital seriousness of the Germanic race and to the deepened contemplation of our enigmatic and perplexing existence."

He could scarcely have found a better way to reach Wagner's heart than through this complete identification with Wagner's views on German shortcomings, and the reaction was an open invitation to visit Tribschen for a prolonged stay whenever he could find the time. "As yet, my experiences with my German countrymen have not been altogether pleasurable," Wagner wrote to him on 3 June. "Therefore, come and rescue my not entirely unvacillating faith in what I, together with Goethe and a few others, call German liberty."

The wholehearted welcome Nietzsche received from both Wagner and Cosima undoubtedly owed a lot to the circumstances of their first meeting. After months of virtual seclusion they found themselves confronted with a young man of outstanding intelligence and as yet undeveloped potential who offered himself as Wagner's unconditional disciple, and who had the additional advantage of being unacquainted with the worlds of music and theatre with which all the other disciples – Richter, Cornelius, Porges and so on – were tainted. Wagner, always

sympathetic to young men of talent on the threshold of their career, saw
in Nietzsche something he did not yet possess: an academic rather than
an artistic disciple. And the fact that he arrived on the scene when all the
others were to a major extent inhibited by the personal breach between
him and Bülow, a problem of which Nietzsche was at the beginning not
even aware, made him doubly acceptable at this period of social as well
as artistic isolation. To Cosima, this last factor was clearly enough in
itself to make her look cordially on their young visitor. As for Nietzsche
himself, he was naturally gratified by being accepted so promptly and
warmly by one world-renowned figure and the daughter of another. In
his letter of 29 May to his friend Erwin Rohde he did not fail to mention
that the "intelligent" Frau von Bülow was the daughter of Liszt.
"Wagner," he went on, "is really everything that we ever hoped for: a
luxuriantly rich and great spirit, an energetic character; he is a
bewitchingly kind person, with a huge thirst for knowledge, etc."

On 22 May Cosima staged the first of those elaborate birthday
celebrations which from now on were to be a regular feature of their
family life. Wagner described it in his letter of 26 May to the king: "I was
awakened early by Siegfried's forest call (from the second act), played on
the French horn: this was Richter, who had come especially from
Munich for this single morning – two nights of travel for half a day. . . .
When I went downstairs for breakfast, I found my living-room
transformed into a flower garden; Rienzi's heralds of peace, four
charming boys (the daughters of our friend) came forward to greet me,
dressed in the ideal costumes envisaged by myself and with sprouting
palms in their hands: the two eldest recited to me ancient Greek poems
in praise of spring. I discovered wishes fulfilled in the shape of little gifts,
delicately thought out." Cosima had secretly invited the renowned
Morin-Chevillard string quartet to come to Tribschen to play three of
Beethoven's last quartets. "My friend knew what enjoyment I already
owed to these four artists; but she also knew that the proud isolation
into which I have withdrawn under your protection, my divine friend,
has caused me the sacrifice, frequently and painfully felt, of never being
able to refresh myself with the impressions of a fine musical performance. And so she succeeded in persuading these four incomparable
musicians to tear themselves from their activities in Paris to come to
Tribschen for this one day and bring the most cherished works of my
great master Beethoven once more to life for me. . . . However deeply it
moved and shattered me, I nevertheless felt happy and restored to new
life."

King Ludwig's plan for the production of *Das Rheingold* had claimed so
much of Wagner's attention that the other project mentioned in his

letter of 10 February – a revival of *Tristan und Isolde* – was virtually dis-
regarded. Wagner was reminded of it by a letter from Bülow which
arrived at Tribschen on 31 May. The king had charged Bülow with the
responsibility for the revival, and he begged Wagner to secure his
release. Wagner, shocked to hear that the main roles were to be given to
Heinrich and Therese Vogl, replied offering Bülow his full support in
preventing the performance and suggesting a meeting in Munich to
discuss tactics. "I am prepared to do anything you wish," he wrote on
2 June, "and in any case, if you do want to talk to me, you need have no
fear that I shall try to persuade you to anything at all. *We are all of us
unhappy enough not to pretend any more, since we can no longer help one another.*"

Bülow replied on the following day: "It is not only the coaching of
Herr and Frau Vogl, who, I must say in all honesty, are displaying a
zealousness bordering on the miraculous, nor all the terrible memories
connected with *Tristan* that are proving the final straw to my nerves, but
the never-ending agglomeration of vexations, disappointments, acts of
all kinds of meanness against me which have for months been souring
and destroying all my pleasure in my life and work. I am finished with
myself as well as with my continued existence in Munich or anywhere
else in Germany. I have no reason for believing that I can be of any
further use to 'art' – and not only here, but anywhere at all." He
enclosed a letter from their mutual friend, Karl Klindworth, who, he
suggested, might take over the music school from him. "I find it impossible to reply to him myself, since there are certain matters about
which I can no longer simulate or dissimulate – because my head is spinning, and a few times daily I feel I am on the best way to going mad or
just turning into an idiot." He ended his letter by thanking Wagner for
suggesting a meeting, which he thought would be best postponed until
after the *Tristan* performances at the end of June.

The time was now approaching for Cosima's confinement, and this
put all other considerations out of their heads for the moment. Wagner
had won the argument about where it should take place: it would be at
Tribschen. And there, in the early hours of 6 June, Cosima gave birth to
her fifth and last child. Wagner described the event in her diary, writing
of himself in the third person, as if the account were hers: "As he hears
Vreneli come in and then hears her exclaim in reply to some words from
the midwife, 'Oh, God in heaven!', R. thinks something terrible has
happened to me and hastens to the landing to find out from Vreneli as
she comes rushing out. But she greets him with a joyful laugh: 'A *son* has
arrived!' Her previous exclamation had simply been one of surprise that
so little was prepared. Now R. went back into the *salon*: from the unconscious mother he heard little more, yet on the other hand he could
clearly distinguish the lusty yells of the baby boy. With feelings of

sublime emotion he stared in front of him, was then surprised by an in-
credibly beautiful, fiery glow which started to blaze with a richness of
colour never before seen, first on the orange wallpaper beside the
bedroom door; it was then reflected in the blue jewel box containing my
portrait, so that this, covered by glass and set in a narrow gold frame,
was transfigured in celestial splendour. The sun had just risen above the
Rigi and was putting forth its first rays, proclaiming a glorious, sun-
drenched day. R. dissolved into tears."

At the time, Nietzsche was staying at Tribschen, the first occasion on
which he spent the night there. Wagner had wished to put him off as
soon as it was obvious that the confinement was near, but Cosima
insisted that the visit should take place, and the birth of Wagner's son
was, according to Nietzsche's sister Elisabeth, "regarded by both as an
auspicious omen for the newly-formed friendship". Pleased as he had
been by the birth of his daughters, the arrival of a son held a special
significance for Wagner. "R.'s son is the heir and future representative
of the father for all his children," he wrote in Cosima's diary. "He will
be the protector and guardian of his sisters. We were very happy." And
Cosima, when she resumed the diary herself, wrote on 13 June: "When
the woman [the midwife] said to me, 'Congratulations, it is a little boy,' I
had to weep and laugh and pray. . . . Now that my happiness lies so
sweetly in reach before my eyes, it seems to me ever more tremendous,
more disembodied, I see it hovering, rising up high above all woes, and
all I can do is to thank the universal spirit which proclaimed to us
through this sign that it is kindly disposed towards us."

Wagner, who had broken off his composition work during the confinement, resumed it on 11 June, and on 14 June the composition
sketch of the third act of *Siegfried* was completed. At the end of it he
wrote, "Properly delivered," and to Cosima he said: "Our son is now
truly born."

It was clear to them both that a divorce from Bülow was now imperative. Cosima, having heard that he had submitted his resignation to
the king on the grounds of ill-health and intended to leave Munich immediately after the performances of *Tristan und Isolde*, decided to write
him a letter in which, as she wrote in her diary, "I shall describe my
earlier, my present and my future relationship with him – if he will
accept it!" Her long letter of 15 June, written in French, does precisely
that, and is thus worth reproducing in full:

"My dear Hans, I learn from Richter that you have submitted your
resignation; from elsewhere I learn that you intend to leave Germany
and that you wish me to give my views about the fate of our children and
the disposal of our property. This gives me the courage to address a few
words to you; I do it with much nervousness and beg you not to upset

yourself if I come on you at an inopportune moment. I have never had much good fortune in my conversations with you: when I have attempted to restore an honourable peace between us, you have answered me with irony, when I have asked you for a definite break, you have not been prepared to listen. Today I beg you to hear me in a spirit of good will, to commune with yourself, free of external preoccupations and remembering what we have suffered together over the years.

"If you are resigning because you feel incapable any longer of enduring the intrigues and unpleasantnesses by which you are surrounded and overwhelmed, then there is nothing more to be said, and all I would wish would be for you to take care to explain this, point by point, so that people might know that you did not accept your present position merely for the sake of having a position, but because you wished to serve your art and now, having been hindered in this by the pettiness and malignity of the people with whom you have to do, you are regretfully leaving the service of the king whose intentions have been of the best. If you are leaving Munich because of the obligation you feel to 'simulate and dissimulate', permit me to say that you are wrong. In whatever way you present your relations with me, no blame nor disgrace can ever fall on you. Your character is well-known, there is nobody who does not respect you, and everything which causes an indignant outcry will be directed towards me. In the first place, I am a woman, who is expected to uphold the moral order; in the second place, I am a mother, and I appear to be sacrificing my children; and in the third place you are a man of honour, whom I married of my own free will. If you tell me that the disgrace to which I shall be subjected will inevitably rebound on you, I can reply – if this is only on account of the sorrow it causes you – that it is in your power to save us from that. In saying that the persecutions which we have suffered in Munich have undermined our private lives to such an extent that we have mutually agreed to separate, you will be presenting the situation from one of its aspects, and, though I shall not be spared the severest blame, at least we shall be saved from disgrace. – As far as I am concerned, I admit that I should have preferred you to remain in Munich (except of course for the matter of your health, which calls for a prolonged leave of absence); I prefer it on account of the children, since I imagine that with your salary you would be better able to put something aside for them, and also on your own account, since you are not made for the vagabond life, and I know no other place, either in Germany or elsewhere, where you would find yourself in a better position. I left Munich in November under the illusion that, the longer you stayed, the more your position would improve, and it would be possible for you to establish a home for our children, while I should be allowed to develop their feelings and their abilities. I was mistaken,

and here we stand now among the ruins, while I have to carry the burden
of a grave accusation – that of being the cause of this collapse. Let me
seek together with you the means of justifying myself and at the same
time of putting in order as far as possible the sad state in which we find
ourselves. In the silence and seclusion of my present life I have
frequently reviewed my past and questioned my conscience; I have never
disguised to myself the nature of my wrong towards you, for you have
none on your side other than that of having married me. I may say that
during the seven months of our separation my whole thoughts and
regrets have concerned only you (and I hope you will listen to me with
sufficient calmness and good will to believe what I am telling you); time
and time again I have asked myself what I could, what I ought to do, and
I swear to you that it has never been selfishness that has prevented me
from hastening to your side. The memory of our private life since the
second year of our marriage is always rising up before me to show that,
whatever my good intentions, I have never made you happy. Nothing I
did ever succeeded: how many times when you were ill did you send me
away from your bedside without my knowing why, and you will
remember that when I was expecting Loulou [Daniela] I did not dare tell
you about it, as if my pregnancy were something illegitimate. Still, I
admit that I should never have left you if I had not met the life which
merged so absolutely into mine that I no longer know how to unravel it.
You will never know the extent of my struggles and sufferings, nor would
it be possible for me to describe my distress at that time, when the plan of
a *vie à trois* was shown to be impossible. It was not the humiliations you
inflicted on me that made me wretched then; I had arrived, believe me,
at the point of finding sorrow almost easier to bear than happiness, and
every expiation of my sins as of my pleasures was welcome to me. Rather
it was the presentiment that things could not go on like this much
longer, and that you yourself were hastening the catastrophe. But,
though I may have left you and you may have been to a large extent
responsible for this separation, what cannot change and will never
change is the concern I have for you and your destiny. You are the only
being in the whole world of whom I am constantly thinking, the only
one whose heavy griefs I share from afar.

"I do not believe that you can scoff at these feelings, which have
always been the same and which will continue, whatever may become of
us. And it is in their name that I ask you whether you have the strength to
separate from me officially, to allow me to bring up our children, and to
remain in contact with me. If you find my suggestion foolish, or if you
scorn what I am saying, answer me without malice or sarcasm, for I have
been speaking to you from the bottom of my heart, and I am not to
blame if my complete withdrawal from the world has nurtured in me

feelings which the world neither recognises nor understands. I feel I have the right to bring up my children because I love them, and because the life I have adopted in cutting myself off from all contact with the outside world allows me to live exclusively for them. Perhaps I could more easily bear the sacrifice of the dearest of my prerogatives (assuming that were demanded of me) if I knew of a single person in your family who could take my place. But your mother – whom I have never allowed myself to criticise since I owed her certain duties and respects – your mother would, I fear, deprive our daughters of their gaiety and their sense of security, since through the rigidity of certain views, arising from unhappy experiences, she has no deep convictions and nothing of that which children need to make life a paradise and sow in them the seeds of a pure and noble existence. The world and your family are within their rights in advising you not to leave the bringing up of our children to me, for they claim the right to see me simply as a woman who has broken her sacred vows to indulge her passion, but I believe you are in a position to see me in a different light and to know that I shall bring them up well, and that in my company they will see and hear nothing which would make them unworthy of you. It is for you that I shall bring them up, so that they can one day be a consolation to you. And for their sakes I ask – if it is not too great a sacrifice for you – that you remain in touch with me. If you agree, I shall bring them to you wherever you may be and shall stay with them in your home, even in Munich, for I fear neither person nor place; in leaving you I have given up everything – except the children. It is for their sakes that I wish you may remain in the position you now hold (with prospects of improvement, of course). It is on you that the task will fall of sending them into the world, everything – your name, your talent, your character – permits you to assure them an honourable position, whereas I, having isolated myself and being in consequence rejected, can do no more than bring them up nobly and piously; and you know me sufficiently well to be confident that no trials and no pleasures can divert me from this task.

"As far as our property is concerned, I should like to ask you to retain it all for the children, and at the same time I would request you to put aside the 6,000 francs I receive from my father and my mother (if you have no need of them yourself). There is nothing more I have to say, and, however sincerely I have opened my heart to you, I always have the feeling that my inspiration is not the happiest, and that I shall have to resign myself to one of those bitter replies which you may feel you have the right to give me, but which I know in my heart and conscience I have not in the least deserved! Cosima."

Bülow's reply to this letter, also written in French, was dated 17 June. It is reproduced with only a few minor omissions:

"Dear Cosima, I thank you for the initiative you have taken, and shall give you no cause to regret it. I feel too unhappy – through my own fault – not to wish at all costs to avoid hurting you with unjust reproaches of any kind. In the very cruel separation to which you have felt yourself committed I acknowledge all the faults on my side, and I shall continue to emphasise them as sharply as I can in the inevitable discussions with my mother and your father on this subject. I have repaid you very badly, very wickedly, for all the devotion you squandered on me during our past life; I poisoned your life, and I can only thank Providence for having provided you with an effective antidote at the eleventh hour, when your courage for the continuation of your drudgery was about to desert you. But, alas, since you left me I have been deprived of my whole support in dealing with life and its struggles. Your spirit, your heart, your friendship, your patience, your indulgence, your sympathy, your encouragement, your advice – and finally, above all, your presence, your gaze, your speech – all these shaped and constituted this support. The loss of this supreme being, whose full worth I only appreciated after the loss, has made me both morally and artistically insolvent – I am now a bankrupt. Do not think that this complaint – I am suffering enough to allow myself to complain, seeing that I abstain from accusing any other than myself as the author of it – reflects any irony, any bitterness towards you. You have preferred to dedicate your life and the riches of your spirit and your heart to a being superior in every way – far from blaming you, I *approve* your action from every point of view, I feel you are entirely in the right. I swear to you that the only consoling thought that has at times cast a soothing light across my inward shadows and outward torments has been this: at least Cosima is happy where she is.

"I have thought it necessary to precede my personal explanations with this preface of a kind, for which I claim the title, or rather the character, of an absolute confession of faith.

"Now I shall have to ask your indulgence (for the last time) if the explanations which are about to follow are not distinguished by complete lucidity or accuracy of expression. Forgive me if I am obliged to boast as always about my activity ('That sacristan has a lot to do,'as Loulou said to you one day in church). Today and tomorrow orchestral rehearsal for *Tristan* from 9 to 2, music school from 3 to 6, correspondence, visits, etc. – and physical frailty such as obliges me every two or three days to spend a whole day in bed doing nothing.

"I handed in my resignation a week ago, that is true. The reason I have put forward is the very rundown state of my health. Everybody can understand that, and Rubner gave me a certificate two months ago. The intrigues, calumnies, obstacles, the bad will . . . have done nothing but increase from month to month. Now, with you no longer there (my

mother to replace you – there is no need for me to dwell on that), I lack a
counterbalance, and my strength, both moral and physical, my inclination to continue a game which is not worth the candle (and that in any
case considerably burnt down) have diminished in inverse proportion.
The few pleasures I might perhaps have to record do not provide any
real compensation, and give me no incentive to continue. My work for
the King of Bavaria brings in only 4,000 florins per annum (I have never
envisaged a rise in my salary), which does not cover my expenses. I have
come to the firm conclusion that to continue my work here and to
resume my position would not in any way aid the good cause of art, and
would at the same time, and for this very reason, only succeed in
bringing about my personal ruin within a single year, or perhaps two.
On top of that, my position is fundamentally unsound – I am basically
seen merely as the favourite of the king's favourite, and the feeling that I
acquired this position of favourite by being a complaisant husband is
fairly widespread. . . . Let us add to this that my enforced preoccupation with *Tristan*, that gigantic but ominous work, is literally in the
process of finishing me off. The public performance will take place on
Sunday, I shall see to it that it is no profanation – I wrote to Wagner
about that a few days ago – and that will see me presiding over the
orchestra for the last time. My stay in Munich will end just as it began –
this will give it a kind of *Abrundung* [rounding-off] – a circle more inevitable than vicious! – and will later help me to look on the succession
of events and sufferings (my punishment for my wrongs towards you) –
framed between these performances of the same work over a period of
four years – in the light of a nightmare. Yes, without reproaching its
great composer, I declare that the finishing stroke *has* been *Tristan*. My
nerves are not as strong as yours, remembering for how many long years
you managed to endure such disheartening intimacy with a character as
evilly born or badly educated as mine, and to survive this punishment!
Poor Eberle [the coach recommended by Richter] went out of his mind
during rehearsals – *because of the work* (we are telling the public it was
because of too much beer). As for me, who admit to having always
lacked the necessary courage in my numerous desires to take my life, I
assure you that this time I should not have been able to resist the temptation if somebody had offered me a few gulps of prussic acid!

"The opportunity did not arise and, though I may curse it, I cannot
help acknowledging the tremendous amount of vitality (*Wille zum Leben*
[will to live]) that there is inside me. But how gratify it, other than by
leaving a town which since your departure has become *hell* for me, and
by starting a new life, I do not yet know where, but certainly *somewhere
else?*

"This separation from you – you had no other choice, keep the introduction to these lines always in your mind – must be a complete one. It is necessary for me to break with all that pertains to you and to R.W., since my previous life had only these two leading threads (to which I might perhaps add your father) – also in my thoughts, as far as this is humanly possible. Do not misunderstand me: I am not on any account suggesting to you the scandal or the vexations of a divorce. If your father is of this opinion, if he prefers your association with R.W. to be given this official sanction, I have nothing against it myself. But since, as you can well imagine, I have no desire or inclination, no whim, to marry again, I have no reasons for proposing a divorce. For the rest, I leave our children to you, I leave their education in your hands, since I also feel that it is the best they are likely to obtain, having nothing better to offer them, and since I share completely your view of the impossibility of entrusting them to my old mother or to any other member of my family (if I can still talk of a family). And if you can find it in your excellent heart to bring up our children, in spite of all the antipathy and the justified bitterness you feel towards their father, I see no reason at all why I should not leave you with my name.

"I feel it would be petty and unworthy of the situation were I to express a sensitivity capable of misinterpretation on the subject of the sacrifices you are making for me. Allow me to give you a firm, simple and short reply. The allowance from your father (and what you receive from your mother too) belongs to the children. Since you are assuming charge of their education, your 6,000 francs should rightly and properly be used to pay the expenses of this education. The companion of your present and future life will certainly be prepared to assume responsibility for the investment of the capital you could, if necessary, raise on this small sum. The fortune of your own which you brought into our dismal marriage – was this not for me, ashamed of my poverty, the first stumbling-block, the first jarring note in the matter of duty and even of love itself ? I can only decline the task of setting myself up as the children's financial adviser with the help of your money. What I myself can (for the moment) set aside for them is just the small legacy from my aunt Frege (5,000 crowns invested in the Frege business itself), which should, if I am lucky, have doubled by the time they come of age.

"You will equally be kind enough, I beseech you, to understand that I cannot regard all our furniture as anything but *your own very personal* property. When I leave here, and that (I very much hope) will be on 1 August, I shall take only those things which are indisputably mine – my clothes, books and music – leaving everything else in the apartment, our lease of which expires on 1 October. . . .

"In leaving Munich and if possible Germany, I have not yet made any plans for the future (if I had, I would not take the liberty of boring you with them), and in any case I regard them as of very secondary importance. The essential and urgent thing is to get going – I wish to take with me as little as possible that could remind me of the past, of my previous life, for it is only by breaking completely and radically with all this that I can visualise the prospect of a new existence. There is only one single thing which I cannot and have no wish to give up, and that is my profoundly grateful memory of all you did for my development as an artist. I shall always be proud of the favours you did me in this regard.

"Allow me to put your mind at rest to some extent (as far as seems necessary) about the manner in which I shall be leaving Munich. I shall remain at the Musikschule till the end of the school year, burdening myself once again with the wearisome work of examinations, that is, if my legs and my head do not refuse too obstinately to allow me. . . . I shall hand in my definite resignation on 1 October, while provisionally accepting the leave which His Majesty is kind enough to grant me. In this way I shall take my departure with as little fuss as possible, without breaking the window-panes. Do not do me the disservice of believing that I am play-acting (R.W. will not hesitate, I fear), and that the promise of a position and secure appointments will make me change my mind and return to a '*Heimat*' [home] which is one of the most farcical imaginable. . . . I feel *no desire at all* to resume work here. I shall be a thousand times happier with the position of piano teacher in some small town. With people like Perfall in charge, it is impossible to do anything but follow a routine, and it is a routine in which one loses one's faculties piece by piece. I have no desire to list all the things I have lost in the course of the past year. And not one sympathetic being – but do not worry, I shall stop moaning. If you remember, I knew exactly what would happen after you left me. Do you recall how determined I was not to return to Munich except in your company? Lord, I am not saying this in an attempt to reproach you retrospectively. You found it impossible to remain here – I understand that, I understand it only too well. All – to recapitulate – I am trying to do is to soften in your eyes the apparent harshness of my resolution, ripening painfully day by day since you left. The task has proved beyond my strength, that (both moral and physical) having for some time become considerably diminished. I immersed myself in work in an effort to forget – an impossibility, above all since my illusions about the usefulness of this work (which would have given me outward satisfaction and through that guided me to an inner calm) vanished one after another. – And so I shall make my departure during the first days of August. I have asked Bechstein for the return of my 2,000 thalers, and on that I shall live quietly and without a care for a year. If by then I have recovered my health and my self-possession, I shall surely find some way of creating for myself an existence of some kind which is not chained to a dependence of any kind. (I shall, however, not forget that the position W. procured for me in Munich will have been the means of my improving myself – but this feeling of dependence is one that I can live with after a fashion.)

"So here is my letter, very badly written and hardly worthy of being read by the author of that letter to which it comes as a reply. Basically it is not a reply. It is a kind of testament, written by a mind and heart that are very sick, half deranged. However, it contains no folly, no irrationality, and I beg you to accept it as a '*Noth-Produkt*' [emergency product]: I beg you also to share for the last time in the feelings that have animated me, and acquiesce in the unalterable decisions inspired by these feelings, and to help me, through your approval and acceptance, to carry them out.

"May God bless and protect the mother of the fortunate children to whom she wishes to continue dedicating herself. Hans de Bülow."

CHAPTER VII

Difficulties with King Ludwig

IN HER LETTER to Bülow Cosima made no mention at all of the birth of her son only a few days before she wrote it. That a deliberate effort was being made to keep the birth secret is suggested by a reproachful letter at the beginning of July from Mathilde Maier, who had heard the news from Robert von Hornstein, a composer who had for a short while during the Zurich years been Wagner's friend. And since Hornstein lived in Munich Cosima was worried about the manner in which Bülow would learn of Siegfried's birth. She still could not bring herself to inform him directly.

When Bülow's letter arrived, Wagner held it back for a whole day, giving it to Cosima only after she had expressed disquiet over his failure to reply. He must have read the letter first, for in handing it to her he remarked that it was "very fine". That was the day (20 June) on which Bülow was conducting *Tristan* in Munich, and Cosima, fearing that in his present state of mind he might not have managed to get through it, sent an anxious telegram of enquiry to Richter. The reply came back: "Bülow came to life during performance, afterwards cheerful, calls of 'Bülow stay', success tremendous."

Bülow sent Wagner a report on the performance the following day, praising the Vogls highly and saying that he himself had conducted the work better than before. He ended his letter with the definite refusal of a meeting with Wagner: "A re-encounter with me would cause you painful embarrassment and certainly bring me in my present state a dangerous emotional upset."

Ludwig, who had seen the new *Tristan* production three times, wrote to Wagner on 24 June making his customary apology for having acted against the composer's wishes. "If you knew the irresistible longing which overcame me to hear this work, the dearest to me of all the works of yours I so far know . . . you would surely not chide me, but exercise consideration and amiably forgive me."

Wagner replied to him on 1 July, expressing his satisfaction with the present arrangement, which enabled him to get on with his composing in peace, while leaving the production of his previous works to others:

"We have recently seen the remarkable success achieved by *Tristan*, which, though performed by the least suitable and most boring of singers, went off all right, and indeed seems to have given a lot of pleasure; this certainly gives cause for reflection, and my reflections usually end in a tolerant smile."

On the other hand, his acceptance of what he called Ludwig's "inspired obstinacy" did not extend to *Das Rheingold*, and he again begged that it should be given the status of a special performance by royal invitation only. It was, however, a comparatively mild attempt to influence the King: his mood at the time was one of sublime contentment over the birth of his son and the simultaneous completion of *Siegfried*. He was now, since 25 June, working on the orchestral sketch, and taking the opportunity to improve as he went along. Wotan's last words to Erda, he told Cosima on 3 July, had turned out "too idyllic", and it took him four days to find a better solution.

She, meanwhile, was wrestling with her conscience and suffering bad dreams, in one of which she and Bülow, begging in the street, were stoned, while in another she was being reproached by George Sand for her misdeeds. On 6 July she noted in her diary that she had decided to write to Bülow, offering to return to him with her four daughters if he really could not find happiness amid all the stir their present relationship was causing: otherwise, she would beg him, for his own sake, to consent to a divorce. "R. says that in this matter he must remain silent," she wrote. And on the next day: "I try to make him understand how – in my sense – the sacrifice of our happiness, indeed even of our life together, could never affect our love. He feels deeply hurt, but as always we have to admit, amid smiles and tears, that it is only the excess of our love which makes us so susceptible."

The letter to Bülow was not written. Wagner, feeling secure in possession of her since the birth of their son, was content to leave it to time to lessen Cosima's pangs of remorse, and confined himself to making her life bearable by frequent declarations of love and little acts of attention towards her.

On 16 July there arrived at Tribschen a trio of young French admirers from Paris, the poet Catulle Mendès and his wife Judith, together with another poet, Villiers de l'Isle-Adam. Judith, the beautiful daughter of yet a third poet, Théophile Gautier, was at that time in her early twenties, and she had first set eyes on Wagner during the rehearsals of *Tannhäuser* in Paris in 1861. She wrote a series of articles about him in a French periodical before the Paris production of *Rienzi* and followed these with a letter to Tribschen, to which Cosima replied. Her visit was the direct outcome of that contact. Cosima found Judith somewhat disconcerting at first, "so lacking in manners that I find it downright embarrassing, yet at the same time good-natured and terribly full of enthusiasm. She literally forces Rich. to play and sing pieces from *Die Walküre* and *Tristan.*" On the following day Mendès and Judith, who were staying at the Hôtel du Lac in Lucerne, came again. "How curious their noisy enthusiasm seems to me!" Cosima wrote. "The woman says out loud all the things I believe in my inmost heart; the fact that she can say them aloud makes her seem strange to me. He is highly cultured and both of them thoroughly kind-hearted."

Judith left an account of this visit in her book of reminiscences, *Le troisième rang du collier.* She was impressed, she wrote, by Wagner's youthful agility, shown by his climbing the highest trees in the garden. She spoke too of the "expression of infinite kindness playing about his lips" and of his volatile nature, which, "so exquisitely sensitive, so highly-strung and impressionable, led to terrible outbursts which made one wonder how he could survive them: one day of worry could age him by ten years; but on the very next day he could again look younger than ever before".

Their visit lasted nine days, during which time they went sightseeing with Wagner and Cosima and the children. Wagner himself was stimulated by their company to such an extent that he overcame his prejudices about their Frenchness and pronounced them to be "a real enrichment of our lives".

They left for Munich on 25 July, armed with a letter from Wagner to Richter, authorising them to attend rehearsals of *Das Rheingold*. With their departure Wagner resumed work on the orchestral sketch of *Siegfried*, which he finished on 4 August, and in the evenings Cosima and he entertained themselves playing Haydn's London symphonies together on the piano. No doubt in reaction against the gaiety that had vanished with Judith and her companions Wagner complained to Cosima that things had changed between them, that she was now no more than "earnestly companionable" towards him. "My happiness lacks but one happiness," he told her, "that you may also be happy." Not even the news, received on 31 July, that Bülow was prepared to set divorce proceedings in motion could restore her spirits. Her main concern was that he might have been brought to this point by learning in a tactless way of Siegfried's birth. It was true that he had heard the news "in passing" (Cosima did not reveal through whom), but her suspicion that he intended divorce as a punishment seems unlikely. His mind was in any case not yet fully made up, and his present proposals amounted to hardly more than an enquiry whether Cosima would consent to a legal separation. Liszt was anxious that he should remain in Munich, and both Cosima and Wagner were convinced that Liszt was largely to blame for Bülow's present indecision. Even the proposal of a legal separation appeared also to have been dropped as a result of Liszt's suggestions, and Cosima expressed her indignation with her father in her letter of 25 August to Judith: "He prefers to see me dragged through the mire by the newspapers and to prolong a false situation than to see an indissoluble union blessed. I thanked heaven when I reached this point with M. de B., and now, by his intervention, he has undone it all, and the newspapers are saying that I am to be granted the favour of not being deprived of a 'name' which for years I have been demanding by might and main to be released from bearing."

Judith, introduced to Liszt at a party in Munich, did not hesitate to ask him promptly what his intentions were with regard to his daughter. According to her reminiscences, Liszt told her that he did not condemn Cosima for leaving Bülow, but he added: "The costume I wear imposes opinions on me which I cannot openly repudiate. I know too much about the temptations of the heart to judge them severely. Convention obliges me to keep silent, but inside I am more concerned than anybody to see this crisis solved legally."

Judith's letter arrived just after Cosima had received news that Bülow had left Munich, "despondent and sad, without saying where". This aroused in her such feelings of remorse that she contemplated suicide. "Oh, children, my children," she wrote in her diary, "remember your mother's words, no suffering is so hard to bear as the wrong we do, remember these words, wrought from pain in the most painful of hours!" To Judith, whose letter also included the news that Bülow had gone to Berlin to expedite the divorce, she wrote on 28 August a grateful reply, telling her that Wagner, seeing the revivifying effect it had on her, sent Judith his blessings: "I know that my father and I are united on a plane beyond the clamours of this world. . . . If I sleep tonight, it will be to you I owe it."

Wagner was meanwhile doing all he could, short of going to Munich, to exercise some sort of control over the staging of *Das Rheingold* in Munich. "With this whole production," he wrote to Richter on 13 August, "I have only one thing in mind: that the score should be translated into sound correctly, in a good and spirited manner. The scenery, dramatic talent – all that I am letting go, but the music must be beyond reproach; then at least the main thing will have been saved." In line with this approach he invited Richter to bring the chief singers to Tribschen for personal coaching, and on 18 August three of them, Betz (Wotan), Schlosser (Loge) and Otto Schelper (Alberich) made the journey to Switzerland together with Richter. On the scenic side his help, though still forthcoming, was of a more negative kind. After the Munich scene painter, Christian Jank, had visited him on 14 July, he wrote to Richter complaining that his previous discussions with Hallwachs and

Brandt had obviously been in vain, and he had had to start again from the beginning. The costume designs, which he received on 26 July, he found to be too classical in appearance. "I want *less* nakedness and more real clothing," he wrote to Richter on 26 July, "also no wild men from the Prussian coat of arms in place of the giants: the gods with attributes, e.g., Froh with a sickle, Fricka with a distaff, Freia, as goddess of flowers and fruits, likewise characterised. No *gold* ornaments of any kind! That should be obvious in a play in which gold is first discovered and made known to the gods."

Something was done about the costumes, but, when on 27 August the time for the dress rehearsal arrived, nothing on the scenic side was ready, and the reason for that, Betz wrote to Wagner, was that Brandt and Hallwachs had been sidetracked and the scenery entrusted to two others who "did nothing, either out of laziness or ignorance". Betz declared roundly that the production was "an act of criminality towards the work", and they would be lucky if they were not laughed off the stage.

Judith, who attended the dress rehearsal, wrote to Wagner the same evening describing the shortcomings in more detail. After praising singers and orchestra highly, she declared the scenery would shame the cheapest variety theatre: "In the first scene a row of dummies reminding one of a marionette theatre, the Rhinemaidens with roses in their hair and dressed in rough, puffed-out gowns which the water never causes to cling, the gold like a dimly lit street lamp. Second scene: the receding water keeps stopping, the backcloth (Valhalla) is not taut, but creased like an old gumboot, the castle in two pieces that do not join . . . Froh dressed like a sugar cupid, Freia looking like a costermonger. Third scene: the *Tarnhelm* of grey sailcloth, shaped like a donkey's hat, Alberich takes it and disappears ten minutes later; his way of disappearing is very simple – he goes off into the wings, and one hears his voice miles away; as for the dragon . . . imagine a piece of chiffon painted green which Alberich places on his back and which does not cover more than half of him. When he turns into a toad, it is also quite simple – he crouches behind a rock. The fourth scene is the final straw, the rainbow a paved path across the sky, above which the light never manages to rise, the gods walk across this granite bridge in single file, looking extremely comical."

A telegram from Richter, received on 28 August, gave further cause for alarm: "Main aim achieved, musical part performed to best possible satisfaction of true friends, cannot deny performance to general public impossible in view of scenery. Orchestra very good, Liszt himself and others expressed approval. Stop performance at all costs."

On receipt of this Wagner immediately sent a telegram to the king, requesting a postponement. On 30 August he wrote a letter to Ludwig setting out his complaints in detail and offering to go himself to Munich to put things in order. However, the letter arrived too late to save the situation. Richter refused to conduct *Das Rheingold* in its present state. Ludwig, enraged, wrote to Düfflipp on 29 August saying that Bülow should be asked to conduct the first public performance on 1 September, after certain weaknesses, which he himself had noticed at the dress rehearsal, had been attended to.

Richter was suspended. Bülow, who was not in Munich, answered Düfflipp's written request for his return with a refusal. Perfall then approached Edouard Lassen, who had come to Munich from Weimar to see the performance, but Wagner stopped this by withholding his consent. Julius Herbeck of Vienna, Hermann Levi of Karlsruhe and Camille Saint-Saëns from Paris, who had also come to Munich for the performance, all rejected Perfall's offer of the conductorship out of deference to Wagner.

It began to look as if Wagner might emerge the victor, but he did not know the extent of the king's rage against him. Ludwig wrote to Düfflipp from Berg on 30 August: "The behaviour of Wagner and the theatre rabble is utterly criminal and insolent: it is an open revolt against my commands, and this I cannot tolerate. Richter may on no account be permitted to conduct, and is to be dismissed immediately – that is final. The theatre people have to obey my orders and not Wagner's whims. . . . Everything must be done to make the performance possible, for, if Wagner's disgraceful intrigues were to succeed, the whole pack would become even bolder and more impudent, and in the end there would be no holding them; the evil must be torn up by the roots. . . . *Vivat* Düfflipp, *pereat* theatre rabble!" And on 31 August: "If W. attempts any further resistance, his salary is to be permanently withdrawn, and no work of his will ever again be performed on the Munich stage."

Ludwig calmed down a little after receiving Wagner's letter of 30 August, which he sent to Düfflipp, saying that his wishes were on the whole reasonable and should be attended to as far as possible. However, he still insisted on a performance on 5 September. "Do all you can to stop him coming here. He need not know that this is my own wish, otherwise all hell will be let loose, and the performance will never come about, neither now nor later."

Hearing of the postponement, Wagner thought that the king had listened to his plea, and on 1 September he hurried to Munich to take over the rehearsals. He was coldly received, and his demand that Richter should be restored to the conductorship was met with a steadfast refusal. Perfall was unwilling to allow the rehearsals he requested, and so on the following day he returned to Tribschen. The one advantage he gained from his trip was a closer understanding with Düfflipp, whose diplomatic skills in cooling inflamed tempers he learned belatedly to admire. And possibly he would have responded to Düfflipp's plea that he should make "a sacrifice to love" by sanctioning the performance as planned if quarrels had not broken out in another quarter.

Betz took exception to certain remarks made to him by Perfall, threw up the role of Wotan, and returned to Vienna. As a consequence of this, Wagner sent a telegram to the king on 3 September, begging him to cancel the performance altogether. Ludwig did not reply, but reports in the newspapers that the performance had been postponed indefinitely gave him the feeling that the king had capitulated. He was wrong: on 10 September Richter arrived at Tribschen with the news that *Das Rheingold* was to be done in Munich in a fortnight's time, with a substantially changed cast and a reduced orchestra under the direction of Franz Wüllner, one of Munich's lesser conductors and a teacher of choral singing at the school of music.

That same night Wagner wrote a furious letter to Wüllner: "Keep your hands off my score! Take my advice, sir, or the devil take you! Go and beat time for choral societies and glee clubs, or, if you must have opera scores at all costs, go and get them from your friend Perfall! And tell that fine gentleman, if he doesn't frankly admit to the king that he is incapable of putting on my work, I will light him a blaze which all the gutter journalists he pays with what sticks to his fingers from the *Rheingold* budget will be unable to blow out. You two gentlemen are going to have to take a lot of lessons from me before you realise that you have no understanding of anything."

Cosima was horrified when Wagner showed her this letter the following morning. "I should have preferred him not to send it," she wrote in her diary, "but it does him good, for bearing things in silence gnaws at his heart." However it may have benefited Wagner, it did not deter Wüllner, who conducted the first public performance of *Das Rheingold* in the Munich opera on 22 September, taking (according to the newspapers) three hours over it, in contrast to Richter's two and a half. The Munich bass singer August Kindermann took over the role of Wotan; Schlosser, who had displeased the king as Loge, was switched to Mime, and Vogl came in as Loge. Otherwise the cast remained substantially as before.

"So there it is," Cosima wrote in her diary on 23 September, "it is always the wicked who triumph. My only consolation is R.'s words: 'I have the feeling that none of it really affects me, inside I remain unscathed; only when I am not in complete harmony with you does the ground tremble beneath me.'"

Richter, now out of work, came to stay at Tribschen while seeking a new appointment. Catulle and Judith Mendès returned from Munich, and at the same time the Irish-French poetess and composer Augusta Holmès arrived with her father from Paris. Augusta, being at this time only twenty years old, was more renowned for her beauty than her art, and she turned Richter's head as she had already turned Mendès's, whose mistress she in fact was. There is no evidence that she had any effect on Wagner, but this did not prevent rumours spreading, after he paid a visit to her father in his hotel, that he had asked for Augusta's hand in marriage. Cosima wrote to Judith on 6 October, after all the visitors had departed: "I confess that the news pleased me because of the omission of my name, which all German journals delight to wound in whatever way they can."

Wagner had done no further work since completing the orchestral sketch of the third act of *Siegfried* on 25 August. On 2 October he came to Cosima bearing the beginning of his work on *Götterdämmerung* – the Norns' scene in the prologue. However, he had not yet reached the stage of continuous commitment. Most of the month of October was spent on the orchestration of the third act of *Siegfried*.

On 14 October a picture of Beethoven arrived at Tribschen. It had been sent by King Ludwig, and was followed eleven days later by a letter. "All the old expressions of love and rapture, and with them a plea for pardon concerning his behaviour over *Das Rheingold* ('my longing was too great'),'' Cosima wrote in her diary. "Then we read in the *Signale* that *Die Walküre* is being prepared in the Munich court theatre; so much for the letter: it really is terrible!"

Ludwig's letter, written on 22 October,* was in fact more revealing than Cosima seems to have realised. The plea for pardon was indeed familiar, but the tone was different, more forthright than ever before: "I despise lying, have no desire to make excuses, and tell you quite openly that I realise my mistake and regret it; I should have conveyed my wishes to you personally, and I felt in my soul deep anger – which was not without justification – against those people who claimed for themselves the right – surely against your intentions – of carrying out your instructions in no very tactful way (to put it mildly). . . . I think (if I may say so) that you imagine my post to be easier than it is. To stand alone, absolutely alone in this harsh and dreary world, alone with my ideas, misunderstood and distrusted, that is no easy matter. In the first years after my accession it was to some extent the charm of novelty that

---

* Cosima's diary entry of 25 October 1869 makes it clear that King Ludwig's "incomplete" letter, ascribed on page 290 of the second volume of *König Ludwig II und Richard Wagner: Briefwechsel* to the middle of November 1869 (No. 438), is in fact the first part of his letter of 22 October (No. 436).

was responsible for my pleasing people – oh, woe to those who have to deal with the masses, lucky those who, like yourself, can deal with individuals! I have learnt, believe me, to know human beings; I approached them with genuine love and felt myself rejected; and such wounds heal slowly, very slowly."

To perceptive eyes there could be no overlooking the change that had occurred in Ludwig. This was no longer the admiring young pupil, full of idealism and enthusiasm, but a man who had found in himself a measure of independence: it was a sign of maturity, but one tinged with misanthropy. The fact that his letter was written at Linderhof, where in that year Ludwig had begun to build the first of the castles in whose design and execution he increasingly immersed himself, would not of course have been seen by Wagner as a significant pointer towards the future (it was too early for that), but the difficulty he found in replying to this letter was an indication that he was aware of the change in Ludwig. It led him to the conclusion, as he declared in his letter of 1 November, that he could not write to the king in any way without giving a false impression. "It would mislead you if I were to attempt to give you an idea of the astonishment that recent experiences aroused in me, for in the end I should have to apply this very astonishment to myself, who am old and experienced enough not to be astonished by anything. But it would mislead you even more if I were to reply to you without mentioning my astonishment, for then you might think that these last experiences had passed by without leaving a terrible impression on me, destroying all illusions. And this incorrect assumption would lead unerringly in the future to further illusions and confusions, which might prove fatal. May the genius of our love protect us from that, as, amid the ruins of the present case, it has once more proved the victor."

Cosima, to whom Wagner read his letter before sending it off, thought he could have been severer. He himself was dissatisfied with it, and wrote again, after much heart-searching and consultation with Cosima, the much more explicit letter which he dated 20 November and despatched on that day. Recalling the difficulties that had come between them before, he wrote that at times he had the feeling that Ludwig wanted something quite different from what he himself wanted: "Then you hold me at a distance, avoid me, even – when there are difficulties which we could quite easily resolve together – ally yourself against me, so that I, completely despised, begin to wonder whether I only dreamed that I had a king for a friend." He begged the king to read once more his Preface to the *Ring*, to recall what this work had been designed to accomplish in the evolution of the ideal theatre, and then reply to "the single question, the answer to which will determine our whole future: *Do you wish to have my work in the way I want it, or do you not?*" If the answer were yes, then he would ask the king to cease for a few years to take any interest in the theatre as it at present existed, "a theatre unworthy of the royal friend and sponsor of Richard Wagner". As a consolation, Wagner would then ensure that he heard all his works privately, as before. "Or do you wish, my gracious king, just to add to *my* difficulties? You will do this if you continue to give your theatre director instructions to produce further performances of my *Nibelungen* works."

To this letter Ludwig made no reply, but his answer was implicit in the fact that the command to prepare a production of *Die Walküre* was not withdrawn. Wagner, already upset by the newspaper reports concerning it, told Cosima that he had no desire to write another note of his *Ring*, and on 31 October he began work on his essay "On Conducting".

This is one of the few of Wagner's literary pieces that deal in a practical, rather than a theoretical way with his musical ideas. Though conducting had occupied only a minor role in his life since his early manhood, his outstanding skill as a conductor, particularly of the symphonies of Beethoven, was generally acknowledged, and thus this account of the technical problems presented by various works by Beethoven and Mozart, and his detailed handling of Weber's *Freischütz* overture and the prelude to *Die Meistersinger*, are as valuable as they are revealing of his own attitude towards music. The essay is, however, uneven in quality, the practical information being interrupted by narrative passages which, though frequently amusing, revert to familiar prejudices such as the dullwittedness of German *Kapellmeister* and the shortcomings of the Jews.

The visit in November of his friend Richard Pohl, a writer on music, reminded Wagner of his autobiography, on which he and Cosima had done no work for some time. He asked Cosima to begin copying out the pages so far written for the king, then on second thoughts decided to have them printed, and he turned to Nietzsche for help. "I am performing an act of the utmost trust in you," he wrote to him on 3 December, "in sending you with these lines a fairly bulky manuscript of the most valuable kind, the beginning of my dictated reminiscences. My object is twofold: I should like you to read through this part, which is as far as we reached with the reading during Pohl's visit, so that, when you come to us again for a long stay – as I hope you will – we can continue with the reading in your presence. But secondly I would like you to have about sixteen pages printed before Christmas, since I want to include them among my presents for our cherished friend [Cosima]."

Nietzsche contacted an Italian printer in Basel, G. A. Bonfantini. It was obvious, Wagner told Nietzsche in his letter of 19 December after reading through the first proofs, that the typesetter was a Roman. "I am sorry, dear friend, that you are presumably being caused unforeseen labour with corrections, etc."

This was not the only extra labour Nietzsche had to perform on behalf of Tribschen. Cosima enlisted his aid and that of his sister Elisabeth in tracking down and buying a portrait of Wagner's revered uncle Adolf, a writer and translator who had been a friend of such celebrities as Schiller and Tieck. Then, pleading her "Lucerne helplessness", she asked him to buy on her behalf a reproduction of a Dürer engraving, some dolls for the children and some dress material. In requesting him to carry out such mundane errands she had to forget, she told him in her letter of 15 December, "that you are a professor, a doctor, a philologist, and just remember that you are twenty-five years old and attached to us Tribscheners". Nietzsche, delighted to have been taken so completely into the family, accepted the little domestic duties that went with it without complaint. Since the birth of Siegfried he had paid five further visits to Tribschen for stays of varying length, had goodhumouredly endured teasing about his vegetarianism and his solitary mountain climbing, and found it quite natural, when he arrived on 24 December for the Christmas holidays, to help Cosima gild nuts for the Christmas tree.

However, Wagner and Cosima were fully alive to his intellectual qualities, which he demonstrated in his inaugural lecture at Basel University. After reading *Homer and Classical Philology* with Wagner soon after its delivery, Cosima wrote to Nietzsche on 26 August: "Herr Wagner asks me to thank you and say that he can only agree with all your views on aesthetic matters. With regard to the subject of the lecture, he congratulates you on having stated the problem so correctly – that is indeed the beginning and perhaps the end of all wisdom, and usually it is given no thought at all. . . . You seem to me to have passed with true artistry from questions of a more general nature to the specific theme, and you have succeeded in containing a very difficult subject within the framework of a lecture with great clarity and sureness of touch."

Nietzsche, gratified by this praise, had his inaugural lecture printed at his own expense and presented a copy to Cosima on her birthday (Christmas Day) with a dedication to her.

This Christmas there was none of the usual exchange of gifts and greetings between the king and Wagner, and Wagner's letter to him of 30 December was in the nature of a cautious attempt to sound the king on the nature of their relations. Ludwig replied on 6 January, pleading preoccupation with state duties as the excuse for his silence. Though he did not answer the question Wagner had baldly put to him in his letter of 20 November, his expressions of undying loyalty gave Wagner the feeling that he might yet avert the dreaded production of *Die Walküre* in Munich, and in his letter of 12 January to the king he put forward a counter-proposal. He himself, he said, would be willing to stage both *Das Rheingold* and *Die Walküre* in Munich in 1871, but only on condition that he were given complete authority. To this proposal the king did not even reply, though a subsequent letter from Düfflipp revealed that he was unpleasantly surprised by it.

It was now clear that Wagner would have to resign himself to what he considered to be the desecration of *Die Walküre*, but at least he could ensure that *Siegfried* did not suffer the same fate by the simple method of not completing the orchestration of the third act. Instead, he turned all his attention to the composition of *Götterdämmerung*, on which he had done some work while simultaneously writing "On Conducting". After completing the essay, he sketched the orchestral opening to the Norns' song on 9 January, and two days later began the orchestral sketch. Entries in Cosima's diary enable us to keep track of his progress:

17 January: "revising his 'Norns' Song' for the second sketch." 4 February: "Siegfried's passage down the Rhine . . . puts us in fine spirits." 7 February: "He plays me the Gibichungs' theme, which came to him in such a clear-cut form that he wrote it down in ink immediately." March 15: "R. in cheerful mood, gets down to Siegfried's arrival, which has caused him a lot of work." 30 March: "R. works and plays for me the wonderfully moving passage in which Siegfried loses his memory of Brünnhilde." 7 April: "He has completed the Oath [Siegfried and Gunther] and is satisfied." 21 April: "R. completes 'Hagen's Watch'." 30 April: "R. works and finishes the intermezzo ('Hagen's Watch' – Brünnhilde contemplating the ring)." 15 May: "R. sketches part of Waltraute's narration." 4 June. "R. shows me in the sketch the theme from the love scene between Br. and Siegfried, which appears like a mirage as S. overpowers Br. and she subconsciously recognises him." 5 June: "R. today finishes the pencil sketch of the first act." The orchestral sketch was completed on 2 July.

Life at Tribschen during these first six months of 1870 was relatively undisturbed. Nietzsche spent two days there in February, and at the end of February Heinrich Porges came for a twelve-day visit, his main hope being, it seemed, to secure Wagner's permission to take over the musical direction of *Die Walküre* in Munich. However, he was too tactful, or too shy to make a direct request. At the end of March, Richter returned from Brussels, where he had conducted the first production of *Lohengrin*: Catulle and Judith Mendès had been responsible, together with a young Belgian disciple, Franz Servais, for bringing this about as a consolation for the loss of his job in Munich.

The divorce proceedings initiated by Bülow the previous autumn were moving in Berlin with painful slowness. Bülow himself had gone to Florence where, with the help of Jessie Laussot, he was busy establishing a new career. News of him arrived occasionally in Tribschen – in April that he had given a concert in Milan, and that he had received a decoration from the King of Italy, in June that he was to play in Nuremberg on behalf of the Hans Sachs monument – but only one direct communication: a letter to Daniela in January thanking her for her account of their Christmas activities. Two discreet congratulatory telegrams from Liszt – one on Cosima's name day on 27 September 1869 and the other on Wagner's birthday in 1870 – showed that he, like Bülow, was now resigned to the inevitable. It was only the lawyers who were so dilatory. "Nature and love are prompt," Wagner told Cosima, "but laws – they creep on all fours!"

However, they could while waiting give thought to the future. "In the evening *Die Walküre*," Cosima wrote in her diary on 5 March, during Porges's visit to Tribschen. "When we subsequently talk of the production of these works, I tell R. he should look up the article on *Baireuth** in the encyclopedia; R. had mentioned this place as the one he would choose. To our delight we read in the list of buildings of a splendid old opera house!"

This passage, seized on by Wagner's and Cosima's first official biographers, Glasenapp and Du Moulin Eckart (both of whom had access to Cosima's diaries), has created a kind of legend, suggesting that the choice of Bayreuth as the site of Wagner's festival theatre was due to a lucky accident: the discovery there of a theatre – the Markgräfliches Opernhaus, built in 1747 – which possessed a stage large enough to accommodate the *Ring*. Though that discovery certainly served to concentrate Wagner's thoughts on the town, Bayreuth, as Cosima herself pointed out, had been in his mind even earlier. He first became acquainted with the town in 1835 during a journey from Karlsbad to Nuremberg, and its charm left a lasting impression on him. In 1866 he expressed the wish (in a letter to Bülow) that the king might give him a pavilion in the palace there as a place of refuge, and later the same year he suggested to Ludwig himself that he might make the Bayreuth palace his favourite residence. Clearly Wagner did not know the Markgräfliches Opernhaus, but it appears that Richter had heard of it through a friend and had once mentioned it to Wagner when they were discussing the possible site of a festival theatre.

Thus the consultation of the encyclopedia on 5 March was more in the nature of a confirmation than a revelation. What is, however, clear beyond all doubt is that Wagner had now decided that Ludwig could no

---

* The old spelling, subsequently changed to Bayreuth.

longer be relied on to carry out his plans for a revolutionary theatre and, if he wanted it, he would have to take the initiative himself. For the moment it remained a pipe-dream. He made no move yet to visit Bayreuth or to find out how suitable the town might be for the realisation of all the plans that had come to grief in Munich.

As the first performance of *Die Walküre* drew near, Wagner made a final appeal to the king. "Once more I implore you," he wrote on 15 June, "have *Die Walküre* performed for *yourself*, but keep the public out. Choose any excuse you like for this decision: have several dress rehearsals (for yourself alone) and then declare that – for personal reasons – you are putting the performance off till later. . . . I can overcome and resign myself to anything, if it is in accordance with your wish, but I shall find it impossible to overcome the deep pain this unprecedented use of my work is causing me: it grips me, despite all vows to the contrary, because it is more powerful than my concern for my tranquillity. May God, who gave me the inspiration for my works, make you understand what I feel and am now telling you; this is not just empty egoism!"

Even this plea failed to move the king, and, to express his displeasure, Wagner could do no more than request his friends and supporters to keep away from Munich. The first performance took place on 26 June, Wüllner again conducting. The cast included Heinrich and Therese Vogl as Siegmund and Sieglinde, Kindermann as Wotan and Sophie Stehle as Brünnhilde. Its great success did nothing to assuage Wagner's bitterness with the king. On the day of the dress rehearsal, 24 June, Cosima wrote in her diary: "R. so beside himself and also so physically worn out that I stand there disconsolate, not knowing what to do." And on the same day he remarked to her: "You are the King of Bavaria's sister, you have joined hands to save my life – he, it is true, as a foolish character, you as a good woman." Ludwig did not attend the first performance of *Die Walküre*, but waited until *Das Rheingold* was revived on 7 July, then saw them both in succession. He did not, as after *Tristan* and *Die Meistersinger*, send ecstatic messages of congratulation, but that was surely only because he realised what effect, in the circumstances, such effusions might have on Wagner.

Marriage in Wartime

DESPITE A FRENCH mother and a brother-in-law, Emile Ollivier, who was at that time heading the French government, Cosima had so completely absorbed Wagner's jaundiced view of France that she found no difficulty in proclaiming her support for Bismarck when, on 17 July 1870, war broke out between France and Prussia.

Wagner's own feelings of gratification were inspired less by hostility towards France than by hope for Germany. King Ludwig's action in immediately mobilising the Bavarian army in support of Prussia earned his warm approval: it raised the war to the level of a struggle for liberation from the cultural domination of Germany by France. Without it, he told Cosima, the German states would gradually sink to the level of Belgium, in which all culture was French and only "the humble people" German in outlook. Wagner's views on France were greatly influenced by the indifference Paris had shown towards him in his early struggles to establish himself as a composer. But his disgust with Germany, with its host of petty kingdoms and principalities, each devoted to its own selfish interests, was just as great, and basically just as subjective. His dream was of a united Germany in which the spirit of Luther, Dürer, Bach, Beethoven, Goethe and Schiller would be revived, and in the banding together of the German states against France he saw the emergence of a great opportunity.

He was anxious to start work on an essay on Beethoven, and he tried to put off the proposed visit of Catulle and Judith Mendès, additionally unwelcome now on account of their French nationality. However, they arrived in Lucerne on 19 July, bringing not only Villiers de l'Isle-Adam with them, but also Saint-Saëns and the composer Henri Duparc. The news of the divorce arrived on 27 July, while the visitors were still there; Bülow's petition had been granted nine days earlier in Berlin. Cosima's reference to it in her diary was brief: "There is no happiness on this earth, my children, for at this news I only had tears."

Nietzsche arrived on 28 July, accompanied by his sister Elisabeth. "I was somewhat confused at finding Wagner such a pigmy compared to Frau Cosima," she wrote in her book *The Nietzsche-Wagner*

Correspondence. "I must admit that I was also unpleasantly impressed by the interior decorations of the old-fashioned country house, which consisted of rose-coloured hangings and *amorettes* in lavish profusion, evidently designed by some Parisian *meubleur.*" However, she eventually found "Wagner and Baroness von Bülow delightful and the children fascinating, especially the little Siegfried, of whose advent I had been kept in ignorance." And Cosima found Elisabeth "a nice, modest girl".

The next arrival was Richard Pohl, who had left Germany hurriedly in order to avoid becoming involved in the war. Wagner, surveying all his guests, compared them with the refugees in Boccaccio's *Decameron*: "As they fled from the plague, so we from the war." But on 30 July the company broke up, Mendès and Judith promising to return in time for the wedding.

This, Wagner was assured by the Protestant parson in Lucerne, Pastor Tschudi, could take place as soon as Cosima received official confirmation of her divorce. The papers arrived on 3 August, the day on which Malwida von Meysenbug paid her first visit to Tribschen, together with her ward, Olga Herzen. Since Malwida had known Minna, Wagner was somewhat uneasy about her reaction to Cosima, but he soon found he had no cause for concern. Malwida, an early champion of women's rights, had no respect for social conventions and admired women who had the courage and independence to take their fate in their own hands.

Three years younger than Wagner, she too had been affected by the revolution of 1848–49 and, after working in Berlin as a journalist, had gone into exile to escape persecution. She went to London, where she became governess to the two daughters of the Russian philosopher Alexander Herzen, and on the death of his wife adopted the younger one, Olga. She met Wagner briefly in London in 1855, having in the meantime read his *Art and Revolution* and other Zurich writings, of which she profoundly approved, then again in Paris during the rehearsals for *Tannhäuser*. There she formed a close friendship with Minna, but, as she wrote in her reminiscences *Memoiren einer Idealistin (Memoirs of an Idealist)*, she saw that Wagner's marriage was foundering on its childlessness and Minna's total inability "to grasp the nature of a genius and the consequences arising from it in his relationship with the world". What Wagner, "a man so totally dominated by his daemon", needed, she decided, was "an understanding woman of lofty intellect, a woman who would see her task as one of mediating between the genius and the world, having understood that between these there is an eternal hostility". Malwida, who had no personal ambitions to assume this task herself, swiftly recognised in Cosima the qualities she had defined. Wagner's regard for Malwida, untouched by amorousness, was unusually firm, in spite of her independent outlook, on which he frequently teased her. He did not normally (and nor did Cosima) approve of women who put a career before marriage.

While Cosima sat with Countess Bassenheim, Malwida and Olga in Lucerne preparing lint and bandages for the German wounded, Nietzsche, on holiday with his mother and sister in the Madaraner valley, was debating with himself what part he could take in the war. His great desire was to volunteer for army service, but, as a condition of his appointment in Basel, he had now become a Swiss citizen, and as such was unable to take a combatant role without giving up his professorship and resuming German nationality. As a Swiss he could, however, enlist as a nursing orderly, and he wrote to Cosima to seek her advice. She was not in favour of his plan. The time to join in personally, she told him in her letter of 9 August, was when German territory was invaded: "The works of peace should not be neglected unless the battle has become desperate; you are a scholar, and I feel you must remain that until it becomes a shameful thing to be a scholar, that is to say, when our dear country is threatened and one can retain one's self-respect only by fighting." She concluded: "I know you will follow your own feelings, and will be right to do so, for it is perhaps better to act incorrectly according to one's own feelings than do the better thing according to the feelings of others."

Richter, now working again as Wagner's copyist, was also restless, but Wagner warned him against joining the army. "It will turn you into an adventurer," he said. "For love of me you have given up your position, now hold out." Richter allowed himself to be dissuaded; not so Nietzsche. He went straight from his holiday to Erlangen for training as a medical orderly.

Wagner and Cosima were married in the Protestant church in Lucerne at eight o'clock on the morning of 25 August, the king's birthday. Wagner wrote to Düfflipp on 21 August: "The possibility of being able to choose this day, which is so inexpressibly significant to us, for our wedding appeared to us as a solemn hint of fate, which we greeted joyfully as a sign of blessing." As birthday presents for the king he sent a poem extolling Ludwig for committing his country to the struggle for Germany, and a copy, made by Richter, of the orchestral sketch of *Götterdämmerung* up to the end of the first act. The effect was all that could have been wished. At the hour of their wedding, Ludwig despatched a telegram from Hohenschwangau avowing that he was more than ever with them in spirit.

Mendès and Judith did not return to Lucerne for the wedding, since, Judith wrote, Catulle would be considered a deserter were he to leave Paris. Nietzsche was by now in France tending the wounded, so the only friends present were Malwida and Richter and their neighbours Count and Countess Bassenheim. Daniela and Blandine also attended the ceremony, and Cosima would have liked the younger children to be there too, but Isolde was in bed with a cold, and Eva was left at home to keep her company.

The wedding seems to have meant little more to them than an official confirmation of an established fact. Wagner did, when they visited François and Eliza Wille a few days after their marriage, express to Cosima his pleasure in now being able to refer to her as "Frau Wagner", but in moments of absentmindedness he could still find himself talking to the servants of the "Frau Baronin", while she had become so used to her life of retirement that she continued to regard excursions into the outside world as an exertion, though there was no longer any social barrier to restrain her. She was quite content to devote herself to providing her husband with companionship and support and bringing up her children. Wagner at times reproved her for taking their education so completely on herself that she was in danger of ruining her already weak eyesight, but she remained firm in her resolve and resisted all suggestions that she should send them to school. It was a decision that arose as much from the emotionally deprived circumstances of her own childhood as from her desire to create a tranquil and settled home in which Wagner could work freely. He too was happy to have the children with him: "Without them we should be too earnest," he declared.

His behaviour towards Cosima showed no signs of diminishing into a marital complacency. He still paid her all the attentions of a lover, and left her in no doubt that she was the very centre of his life. "Dear indispensability", he called her, and between the pages of her diary she sometimes pressed wild flowers that he had picked for her. Her own comment on her second marriage, written on 9 September, was: "My union with R. is like a palingenesis, a reincarnation which brings me nearer to perfection, a deliverance from a previous erring existence."

In their sexual relationship their differing attitudes are reflected in Cosima's diary entry of 16 May: "If only we could curb passion – if only it could be banished from our lives! Its approaching now grieves me, as if it were the death of love." And on 14 February 1871 she wrote: "Great ardour on R.'s part puts me into a despondent mood; best of all I should like to live my life here unnoticed, reaping only beaming glances; I have suffered too much to be susceptible to other pleasures!" On 6 December she told him that she was pregnant again. It turned out to be a false alarm. "This moves him to tears, for he had been pleased and had thought that Fate desired me to bring a child into the world without fear and in the full happiness of love."

In later years they looked back on their life in Tribschen as the time of their greatest happiness, but it was only in the few months after their marriage that they enjoyed the unworried tranquillity with which Tribschen was associated in their memories, and even these months were overshadowed by the war, whose progress they followed anxiously. Within their home, however, all was peace as Wagner worked on his Beethoven essay and, when that was completed on 7 September, on the orchestration of the third act of *Siegfried*, while Cosima gave lessons to the children. In the evenings they would either make music with Richter, or Wagner would pursue his favourite pastime of reading aloud. There was no conscious pattern to their reading, and the range was wide: during these months it included Xenophon's *Symposium*, plays by Aristophanes and by Shakespeare (*King John* and *Henry IV*), Byron's *Don Juan*, Goethe's *Wilhelm Meister*, and stories by E. T. A. Hoffmann and Ludwig Tieck.

There were occasional excursions to visit friends: the Willes (François having become more cordial now that his anxiety about Wagner's designs on his wife had been removed); and Jakob Sulzer, a Swiss cantonal secretary who had helped him financially in his Zurich years. They also visited the Wesendoncks, though the prospect of this reunion caused Wagner a certain amount of apprehension. Always anxious to play down to Cosima the importance to him of his previous loves, he had to remember that Cosima had been a witness to the upheavals with Minna in Zurich on Mathilde Wesendonck's account. That in the meantime Mathilde had changed the colour of her hair from blonde to brunette helped them both, when they saw her again in her home in Zurich, to regard her as a different person.

On the whole, however, it was a time of forming new friendships, and these included, besides Nietzsche himself, two of his friends who had been fellow students, Erwin Rohde, a lecturer on philology at Kiel University, and Karl von Gersdorff. The first of these Nietzsche brought to Tribschen on 11 June, and after the visit Cosima wrote in a letter that Wagner had been impressed by "his manly earnestness, his understanding, and the genuine friendliness which now and again illumined his severe features." Gersdorff, who served throughout the war as a German officer, they did not meet till later, though they exchanged a few letters. These three young men, together with Richter, clearly formed the nucleus in Wagner's mind of the future artistic community which was thought of, though still vaguely, as Bayreuth.

Nietzsche's war service did not last long. He was sent to look after the wounded at the battle of Wörth, and, returning to Karlsruhe with six of them in a cattle-truck, he contracted dysentery and diphtheria simultaneously. After a week in hospital he was sent home to Naumberg to be nursed back to health by his mother and sister. He returned to his post in Basel on 21 October.

Wagner began his essay on Beethoven on 25 July 1870 and finished it on
7 September. His primary reason for writing it was his desire, in the
centenary year of Beethoven's birth, to provide a memorial to the
composer whom he regarded above all others as his spiritual ancestor.
The human Beethoven he presented was a man very like himself,
isolated, single-minded, independent, asking nothing of the world
except that it should unconditionally provide him with the means to
pursue his difficult path in his own way. Music, as Wagner defined it –
admittedly arriving at his conclusion with somewhat obscure
philosophical arguments – is a direct expression of the inner being: a cry
of joy or of horror is music in its most primitive form, and as such instantly understandable to all, whatever their language. As music grew
more sophisticated it came increasingly to be contained within formal
patterns, and with the passage of time these patterns had come to be
mistaken for music itself. Beethoven was no formal innovator: he
retained the patterns, yet was able to make them the servants and not the
masters of his musical expression, thus restoring to music its profound
original function. It was something, Wagner declared, that – in a
different art form – only Shakespeare had ever done: a manner of using
existing patterns in such a way that one loses sight of the form and
responds directly to the essence of what is being expressed.

In his essay Wagner made no reference to his own artistic aims, but his
views on Beethoven's *Fidelio* throw an interesting light on them. What is
this opera, he asked, other than an "almost repulsive dilution" of the
drama expressed in the third *Leonore* overture? The idea that in opera
music heightens the effect of words is wrong: in fact, music usurps the
words and expresses the dramatic aim by itself, through its direct appeal
to the inner consciousness. "We should not go far astray were we to at-
tribute entirely to music the human ability to fashion drama." He
applied this assertion to his own work in a remark made to Cosima on 22
January 1871, a few months after completing his essay: "I am no poet,
and I don't care at all if people reproach me for my choice of words, in
my works the action is everything."

Curt von Westernhagen suggests in his book *Die Entstehung des "Ring"*
(*The Forging of the "Ring"*) that the lapse of a complete year between the
finishing of the first act of *Götterdämmerung* and the beginning of the
second on 24 June 1871 might have had something to do with the
Beethoven essay, "which is relevant here for its clarification of the
change that had taken place in his view of the relationship between
music and text in his drama. Whereas the emphasis in *Oper und Drama*
had been on the role of the text, he now acknowledged that music
enshrined 'man's *a priori* ability to create dramatic forms at all'."
However, there is no evidence to suggest that this recognition of a shift

of emphasis seriously affected his view of the *Ring* as it had progressed so far (and certainly he made no attempt to revise the parts already written), nor was there any discernible change of direction when he eventually came to resume *Götterdämmerung*. It therefore seems questionable whether anything in the nature of a conscious artistic crisis occurred to impede progress. The explanation may perhaps be sought rather in the circumstances of Wagner's life at that time, in his simple enjoyment of the family life which his marriage had now made secure, and the background of war, with the atmosphere of uncertainty and impermanence it inevitably engenders. There was now also the feeling that, once the war ended, there would be no return to life as it had been. Munich was now definitely behind him, and the future belonged to Bayreuth, still no more than a vague symbol of a new beginning. It is possible to see in all this a deliberate resolve on Wagner's part to delay the completion of *Götterdämmerung* until he knew more of the practical realities of "Bayreuth".

On 2 October he drafted a "proclamation and invitation to the friends of my art" in which he revealed his intention of producing the *Ring* at a special festival. He mentioned no locality: "At the moment I feel I may do no more than appeal for the active support of genuine friends of my art and my artistic ideas, and ask them to provide assistance in carrying out my intention to produce my great stage festival in my own way."

Next he occupied himself with the writing of a one-act farce, *Eine Kapitulation (A Capitulation)*, a reflection of his elation with the progress of the German army which, following the surrender of Napoleon III at Sedan on 1 September, was now besieging Paris. He had recently been reading the comedies of Aristophanes, and, when he read in the newspapers that balloons were being used to evacuate refugees from Paris, he discerned in the idea of a French government taking to balloons ("up in the air in both senses") a subject for an Aristophanic comedy. Though originally thought of as a task for another writer, he eventually decided to do it himself, and completed the play within a week in the middle of November. The loyal Cosima described it as excellent, but she was almost alone in this opinion: even he himself was doubtful, and confessed to her that he wrote it "without much pleasure". A man of great humour, as both *Die Meistersinger* and the testimony of his friends prove, Wagner lacked the lightness and sharpness of touch necessary to a satirist, and the comedy, which brought to the stage not only a balloon, but also Victor Hugo, Jacques Offenbach and members of the new French government, gave the impression of being little more than a mocking gibe at defeated enemies.

Wagner decided that his authorship of the play should be kept secret

(the author's name was given as Aristop. Hanes), that Richter should
write the music for it, and that it should be offered to the little popular
theatres of Germany for production. Richter consented with reluctance,
wrote a few musical numbers, and the play was sent to Betz in Berlin to
place. Both Richter and Betz were somewhat embarrassed by the whole
affair. They eventually claimed that the play was turned down by theatre
managers on account of the expense of its production, but this may have
been an excuse to extricate themselves from it.

Wagner apologised to Cosima for abandoning more serious work in
order to write his farce. The serious work he was talking about was the
orchestration of the third act of *Siegfried*, which he had taken up again on
6 October. On 23 November, after the completion of *A Capitulation*, he
told her that he had begun to make sketches for the second act of *Götterdämmerung*. However, it would be unwise to regard Cosima's diary as a
reliable source in relation to his musical activities at this period, for he
was in fact working on a piece which was intended as a complete surprise
for her, and he did his utmost to put her off the scent. This was the
Siegfried Idyll, that delicate and moving tribute to a beloved wife
which was based on themes first noted down in Starnberg (and subsequently incorporated into the *Siegfried* love duet) and a little nursery
song written for his children in December 1868, as well as on themes
from *Siegfried*. Later he told her that "all he had set out to do was to work
the theme which had come to him in Starnberg (when we were living
there together), and which he had promised me as a quartet, into a
morning serenade, and then he had unconsciously woven our whole life
into it – Fidi's birth, my recuperation, Fidi's bird, etc. As Schopenhauer
said, this is the way a musician works, he expresses life in a language
which reason does not understand." Fidi, incidentally, was Siegfried.

Wagner finished the *Triebschen Idyll*, as it was first called, on 4
December and entrusted Richter with the task of assembling the instrumentalists (flute, oboe, two clarinets, trumpet, two horns, bassoon
and strings) and rehearsing them, for the sake of secrecy, first in Zurich
and then in the Hôtel du Lac in Lucerne.

Wagner invited Nietzsche to attend the final rehearsal on Christmas
Eve at the Hôtel du Lac, and they arrived at Tribschen together, to find
Cosima busy preparing the Christmas tree and the presents for the
children. For the first time, owing to shortage of money, Wagner and she
had decided not to give each other Christmas presents – for him a convenient subterfuge, since, owing to the accident of her having been born
on Christmas Day, the *Idyll* could be looked on as a birthday and not
a Christmas present.

At seven o'clock in the morning the musicians stationed themselves
quietly on the stairs outside Cosima's room and began to play. "As I

awoke in the light of dawn, my mind passed from one dream into another," she wrote to Eliza Wille on 15 January 1871. "Familiar sounds from *Siegfried*, though now transformed and, it seemed, transfigured, stole on my ears; it was as if the house, or better still our whole existence, was rising up in music and ascending to heaven; sacred memories, birdsong and sunrise, woven into the music of *Siegfried*, settled like a balm on my heart, and slowly, gradually I began to realise that I was not dreaming and yet was experiencing the most blissful of all dreams."

"I was in tears," she wrote in her diary, "but so, too, was the whole household." The work was played twice more in the course of the day, during which Sulzer joined Nietzsche as a guest. "Now at last I understood all R.'s working in secret, also dear Richter's trumpet (he blazed out the Siegfried theme splendidly and had learnt the trumpet especially to do it), which had won many admonishments from me. 'Now let me die,' I exclaimed to R. 'It would be easier to die for me than to live for me,' he replied."

The German states, having fought together successfully, began, now that the defeat of the French was imminent, to consider the idea of forming themselves into an empire. Ludwig, fearing for the independence of Bavaria, was reluctant to see further power placed in Prussian hands, but it was he who, yielding to his ministers' arguments of political tact, made the proposal that the imperial crown should be offered to the Prussian king. Ludwig's objections were as much personal as political, for he hated the Prussian royal family, to which his own mother belonged.

Wagner too looked on Prussian dominance with misgiving, for his experiences in Berlin had convinced him that the Prussians had no interest in the arts. He admired their military skill, but he considered that Bismarck had little imagination, and he thought it might be a good idea, when the war ended, to send him a copy of his *German Art and German Politics* in order to give him the right ideas about the importance of the theatre in the new empire. Nietzsche, too, was gloomy about the cultural future of Germany, which he prophesied would be dominated by militarism and pietism.

The need for "Bayreuth", for a community dedicated to upholding and strengthening the traditions of German art, became even more pressing. Nietzsche sought to convince his friend Rohde of its necessity in his letter of 15 December: "You know of course about Wagner's Bayreuth plan from your visit to Tribschen. I have been quietly reflecting in my own mind whether at the same time there should not also be *on our side* a break with traditional philology and its *educational* outlook. . . . A book on Beethoven by Wagner, which has just been published, will give you some idea of what I want from the future. Read it – it is a revelation of the spirit in which we – we! – shall live in the future. If, as is possible, we find few to share our feelings, I still believe that we shall be able – of course with some sacrifices – to fight free of the currents and reach a little island on which we shall no longer have to stuff wax in our ears. We shall then teach each other, our books will be just fishing-hooks to win new recruits for our monastic-artistic brotherhood. We shall live, work, enjoy, for each other – perhaps this is the only way to work for the sake of the *whole*. To show you how seriously I mean this, I have already begun to reduce my personal needs, so as to save a little part of my means."

Money was indeed a major problem in turning the Bayreuth plan into reality. Wagner's inability to economise was notorious (even Cosima admitted it), but it could not be maintained that he was guilty of any irresponsible extravagance at this time. He now had a wife and five children to support, and his income was no greater than it had been for himself alone in Munich, for, though his allowance from the king had been raised, he was still paying back from income the advance he had been granted to take out an insurance. The sale of his books brought him next to nothing. Since there was no copyright act then in operation, the frequent performances of *Rienzi, Der Fliegende Holländer, Tannhäuser* and *Lohengrin* earned him nothing from theatres which had already paid a lump sum for them in the past. He received from Munich no royalties for performances of any of his works. Only *Die Meistersinger* in Dresden, Berlin, Vienna and a few smaller theatres provided an addition to his income, but not on a level to help much with the expenses of his household, which included Richter as well as an array of servants. They lived comfortably, but not extravagantly, making do with one carriage and a single horse, the elderly Fritz, who was replaced during 1870 by Grane, a present from Ludwig on Wagner's birthday. Cosima's little income, consisting of allowances from her father and her mother, was being saved to provide dowries for her four daughters.

Certainly, if they had wished to follow Nietzsche's example of abstemiousness, they could have cut down on wine and cigars, but this would scarcely have met the financial needs of their Bayreuth plan. For this Ludwig still remained their best prospect, and Wagner wrote him a dutiful letter on 28 December, expressing his good wishes for the coming year. It was written, Cosima noted, "with an effort", and the stilted expressions of undying loyalty confirm it. Of his own future he wrote merely: "My plans for the performance of the whole [*Ring*] are maturing and, as soon as your royal graciousness provides permission for carrying them out, I shall feel it my privilege to place them in more detail before my noble lord."

Though still recognising his dependence for practical purposes on

King Ludwig, Wagner was exhilarated by the emergence of a larger, united Germany, of which King Wilhelm I of Prussia was proclaimed emperor on 18 January. Wagner saw the new empire as a revival of the Holy Roman Empire, which in its days of greatness had reflected the true German spirit, so sadly lost since. This feeling inspired him to write, shortly after the coronation in Versailles, a patriotic poem, "To the German Army". Cosima advised him not to publish it in a newspaper, but to send it directly to Bismarck as the architect of Germany's re-emergence, and she herself undertook to ensure through her friend Lothar Bucher in Berlin that the poem should reach Bismarck, whose close associate he was. In time a letter arrived from Bismarck thanking him for the poem. Cosima admitted in her diary on 25 February her "childish joy" in the handwritten letter: "The children gaze with curiosity on the colossal sweep of the writing, and R. says his own *Leubald und Adelaïde* was written in a hand something like that." (Wagner had written *Leubald und Adelaïde*, his first play, at the age of fourteen.)

The publishing house of Peters had invited Wagner at the end of 1870 to write a coronation march for the ceremony in Versailles, but he had no inclination for writing to order and refused the offer, preferring to devote his time to the orchestration of *Siegfried*. The capitulation of Paris on 28 January, and with it the end of the war, brought his thoughts back to a celebratory march – a task all the more attractive for having attached to it a fee of 1,500 francs. Shortly after completing the orchestration of *Siegfried* on 5 February, he began his *Kaisermarsch*. Yet the writing of it gave him little pleasure. "I can't do things when I can't imagine something behind it," he told Cosima. "And if I imagine something, it gets out of hand. A march is an absurdity; the most it can be is a popular song, but it is not meant to be sung, which is nonsensical. I must have some great vehicle, on which I can reel off my music."

He did, after completing the orchestral march, come on the idea of writing a popular song to be attached to it, and he wrote a patriotic verse, beginning "Hail! Hail to the Emperor", which he set to a popular melody that could be sung by the German soldiers as they marched into Berlin in triumph on their return from France. This was certainly a "vehicle" of sorts, but hardly of the kind Wagner had in mind when he made his remark to Cosima. He himself thought little of either the *Kaisermarsch* or its choral adjunct, the "Kaiserlied", and whether they were performed together or separately mattered not at all to him.

On 7 May 1869 Wagner had been elected an honorary member of the Royal Academy of Arts in Berlin – the first academic honour ever to be offered him. The war had presented him with a convenient excuse for not going to Berlin to receive it, but, now that the war was over, he saw the practical advantage of combining his long-delayed exploratory visit to Bayreuth with a lecture at the Berlin Academy, in which he would expound his ideas on the future of the operatic stage and disclose his own plans for putting them into practice. Before beginning work on this lecture, entitled "The Destiny of Opera", on 5 March, he wrote a very long letter to Ludwig, in which he went into more detail about his plans, while still concealing that they were centred on Bayreuth. All he was prepared to tell Ludwig at this stage was that the place of his choice was in Bavaria, and that its great advantage was that it already possessed a suitable theatre. His reason for silence, he told the king, was that he had learnt from bitter experience how easily over-hasty disclosures could lead to the thwarting of plans.

The first part of his letter, dated 1 March, contained a long description of the circumstances in which he had come to write the *Ring*, and the difficulties he had experienced in keeping his inspiration alive over all the years of its composition. The production against his wishes of both *Das Rheingold* and *Die Walküre* in Munich had aroused in him the feelings of a father seeing his child snatched from him to be delivered over to a life of prostitution. Despite this setback to his inspiration, he had managed to compose "a large and particularly difficult part" of *Götter-dämmerung*, but he now again found himself unable to continue. "How can I translate a spiritual conception into living sound when all I see is just notation lines staring at me? . . . So what is to become of me? What is to become of my work, for which you are continually arousing my enthusiasm by praising it so highly, by regarding it as the greatest ever conceived by a mortal brain? – Certainly things cannot remain as they are: if I am to recover the will and ability to complete it, I must be able to see before me a definite prospect of my demands for the only possible staging of my work fulfilled."

Finally he attempted in his letter to put new courage into Ludwig, who had admitted to him in his letter of 18 February that the "political torments" he was undergoing in connection with the founding of the empire had again raised in him thoughts of abdication. Germany, Wagner told him, had been saved from the fate of becoming another Alsace under French domination: "If we have saved Germany's body, the task is now to strengthen its soul. Oh, my king, the German spirit still looks to you! Now for the deed! Do not once again allow it to be wrested from you. Set the example!"

With this letter Wagner finally committed himself inwardly to Bayreuth – not the town so much as the idea. "If Bayreuth is refused us," Cosima wrote on 21 March in her diary, "we shall think of Strassburg." As they waited anxiously for Ludwig's reply to his letter, Wagner worked on his lecture, and Cosima occupied herself re-establishing contact by letter with the French relations and friends from whom they had been cut off by the war. She had antagonised many of them with her pro-German proclivities, but Wagner was less apt to allow political views to influence personal feelings. He wrote to Catulle Mendès at the time of the battle of Sedan: "Luckily there is one region of life in which we are and will always remain united. . . . We are in perfect accord on these two great principles: love and music." Mendès agreed.

Cosima had kept up a correspondence with her mother throughout the war, but it was an uncomfortable one, since Marie d'Agoult was as uncompromisingly pro-French as her daughter was pro-German. However, life in Paris being difficult after the capitulation, and her own future being in doubt, the countess decided to pay a visit to Tribschen, where she arrived on 24 March. Cosima, seeing her for the first time in seven years, found difficulty in establishing a cordial relationship with her. Wagner, on the other hand, felt tender towards the countess for the sympathy she had always shown towards him and Cosima, and he demonstrated his gratitude by singing to her passages from his works. Her pleasure in her grandchildren melted Cosima in the end, and after her departure on 2 April she wrote to Nietzsche: "I was nervous of our reunion, but found her to my surprise robust and in good spirits, and I saw in her that fine feature of the former French character, a heroic recklessness. When Wagner sang the prayer from *Lohengrin* to her, she burst into tears, and I had the feeling that she realised that this power was bound in the end to triumph. Triebschen made a great impression on her; she said it was life as she had always dreamed it."

It was now nearly a month since Wagner had written to the king, but still no answer came. Then Richter received a letter from Munich saying that people there were talking of an arrangement between Tribschen, King Ludwig and Emperor Wilhelm I to present the *Ring* at Bayreuth. "We compare this piece of news with the silence towards us and ask ourselves what it means," Cosima wrote in her diary on 26 March. "Is there some mischief brewing? I am fearful." She did not mention from whom the letter came, but it seemed ominous that, while Wagner had been careful to conceal the name of Bayreuth from the king, it should have become a subject of common gossip in Munich. In fact, it was not so surprising, for the name was in open use at Tribschen; it would certainly have been known, for instance, to Porges, who at the beginning of the year had been appointed musical director at the Munich opera (a short-lived appointment, incidentally, since he proved an incompetent conductor).

At last, on 4 April, a letter arrived from Düfflipp. The king, he said, had been offended by Wagner's remarks about the Munich performances of *Das Rheingold* and *Die Walküre*, and he was now calling for *Siegfried*. Neither Ludwig nor Düfflipp knew that *Siegfried* was now finished, for

Wagner had been careful not to reveal in his letter that the orchestration had been completed. That the king should choose this moment to remind Wagner of his rights aroused further apprehensions. "Over beer we discuss our prospects," Cosima noted on 9 April. "My heart feels very heavy – God knows what now lies before us! All that remains for me is to be worthy of R. and never to show him any signs of faint-heartedness. Today I had to weep on his shoulder."

In spite of her resolutions she was not at all eager to accompany him to Berlin, but he insisted, telling her that he could no longer bear to be separated from her. "You are my buskin, my crutch, my little *stilt*," he told her. They set off on 15 April and made their first stop in Augsburg. There they met Düfflipp, who came at Wagner's request and with the king's consent, to discuss the plans he had outlined in his letter of 1 March. Düfflipp told them that, since the last act of *Siegfried* was not yet available, the king was thinking of having the first two acts performed in Munich. Before he would consent to that, Wagner told Düfflipp, he would burn the complete score and go out begging. When on the following day he and Cosima left Augsburg for Bayreuth, it was in the clear knowledge that, if he were to carry out his resolve to present the *Ring* himself and in his own way, it would be in spite of Ludwig rather than with his help.

CHAPTER IX

APRIL 1871 – APRIL 1872:

The End of Tribschen

BAYREUTH, LYING BETWEEN wooded hills in Franconia, the northern part of Bavaria, close to one of the sources of the river Main, is an old town, dating back to the twelfth century. Active mainly in agriculture, pottery and flax spinning, it reached the height of its prosperity in the eighteenth century under the margrave Friedrich, whose wife Wilhelmine was a sister of Frederick the Great. It was she who was responsible for giving the little German market town its aristocratic air, bringing in French and Italian architects to build first a rococo opera house, then a new palace in classical style in the town, as well as a fanciful summer palace, the Eremitage, just outside it.

After her death the town gradually declined, but its fine buildings still stood, and it was these that impressed themselves on Wagner's memory when he passed through Bayreuth in 1835, and caused him in later years to recall it as the "beautiful wilderness, far from the smoke and industrial odours of civilisation" which he described in his Preface to the published text as the place he required for the production of *Der Ring des Nibelungen*.

He arrived there with Cosima on 17 April 1871, and on 19 April they went to inspect Wilhelmine's opera house, whose stage, as the encyclopedia had told him, was one of the largest in Germany. However, he saw at once that the Markgräfliches Opernhaus would not do for the *Ring*. He wrote to Düfflipp the same day: "This theatre is probably the most fantastic example of rococo to be found anywhere, and not the least little thing in it may be changed. . . . For the rest, I shall just say today that Bayreuth and its surroundings fully live up to my hopes, and I still retain my wish to settle down here and in that connection am still thinking of carrying out my great undertaking."

It was clear that a theatre would have to be built, and, after touring the town in a search for a suitable residence, Wagner and Cosima decided they would have to build themselves a home too. They discovered a likely site for that adjoining the grounds of the New Palace, and not far from it a place for the theatre. On the following day they left Bayreuth, having as yet made no official contacts.

They went to Leipzig, where they visited Wagner's sister Ottilie and her family. Her husband, Hermann Brockhaus, an orientalist who taught at Leipzig University, was Wagner's favourite among his brothers-in-law; "an engaging, eloquently intellectual, reserved character", he called him, and at this time of his life Wagner was happier in academic than in theatrical surroundings. He also had a great liking for Ottilie's sons, Clemens, a clergyman, and Friedrich (Fritz), who, after studying law, had recently (with Nietzsche's help) obtained a teaching post at Basel University. In Leipzig Wagner attended a rehearsal of his *Kaisermarsch*, which was to be given its first performance on 23 April under the conductor Gustav Schmidt. They did not wait for that, but journeyed on to Dresden, where Wagner's sister Luise lived with her husband Friedrich Brockhaus, a brother of Hermann and a publisher. Wagner showed Cosima the house in which he had written *Tannhäuser*, then went with her to visit Pusinelli and his large family, and in the evening they went to the opera, housed temporarily in a wooden barn following the burning down of Semper's theatre in 1869. Wagner did not dislike the barn: "It holds a lot of people," Cosima wrote in her diary. "He observes everything with an eye to Bayreuth."

On 25 April they arrived in Berlin, where they were met by Marie von Schleinitz, Cosima's close friend in the first years of her marriage to Bülow. Wagner had met her only briefly, when in 1863 she attended the concert he conducted in Breslau. She was then Marie von Buch, but shortly afterwards she married Count Alexander von Schleinitz, the Prussian Minister of the Royal Household: she was five years younger than Cosima, her husband six years older than Wagner. A woman of great beauty and charm, she was utterly devoted to Wagner's music and had already shown in her activities on behalf of the production of *Die Meistersinger* in Berlin that she was prepared to exercise her considerable influence in court circles on his behalf.

It was a matter of simple common sense that Wagner, knowing of King Ludwig's hostility towards his plans for Bayreuth, should seek an additional centre of support in Berlin, now of even greater importance than before through having become the capital of the German Empire. On the musical side he had good friends and allies there in the persons of Karl Eckert, musical director of the opera house, the singer Betz and the pianist Karl Tausig, while Cosima, through her friendships with Marie von Schleinitz and Lothar Bucher, had access both to the court and to the government. On the other hand, there were powerful adversaries, particularly on the musical side. Wagner had an unfortunate habit, arising from his views on the proper function of the theatre, of making enemies of theatre directors, and he considered the Berlin intendant, Botho von Hülsen, to be among the most malevolent of them. The head of the Royal Academy of Music was the violinist Joseph Joachim, now fully identified with Brahms and other musicians of the post-Schumann era, for whom Wagner had no respect at all.

Joachim, highly regarded in Berlin, was among the audience which came to the Berlin Academy on 28 April to hear Wagner's lecture, "The Destiny of Opera". This, as he himself stated in a foreword when he came to publish it in his collected writings, was a bare summary of ideas dealt with at much greater length in his book *Opera and Drama*, some of them qualified by later reconsideration. It led up to the conclusion that the ideal opera would have the highly developed improvisatory character of a Shakespearean drama and a Beethoven symphony combined, but it would demand, to be fully effective, actors who would have to be educated to take their task more seriously than now.

The lecture, kept in these general terms, injured no susceptibilities, nor was it intended to, for during this visit Wagner was seeking support, not controversy. While still in Berlin he wrote to Düfflipp, quoting figures to show that the sort of temporary theatre he wished to build in Bayreuth would not prove unduly expensive. The king's present objections, he suggested, were due simply to a fear of possible practical inconveniences to himself, and he assured Düfflipp that he had no intention of seeking financial help from anyone but private persons and would invite no other German sovereign to his festival beside King Ludwig. The king's own productions in Munich could continue as a separate venture, and all he asked was that further stagings should be delayed until he had staged his own festival and set an example.

He held firmly to his intention, he continued, to build his theatre and home in "quiet and charming Bayreuth". All he required from the king was permission to carry out his plan and the granting of a financial loan to tide him over until the first payments from his supporters arrived in the following year, when the money would be repaid. He also asked for Semper's plans for the abandoned theatre in Munich to be placed at his disposal, pledging himself to use only those parts of them that were based on his own ideas.

He read his lecture again to a mixed gathering at the home of the American ambassador, George B. Bancroft. But the social highlight of his visit was his meeting with Bismarck, now, in recognition of his services to Germany, raised to the rank of prince. The meeting took place, at Bismarck's invitation, on Wednesday, 3 May, and Wagner went alone to the ministry. On his return he told Cosima that he was enchanted with Bismarck: "Not a trace of reticence, an easy tone, the most cordial communicativeness, all of it arousing trust and sympathy." However, his doubts of Bismarck's interest in cultural matters persisted. "We can only observe each other, each in his own sphere," he said. "To have anything to do with him, to win him over, to ask him to support my cause, would not occur to me." Bismarck was equally impressed by Wagner. He told Lothar Bucher afterwards that never before had he met a man with such self-assurance.

The heavy round of engagements culminated on 5 May in a concert in the opera house, at which Wagner conducted Beethoven's Fifth Symphony, the *Kaisermarsch* and extracts from *Lohengrin* and *Die Walküre* before Emperor Wilhelm and the assembled court. Count von Schleinitz told Wagner the following day that the emperor had declared he had never heard anything so perfect.

More important, however, than all this social success were the discussions held in Count von Schleinitz's house concerning ways and means of raising money for the Bayreuth venture, and it was here that the plan was devised of offering *Patronatsscheine* (certificates of patronage) at 300 thalers each (900 German marks, the value of the mark at that time being twenty to one pound sterling). Subscribers would be entitled to attend performances at the festival free of charge, and seats would be obtainable in no other way. The task of organising the fundraising was assumed by Marie von Schleinitz and Tausig. He, a Jew of mixed Bohemian and Polish descent, a pupil of Liszt and a protégé of Wagner since his precocious boyhood, had a strong streak of independence, and never became so completely enslaved by Wagner as Bülow or others of the young disciples. However, their friendship was maintained during the Vienna years and, their careers having gone different ways in the meantime, was swiftly renewed in Berlin.

As a result of the discussions with Tausig and Marie von Schleinitz, it was decided to set up a committee, and Cosima paid a visit to Otto Wesendonck, who was in Berlin at the time, to invite him to join. He declined, but that was only a minor setback: the Berlin visit had revealed a large contingent of influential wellwishers.

Dürflipp, in his reply to Wagner's letter, informed him that King Ludwig was prepared to give 25,000 thalers towards their venture, but otherwise wished to have nothing to do with it. This news, which arrived just before they left Berlin on 8 May, was not as good as they had hoped, but at any rate it showed they need no longer fear active opposition from the king. In Leipzig, to which they returned, Wagner felt sufficiently confident to issue on 12 May a public announcement that his festival would take place in the summer of 1873, and for the first time in public he stated where: in Bayreuth. On the day before his announcement he wrote to Dr Karl Landgraf, a Bayreuth physician who had treated him for a slight indisposition on his arrival there, telling him that in due course he would approach the town authorities, "on whose willingness I believe that I can reckon, when one considers what prestige and significance I shall be bringing to Bayreuth".

On the return journey Wagner and Cosima stopped at Darmstadt to visit Karl Brandt. Though engaged as technical director at Darmstadt, one of the lesser court theatres in Germany, Brandt was Germany's leading stage machinist, and Wagner was eager to secure his services, not only to design and construct the machinery for his production of the *Ring*, but to help from the beginning in the construction of his festival theatre stage.* He had made sure that Semper's plans were in Brandt's hands by the time he himself arrived in Darmstadt, and Brandt, having studied these, had no hesitation in accepting Wagner's invitation.

One of Wagner's first acts after returning to Tribschen on 16 May was to write a reassuring letter to the king. This letter is not included in the published correspondence, and the knowledge that it was written and sent off on 20 May we owe to Cosima's diary. Exactly what he wrote to Ludwig is unknown, but the king's reply, written from the Hochkopf on 26 May, shows that it was effective: "I was able to see from it that you are still building your hopes steadfastly on me, as before (and how right you are to do so!)." Ludwig confessed to having been hurt by Wagner's suggestion in his last letter to Düfflipp that an estrangement had arisen between them. "Such a thing is absolutely impossible, as impossible as if you, dear friend, were to abandon your ideals and start paying homage to Offenbach's pseudo-muse. . . . Your plan for producing your *Nibelungen* in Bayreuth is divine." Ludwig's initial reaction to the Bayreuth plan, as expressed to Düfflipp on 19 April, had been in sharp contrast: "I dislike this plan very much." But it is perhaps too facile to regard his words to Wagner as complete hypocrisy. Ludwig was hurt by Wagner's decision to take things out of his hands, but, since his own efforts on Wagner's behalf had brought him little but suffering, he might on reflection have felt some relief at having the burden lifted from him, especially since his main desire – to witness a performance of the complete *Ring* – was not endangered. On the contrary, the prospect was enhanced: Wagner would now at last complete the *Ring*, and, if his own

---

* Karl Brandt had supervised the enlargement of the stage in the Munich opera house that preceded the production of *Das Rheingold* in 1869, and it was presumably this fact that misled Glasenapp and after him all leading Wagner biographers, including Newman, into stating that it was he who prepared the machinery for that production and for the production of *Die Walküre* in 1870. Wagner had indeed suggested he should do so, but Perfall ignored his request (see Wagner's letter of 3 September 1869 to Düfflipp in vol. 5 of *König Ludwig und Richard Wagner: Briefwechsel*) and gave the task to Karl Brandt's younger brother, Friedrich Carl Brandt, who had been machinist at the Munich court theatre since 1865.

festival failed to materialise, the work would at any rate be there for Munich to produce.

By now Ludwig had learnt to distinguish between Wagner's works and Wagner the man; he no longer yearned for Wagner's presence, and, when Wagner requested an audience in Munich on his way back to Tribschen in May, he found reasons not to receive him. He was already preoccupied with his castles, of which Linderhof was now habitable, and work had begun on Neuschwanstein. For recreation he had started this year to attend play rehearsals in his court theatre in Munich, where, with the removal of the Wagner "clique", he was in no danger of having his desires thwarted. But most of his time was spent in the mountains with only his equerry, Richard Hornig, for company. Hornig had become his most intimate companion since Paul von Taxis forfeited his court position and princely title in 1868 by marrying an actress.

Wagner's birthday was celebrated in the usual picturesque fashion that year, the girls dressed up as characters from his works and Cosima herself appearing as Sieglinde with Siegfried in her arms, a sight that deeply moved Wagner. Nietzsche was present, and he told them that he was now busy preparing a periodical which would start publication in two years' time under Wagner's auspices.

Wagner did not immediately resume work on *Götterdämmerung*, but occupied himself going through his early essays and stories for an edition of his collected writings. He told Cosima that he did not intend to include *Judaism in Music* among them – but he subsequently changed his mind about that.

A series of letters from Marie von Schleinitz and Tausig brought news of the fund-raising committee, most of it hopeful. More disturbing, from a personal point of view, was Marie's notification that Liszt was to join the committee and wished Cosima to write to him and arrange a meeting in a neutral place. She was unwilling to comply, firstly, because she still felt hostile towards her father, and secondly, because she felt that a reconciliation between them might offend Bülow. If there was to be a reconciliation, she felt her father should take the first step, and she resisted his appeals for a letter, conveyed once again by Marie von Schleinitz and then by Tausig. But finally she yielded to a plea from Marie Muchanoff, who told her that Liszt's dignity did not allow him to make the first move. On 21 June she wrote to him, "not emotionally . . . but simply and soberly". The letter has not been preserved, and in fact it never reached its destination. Marie Muchanoff, to whom Cosima had sent it with instructions to pass it on, returned it a week later unread, since in the meantime Liszt had changed his mind, deciding it was still too early for the breach to be publicly healed. That Liszt inwardly wished for a reconciliation is clear from the persistence with which he asked his friends to arrange it.

Wagner's thoughts now began to return to *Götterdämmerung*. On 11 June he played to Cosima the beginning of the scene between Alberich and Hagen with which the second act begins, and on 20 June Cosima noted that he was girding himself for composition: "His first act both pleases and dismays him: 'Shall I continue like this?' The scene between Waltraute and Brünnhilde he finds 'utterly incomprehensible', so completely did he forget it. He says: 'I should be uneasy if I did not know that everything I do passes through a very narrow door; I write nothing which is not entirely clear to me.'"

Such remarks, numerous in Cosima's diaries, are immensely useful for the light they throw on Wagner's composing methods, a subject which has not hitherto received the attention it deserves, mainly because such evidence as exists has not been easily available. The publication within recent years, both of Cosima's diaries and of Curt von Westernhagen's book *The Forging of the "Ring"*, which is based on a close study of the existing material from the earliest jottings of isolated themes through the various stages of composition of the *Ring* up to the final score, has done much to fill the gap. It is, however, important to bear in mind that Wagner's remarks to Cosima while actually engaged on his composition are not considered explanations, but impulsive outbursts occurring usually at times when he came up against a problem. But behind the mostly humorous, self-deprecating tone there is very likely more than a grain of truth. "I am now sketching out a big aria for Hagen, but only for the orchestra," he told her on 23 June. "It is incredible what a bungler I am — I can't transcribe at all. With me, composing is a curious affair; while thinking it up, I have it all in my mind, endless, but then comes the job of writing it down, and the mere physical actions get in the way. It becomes 'How did it go?' instead of 'How is it?'; not 'How is it to be?' — but 'How was it?' — and then having to search about till one finds it again. Mendelssohn would raise his hands in horror if he ever saw me composing." In the process of "finding it again" Wagner made copious use of the piano, but this, he once explained, was as an aid to memory: "I get no new ideas there."

He began continuous work on the composition sketch of the second act of *Götterdämmerung* on 24 June, and it kept him occupied until 25 October. The orchestral sketch was begun on 5 July, the two processes being as usual worked on simultaneously. The great scene in which Hagen summons the vassals up to the end of their chorus greeting Gunther's arrival with Brünnhilde caused him a great deal of trouble, and the number of alterations in the sketches and rough notes on the back of their pages is unusually high. Hagen's summons was rewritten entirely: the first version, he told Cosima, sounded "too composed". The whole scene, one of the most vivid and seemingly spontaneous in the whole of *Götterdämmerung*'s rich score, was the result of dogged hard work, and it took Wagner a full month to achieve. He told Cosima on 1 September: "The peculiar thing about me as an artist . . . is that I look on each detail as an entirety and never say to myself, 'Since this or that will follow, you must do thus and such, modulate like this or like that.' I think, 'Something will turn up.' Otherwise I should be lost; and yet I know I am unconsciously obeying a plan. The so-called genius of form, on the other hand, reflects, 'This or that follows, so I must do such and such,' and he does it with ease." What turned up was sometimes in advance of its appointed time: on 29 September he told Cosima he had composed the orchestral interlude to follow Siegfried's death in the third act, and he described what we now call "Siegfried's Funeral March" much as it finally emerged; and on 18 October he said he already had the theme for the Rhinemaidens in Act Three.

His work on the second act, though uninterrupted, was not without its setbacks and distractions, sometimes due to ill health. The severest blow occurred on 17 July with Tausig's death in Berlin from typhus, but its effect on his emotions was blunted by his absorption in his work. He was rather ashamed of his reaction and said to Cosima: "I am so churned up inside that even something like Tausig's death goes in one ear and out the other, and that is not good."

During the months he was engaged on composition Wagner left it entirely to the committee in Berlin to sue for subscribers to the certificates of patronage. A new line of approach was initiated by a music dealer in Mannheim, Emil Heckel. He wrote to Wagner shortly after the announcement of the Bayreuth plan, pointing out that among the lovers of his works there were many who would be unable to afford the cost of a certificate of patronage. He asked for permission to set up in Mannheim a Wagner Society, which would collect money from these people and with it purchase certificates on their behalf, the seats for performances thus acquired to be shared out between them. Wagner gave his approval to this idea, which, once put into practice in Mannheim, was swiftly followed by other towns. It provided a welcome addition to the prospective funds, which as yet, as far as individual donors were concerned, had scarcely progressed beyond a number of vague promises.

Nietzsche was a regular visitor to Tribschen during these months, and on 30 July his friend Karl von Gersdorff, now released from the army, paid his first call. Wagner and Cosima accepted him at once into the fold: "He has all the noble and earnest characteristics of the North German," she wrote in her diary. The two nephews Clemens and Fritz Brockhaus also came to stay, and it is evident that these young men, together with Nietzsche's friends Rohde and Gersdorff, represented the idealistic nucleus of the Bayreuth venture. About Nietzsche himself, however, Cosima began to feel some misgivings: "A not quite natural reserve makes his behaviour in many respects most displeasing," she wrote in her diary on 3 August. "It is as if he were trying to resist the overwhelming effect of Wagner's personality."

On 6 August Karl Brandt came to confer on the building of the theatre with Wagner and Wilhelm Neumann, an architect and inspector of royal buildings in Berlin whose wife was a friend of Cosima's. "The conference with the machinist in particular was very productive," Cosima wrote to Nietzsche on 17 August, "and I believe we shall all be wide-eyed when we one day really find ourselves sitting in the artwork of the future." On 21 August Marie von Schleinitz arrived with her husband and Baron August Friedrich von Loën, the director of the court theatre in Weimar, who had volunteered to replace Tausig on the fund-raising committee.

Cosima, who might have been expected to take a more active part in the preparations for Bayreuth, in fact did little beyond writing a few letters on Wagner's behalf, confining her activities, while he was composing, to teaching the children and translating his earlier essays in the *Gazette musicale* from French into German for the collected writings. It was not lack of interest that restrained her, but apprehension that the Bayreuth venture might rob her and her family of their cherished tranquillity and plunge them into an uncertain, perhaps even disastrous future. As a loyal wife, she preferred to suppress her anxieties, even in her diary (which Wagner frequently read). However, her feelings sometimes overcame her discretion, and she noted on 7 October: "I realise with sorrow that in this matter I cannot share R.'s cheerful spirits, I would rather do without even the most important things than be in debt; also, I have no confidence about the earnings R. expects to make . . . but how hard life is, how dismal!"

At last Liszt took it on himself to make the first step towards a reconciliation. He seized the occasion of Cosima's name day to write her a letter of congratulation. Name days, he told her, were a Catholic institution, and it was Catholicism that divided them – a remark that stirred Wagner and Cosima to laughter. She found difficulty in replying to him, destroying her first letter on Wagner's advice, but on the following day she sent off an answer whose contents she did not divulge in her diary. The reconciliation could hardly be described as a complete one, but at least a contact had been re-established.

It was not until 1 November that Wagner made his first approach to the town authorities in Bayreuth, and he addressed his letter to Friedrich

Feustel, a local banker who was chairman of the town's committee of authorised representatives (*Gemeindebevollmächtigte*). Feustel was distantly connected by marriage with Wagner's sister Ottilie, and, before Wagner wrote his letter, she made sure that he would be willing to receive it favourably. In his letter Wagner explained his reasons for selecting Bayreuth as the place in which to build his theatre, and assured Feustel that he was not expecting from the town any financial support for his enterprise. He gave the impression that this was a purely private matter, of concern to the town only in connection with its ability to provide accommodation for two hundred performers and two thousand visitors during the summer. He asked for confirmation that this would be possible.

The response of the town councillors was immediate and enthusiastic, and went much further than Wagner had asked for or expected: they resolved that he should be helped in every way and a site for his theatre placed at his disposal free of charge. Of course they already knew of his intentions, since he had announced them publicly in May, and no doubt they had felt some anxiety over his delay in approaching them officially, for there was no lack of small towns in Germany eager for the privilege of housing the eminent composer and his theatre: Baden-Baden, Bad Reichenhall and Darmstadt were three that indeed offered their services after the announcement was made. Bayreuth, in promptly promising Wagner even more than he requested, was determined to prevent his going elsewhere.

Wagner completed the orchestral sketch of Act Two of *Götterdämmerung* on 19 November, and the time was opportune for a second visit to Bayreuth to meet the mayor and town authorities and decide on the site for the theatre. Nevertheless, he viewed the prospect without eagerness, mainly because Cosima was not this time to accompany him.

His departure from Tribschen on 9 December plunged them both into the deepest gloom: it was, after all, the first time they had been separated for two years. But the main cause of their pain was that they parted in an atmosphere of disharmony. This emerges from one of the few letters written by Wagner to Cosima that have survived, and he wrote it from Zurich on the day of his departure. As Cosima's diary shows, she had been worried about her children's behaviour during the preceding days, their lying and untidiness, and she had punished them with a strictness Wagner found excessive: "Youth and virtue do not mix," he told her. It had led to differences between them which had not been resolved before he left.

"What, my wonderful wife," he wrote to her, "was I to understand from our parting? You seemed utterly cold towards me and to avoid my touch. . . . If everything should not go right on this journey, it would be a punishment for my presumption in always solemnly declaring that I shall make no more journeys, nor do anything else, without you. Now I have had to break my vow for love of you. And how it affects me only God knows, for I am already nothing but worry, and in this worry as foolish as I always am when I torment you. There is only one remedy for this – constant, *prompt* news from you about everything that comes your way: for, heavens, from how many directions can you always be assailed, poor you, who have so much love for me to atone for! Certainly I hope that since the '*Benedix*' [evidently a private word for a pious lecture to the children] there has been better behaviour at home; but your house of afflictions is so capacious! . . .

"Be as blessed as you are loved by me, my wife, my dear, splendid wife! – Kiss all the children for me, all who – wept for me! Be kind and also optimistic about the things that cause you the blackest worry: one saved, all saved: 'who can love? ?' That is the question. And my hope at any rate is sure – *everyone* loves *you*! . . . Take comfort, be confident, and then you too will no longer look on leniency as weakness. . . . Farewell, and a thousand heartfelt kisses from your Richard."

From another letter to Cosima that has survived a further reason for his solitary journey emerges: he wished Franz Lenbach to paint a portrait of him as a birthday surprise for her, and the date of his departure had been to some extent dependent on Lenbach's availability. Owing to the atmosphere of disharmony in which they had parted, he thought it wise to abandon the secrecy, in order to prevent her coming to wrong conclusions about the reason for his lengthy stay in Munich. In his letters of 10 and 11 December he wrote amusing accounts of his sittings in Lenbach's studio, where he posed simultaneously for three artists – Lenbach, the Swiss painter Arnold Böcklin and the German sculptor Lorenz Gedon: "These three, after assuring me all together that they were the three leading artists of our time, continually crying out and vowing that with my portrait they would be producing their best work. Lenbach continually: 'Excellent!' . . . Eternal raptures over my patience and quiet posture. . . . All three wildly smeared and sticky."

During his visit Wagner had a meeting with Düfflipp. "God forgive me, but I must regard this curious being as my friend," he wrote to Cosima on 10 December. "He was very moved, in fact quite beside himself, to see me. . . . I explained everything to him in great detail and discovered a very definite willingness to support my wishes, indeed, I received a promise of putting them into effect. . . . I feel thoroughly encouraged."

Purely by chance Feustel was in Munich at the same time as Wagner, and they were able to travel together to Bayreuth, where they arrived on 14 December. This gave Wagner an excellent opportunity of getting to know the Bayreuth banker, eleven years younger than himself, who was to become a firm personal friend as well as the leading figure in the organisation and administration of his festival. He was taken to meet the mayor, Theodor Muncker, and the district president of Upper Franconia, Baron Ernst von Lerchenfeld, who had his residence in Bayreuth. Both expressed their lively interest in the festival undertaking.

Wagner wrote to Cosima on 15 December: "I shall have a lot to tell you about the people: Feustel is a child of nature of great and cheerful energy, the mayor enthusiastic. . . . A curious element for you! But we shall get used to it, for ultimately *we* shall become everything here. . . . I am now the complete Hans Sachs – soon I shall be fetched and taken to the meadow."

The "meadow" in this case was the site the town authorities had selected for the festival theatre, Wagner's own first choice close to the palace gardens having proved technically impracticable. The new one was on the Stuckberg, a hill in the district of St Georgen, and, a few hours after Wagner, in the company of Neumann and Brandt, had seen and approved it, the town council met and resolved unanimously "amid acclamation" to buy both the site and the land necessary to construct an approach road, and to place them freely at Wagner's disposal. Feustel undertook privately to attend to the purchase of the site Wagner and Cosima had chosen for their house, this to be paid for by Wagner himself.

He left Bayreuth the following morning for Mannheim, where, in gratitude for Heckel's initiative in starting the Wagner Societies, he had agreed to conduct a concert (including Beethoven's Seventh Symphony) in aid of the funds for Bayreuth. It had been arranged that Cosima should join him there, together, Wagner hoped, with Daniela. As a punishment for telling lies Cosima decided that she should remain at home and, at the risk of prolonging the discord which her strictness with the children had caused between them, Wagner pleaded earnestly on her behalf in one of his letters from Munich: "Look for a moment beyond the circle of imaginings which cause you so much worry – there is another side to it." However, when she met him on 17 December on the railway platform at Mannheim – "standing there like a saga", he told her, "so earnest and long" – she was alone. For the friends assembled in Mannheim for the occasion, who included Nietzsche, Pohl, Wagner's niece Franziska and Alexander Ritter, her husband, he conducted the *Siegfried Idyll* at a rehearsal in the morning. "Great sorrow on my part to see it performed in front of so many strangers," Cosima wrote in her diary.

Wagner's birthday gift to Cosima that year was Lenbach's portrait of himself. She wrote in her diary on 3 January 1872 that she was coming increasingly to like it, "although I know that R. can also look quite different, as, for example, when I saw him on the railway station in Mannheim, beaming, transfigured, and with such a sweet expression on his face that his features looked small and delicate; here everything is sharp and energetic, unyielding." She recorded his own comment, after she had come on him contemplating his son with tears in his eyes: "You and the family are my sunshine. Now I understand Lenbach's portrait – a person who is as happy as I am dares to face life, and he accepts the world's challenge; he neither makes melancholy eyes nor lets his head hang; the only trouble is that I do not want to die."

On 4 January he began work on the composition sketch of the third act of *Götterdämmerung*. But only four days later he was interrupted. Feustel and the mayor of Bayreuth came in person to tell him that one of the owners of the Stuckberg site refused to sell, and consequently they had sought and found another site for the theatre. In spite of their assurances that it was in every way a better one, Wagner angrily refused to listen to their explanations and threatened to abandon the whole venture. Muncker and Feustel retired in confusion to their hotel in Lucerne and finally decided to make another attempt. They returned to Tribschen, taking the precaution this time of approaching Cosima first. It was she who persuaded Wagner to listen calmly to what they had to say, and in the end he grudgingly accepted their offer of a new site.

His desire to see it, coupled with disquieting reports about the efforts of the fund-raising committee and uncertainties concerning the activities in Berlin of the "Wagneriana", a society set up by a financier, Bernhard Löser, with the aim of establishing a Wagner festival there with its own orchestra, convinced Wagner that he must make a journey to Berlin and Bayreuth at once, in order to disentangle the muddles. He left Tribschen on 24 January, after telling Cosima: "I complained of having to compose, now things see to it that I can't continue. But this doesn't touch the vital nerve – that is safe; you are the driving force and embryo for everything, and I have you."

His talks with Loën could not satisfy him that the financing of his enterprise was in safe hands, and as for the grandiose plans in Berlin, these turned out, after a discussion with Löser, to be nothing more than what he called "the usual Jewish fog". It was Feustel who came to rescue him from his exasperation, justifying with his third surprise appearance Wagner's feeling that they had been brought together by Fate. He had come to Berlin to confer with Neumann on the building of the theatre and, hearing that Wagner was also there, visited him in his hotel. His proposal, after hearing Wagner's account of his difficulties, was to set up in Bayreuth a management committee under himself and Muncker, and to entrust to it the entire task of managing the finances, supervising the erection of the theatre and organising the festival. "Now everything is settled," Wagner wrote to Cosima on the following day. "Nothing will be changed, but now everything will follow a somewhat staider course. Feustel is divine."

He arrived in Bayreuth on 31 January, inspected and approved the new site for the theatre, set up the management committee, and on 5 February returned home. From then until 10 April he worked relatively undisturbed on the composition sketch of the third act of *Götterdämmerung*, and from 9 February on the orchestral sketch as well. "I have cut several things, for example, '*Glücklich in Leid und Lust*', etc.," he told Cosima on 4 April. "I shall retain it in the reading text, but what is this maxim doing in the drama? One knows it anyway, having just gone through it all. It would seem childish if she were yet again to turn to the people to proclaim her wisdom." He finished his pencilled composition sketch on 9 April, but the date he wrote on it was 10 April, and he set above it the words: "Thus accomplished and concluded on the day on which seven years ago my Loldchen [Isolde] was born."

The third act, though completed in a comparatively short time by Wagner's standards, had not been altogether easy. His health was poor, and there was a lot to be done in the preparation of the ceremony accompanying the laying of the theatre's foundation stone, which had been fixed for his birthday on 22 May. He had decided, at Cosima's request, to conduct a performance of Beethoven's Ninth Symphony in the Markgräfliches Opernhaus, and this entailed much correspondence in assembling an orchestra, chorus and soloists, all of whom were expected to give their services free. The replies proved either too enthusiastic (the mayor of Schweinfurt, for instance, volunteered to play a drum) or too grudging (only 38 chorus singers from Berlin instead of the requested 200), arousing a mood of exasperation. A final flurry of alarm came at the end of March, when a letter from Düfflipp informed Wagner that the king was worried that the cost of the Bayreuth theatre would much exceed the estimates. Düfflipp also observed that the building of his home in Bayreuth was again causing mutterings in Munich about Wagner's extravagance. And finally Düfflipp conveyed a message from the king, reminding him that *Siegfried* was Ludwig's by right of purchase: he demanded immediate delivery of the complete score.

It was on Cosima's advice that Wagner replied to Düfflipp telling him to cancel the purchase of the site for his house (which was to be paid for out of the 25,000 thalers promised by the king as his sole contribution towards the Bayreuth undertaking), and persisting in the untruth that the score of *Siegfried* was not yet finished. He also wrote to Feustel, telling him that, if there were any doubts in Bayreuth about the feasibility of his enterprise, he would prefer to abandon it entirely. Feustel hastened to assure him that, as far as the town was concerned, there were no misgivings, and Düfflipp wrote too, chiding him for making such a fuss. Everything, he said, would remain as it was before.

The day before Wagner left for Bayreuth on 22 April, a young Russian musician arrived at Tribschen. A few weeks previously Josef Rubinstein had written to him from his home in Kharkov declaring that, after reading *Judaism in Music*, he had come to the conclusion that the only alternatives open to him were to commit suicide or to seek deliverance from his "Jewish deficiencies" by serving the man who had so revealingly shown them to him. Wagner had sent him a sympathetic reply, as a result of which Rubinstein hurried to Tribschen, together with a medical attendant who, "concealed in the boathouse without the young man's knowledge", as Cosima noted, begged that he should be treated with great consideration. This apparent evidence of mental instability did not deter Wagner from inviting the young musician to join him later in Bayreuth.

To Cosima fell the task of packing up the household belongings after Wagner's departure. Nietzsche joined her at Tribschen on 25 April and stayed two days, helping her pack, and in the evening playing the piano to her. "Tribschen has now ceased to be," he wrote to Gersdorff on 1 May. "We went around as if in a pile of ruins, sadness everywhere, in the air, in the clouds, the dog would not eat, the family servants, whenever one spoke to them, in constant sobs. We packed the manuscripts, letters and books – oh, how disconsolate it all was! These three years I spent close to Tribschen, which I visited 23 times – what they mean to me! What should I have been without them?"

Cosima wrote to Marie von Schleinitz during the final days: "Ultimately it is not a good thing to set everything on a single card, to live only in one's heart, since the outside world, which contributes nothing, comes along and takes. Forgive my melancholy, dearest; when I fled here, I believed I should never need to do more than live for Wagner and the children, and that in the strictest seclusion. The change – not of the task, but of the outward circumstances in which it is to be carried out – affects me more deeply than I had imagined, and my words are in consequence as melancholy as my feelings. Be kind and understanding, and let us say no more about it, everything must come to pass as it is ordained."

It was a parting, not only with a beloved house, but with the faithful Vreneli and her husband Jakob, who chose to remain in Switzerland.

With the five children, the nursemaid Käthchen, her personal maid
Anna and Wagner's Newfoundland dog Russ, she left Tribschen on 29
April, and on the following day they arrived at the Hotel Fantaisie in
Donndorf, near Bayreuth, where Wagner had taken rooms until the end
of summer.

The Bayreuth Beginnings

THE SITE CHOSEN by the town authorities for the festival theatre, the "green hill" on which it still stands today, lay just outside the town boundaries on the road leading past a guest house, the Bürgerreuth, to the Hohe Warte, the highest hill on the north side of Bayreuth. Visible for miles around, the site really called for a monumental building such as Semper had designed for Munich, but Wagner had no desire to squander his limited resources on the theatre's exterior. What he was now about to put up, he wrote to Feustel on 17 April, before his departure from Tribschen, was a temporary structure that could serve as a model for a more massive permanent theatre later. "I should even approve a completely wooden structure, however much this might vex our dear citizens of Bayreuth. . . . For the auditorium I require nothing more, if needs be, than one of those erections which are nowadays so frequently used for musical festivals, etc.; I shall even accept a rafter framework, for the sole aim is to illustrate the idea. On the other hand, the heavy and important technical apparatus must be completely *solid*, since it, together with the foundation works, will – God willing – long outlive our flimsy temporary building."

The large stage was designed to occupy a full half of the building and to have ample room above and below to allow for elaborate scene changes both between and during the acts. This part of the theatre's design was Brandt's province. Wagner concerned himself more with the area front of stage and ways of constructing an auditorium that would create the conditions necessary for complete concentration on the drama, undistracted by the "realities" of the technical apparatus involved. To help in creating that "visionary state" in which the scene before the onlooker's eyes would "appear to be an utterly true reflection of life itself" (to borrow Wagner's own words from his article "The Festival Theatre in Bayreuth"), he drew on his own experiences, two of the most significant of which belonged to his early life. In Riga, where he had worked as conductor from 1837 to 1839, he had been impressed by the steep rake of the auditorium and the near invisibility of the orchestra; in Paris, two years later, he had been struck, while listening to a Beethoven symphony from the other side of a partition separating him from the concert hall, by the "compact and ethereal sort of unity" of the sound when freed of all mechanical side-effects. These were the origins of the amphitheatrical auditorium and the invisible orchestra, two of Wagner's reformative ideas which had been translated into practical terms by Semper, and which Wagner was now about to realise in Bayreuth with the help of another architect, Otto Brückwald of Leipzig, he having been brought in on Brandt's recommendation when Neumann proved inadequate for the task.

For the first months after they moved to Bayreuth from Tribschen Wagner and his family lived in the modest Hotel Fantaisie adjoining the summer palace of that name in Donndorf, a village a few miles to the west of the town. After her arrival with the children on 30 April Cosima scarcely had time to acquaint herself with the magnificent and romantic palace grounds, of which the owner, Duke Alexander of Württemberg, gave them the freedom, before Wagner took her off on 6 May to Vienna.

Their visit there was designed to raise interest in the Bayreuth venture. His most active supporter in Vienna was Countess Marie Dönhoff, wife of the first secretary in the German Embassy, Count Karl Dönhoff. Aged twenty-four, this petite and charming lady was the daughter of that Italian Princess di Camporeale who had so impressed Wagner in Paris in 1861 when she sang Isolde's "Liebestod" to him. From Marie Dönhoff and from the head of the Wagner Society in Vienna, Theodor Kafka, they learned that in general the attitude of the Viennese aristocracy towards Bayreuth was one of complete passivity. However, its members expressed their pleasure at seeing him again in Vienna by showering him with laurel wreaths after the concert he conducted on 12 May, the programme having consisted of Beethoven's "Eroica" Symphony and extracts from *Tannhäuser*, *Die Walküre* and *Tristan*.

They returned to Bayreuth together with Richter, who was now conductor at the opera house in Pest. With only a week to go before the foundation stone of the theatre was to be laid, there was still some uncertainty about who would take part in the performance of the Ninth Symphony in the Markgräfliches Opernhaus, the main feature of the ceremony. But already the supporters were beginning to arrive. First, Nietzsche came with Gersdorff, then Alexander and Franziska Ritter, Heckel, Cornelius, Porges, Marie Schleinitz, Marie Dönhoff, Malwida von Meysenbug, Rohde, Joseph Standhartner (his doctor friend from Vienna) and many others.

Liszt, however, still held aloof. Wagner wrote to him on 18 May: "My dear great friend, Cosima maintains that you would not come – even if I were to invite you. That we should have to bear – as we have had to bear so many things! But to send you an invitation is something I cannot omit. And what am I calling to you when I say 'come'? You entered my life as the greatest man I have ever been permitted to address as an intimate friend. You separated from me – perhaps because I had not grown as close to you as you to me. In your place there came to me your inner self reborn – and satisfied my longing to feel myself close to you. And so you live in all your beauty beside and within me – and we are united beyond the grave! You were the first being to ennoble me through your love. Now I am wedded to Her in a second higher life – and able to do what I could never have done alone. And so what a tremendous advantage I have over you! When I now say to you, 'Come', I am saying come back to yourself – for it is yourself you will find here. My blessings and love, however you decide. Your old friend Richard."

Before receiving this letter Liszt, who was in Weimar, had decided to send Adelheid von Schorn, Princess Wittgenstein's confidential friend, to Bayreuth as his representative. He gave her a letter addressed to Cosima, in which he declared that, if he could not be there himself, he could at least ensure that those closest to him were.

Rehearsals of the symphony began on 20 May and demanded much hard work, for both orchestra and chorus had been assembled from all parts of Germany (the leader was August Wilhelmj, already at the age of twenty-seven famous as a solo violinist), and neither they nor the four soloists – Marie Lehmann, Johanna Jachmann-Wagner, Albert Niemann and Franz Betz – were familiar with Wagner's ideas on Beethoven's Ninth. Johanna Jachmann-Wagner, the adopted daughter of Wagner's brother Albert, and his first Elisabeth in *Tannhäuser*, did not even know her part, and Richter had to be delegated to give her some intensive coaching. As always, Richter was ready to do anything that was asked of him. "On account of non-arrival of the Berlin trumpeter," he wrote in his diary, "I took over the second trumpet in the symphony, also the triangle in the *Kaisermarsch*; in the last movement of the Ninth I beat the big drum."

The final rehearsal was on the evening of 21 May. Cosima wrote that, driving home after it, "we see columns of people making a pilgrimage to the Fantaisie; singers of both sexes in open farm waggons, since there is nothing else to be had. The choral society sings a serenade to R. We go down to join the people, which pleases them greatly, and, although he is hoarse, R. speaks a few words to them in his uniquely affecting way. In our apartments upstairs many friends, and we part in a general mood of joyous uplift."

On the following day the weather did its best to dampen the rejoicing, for it rained solidly all morning. In spite of it, hundreds of people tramped up the green hill to see Wagner lay the foundation stone of his theatre, beneath which he placed a metal casket containing some documents, coins, a telegram from King Ludwig which arrived that morning, and a dedicatory verse of his own. The king's telegram read: "From the deepest depths of my soul I send you, dearest friend, my warmest and sincerest congratulations on this day that means so much for all Germany. Greetings and blessings for next year's great undertaking! Today I am more than ever united with you in spirit." Wagner's quatrain might be freely translated thus:

> Here for centuries shall lie
> The secret I have therein sealed:
> As long as stone shall hold it dry,
> It to the world will be revealed.*

While a military band played the *Huldigungsmarsch*, Wagner took the hammer and tapped the stone three times, saying: "Blessings, my stone, stand long and hold firm!" Cosima made no attempt in her diary to describe his actions or appearance at this ceremony, but Adelheid von Schorn related that he was deathly pale and his eyes full of tears, and Nietzsche, in a well known passage in his book, *Richard Wagner in Bayreuth*, written four years later, spoke of his silence and inward-looking gaze as he drove from the building site to the Markgräfliches Opernhaus, to which, on account of the rain, the remainder of the ceremony had been transferred. There Wagner insisted that Cosima and the five children should sit beside him on the stage.

In his speech to his assembled supporters Wagner said: "When we next meet here on this spot, you will be greeted by a building in whose features you will be able at once to read the history of the thought that lies behind it. . . . In the proportions of the interior and in its seating arrangements you will find the expression of an idea which, once grasped, will transform your expectations into something quite different from what you have ever before experienced in visiting a theatre. If this effect is fully achieved, the mysterious entry of the music will now begin to prepare you for the unveiling and display of scenic images which, by appearing to emanate from an idealistic dream world, should demonstrate to you the complete reality of the simulating powers of a noble art." He was not, as had often been claimed, attempting to erect a German national theatre in Bayreuth, for where was the "nation" which as yet felt the need for such a theatre? It was the personal idea of an individual, and it was only in his friends and supporters that he could for

---

* In the original German:
> Hier schliess' ich ein Geheimnis ein,
> da ruh' es viele hundert Jahr':
> so lange es verwahrt der Stein,
> macht es der Welt sich offenbar.

the time being recognise the foundation on which the edifice of their noblest German hopes would be erected. "If it should for the moment be a provisional one, it is that only in the same sense that for centuries all outward forms of the German character have been provisional. But this is the nature of the German spirit – that it builds from within: the eternal God must live firmly inside it before it builds the temple to honour him."

The company, after hearing the "Wach' auf" chorus from *Die Meistersinger*, broke off until five o'clock, when the concert was due to begin. During the afternoon another delegate from Weimar arrived. This was Baroness Olga von Meyendorff, and she came bearing Liszt's reply to Wagner's invitation, which had been delivered after Adelheid von Schorn's departure. "Dear and noble friend," Liszt wrote, "deeply moved by your letter, I cannot find the words to thank you. But I ardently hope that all the shadows and considerations which keep me away will disappear – and we shall soon meet again. Then you too will come to see how inseparable I remain within my soul from you both."

However, these words did not lessen Wagner's annoyance at Liszt's absence, and at the banquet in the Hotel Sonne which followed the concert he treated both ladies from Weimar with considerable discourtesy. Cosima did her best to make amends, but she found Olga von Meyendorff, who was the same age as herself and had been Liszt's close companion for some time (she was of Russian birth, and her deceased husband had been the Russian envoy in Weimar), "very unpleasant", her manner "cold and disapproving". Her dislike was further increased by the baroness's insistence on talking French, which induced an angry mood on Wagner's part and sorrow on hers. Wagner's annoyance can perhaps be understood: to him Liszt's emissaries were spies and interlopers, and they alone cast a shadow over the auspicious day, unless the behaviour of Niemann and Betz in quitting the banquet early because of some imagined slight might be considered another. Used as he was to the tender susceptibilities of singers, Wagner was nevertheless hurt, and that night he dreamed of being obliged to enter a door marked "*Ici on parle français*", then of a quarrel with Betz and Niemann.

However, these were only tiny blemishes on an occasion which filled him with optimism for the future. The money so far received from the sale of certificates of patronage was perhaps modest, but the enthusiasm of the supporters who came to the stone-laying ceremony, and the unanimous decision of the patrons and delegates of the Wagner Societies on the following day to proceed with the building of the theatre, suggested that the target would be reached. There were prospects, too, of money from another source. The German copyright act of 1870 had introduced the principle of royalty payments, and on 24

February 1872 Wagner signed an agreement with a theatre agent in Mainz, Karl Voltz, and his partner, Karl Batz, empowering them to collect royalties on performances of *Rienzi, Der Fliegende Holländer, Tannhäuser, Lohengrin* and *Die Meistersinger*. Cosima remarked on 1 May that Voltz and Batz were conducting themselves splendidly, and had extracted 1,500 thalers already from Leipzig.

Nietzsche's first major work, *The Birth of Tragedy out of the Spirit of Music*, had been published at the beginning of the year, and it made a very great impression on both Wagner and Cosima. "You have now given to the world a work which is unequalled," Wagner wrote to him on 10 January. "Every outside influence that has been brought to bear on you has been rendered practically negligible by the entire character of this work, and, above all, your book is characterised by an assurance so consummate as to betoken the most profound originality. In what other way could my wife and I have realised the most ardent wish of our lives, which was that some day someone might come to us from without and take full possession of our hearts and souls!"

He then went on to express the value he placed in general on Nietzsche's friendship. "You see and perceive everything, so that it has been a hitherto undreamed-of delight to be permitted to see and perceive through your eyes. I have also gained a much better understanding of many things now engrossing your attention in connection with your vocation – for example, with your ideas in regard to pedagogy. . . . Through you I have gained a wide and sweeping perspective, and immeasurable vistas of promising activity open up before me – with you at my side!"

Wagner did his utmost to ensure that copies of the book reached all his friends, influential and otherwise, including King Ludwig. The book also set him thinking of the role Nietzsche might play in Bayreuth. He told Cosima on 3 January that he hoped to start a periodical there, and Nietzsche could edit it. Nietzsche also considered his future to lie with Wagner. He wrote to Gersdorff on 24 January: "Bear in mind that we two are called upon to fight in the front ranks of a cultural movement. . . . On the whole, I have always felt that we were not born into this world to be happy, but simply to perform our duty, and we may consider ourselves thrice blessed if we know and realise just where this duty lies."

He felt that Wagner, in putting the Bayreuth venture into practice, was having to bear too much on his own shoulders. Immediately after writing to Gersdorff, he wrote to Wagner offering his services: "I feel my present existence as a reproach, and I ask you sincerely whether you can make use of me."

Wagner, as previously in the case of a similar appeal from King Ludwig, saw more value in Nietzsche's remaining in his present position than helping him directly, and he did no more than thank him for his offer. The tactical advantage he saw for the larger cause in a distinguished ally in independent academic circles was, however, threatened by Nietzsche's book itself. In its first version it had dealt in general terms with the subject of Greek tragedy, but before publishing it Nietzsche added extensively to it, bringing in Wagner's works and ideas directly, as an expression, he told Rohde, of the tremendous obligation he felt towards Wagner. As a result the book, though making an impression on the public at large (and Wagner's supporters in particular), aroused great resentment among philologists. At the beginning of June one of them, Ulrich von Wilamowitz-Moellendorf, published a pamphlet under the title *Zukunftsphilologie* (*Philology of the Future* – a play on the nickname, "music of the future", applied to Wagner's music by his opponents). In this he attacked the book and accused Nietzsche of being unscientific. Wagner hastened to Nietzsche's defence, and in his "Open Letter to Friedrich Nietzsche", published in the *Augsburger Allgemeine Zeitung* on 12 June, he poked fun at academic philologists, producing their learned treatises that were incomprehensible to any but themselves, and praised Nietzsche for addressing a wider public. Such a man as he was sorely needed, he declared, if German culture were ever to achieve the noblest aims of the reborn nation.

His concern about Nietzsche himself, and the dangers he faced in his academic career through his association with him, were expressed in a letter dated 25 June: "Day after day I have carefully reread the *Birth*, and at each reading I say to myself: 'If only he regains his health and keeps it, and everything goes well with him in other ways! – *But things must not go wrong with him.*' How gladly would one do something to help matters along! This has set me thinking anew how a beginning might best be made, and it is this uncertainty which causes my anxiety. But – hold out a little longer, and sooner or later the right way is sure to be found."

Wagner's present main concern was to complete *Götterdämmerung*, and he resumed work on the orchestral sketch of the third act on 16 June. Cosima returned to her lessons with the children, frequently, since the weather was fine, using the Fantaisie grounds as her schoolroom. Though she was enchanted with the peaceful countryside and was establishing friendly contacts with the people of Bayreuth, her mood was more melancholy than otherwise, for Wagner, as usual when hard at work, suffered from various ailments, and his temper was uncertain. Josef Rubinstein arrived on 13 July and pleased Wagner and Cosima with his piano playing. He was in truth a considerable pianist: he studied in Vienna with Joseph Dachs (a pupil of Czerny) and gave his first concert there in 1865 at the age of eighteen. Four years later Grand Princess Helene of Russia (a devoted and influential supporter of Wagner) appointed him her pianist, and while with her he came into contact with Wagner's later works. He was urged by another friend and supporter, the Russian composer Alexander Serov, to study *Tristan* and *Die Meistersinger*. It was this study that led him to make his first approach to Wagner personally, just before the departure from Tribschen.*

Wagner, when Rubinstein presented himself at the Fantaisie, immediately recognised his musical talent and started educating him in his own works. He also set him to copying out the orchestral sketch of the third act of *Götterdämmerung*, his gift for King Ludwig's birthday in August. Wagner was not satisfied with the orchestral finale of *Götterdämmerung* as he had left it in his composition sketch, and he made several alternative versions. At last, however, on 22 July, the orchestral sketch was completed to his satisfaction, and he wrote beneath it: *"Schluss! Alles Cosel'n zu Gefallen"* ("The end: all to please Cosel").

"I tell him how in earlier times I had considered how I should celebrate the completion of the *Nibelungen*," Cosima wrote in her diary, "but now I could do nothing. 'So it is not enough for you,' says R., 'that you alone gave me the strength to complete it, you alone made it possible for me? There must also be some outward sign – how vain women are!'"

He himself was well satisfied with his work: "I am glad that I kept back Sieglinde's theme of praise for Brünnhilde, to become as it were a hymn to heroes," he told Cosima on 23 July, and on the following morning: "So now after all I have set this whole poem to music from beginning to end; previously I never believed it, not only on account of the impossibility of performing it, but also my inability to remain so persistently in the right mood; but I did remain in it – right up to the last verse I was as moved by it as at the very first word."

The whole of *Götterdämmerung* had still to be orchestrated, however, and he did not begin on it straight away. Indeed, nearly a year was to pass before he found the energy or the opportunity to begin. Instead, he turned to literary work. There were proofs of *My Life* to read, and these inspired him to continue work on the third volume. He dictated to Cosima on 31 July and the following two days, bringing his autobiography to the point at which Minna joined him in Paris in 1861. With these, the final pages of the third volume, he again put the work aside and began an essay, "On Actors and Singers". This was intended

* These biographical details of a somewhat underestimated figure in Wagner's life come from a letter in Rubinstein's own handwriting preserved in the Wagner archives in Bayreuth. The letter, written in Bayreuth in July 1876, was addressed to an unknown correspondent, and the information contained in it was intended for an encyclopedia, the *Schuberth'sches Musik-Lexikon*.

to form part of the ninth volume of his collected writings, and there will be more to say of it later. Six volumes of the collected writings had now appeared, and his publisher, Ernst Fritzsch, wrote that they were selling very well.

Work on the theatre had begun immediately after the laying of the foundation stone, and Wagner was already beginning to think in practical terms of his production. On 30 July he wrote to Joseph Hoffmann, a Viennese artist who had shown interest in working for Bayreuth, inviting him to design the scenery. He toyed with the idea of establishing a permanent orchestra. It could play in Bayreuth in the spring and summer, he wrote to Wilhelmj on 16 July, and in the autumn and winter take on engagements elsewhere. Other theatres wishing to repeat the Bayreuth productions would, he thought, be delighted to have a fully rehearsed orchestra placed at their disposal. "In short, I am hatching out a plan for the establishment of a large German orchestral school, to set beside a school of dramatic singing with equal status."

For the moment, however, his choice of singers and instrumentalists was confined to those he knew and those who voluntarily offered their services. Among the latter were Karl Hill, who had written to him from Schwerin before he left Tribschen, and Franz Diener, a young tenor from Cologne. Diener came to Bayreuth that summer, and Wagner spent much time coaching him. Of the singers he already knew, Betz was firmly fixed in Wagner's mind for the role of Wotan. In spite of his previous bad experiences with the temperamental Niemann, he wanted him for Siegmund, and they went through the role when Niemann visited Bayreuth in August. Other visitors during that month were Marie Lehmann's sister Lilli ("a possible Sieglinde", Cosima wrote to Nietzsche on 22 August) and the conductor Hermann Levi, who earlier in the year had left Karlsruhe to become musical director in Munich. Wagner welcomed the appointment and wrote to him on 29 April: "As far as I am concerned, I am thoroughly happy with the thought that after Bayreuth you will conduct the *Nibelungen* pieces there (for the King of Bavaria must be the first to get these). But – Munich? – Hm, hm!"

That summer Bülow, whose existence had now become the nomadic one of a concert pianist, returned to Munich at the king's invitation to conduct *Der Fliegende Holländer* and *Tristan und Isolde*. Marie Muchanoff, writing from there, told Cosima that Perfall had approached Bülow with a view to bringing about a reconciliation with Wagner. "Our astonishment makes us laugh," Cosima wrote in her diary on 25 August. "Probably he wants with this manoeuvre to keep Hans, whom he hates, at a distance, just as he engaged Levi for the same purpose." The line of thought is perhaps somewhat tortuous, but her reaction indicates how far Wagner and she were from even contemplating the possibility of bringing Bülow back into the fold of active supporters. He, for whom the propagation of Wagner's music was an essential part of his life's work, could now pursue it only at a distance, helping with piano recitals to raise funds for the great venture in which he could play no direct part.

With Liszt there had been no correspondence at all since the stone-laying ceremony, due, Cosima suspected, to Olga von Meyendorff's displeasure over the hostility of her reception in Bayreuth. But Marie Muchanoff continually insisted that Liszt was yearning for his daughter to visit him in Weimar. Cosima still hesitated, and it was Wagner who eventually broke through their barrier of pride by writing to Liszt on 29 August, asking him point blank whether a visit from them would be welcome. Liszt's relieved assent arrived on 1 September, and on the very next day Wagner and Cosima set off for Weimar.

Liszt had now begun what he liked to call his "*vie trifurquée*", dividing up the year between Rome, Weimar and Budapest, in the first of which he tended to spend his time composing, while in Weimar and Budapest he concentrated on teaching. In all three he lived modestly, with only a single manservant to look after him. Yet despite his deliberate abstemiousness, he was still the magnetic figure he had been from his earliest years, and his power over women was still unimpaired. Indeed, he had only recently emerged from a turbulent encounter in Budapest with one of his pupils, the "Cossack countess" Olga Janina. This young lady had come to his apartments in Budapest in November 1871, armed with a revolver and some phials, and she threatened to shoot him and then poison herself. He had to hold her at bay for two hours before rescue came.

This was the man whose "weariness of soul" so upset Cosima when she and Wagner visited him in his little four-roomed apartment in the court gardens at Weimar. "In the evening, when he scarcely spoke and I related all sorts of things, and R., in order to do his bit towards sustaining a cheerful atmosphere, jokingly disputed with Baron Loën about his (R.'s) supposed popularity, I saw the tragedy of my father's life as in a vision – during the night I shed many tears!" However, with the help of Wagner's gaiety and the company of Liszt's friends, a semblance of the old intimacy was restored. On the last day of their three-day visit, Cosima noted, her father again withdrew into his shell, and she put that down to Olga von Meyendorff's jealousy of the affection he had shown for her the previous day. She did not hold that against Olga. "All her little ruses and underhand methods are excusable," she wrote to Marie von Schleinitz, "for they arise from the sufferings of love, and I believe her spirit and her heart are noble, but tormented, hence uneasy and incomplete." Wagner too had been uneasily watching the re-emergence of

Dammallee 7, Bayreuth, water colour by G. Küneth

The Bayreuth festival theatre in 1876

Above: Wahnfried shortly after completion

Below: The *salon* at Wahnfried. The pictures (from left) are
Lenbach's portraits of Wagner and of Cosima; Joukowsky's
"The Holy Family" and portrait of Cosima; Ludwig Geyer's
portrait of Adolf Wagner; and Lenbach's portrait of
Schopenhauer

1876 (the year of the first festival at Bayreuth)

Above left: Marie von Schleinitz

Above right: Richard Fricke

Left: Karl Brandt

Below left: Heinrich Porges

Below right: Hans Richter

Above left and right:
Richard and Cosima
Wagner in London, 1877

Below right: Judith Gautier

Below left: Self-caricature
by Edward Burne-Jones
in a letter to Cosima, 1877

Cosima's former intimacy with her father, and on the train journey home she had to cope with an outburst of jealousy from him.

On 21 September they left the Hotel Fantaisie to take up residence in a rented house in Bayreuth pending completion of their home, on which work had now begun under the supervision of the municipal architect, Carl Wölffel. Dammallee 7 was a large villa in a quiet street at the edge of the old town. Their first visitor there, while they were still in the throes of changing house, was their nephew Fritz Brockhaus, and he was followed on 15 October by Liszt. Since the reunion in Weimar he had come under heavy attack from Princess Wittgenstein in Rome, and his visit was in essence an act of defiance. "I am very upset that my father should be tormented like this," Cosima wrote in her diary on 17 October; "he is so tired and is always being so torn about! Particularly this wretched woman in Rome has never done anything but goad him – but he does not intend to give me and us up. This conversation keeps me long at my father's side, and unfortunately R. is offended by my leaving him alone so long; I do not find it easy to ask his pardon, and a slight shadow of discord persists between us all day."

In spite of his jealousy, Wagner was very proud of his renowned friend and took every opportunity to show him off to the dignitaries of Bayreuth. He took him to a meeting of the *Kränzchen*, a private club of prominent citizens, eight to ten in number, who met every Thursday in each other's houses to discuss political and social issues, and on 18 October gave a party in his home at which Liszt played the piano to a gathering of about twenty Bayreuth citizens. At a more intimate gathering on the following evening Wagner read aloud his draft of *Parzival*, which drew from Liszt the remark that it was his finest conception – "and all this time you are still romping about with singers and actors!"

The remark contained a hint of Liszt's basic attitude towards the Bayreuth venture. Having himself put all activity in concert and theatrical life behind him, he was pained to see Wagner, whose creative talent he recognised as so much greater than his own, waste his time trying to ensure ideal performances of his works, which were quite strong enough to make their way on their own. It was a fundamental difference in their characters: the single-minded striving for perfection which possessed Wagner, both in the creation of his works and in their presentation, and the difficulties and unpleasantnesses he was prepared to face in order to achieve perfection, was something quite foreign to Liszt, who creatively was an impulsive, improvisatory artist, quite content to leave things as they were so long as people were satisfied.

Both Wagner and Cosima tried to persuade him to settle permanently in Bayreuth, but with little confidence of success. "As far as such a thing is possible, we have come to a clear understanding with this wonderful man," Wagner wrote to Nietzsche on 24 October, "and we regret all the more profoundly that we had – and have – very little hope of being able to do anything for this ruined life." By "ruined life" he presumably meant what he saw as Liszt's loss of the will to fight for his ideals and his capitulation to the world's values.

The temptation was nevertheless one he could understand. Though he did not share Liszt's hankering to move in aristocratic circles, he did see in the solid citizenry of Bayreuth the model of a quiet and contented family existence which had its attractions for him. "I have come back to the point from which I started," he told Cosima on 7 June, a few weeks after their arrival in Bayreuth. "My childhood surroundings were like these people and these houses: plain middle class, with, if you will, a limited outlook, and yet vital and with a sound core. I could imagine my uncle Adolf here among us." And on 24 July he observed: "I have been thinking whether I should not become choirmaster here, learn the organ, and play it, in order to be of some use to the people."

Clearly such remarks need not be taken too literally. They were dreams emanating from that side of his nature that craved rest, but they are significant for the indication of the level at which they aimed. The world he idealised was the world of Hans Sachs and the mastersingers, the world of bourgeois respectability; the world he held in contempt was the world of power or, more precisely, the people who currently exercised it: petty princes, the Catholic hierarchy, Jewish financiers and the press. For him the true German spirit resided in such stalwart figures as Feustel and Landgraf, in Lorenz Kraussold, a church councillor who had formerly been a member of the patriotic students' *Burschenschaft* and whose wife received Cosima in her vegetable garden. Most respected of all, by both Wagner and Cosima, was Dean Dittmar, whose lack of musicality (he preferred the *Kaisermarsch* to the Ninth Symphony in the foundation-stone ceremony concert) did not disturb them in view of his wide literary interests and the sincerity of his religious views.

Cosima had at last decided to adopt the Protestant faith. The intention had long been in her mind, but she had held back because of her fears of the effect of such an act on her father, fears which her recent meetings with Liszt had apparently allowed her to set aside. Dean Dittmar prepared her for confirmation and carried out the ceremony on 31 October, during which she received the sacrament together with Wagner. She wrote in her diary: "A deeply moving occasion, my whole soul trembles, our dean speaks from the depths of his heart. R. is profoundly touched. What a lovely thing religion is! What other power could produce such feelings? . . . As we embraced, R. and I, I felt as if our bond had only now been truly sealed, that now we were united in Jesus Christ.'' Two days later she recorded Wagner's views on the ceremony: "How beautiful it was in that little vestry, how powerful the voice of our dean sounded – like the voice of a lion emerging from a cave! What substitute could there be for the feelings aroused in one when the indescribably moving words 'This is my body' are spoken! . . . I could almost say – if I did not shrink from the word in this connection – that it all made an artistic impression, even the little acts of pouring wine, etc.''

There was, as these two reactions suggest, a marked difference between the feelings of Wagner and Cosima on religion. His attitude towards the Christian faith was a detached one: he saw Jesus Christ as a historical figure – in much the same light, in fact, as Ernest Renan, whose *History of the Origins of Christianity* he read with approval as each new volume was published. He revered Christ as a philosopher, yet felt his ideas to be too insubstantial to support the weight of an organised religion. He admired the early Christians and the saints for their fortitude and single-mindedness rather than for their beliefs, whereas the established church repelled him by what he considered its hypocrisy and cynicism. Martin Luther was one of his heroes, not on account of his doctrines, under which he had been brought up, but because Luther was a true German, the founder of the German language and a sturdy opponent of Catholic hypocrisy. Wagner was no churchgoer and no theist – God hardly existed in his vocabulary; his line of thought was metaphysical, and he both read and admired Charles Darwin. In line with Schopenhauer's philosophy he believed in man's power to influence his destiny, and his whole approach was intensely moralistic. Collective human wisdom was embodied for him in myth and legend, and religious doctrine – not only Christian, but Hindu and Buddhist as well – interested him primarily from its legendary aspect. His hesitation in admitting that it was the theatricality of church ceremony that most impressed him resulted probably from his fear of wounding Cosima rather than from any shame about his own feelings. Religion and art were for him truly synonymous terms.

Cosima never abandoned in spirit the devout Catholic faith in which she had been brought up since childhood. Her conversion to Protestantism was a sacrifice she made to Wagner as part of her effort to identify herself wholly with him. It was also a sacrifice to her children: "The Reformation saved the German spirit," she wrote in her diary (2 June 1871), "and I want my children to be true Germans." Only Siegfried had received a Protestant baptism, the four girls being Catholics under the terms of Cosima's marriage to Bülow, and she had to ask him to give his consent to the change. He did so in his letter of 28 November 1871, which he ended with the words: "In the middle of the most infernal

hours of my life I have always extracted a certain comfort from my conviction of the necessity, the providential loftiness of the mission you have
to fulfil, close to the majesty of the greatest genius of our century, a
mission which would have been utterly impossible for you to fulfil
without the inspiring ardour of an earthly passion. Perhaps all the
wrongs against you with which I have to reproach myself, the wrongs
which provoked and facilitated this ardour, have also had something of
the nature of a 'providential mission', leading indirectly to the goal of
your own.''

Bülow's habitually supercilious phraseology always conveys a slight
hint of mockery (it is possibly only self-mockery), but Cosima took it at
its face value and was gratified to find her awareness of the divine
mission entrusted to her confirmed. Yet, in spite of her self-sacrifice and
the devotion with which she followed her new Protestant faith, her
religious feeling remained basically Roman Catholic: her diary shows
her constant preoccupation with prayer, with penance and atonement,
confession and absolution. However carefully she strove to conceal her
inner beliefs from Wagner, he was not deceived, but he regarded them
with tolerant amusement. "Today you are wearing your Catholic
expression," he sometimes said to her.

Hopes and Setbacks

WAGNER'S ESSAY "On Actors and Singers", completed just after their return from Weimar and published immediately as a brochure, was an attempt to clarify in his own mind, before setting off on a tour of the German opera houses, exactly what qualities he was looking for in his search for participants in his festival. In the end he discovered that he could sum them up in a single word: truthfulness, and he dedicated his essay to the memory of the singer who above all others in his experience had embodied this quality: Wilhelmine Schröder-Devrient.

He began with Shakespeare, whose unique greatness as a dramatist he attributed to the fact that he was himself an actor writing for actors: "In him every conscious style – that is to say, every preconceived leaning towards form and expression taken over from others or the result of deliberation – is merged in that one basic law from which the actor's natural gift of imitating what he sees in real life derives its wonderful power to deceive. Shakespeare's ability to bring to life, through the masks of his players, every human individuality perceived by him in the manner most natural to it – this ability also enabled him to recognise and express in apposite behaviour all that lay outside his experience. All his figures bear the stamp of exact truthfulness to nature, with so much clarity that for the task he set nothing seems necessary initially but a complete absence of affectation; but what this demands in fact will be evident to anyone who reflects that our whole modern theatre, and its highflown pathos in particular, is based on affectation."

An actor, Wagner continued, works by providing an example, and to do this he must efface his own personality in the interests of the assumed one. Opera singers in Germany were originally identical with dramatic actors: only when a special *coloratura* technique was required was a singer engaged specially for the role, and this led in time, as vocal demands increased, to specialist singers, seeking and being given applause for their technical prowess and the quality of their voices, rather than for the truthfulness of their acting.

This was a deplorable development: "Now that I am about to set off in search of singers for as correct a production of my dramatic works as I can possibly achieve, it is not any shortage of 'voices' that worries me, but the bad manner, presumably widespread, in which these voices have been trained, resulting in a delivery which totally precludes all healthy speech. Since our singers do not pronounce their words naturally, they are for the most part quite incapable of understanding the sense of what they are saying, and in consequence the nature of the role they are to play comes through to them only in shadowy general outlines, viewed in the light of certain banal operatic conventions. . . . What the German singing actor (for that is what I wish to call him here) needs, apart from encouragement to rediscover his shamefully neglected naturalness, in speaking as in singing, lies exclusively on the *intellectual* level of his education.''

The actor's power to understand his role and reproduce it faithfully must not be reduced by attempts on the author's part to tell him exactly what to do. The markings in his scores, Wagner declared, were intended only to help the singer or musician to "recognise the picture I am holding up for his interpretation", leaving all else to his natural instincts. In dramatic art the author has to be as self-effacing as his actors, since it is only the final spectacle, the result of their combined efforts, that is important.

With these precepts in mind Wagner set off on 10 November with Cosima on his first journey of discovery. It was bound by its very nature to be a long and wearisome process, firstly, because Wagner, having for so many years been out of touch with the theatre in Germany, knew few singers, and secondly, because Germany possessed an enormous number of opera houses – each of its many monarchs and lesser princes taking pride in the possession of a theatre and a company of his own. Since Wagner, for reasons his essay made clear, was not interested in pampered "star" singers, he was as likely to find individuals he could work with in the smallest as in the largest companies – and in consequence must visit them all.

The first of his journeys lasted until 15 December and took him and Cosima successively to Würzburg (where he saw *Don Giovanni*), Frankfurt (Meyerbeer's *Le Prophète*), Darmstadt (Auber's *Le Maçon*), Mannheim (*Der Fliegende Holländer*), Stuttgart (Meyerbeer's *Les Huguenots*), Karlsruhe (*Tannhäuser*), Mainz (*Fidelio*), Cologne (*Die Zauberflöte*), Bonn (Auber's *La Muette de Portici*), Düsseldorf (Handel's oratorio *Solomon*), Hanover (Weber's *Oberon*), Bremen (*Die Meistersinger*) and Dessau (Gluck's *Orfeo*).

In most of these towns the reception was the same: banquets, serenades by the orchestra outside their hotel, audiences with the reigning prince; even in those towns they planned to visit incognito, the news of their presence invariably leaked out. Wagner told Cosima that he felt like hitting out in fury whenever he saw "the usual rows of bottles, the rolls, and the folded napkins laid out for dinner".

Immediately on their return to Bayreuth on 15 December Wagner wrote an article, "A Glance at the German Operatic Stage of Today", which was published in Fritzsch's *Musikalisches Wochenblatt* in the following month. Though amusingly written, it was a sweeping condemnation of the prevailing artistic standards, for which Wagner held the conductors and producers mainly responsible. Just one of the productions he saw earned his unreserved praise, and that was *Orfeo* in Dessau: "I loudly assert that I have never seen a nobler or more complete overall performance in any theatre. . . . Every aspect of scenic life, the grouping, the scene painting, the movements, the rhythmic flow, contributed to that ideal deception which holds us enclosed within a kind of dawning fancy, a prophetic dream beyond the realms of experience. . . . I was certainly not mistaken when I ascribed the outstanding excellence of the entire musical ensemble, chorus and orchestra included, to the effect of this wonderful concern for the scenic background."

It was the choreographer of this production, Richard Fricke, whom Wagner chose to help him with his own production of the *Ring* in 1876. Otherwise, the first journey yielded only one singer of note: Luise Jaïde of Darmstadt, whom he looked on initially as a possible Brünnhilde. On the other hand, Diener, whom he heard in both Cologne and Düsseldorf, disappointed Wagner so severely that he dropped him entirely.

They set out on their second journey on 12 January 1873. The news they had received from Feustel that payments for certificates of patronage were slow in arriving, and in consequence the building work on the theatre was in danger of coming to a halt, caused Wagner to alter his arrangements and this time to undertake a few conducting engagements in order to raise some immediate cash. These, and other social functions designed to make publicity for the Bayreuth enterprise, took precedence over visits to theatres. From Dresden (*Rienzi*) they went to Berlin, where on 17 January Wagner gave a reading of the *Götterdämmerung* text. Marie von Schleinitz, in whose home the reading was held, thought it wise to ask Wagner to remove references to the incestuous love between Siegmund and Sieglinde and Sieglinde's pregnancy from his introductory remarks, for fear of offending prudes. Whether or not as a result of this precaution, a distinguished and select audience, which included Field Marshal Moltke and most of the foreign ambassadors in Berlin, departed well satisfied. From there he and

Cosima went on to Hamburg, where besides seeing a performance of *Die Meistersinger* Wagner conducted two concerts (Beethoven's Fifth Symphony and extracts from his own works).

The ensuing visit to Schwerin brought the main discovery of this second journey. Karl Hill, who, as already mentioned, had signified his interest in Bayreuth some months previously, sang the main role in *Der Fliegende Holländer*, and Wagner at once recognised in him the kind of singer he was looking for.

Back then to Berlin, where Wagner conducted a concert of his own works, with Betz and Niemann as soloists. After the concert, at which Emperor Wilhelm and Empress Augusta were present, Olga von Meyendorff wrote to Liszt: "Your daughter achieved great success everywhere through the charm and particularly the distinction with which she captivated the ladies and the prominent people who did not know her before. . . . I myself also capitulated to the charm she radiates." Cosima was sufficiently her father's daughter to enjoy moving in aristocratic circles; Wagner, though quite able to deport himself correctly in high society, took no pleasure in it; for him the main gratification of the Berlin visit was that the concert raised 16,000 marks towards the Bayreuth funds.

They returned home on 8 February via Dresden, where Wagner wished to hear a rising tenor, Ferdinand Jäger, sing Lohengrin. Since yet another journey was looming in April, he felt no inclination to start on the orchestration of *Götterdämmerung*, but devoted his attention to literary work. He wrote his essay, "On Performing Beethoven's Ninth Symphony", and resumed dictation of *My Life*, which he brought up to his departure from Paris following the *Tannhäuser* production of 1861.

His earnings from his concerts in Hamburg and Berlin, a total of 36,000 marks, were soon swallowed up by the builders, and Feustel was obliged to go in search of a temporary loan to tide them over until the money from the sale of certificates of patronage was paid over. He found nobody prepared to help, and it became clear that the original aim of holding the festival in 1874 could not be realised. Wagner was nevertheless reluctant to announce a postponement, knowing that such an admission would be eagerly seized on by his enemies, and fearing that it would tend to make his patrons even more dilatory in paying for their certificates.

There were other arguments in favour of postponement apart from the financial ones. Wagner had engaged four young musicians, Anton Seidl, Franz Fischer, Emmerich Kastner and Hermann Zumpe, to prepare the individual parts of his score for performance. They started work in October 1872, but in six months had not managed to reach the end of *Die Walküre*, while he for his part still had the whole of *Götter-*

dämmerung to orchestrate. Wagner saw that, if the work were to be finished in reasonable time, the travel would have to stop. The trip to Cologne, where on 24 April Wagner conducted a concert containing the "Eroica" Symphony, marked the end of it (and brought in a further 9,000 marks for the builders). He began work on the final score of *Götterdämmerung* on 2 May.

Cosima was worried by the effect her preoccupation with festival work was having on the education of her children. On account of her frequent absences, she had sent Daniela and Blandine to a local school, and their end-of-term reports were very disappointing. She wrote in her diary on 9 May: "Gloomy weather and gloomy thoughts: the children – the two elder ones – do not conform to my efforts and my wishes, they do not make my difficult task easy, and I have the feeling that, people being so malicious, ugly accusations will be made about my methods of bringing them up, or I shall be reproached with neglect. A great struggle within me – whether I should approach the children's father and ask him to send them to a school, for I am not strict enough, I quite see that. Or is this perhaps just vanity on my part, an attempt to rid myself of a responsibility from which I now feel I can gain little praise? Resolve to continue to do what I can and accept all trials – both present and future – as an atonement!"

That year she planned and carried out a celebration of Wagner's sixtieth birthday which, even by her standards, was unusually lavish. She invited Cornelius in Munich to write linking words for a series of *tableaux* based on pictures by Genelli depicting the vices and virtues. Karl Brandt's son Fritz came to Bayreuth to arrange the lighting of the *tableaux*, performed by local volunteers, whom Cosima rehearsed herself. On the evening of his birthday she persuaded Wagner to go with her to the Markgräfliches Opernhaus where, she pretended, the amateur music society had prepared a little celebration for him. What he in fact found there was an orchestra of players from Bayreuth and Würzburg, conducted by Alexander Ritter, which opened the evening with his Concert Overture of 1831 (a work he did not immediately recognise). This was followed by *Der bethlehemische Kindermord* (*The Massacre of the Innocents*), a play by his stepfather Ludwig Geyer which Cosima had persuaded a professional company of actors then appearing in Bayreuth to perform. The final item was Cornelius's piece, *Künstlerweihe* (*An Artist's Consecration*), the *tableaux* being displayed against the music of Wagner's New Year Cantata of 1835. "Wagner was greatly moved and surprised," Cornelius wrote afterwards to his sister, "and Cosima celebrated a great triumph."

At a party in the Dammallee the following evening Wagner played the *Siegfried Idyll* to their guests, and afterwards he said jokingly to Cosima: "I suppose it would have pleased you better if things had not progressed beyond my first poem to you, if there had never been an idyll – you would certainly have found it more interesting!" Her comment in her diary on that was: "What I want and what I should have wished for I do not know – but certainly that he should be happy, calm, and contented, and that I should no longer be conscious of my miserable ego in any shape or form."

The intensity of their emotional relationship sometimes disconcerted their friends. Dean Dittmar teased Wagner about his reluctance to go anywhere without Cosima, and the mayor was horrified when he heard of their intention to build their tomb in the garden of their new house. Wagner, Cosima recorded, admitted to him that people really should conform with communal practices, "for what remains of us we have in common with everybody – but it is nice to imagine ourselves remaining united here below as well, in our earthly guise." He also mentioned the grave in his letter of 2 June to King Ludwig: "We find an indescribable pleasure in knowing its exact position and daily tending the place which will receive us for our eternal rest, in the soil that we owe to the magnanimity of your love, and which one day will be passed on to my son as his permanent home."

His letter, ostensibly thanking Ludwig for his good wishes on his birthday, was designed to prepare the king for the call for financial aid he felt to be unavoidable. Hoping to arouse in Ludwig a more positive interest in the festival, he described the preparations in their most flattering light: "Already Bayreuth is ceasing to be the quiet and remote place it was: almost daily the hotels are alive with visitors, drawn here by curiosity. And already the name 'Bayreuth' is frequently heard resounding overseas, where societies have been formed to promote the work being prepared here. Artists are also turning up; the best singers come to me for an audition; excellent instrumentalists come periodically to be instructed by me during my leisure hours in the performance of German masterpieces. I have every reason to wish to live to an exceptionally ripe old age, for it is only now that I shall be in a position to exert an enduring influence on the future of German art, so long held back by the wretched artistic conditions in Germany. All of this – and particularly if I reach the old age which now seems to me so desirable – is *your* work, my great and noble and splendid friend, my gracious benefactor and protector. To proclaim this to the world for all time – that is my heart's inextinguishable desire!" A few days later Ludwig received a magnificently bound copy of the printed orchestral score of *Das Rheingold*, which had just been published by Schott, the title page bearing the simple inscription: "Conceived in trust in the German spirit and completed by

Richard Wagner to the glory of his noble benefactor, King Ludwig II of Bavaria."

Ludwig, replying to him on 21 June from the Kremelsberg, one of his mountain retreats where he was "torn free of the sober, oppressive world of daily routine with its prosaic political cares", was highly pleased with Wagner's letter and with the dedication, "which fills me with joyful pride and an inexpressible feeling of happiness, as does the form you gave to it." His professions of love and undying loyalty might by now have lost some of their force by constant repetition, but this time they sounded sufficiently sincere for Wagner to approach him again a few weeks later with a more realistic assessment of the financial position of the festival and a direct request for help. Though it contained no downright falsehoods – Wagner Societies had by now been set up in London and in New York, and singers and instrumentalists were indeed coming to Bayreuth for auditions, if not quite in the numbers suggested – his previous letter certainly erred on the side of optimism.

The letter of 11 August was more sober in tone: "The princes turn out either to be firm in their refusals, or their aid is abnormally frugal. The more affluent nobility has forgotten its German soul and squanders its money on either Jewish or Jesuitical undertakings. Our stock exchange millionaires want to have nothing to do with me, unless I would be prepared to transfer my undertaking to Berlin or Vienna, in which case sums up to one million could be placed at my disposal." The only people who were achieving anything, he said, were Frau von Schleinitz in Berlin and Countess Dönhoff in Vienna, who alone kept things moving, and the fact that they had to call on the Sultan of Turkey and the Khedive of Egypt to achieve even this much struck him as curious. He paid tribute to the sterling support of Muncker and Feustel in Bayreuth, but even they had not been able to prevent building delays owing to lack of funds, and, if he himself had not earned money by his conducting, there would be no prospect of completing the outer shell of the theatre by the coming autumn, the target date. Since, when that was done, Brandt would require some time to design, install and test his stage machinery, there was nothing for it but to postpone the performances for a year. The earliest possible date for the festival would in consequence be the summer of 1875, and even that could be achieved only by raising a loan pending the payment of the certificates of patronage. To do this it would be necessary to provide a formal guarantee, which would in fact be of merely moral significance, and Wagner asked the king to send Düfflipp to Bayreuth to look into the accounts and satisfy himself that the enterprise was sound. The purpose of this invitation was plain: that Ludwig himself should provide the guarantee.

Despite these worries his mood remained buoyant. The sculptor

Gustav Adolph Kietz, a brother of Ernst, Wagner's friend in Paris in the early days and himself an acquaintance during the Dresden years, was in Bayreuth that summer to make a bust of him. During the sittings, Kietz told his wife in a letter, "Wagner was very lively, singing snatches from symphonies, quartets and operas. It also happens quite frequently, just as I am working silently and busily and then glance at him to observe some feature more precisely, that I find myself confronted to my dismay with some terrible grimace, the mouth stretched wide with both fingers, the eyes turned up – a real Leipzig street urchin's face! When on one such occasion Frau Cosima came in and exclaimed in shocked tones, 'Richard, really – !', he replied: 'Well, what of it? They are just reminders for Kietz: he comes from Leipzig too'!"

The roof-raising of the festival theatre on 2 August was a modest and purely local ceremony, though Liszt attended it as a member of the family. Dean Dittmar and Wagner read poems written for the occasion, and a local band played the march from *Tannhäuser*. Cosima wrote to Marie von Schleinitz: "From the high scaffolding, on which I stood with my father and the children, the world's reality looked like a dream, and the artist's dream assumed reality. . . . When we sang 'Now thank we all our God', I had the feeling that no victory could have caused me to sing it so from my heart as this taking of the first position – too soon yet to be called a victory. When the glass, hurled through the air in a bold arc, reached the ground intact, I felt it as a sign that our work would be immortal – in fact, all the signs were good."

Liszt stayed nine days, using the occasion to become better acquainted with his grandchildren. He went on outings with them, described Siegfried as "a remarkable boy", and while still there wrote to Bülow: "Loulou and her sisters are progressing splendidly. Impossible to have better manners and better behaviour than they have. An observant person said to me, 'They are not ordinary children,' and I agree entirely." Bülow, he told Cosima, now had brilliant prospects in England, where he had given some piano recitals.

On 17 August, twelve days after Liszt's departure, Malwida von Meysenbug came to live in a house only a few steps away from the Dammallee. It was Wagner's suggestion that, when they moved into their new house, she should come and live with them. "We have great plans for her," Cosima wrote to Nietzsche, "setting up educational establishments, kindergartens, etc." For Liszt, too, a room was to be set aside for his exclusive use.

Malwida, arriving from Munich, brought tales, which disturbed them greatly, of the growing eccentricity of King Ludwig's behaviour. Recently, she told them, he had ordered a dinner for twelve persons, then sat down alone at the table after bowing to the empty seats; he never went out of his palaces through the doors, but only through the windows.

The king had made no response to Wagner's letter of 11 August, and when, on 19 August, Feustel announced that work on the theatre must be suspended unless 10,000 florins could be found by October, Wagner in alarm arranged for him to visit Düfflipp in Munich. Before that meeting took place, the crown prince of Prussia paid an official visit to Bayreuth, and the mayor decided that the festival theatre should be floodlit for the occasion. The crown prince did not visit the site (because, they were told later, of his fear of arousing King Ludwig's jealousy), but, seeing the theatre bathed on the evening of his visit in a red light, Wagner said to Cosima: "It is coloured red with our blood!"

On 14 September Feustel returned from his interview with Düfflipp in Munich in optimistic mood, but a letter to Wagner from the court secretary soon extinguished that hope. "His Majesty has not responded to your request for the guarantee of an intended loan," he wrote on 24 September, "probably remembering your previous declaration, when the 25,000 thalers earmarked for the Bayreuth undertaking were put to your personal use, that you would feel bound quite definitely to refuse any further material participation on the king's part." The king, Düfflipp added, was now anxious to avoid anything that might possibly hinder his own plans.

Faced with the unpleasant realisation that, as far as his festival was concerned, King Ludwig had abandoned him, Wagner decided to call a meeting of his patrons to discuss an appeal to the nation for the guarantee. He suggested to Nietzsche that he might care to write this appeal.

Nietzsche, though (as he told Rohde) terrified by the prospect, was anxious to dissipate the slight ill-feeling that had arisen as the result of his refusal of an invitation to spend the previous Christmas at Bayreuth. A visit, together with Rohde, in April did not appear to Nietzsche to have entirely healed the rift; he felt that at a time when Wagner was struggling with the financial problems of his undertaking, his own preoccupation with remote regions of Greek philosophy must have seemed hollow. "I realise clearly, dearest master, that such a visit can be no refreshment for you," he had written then on his return to Basel, "in fact that it must at times be almost unbearable. I have often wished for the appearance (at least) of greater freedom and independence, but in vain. Enough! I can only implore you to accept me as your pupil, if possible with pen in hand. . . . It is true that I grow more melancholy each day in realising how utterly incapable I am of contributing anything to your diversion and recreation, however gladly I would be of the slightest service to you."

In the first of his *Thoughts out of Season,* about the German religious writer David Strauss, written that summer despite severe eye
afflictions, Nietzsche did attempt to return to the topical cultural battle,
but clearly the writing of a direct appeal on Wagner's behalf gave him an
even better opportunity to relieve his conscience. Undeterred by
Rohde's refusal to join in an effort he regarded as hopeless, Nietzsche
wrote his "Appeal to the German Nation", designed, as he told Wagner,
"to castigate the wicked and *through this fury* to bring together and spur on
the good". He himself arrived in Bayreuth on 30 October, and next day
they went through the appeal together. Cosima thought it "very fine",
though she had doubts about the wisdom of issuing it: "But what use is
wisdom to us? Only faith and truth can help." The management committee and the delegates from the Wagner Societies, meeting later that
day, asked themselves the same question, but came to a different answer:
they felt they had no right to use such bold language, and indeed
Nietzsche's tone was bold, with its opening sentence, "We insist upon
being heard, for we speak as an admonisher, and the voice of warning
has always the right to be heard." He then proceeded to denounce the
Germans for their obtuseness and apathy: "You do not wish to know
what is going on, and out of sheer ignorance are about to prevent a great
deed from being accomplished. . . . What is needed here is *not* merely a
sense of national honour, nor the blind fear of the disparaging verdict of
a critical posterity; you should be willing to become co-workers, co-
sympathisers, co-learners, and, simply by resolving to help in this great
work, learn to rejoice with us from the bottom of your hearts. . . . We
regard it as our solemn duty to remind you of your duty as Germans at a
time when we are called upon to rally to the support of the great art work
of a German genius."

Wagner was delighted with this vigorous onslaught and much
incensed by the refusal of the delegates to make use of it. It was Nietzsche
himself who strove to calm him down, proposing at the same time that
Adolf Stern, a professor of literature, should write a new appeal,
confining himself to a simple request for contributions. This was duly
done, and Stern's appeal was printed and sent to book and music shops
throughout Germany. Whether Nietzsche's hectoring approach would
have had more success is impossible to say, but it could hardly have had
less. The outcome of the whole action was the sum of six thalers, sent by
a group of students.

Wagner did, however, send a copy of Nietzsche's appeal to the king,
along with Stern's, in a new attempt to persuade him to change his mind
and take over the guarantee. In his accompanying letter of 6 November
Wagner once again assured the king that the guarantee would not
involve him in any expenditure at all, and he asked Ludwig to grant him

and Feustel an audience. The reply came back from Düfflipp on 11 November: the king was in the process of moving to Hohenschwangau and did not wish to be disturbed. Despite this, Wagner and Feustel went to Munich on 20 November. They returned two days later, having seen only Düfflipp, who, Wagner told Cosima, received him very affectionately and held out hope of a favourable decision. However, the news of the king himself was alarming: he no longer went out of doors, rose late, took lunch at seven in the evening and dinner at eleven, then, unable to sleep, swallowed sleeping pills; he would see nobody except his equerry Hornig.

The arrival of Joseph Hoffmann on 28 November with his sketches of the scenery for the *Ring* was embarrassing in view of the present precariousness of their situation. Hoffmann was asking 1,500 thalers for the work he had so far done and then, while preparing the scenery from his sketches, a salary of 300 thalers a month. Not only was there no money to pay the first sum, but it was impossible in the circumstances to give him a definite commission, however much Wagner admired his sketches. If the king did not grant the guarantee by the end of the year, the festival would in any case have to be postponed until 1876.

Hoffmann and Brandt, who came to Bayreuth with him, had therefore to be temporarily kept satisfied with friendly words and promises, and Wagner turned his attention back to the only clear task before him, the orchestration of *Götterdämmerung*. He completed the first act just in time to present it to Cosima on 25 December as a birthday gift. Another gift was a little song for four children's voices and piano which he had composed especially for the occasion. Cosima called it the "Kose- und Rosenlied", for in his favourite punning style Wagner had equated the roses that bloom in May with the *Kose* (caress) that blooms at Christmastide, *Kose* of course standing for Cosima. The song, now known as "Kinderkatechismus" ("A Children's Catechism"), was sung outside her bedroom by the four girls, then Siegfried recited the text to her at her bedside. The day was fine and sunny, and Cosima wrote an account of their doings in her diary: "I ask R. to take me to the theatre, and he does so; planks bar the entrance to the stage, no watchman is on hand, I clamber over them – in spite of satin and velvet finery – and succeed amid great laughter in reaching the main stage. Grandiose impression, the whole rising up unrestrained like an Assyrian edifice, the pillars ranged like sphinxes below, the side wings spread out like secret passages; the whole thing seems more past than future, yet today it has a magnificently exhilarating effect on me. . . . After the visit to the theatre, we went to the new house and wandered, R. and I, in the conservatory; joy in the lovely plants, dreamlike gaiety. . . . In the evening I ask him to play me the *Idyll*, we think of that morning in Tribschen, then of the

Tristan time in Munich, all the bliss and all the sorrow. We go to our beds, I restraining by force my overwhelming emotion, laying the *Idyll* and the 'Koselied' beneath my pillow before giving myself up to gentle slumbers. A happy day."

Richter came for a short stay on 27 December, bringing with him Franz Glatz, a tenor he had discovered in Budapest. Glatz was a budding lawyer whose tall figure and powerful voice suggested they might have found in him their future Siegfried. But still no word came from the king. Casting around for possible alternatives, Wagner came on the idea of asking the emperor to proclaim the festival of 1875 a national celebration of peace with France, and to subsidise it with a contribution of 100,000 thalers. However, before taking any steps in this direction, he sent a telegram to Düfflipp on 6 February 1874, asking him to state clearly whether or not King Ludwig would take over the guarantee. Düfflipp's reply arrived by telegram the same day, and it seemed final: the answer was no. Wagner at once summoned Heckel to Bayreuth, and they decided that Heckel should approach the Grand Duke of Baden, and attempt to persuade him to organise a petition to the emperor in Berlin.

During this visit Wagner learned from Heckel the possible reason for the king's strange silence: Ludwig was annoyed with him for refusing to set to music a poem written in his praise by Felix Dahn. Dahn had sent Wagner his ode the previous summer, intimating that King Ludwig would like to see it set to music. Wagner, who was quite used to such requests from unknown poets, simply took it for a vain boast and ignored it.

He explained this in a letter to Ludwig on 9 January: "Perhaps on this occasion I judged wrongly: but, if I had been in any doubt about it, I should have asked Your Majesty to allow me to write my own words to any music that might have been required of me, since I should have found it utterly impossible to write music, in the only way I can, to the antique metre, so artificially imposed on the German language, which F. Dahn employed. Should F. Dahn be in the right and, by notifying Your Majesty of my refusal, have brought about an estrangement between us, I should have to regard this as a great misfortune, though for me in my complete ignorance an undeserved one."

In the same letter he informed Ludwig that he had been forced by financial considerations to abandon the projected performances of the *Ring* entirely: "I shall therefore rest content with having, together with my friends, erected the theatre in which alone my work is one day to be presented for the first time, and assuage my distress with the thought that for me too the performances have lost their significance, since they are no longer able to win the sympathy of the royal benefactor for whose pleasure and glory above all I had wished to bring them to life."

Ludwig waited fourteen days before he replied. His letter arrived at Bayreuth on 27 January, and Wagner could not bring himself to open it. He handed it to Cosima and asked her to tell him what it contained. Ludwig began by excusing his long silence, which was due to immersion in his "historical works", and declared that it would be madness to believe in a flagging of his ardent interest in Wagner and his great undertaking: "No, no, and *no* again! It cannot end like this! Help must be found – our plan cannot be allowed to founder! Parzival knows his mission in life and will offer whatever lies in his power. . . . Do not lose heart!"

He went on to explain that his budget was at the moment in a bad way, and he was obliged to exercise delay, which was not his usual habit. He then passed to other subjects: *A Capitulation*, which he had just read with interest, and a request for a photograph of Wagner and his family. Then, almost as an afterthought, he mentioned the Dahn affair: "I understand completely why you felt no desire to set Dahn's verse to music, and I think you were quite right." Dahn, he explained, had written the poem after being granted a dispensation in the matter of his marriage, and at an audience with the king had mentioned his desire that Wagner should set it to music: "I did not wish to say anything unpleasant to him, so expressed myself rather in favour than otherwise – *voilà tout*. So do not think me so petty as to be annoyed with you over your refusal: you are, thank God, destined by your genius for higher things than providing musical illustrations for sycophantic poems!"

This letter – and particularly the phrase "No, no, and *no* again! It cannot end like this!" – is frequently quoted as if it dispelled all Wagner's financial worries at a single stroke. It did not have quite that effect on Wagner and Cosima, who noticed straight away that it gave no idea what help was in fact to be offered. "Still we are left in uncertainty – will he grant the guarantee or will he not?" Cosima wrote in her diary.

As for the Dahn affair, Feustel expressed surprise at the king's account of it. He himself had learnt from Düfflipp at a meeting in Munich of the king's annoyance, and had even been shown telegrams confirming it. He had not mentioned it to Wagner at the time, Feustel said, since Düfflipp had enjoined him to silence.

Wagner, in his letter to Ludwig of 3 February, tactfully refrained from mentioning the matter at all, confining himself to expressing his joy at being able to correspond again with Ludwig: his letter had shown that they were still pursuing the same goal. "Thus, I hope, I may interpret the magnificent assurances your gracious letter expresses to me?"

He then turned to more general matters, having decided to leave it to Feustel and Düfflipp to discover what the king was in fact offering, while he himself concentrated on the orchestration of the second act of *Götter-dämmerung*, which he had begun on 20 January.

Agreement was not reached until 20 February, when Feustel returned from Munich and reported that, though the king was unwilling to give the guarantee, he had sanctioned a loan of 300,000 marks, to be spent on stage decorations and machinery, gas lighting and interior furnishings, the money to be advanced during the next eighteen months as it was required. The complete proceeds of the sale of certificates of patronage during this period would go to the royal treasury in repayment of the loan.

"R. returned from the conference in an ill humour," Cosima wrote in her diary. "The committee was downhearted, because of the impossibility of keeping to the original year, and Feustel once more talked of concerts. – Feustel remarked that Düfflipp had been in a very bad mood. In short, nothing good, and especially no joy."

Thus the great rescue action appeared at the time, and Wagner could not comfort himself that his financial worries were now over. However, the immediate obstacles to progress had been removed, and there was no course open but to press on hopefully.

CHAPTER XII

APRIL 1874–AUGUST 1875:

Concerts and Rehearsals

THE NEW HOUSE, though not yet finally completed, was sufficiently habitable for the family to move in on 28 April 1874. On the afternoon of that day a conference was held in the dining-room, attended by the management committee, Hoffmann, Brandt and Brückwald, and it was decided to give the task of preparing the scenery for the *Ring* from Hoffmann's sketches to the scene painters at nearby Coburg, the brothers Gotthold and Max Brückner, who were also present. "R. tells me about the fine mood which prevailed throughout, and how everyone was filled with a spirit of complete dedication to the cause," Cosima wrote in her diary. "The house could have been accorded no finer consecration. Cosy supper; the three little ones, Eva as leader, thank us for having given them such nice rooms. . . . Moonlight; going out on the balcony, R. and I see the grave, and he christens the house: '*Zum letzten Glück*' ['The Final Happiness']."

The name he eventually chose for it, Wahnfried, occurred to him on 4 May, when he told Cosima that there was a village in Hesse of that name, and the juxtaposition of the two words *Wahn* (illusion) and *Frieden* (peace) had always touched him: he found it so mystical. This, as with "Triebschen", was a case of his reading into a name more than was actually there, for the village in Hesse is in fact called Wanfried, a name that has nothing to do with illusions. He wrote a little verse to explain what the name meant to him, and this he had engraved above the front door. It runs: "*Hier, wo mein Wähnen Frieden fand, 'Wahnfried' sei dieses Haus von mir benannt*" (in Ernest Newman's translation: "Here where my illusion found peace, be this house named by me 'Peace from Illusion'.") Above this he set up a large *sgraffito*, designed by the painter Robert Krausse, depicting in allegorical form the essence of music drama: in it the facial features of his closest associates, past and present, were used: Ludwig Schnorr represents Germanic myth, Wilhelmine Schröder-Devrient classical tragedy, Cosima music and his son Siegfried the future.

Wahnfried was (and still is, for it is now a museum) a square building consisting of two and a half storeys and a basement. The front door, reached by a short flight of steps, opened into a vestibule from which a modest staircase led to the upper rooms. Beyond the vestibule were the twin glories of the house: a large hall rising right up to a glass roof and surrounded at the level of the upper floor by a gallery. Beyond it lay the *salon*, of greater length and breadth than the hall, but lower in height, and with a wide bay window overlooking the garden at the back and the palace gardens beyond. To the right of the hall was the modest dining-room, to the left Cosima's equally small private sitting-room, the "lilac *salon*". To each side of the main *salon* were rooms for guests. By having his guest rooms on the ground floor Wagner, who designed the house himself, did away with the need for a wide staircase, and the upper rooms of the house were reached by the stairs in the vestibule and spiral staircases to each side of the *salon*. The mezzanine floor consisted of dressing-rooms and – a much-prized innovation – a bathroom. Above these, connected by the gallery, were a living-room for the children (this the room above the *salon*, with a balcony on top of the *salon*'s bay window), a work-room each for Wagner and Cosima, and the bedrooms.

Cosima's pleasure in their new home was overshadowed by the news that Marie Muchanoff was dying of cancer, and for weeks she was torn between the wish to hurry to her friend's bedside in Warsaw and the heavy domestic duties imposed on her by the move. Marie herself solved that problem by refusing all visits, but her death on Wagner's birthday came as a shattering blow. Cosima wrote to Marie von Schleinitz shortly afterwards: "For the first time in my existence I felt no desire to celebrate 22 May, I prepared no little gifts, did nothing at all, I did not know why myself." Her grief over the death of a friend who had never been particularly close to her was, as she herself evidently felt, somewhat excessive, and could perhaps be attributed to the fact that it came in a period in which all seemed black to her, for at the same time she read in a newspaper that Bülow had fallen ill in Moscow, and she learned that the clergyman who officiated at her wedding to Wagner had also died. Yet another death, that of Wagner's publisher Franz Schott, occurred on 8 May. But underlying all this was her anxiety, on moving into the large new house, over the expense in which they had become involved. She wrote on 27 May in her diary: "Today I have to sign a paper permitting R. to make what use he pleases of the money I have saved, for payments on the house. I am deep in worries, for R.'s condition is also causing me great concern, and I fear we might overstep our material resources. R. reproaches me for not having given him a birthday present." There was in fact no need for concern over Wagner's health: he was suffering from digestive troubles, but these were now habitual with him, and a course of Marienbad waters, taken each morning, soon restored him. The real question at issue was the difference in their attitude towards money, though there was in fact at the moment no immediate cause for concern over their personal finances.

At the end of the previous September Schott had paid Wagner 10,000 florins, the agreed advance on *Götterdämmerung*. On 23 January Wagner wrote to Schott again: "I need 10,000 florins to get straight with my house and garden. If you would advance me this sum at once against compositions to be delivered, I on my side would pledge myself to provide six substantial works for orchestra, each of the size and significance of a large overture, at six-monthly intervals, and to send you the first by the end of this year, 1874, at the latest." The works, he told Cosima, would be *Lohengrin's Ocean Voyage, Tristan the Hero, Epilogue to Romeo and Juliet, Brünnhilde, Wieland the Smith* and another not yet decided, and he would start to write them next year.

Schott's experiences of Wagner's failure to fulfil his promises led him to greet this latest proposal cautiously. He did respond to Wagner's request for an advance, but took the opportunity to work out a new agreement, covering works both past and future, and tidying up the many discrepancies in their business dealings which had arisen along the way. Wagner's letter of 9 February, in which he spoke of his sincere delight in signing the new agreement, was the last Schott received before his death.

It did not, and could not, solve all Wagner's contractual difficulties, either with Schott or with virtually all the other people with whom he signed agreements. Though Cosima wrote admiringly of his business prowess, impressed by the amount of attention he gave to every tiny detail, he had no real talent for it and was never very clear about the full implications of the often very complicated agreements he signed. In offering Schott six overtures of which he wrote not a single one, he might perhaps be reproached with a deliberate attempt to deceive, but this would probably be an over-harsh judgment. No doubt he fully meant what he said at the time he said it, for he spoke frequently of his desire to write a series of symphonic works once the *Ring* was completed and produced. What he could never do, however, was to complete a work within the time limit he himself proposed, and this was certainly Schott's reason for paying an advance not on six overtures specifically, but on "compositions whose value shall be determined by Richard Wagner's delivering them to the firm of Schott at a price twenty per cent below that which another publisher can be shown to have offered, until the whole advance has been repaid". Schott, as can be seen by this, was well aware of Wagner's shortcomings as a negotiating partner, but equally alive to his value as a long-term investment.

The immediate debts on the house thus covered, Wagner was able to turn his attention to artistic matters, and he set about selecting the singers for his festival, now fixed to take place in the summer of 1876. To help him with the preliminary auditions and coaching he had his "Nibelungen Kanzlei", the nickname he had given the copyists, who were now living in the still uncompleted festival theatre. Of the original quartet, Kastner had been found unsatisfactory and dismissed, and he had been replaced by Demetrius Lalas, a young Greek musician recommended by Richter. They were joined on 1 June by Josef Rubinstein, who had spent the previous winter in Budapest, taking piano lessons from Liszt. These, though they had improved his technique, earned him some reproofs from Wagner, who objected to what he called his "virtuosic capers". Richter, who had arrived on 20 May, was sent off almost immediately on a tour of those German opera houses which Wagner had not visited himself to find promising singers.

By the end of the summer Wagner had selected a large part of his cast, and on 1 October he wrote Ludwig a glowing account of the excellent qualities they had shown as a result of his preliminary coaching. They included, in the order he named them, Hill (Alberich), Schlosser (Mime), Betz (Wotan), Emil Scaria of Vienna (Hagen), Niemann (Siegmund), Amalie Materna of Vienna, recommended to him by Scaria (Brünnhilde), Friederike Sadler-Grün of Coburg, discovered by Richter (Fricka), Lilli and Marie Lehmann, Minna Lammert (Rhinemaidens), "to whom I shall probably entrust the Norns as well." He had hopes of securing the famous Christine Nilsson for Sieglinde, he told the king, and Glatz, though still untested, was the most likely prospect for the role of Siegfried. The orchestra, to be recruited from a number of court theatres, would have Wilhelmj as leader. Other singers who came to Bayreuth that summer, but were not mentioned in Wagner's letter to the king, were Marianne Brandt, who rejected the part of Waltraute as unworthy of her status as a principal singer; Luise Jaïde, of whose staying power Wagner had some doubt; and Georg Unger, recommended by Heckel and provisionally set down for the role of Loge.

After the long years of isolation from the practical world of theatre, Wagner found these months of assembling and coaching his cast exhilarating, if exhausting. He loved actors, and he knew instinctively how to treat them, mixing flattery and cajolery, criticism with encouragement, demandingness with gratitude. Cosima did not share his pleasure in the acting profession; indeed, nothing inspired more horror in her than the thought that any of her children should adopt a theatrical career. However, there were other visitors to Wahnfried whom she found more congenial, among them Lenbach, always her friend rather than Wagner's (Wagner was slightly jealous of him on that account),

Countess Dönhoff and Standhartner. Klindworth arrived on 4 August from Moscow. He was making the piano arrangement of *Götter-dämmerung* and, his version of the second act having been lost in the post, there was nothing for it but to come to Bayreuth and do it again. Nietzsche arrived on the following day, but his visit was anything but a success. He came bearing a copy of Brahms's *Triumphlied*, a choral composition completed two years earlier to commemorate the Franco–Prussian War, and made Wagner angry by praising it.

"Wagner himself described the entire scene to me some months later," Nietzsche's sister Elisabeth wrote in *The Nietzsche–Wagner Correspondence*, "in the rare way he had of speaking ironically of himself: 'Your brother laid the red-bound book on the piano, so that my eye fell upon it every time I came into the room and enraged me as a red rag does a bull. I knew perfectly well what Nietzsche wished to say to me: See here! Here is someone else who can also compose something worthwhile! I stood it as long as I could, and then one evening I let go of myself, and how I did rage!' Wagner laughed heartily as he recalled this scene. 'What did my brother say?' I asked anxiously. 'Not a word,' was Wagner's reply, 'he grew red in the face and stared at me with a look of astonished dignity. I would give a hundred thousand marks all at once if I were as well-bred as Nietzsche; he is always the aristocrat, always dignified.'"

Elisabeth commented: "It has always remained a mystery to me why my brother did not tell me of this incident. It must have been because he took it much more to heart than Wagner would have me believe. When I later questioned him about it, he was silent for a moment and then said softly: 'Lisbeth, at that moment Wagner was not great!'"

It might be claimed in Wagner's defence that Nietzsche chose an unlucky moment to attempt to interest him in anything outside the immediate practical problems by which he was at that time besieged. There was trouble with Hoffmann, who, resenting changes made in his scenery sketches for the sake of technical convenience, was soon at loggerheads with Brandt and the Brückner brothers. In the end Wagner found himself obliged to exclude Hoffmann from taking any part at all in the practical work, whereupon he demanded immediate payment for work already done. Since money was still in short supply, Wagner had to appease him with promises for the future.

Repayment of the loan granted by King Ludwig swallowed up all income from the sale of certificates, thus leaving no money with which to pay expenses not specifically covered by the loan, and these included the main building works as well as the incidental costs of rehearsals. Wagner made an attempt in his letter of 1 October to persuade the king to suspend the repayment clause for the time being, but Ludwig refused, on the grounds that his building budget was fully stretched. As a small concession he agreed to waive the repayments due on Wagner's personal loan for pension purposes for a further year, and to pay his allowance in full. He also decided to make Wagner a present of the bronze bust of himself which, as Wagner had told him (probably with this hope in mind), he wished to place in the front garden of Wahnfried.

In his letter of 1 October Wagner described in minute detail, at the king's request, his daily life in Wahnfried. Now at last, he said, his life had a meaning it had never had before, and his only regret was that he was not ten or fifteen years younger. After thirty years of unfruitful marriage he had a son: "And I have a prudent wife who keeps everything in order for me, gives it life and soul." The day would begin, after taking a bath, with breakfast with Cosima in her room upstairs, and he would go down to the *salon* at about ten o'clock. "This holds all my possessions: the walls are lined with my book collection; our pictures hang above them, little cupboards standing all around contain our papers and documents; here stands the grand piano, there my large desk with a fine top of Bayreuth marble; opposite it Cosima's smaller desk; somewhere else a large table full of presents and mementoes, all around comfortable furniture for the reception of our still so numerous guests. . . . Here I work, when other business does not prevent me. At one o'clock the bell rings for lunch. . . . I go with Cosima through the hall to the modest dining-room, where I find the children seated around the table and where, after all have been suitably caressed, the family meal is taken. Unless indisposition or ill humour resulting from disagreeable business matters have gained the upper hand, this family meal is usually the source of much merriment. It gives me feelings of the greatest pleasure to see the children of my poor friend Bülow, who were something of a burden to him, flourishing under the painstaking care of their mother as splendidly as it lies in their capacities to do. My son is almost passionately loved by all the children: everyone has ears only for the droll fancies with which he keeps the little company in a constant state of laughter. These usually have their effect on me too, and a deeply grateful glance at his mother concludes the cheerful meal, after which coffee is taken in the garden, the *Bayreuther Tageblatt* (the only newspaper I now allow into my home and read) is glanced through, and some interesting theme from art, philosophy or life is usually discussed by me and Cosima. There follows then a short rest, after which, back in the large *salon*, we look to see what has arrived in the post or from elsewhere. . . . Once all is settled, the morning's work can then be resumed for a while, or a page of orchestration done. Then for a walk, or, if the carriage from the Sonne . . . is available, we make a trip with the children to the Eremitage or the Fantaisie, where what they call 'voyages of discovery' are undertaken. . . . At seven o'clock a simple meal with the children. At eight o'clock withdrawal with Cosima into the *salon*, where we regularly occupy ourselves with a reading, unless permission has been given to my numerous guests to visit us then, in which case we converse or make music."

During that busy summer Wagner had continued to work whenever he could on the orchestration of *Götterdämmerung*. He completed the second act on 26 June, just before the singers started to arrive, and began the third act on 10 July. Progress was of necessity slow, and after the last of the singers had gone he was too exhausted to resume work at full pressure. He began the final spurt on 29 October, and at last, on 21 November, the "thrice sacred, memorable day" arrived on which he wrote the last note of his score.

It was a supreme moment spoilt for them both by a trivial misunderstanding. "Towards the hour of noon," Cosima wrote in her diary, "R. calls to me upstairs, asking me to bring him the newspapers; since he had yesterday complained how worn out he felt and had also assured me that he would not finish before Sunday, I thought that tiredness had prevented his working any longer, but I was too shy to ask him; to distract him, I put down my father's letter, which had just arrived. . . . The noon hour strikes, I find him reading the letter, he asks me for explanations, I tell him what I intend to reply to it, and purposely refrain from looking at the page of the score, in order not to offend him. Offended, he shows me that it is finished, and then says bitterly to me that, when a letter arrives from my father, all thought for him is entirely swept away. I repress my pain at lunchtime, but when afterwards R. repeats his complaint, I cannot help breaking into tears, and I am still weeping now as I write this. Thus I have been robbed of this my greatest joy, and certainly not because of the slightest bad intention on my part! . . . The fact that I dedicated my life in suffering to this work has not earned me the right to celebrate its completion in joy. Thus I celebrate it in suffering, bless the fair and wonderful work with my tears, and thank the malicious God who ordained that I must first atone in suffering for its completion. . . . The children see me weeping and weep with me, but are soon consoled. R. goes to his rest with a final bitter word, I search the piano for *Tristan* sounds; every theme is, however, too harsh for my mood, I can only sink down inside myself, pray, worship! . . . Greetings, eventful day, greetings, day of fulfilment! If a genius completes his flight at so lofty a level, what is left for a poor woman to do? To suffer in love and rapture."

Later that day Wagner succeeded in bringing about a reconciliation, telling Cosima that the cause of their suffering was the intensity of their love for one another, but the wound had gone so deep that it was twelve days before she could bring herself to write in her diary again. It was perhaps in an attempt to make amends that he prepared a new arrangement for childrens' voices and small orchestra of the "Kose- und Rosenlied" ("Kinderkatechismus"), adding at the end a quotation from the finale of *Götterdämmerung*. This he rehearsed in secret in the Hotel Sonne with the children and members of the orchestra from nearby Hof. Cosima woke up on her birthday to the sound of the *Siegfried Idyll*, followed at once by the new "Kinderkatechismus", and during breakfast in the *salon* the little orchestra played pieces from *Lohengrin*, *Tannhäuser* and *Die Meistersinger*. At the end of the day she told Wagner it had been the happiest of her life. When he asked her why, she replied: "Because *Götterdämmerung* has been completed and thus the real worry of our life removed."

The first weeks of 1875 were spent in working out time schedules for the following two summers, writing to the singers and orchestral players already decided on, and explaining to them what was expected of them in terms of time and effort. Since there was no question of a profit being made, he offered no fee, though money would be available for living expenses to ensure that no singer would suffer financially from taking part. This was a proviso Wagner could make, confident that he could find singers to whom the honour of appearing in his festival would provide sufficient reward, and on the whole he was proved right, though the varying claims made by the singers did eventually lead to a few difficulties. With the members of his orchestra he took a different course, since their function was more anonymous, and in his circular letter to them, sent off at the same time, he offered a fixed payment at the rate of 180 marks per month, together with free accommodation and travelling expenses.

In the weeks spent dealing with these organisational matters Wagner found little opportunity for musical work. He did give some thought, Cosima noted on 3 January, to an overture in the series promised to Schott, and at the end of the month he wrote an *Albumblatt* for piano as an expression of gratitude to Betty Schott, now since her husband's death the owner of the publishing house, for her efforts in raising 6,000 marks for Bayreuth with a lottery in Mainz. He also arranged some pieces from *Götterdämmerung* for use in the concerts he was shortly to conduct in Vienna and Berlin in aid of the festival funds. Glatz had been engaged to sing in these, and he came to Bayreuth in January to rehearse with Wagner, while Rubinstein was despatched to Vienna to rehearse with Amalie Materna.

Glatz had in the meantime been studying singing with Richter's mother Josephine, a former singer, and had fallen into what Wagner considered bad habits, so that his hopes for him began rapidly to wane. Richter himself arrived in Bayreuth while Glatz was still there, bringing his young wife, whom he had married on 28 January. The visit was not as happy as his usually were: Richter, loyal to his mother, was unable to share Wagner's misgivings about Glatz, while Cosima had reservations about his wife Marie, the daughter of a Hungarian landowner, Vilmos von Szitányi. "She is to my mind strange, a decidedly Jewish type," Cosima wrote in her diary on 5 February, and on 7 February: "I have the very definite feeling that Richter will now be pursuing other paths."

Nietzsche's sister Elisabeth came to Wahnfried to look after the children when Wagner and Cosima left for Vienna on 19 February, and from Standhartner's house, where they were staying, embarked under the wing of Marie Dönhoff on the usual social round which Wagner always found so trying, but which Cosima secretly enjoyed, listing in her diary all the many aristocratic people with whom she came into contact. For Wagner the main social reward was the meeting (arranged by Lenbach) and reconciliation with Gottfried Semper, now working on the erection of a number of important buildings in Vienna, including the Burgtheater.

The concert on 1 March, consisting of the *Kaisermarsch* and excerpts from *Götterdämmerung*, was a great success, and it was repeated a fortnight later. In the meantime Wagner and Cosima paid a visit to Pest for a concert, arranged by Richter, in which (on 6 March) Wagner and Liszt appeared together for only the second time in their lives (the first had been in St Gallen in 1856). Liszt conducted a new work of his own, *Die Glocken des Strassburger Münsters* (*The Bells of Strassburg*), and was also the soloist in Beethoven's "Emperor" Concerto, conducted by Richter, while Wagner contributed excerpts from the *Ring*.

While still in Vienna Wagner received a letter from King Ludwig thanking him profusely for his "heavenly" letter of 1 October 1874. "What a tremendous change must have taken place in your outlook!" he wrote on 7 March, "what pleasure in your work, what confidence in the attainment of all you are striving for lies in your last letters to me, and how happy it makes me: such a difference in comparison with so many of those letters and remarks which I was previously, to my deep distress, obliged to receive from you – may the mood of disheartenment have left you for ever!" He expressed his great gratitude to Wagner for the offer he had made in his letter to perform the *Ring* for him alone, thus freeing him from having to do the honours to "inept princely colleagues", but he requested that he should be allowed three whole performances for himself instead of just one. And he made an even more far-reaching plea: "I fervently beg you, dearest master, to set to music those words you originally intended for Brünnhilde and which I love so passionately

– the lines beginning '*Verging wie Hauch der Götter Geschlecht*' and ending '*selig in Leiden und Lust lässt die Liebe nur sein!*' It would give me immense delight to hear those words sung in the performances for me, those words, so deeply significant, so full of truth, that noble and magnificent gospel of love which Brünnhilde bequeaths to the world on her death."

How incalculable in his moods Ludwig had now become was demonstrated to Wagner when his offer to repeat the concert of *Götter-dämmerung* excerpts in Munich and to visit the king on his way back to Bayreuth from Vienna was declined. Another sign was Ludwig's refusal, shortly afterwards, to allow *Tristan und Isolde* to be performed in Munich so that Wagner could hear Therese Vogl and consider her suitability for the role of Sieglinde: Ludwig, he was told, could not bear the thought of *Tristan* being performed at a time he himself would be unable to hear it. However, Wagner thought it expedient to send a cordial reply to Ludwig's letter, agreeing to provide the three requested private performances of the *Ring* and even to set Brünnhilde's words to music and include them in these performances. He assured the king that the festival would take place in 1876 as planned – provided that in the meantime he could earn sufficient money to pay his artists.

Wagner and Cosima spent only a few weeks in Bayreuth before again setting out on their travels. Cosima had decided that, in the present un-settled state of their life, she could not continue the education of her two elder daughters herself, and on 8 April she accompanied them to the Luisenstift, a boarding school in Dresden. "The little ones weep bitterly as they take leave of their older sisters," she wrote in her diary. "Fidi literally screams. . . . Gloomy mood, how hard the path! – I am worried about R. – 'One feels at times like a complete fool,' he says, thinking of his undertaking."

She joined Wagner in Leipzig the following day and they travelled together to Berlin, where the concert of *Götterdämmerung* excerpts was given on 24 and 25 April, with Amalie Materna as Brünnhilde and Niemann taking over Siegfried, Glatz having sung so unsatisfactorily in Vienna that Wagner decided to drop him entirely. Niemann was eager to take on the role of Siegfried as well as that of Siegmund in the festival performances, but Wagner disliked the idea of one singer playing both roles, and he felt Niemann's baritonal tenor lacked the bright and boyish quality he wanted for Siegfried.

From the point of view of the festival, the visit to Berlin was chiefly notable for their first meeting with Carl Emil Doepler, whom Wagner had invited to design the costumes, presumably on the grounds that he was a specialist in the period of Germany's legendary past. In his letter of invitation to Professor Doepler, dated 17 December 1874, Wagner was rather vague about what he wanted. More attention could be paid, he felt, to the descriptions of Roman historians who had come into contact with the ancient German tribes, and he suggested that the task offered great scope for an inventive artist with a taste for research. Cosima, who was greatly interested in the subject of costume, joined Doepler in an exploration of the Berlin museums.

They returned to Bayreuth on 27 April, but it was only for a few days, for there was another concert to be conducted in Vienna, and for that Wagner sat down to write a concert ending for "Hagen's Watch", which was to be sung by Scaria. During those few days they were greatly distressed by the death of their dog Russ. Cosima wrote to her daughters in Dresden: "Yesterday he was still running behind our carriage on the way to the theatre, happily springing around and barking. . . . With him a good spirit has left our house. . . . Tomorrow our old friend is to be buried at the foot of our grave." A stone still marks the spot.

Wagner's birthday was less elaborate than usual this year for the obvious reason of lack of time to prepare it. Just before it, two new Newfoundland dogs arrived to replace Russ, and Wagner gave them the names of Marke and Brange. The main feature of the birthday itself was a firework display in the garden to the strains of Strauss waltzes, works for which Wagner had a great liking; they were played by the members of the Nibelungen Kanzlei. And in the hall of Wahnfried there hung sixty-two illuminated balloons, one for each year of his life.

"My friends seem to find it very affecting," Wagner wrote to Ludwig on 30 May, "to see me, at an age when everyone else is thinking only of enjoying what he has already gained or of complete resignation, still in the midst of carrying out undertakings of which a man in the first flush of youth would scarcely feel capable." And for the king's benefit he copied out a birthday letter from Nietzsche which, he said, filled him with encouragement. Nietzsche, writing in ill health, expressed his admiration of Wagner's resilience: "When I think of your life, I always have the feeling how *dramatic* is its course: as if you are so much the dramatist that you yourself can live only in this way, and certainly could not die until the end of the fifth act. When everything is pressing and storming towards a goal, chance stands aside, seems to become fearful. . . . Truly, dear master, to write to you on your birthday means simply to wish *ourselves* good fortune and good health, in order to be able to enjoy you to the full. For really I feel that it is ill health, and the egoism lurking in illness, that forces people to think always only of themselves, whereas the genius in the fullness of his health thinks only of others, involuntarily blessing and healing wherever he lays his hand."

Wagner, reflecting ironically on these remarks, continued his letter to Ludwig: "Often, when I am enjoying my home and my family, I suddenly find myself wondering why I do not rest content with what I have gained, but always feel impelled to put it all at risk by striving for something for which my fellow beings feel not the slightest desire. But so it is! Schopenhauer once made a very fine distinction between 'talent' and 'genius', attributing to 'talent' the capacity to reach a goal which others may see but are unable to achieve themselves, whereas 'genius' reaches the goal which others are unable even to perceive. And thus it is, alas, with my great work! At best – and this goes for most of my friends – they substitute for the goal I perceive a goal they think they perceive, though mine goes far beyond theirs." The singers, he felt, saw his festival only as a preliminary rehearsal of roles which they could then sing in proper performances in their own theatres, year after year. And, as for the financial supporters, "how few of them really see themselves as patrons of an undertaking designed to advance the nation's culture! Most of them feel they are just subscribers to a series of performances to be held in very exceptional circumstances, something at which their presence is vitally necessary, as at the opening of a world exhibition or something of that sort."

There was no doubt an element of ulterior motive in this letter: Wagner was hinting flatteringly to the king that he was different from the others and able to appreciate the true magnitude of the goal. Stressing the physical strain to which its achievement was subjecting him, he added: "There is so much time-consuming preparation involved with the undertaking that I necessarily require financial credit. Oh, if only someone had granted me this in full for the whole enterprise up to the performances, how many hairs would he have helped to preserve on my ageing head!"

Ludwig did not take the hint.

Unger arrived in Bayreuth on 31 May for some preliminary coaching before the rehearsals began. Cosima wrote in her diary that day: "Is he our Siegfried?" Though now in his thirty-eighth year, Unger at least had the right appearance, being tall and fair. However, on his arrival he began to rehearse with Wagner the role of Loge for which he had been engaged, though not to Wagner's entire satisfaction. Cosima went to Weimar on 16 June to attend a memorial service for Marie Muchanoff, and while there she saw a production of *Tristan und Isolde*, the first to be staged outside Munich. The main parts were sung by Heinrich and Therese Vogl, and Cosima was sufficiently impressed to ask them to come to Bayreuth. Her recommendation caused Wagner to reconsider his plans for Unger: if Therese Vogl were to take the role of Sieglinde, he would have to find a part for her husband, and Loge, which Vogl had already sung at the first performance in Munich, was the obvious choice.

Wagner thus began to think more seriously of giving the role of Siegfried to Unger, but, aware of his faulty voice production, decided first to consult Julius Hey, a singing teacher at the Munich school of music whom he had known since 1864. Wagner had already invited him to act during rehearsals as his adviser on vocal matters, and now he summoned him to come at once to Bayreuth and give his opinion on Unger.

In his book *Richard Wagner als Vortragsmeister (Richard Wagner as Teacher of Interpretation)* Hey provided a fascinating picture of Wagner at work during the preliminary rehearsals of 1875. He arrived in Bayreuth on 27 June, to be greeted by Wagner with a hearty hug, and "even his wife was a few degrees warmer than she was previously wont to be", he wrote to his own wife the following day. After hearing Unger sing excerpts from *Lohengrin* and *Tannhäuser*, Hey felt that his singing technique was so defective that there was little hope of making an acceptable Siegfried of him. In expressing his doubts, however, Hey realised that this was not what Wagner wished to hear; he had made up his mind that, given the will, Unger's vocal failings could be overcome. Unger, whom Hey found to be a man of intelligence, refreshingly lacking in vanity, also had his misgivings, but neither he nor Hey could stand out against Wagner's confidence: "His tremendous, inborn will-power, his fatalistic attitude, refused to acknowledge the possibility of having to reckon with an 'experiment' going astray. It was his *wish* – and Unger's *duty* to carry it out!"

Wagner's reliance on his instinct rather than a proved record of success was demonstrated also by his choice of Amalie Materna as Brünnhilde. She had made a name for herself in operetta, a form of singing in which good diction and attack was essential – valuable qualities indeed, but hardly sufficient in themselves to sustain the huge dramatic demands of the role of Brünnhilde. Hey, watching her at rehearsal, had doubts about her at least equal to those about Unger, with whom he was now working intensively. However, he kept his opinions to himself, though there were others, he noted, who were less reticent: "That could not upset Wagner's faith in the least. He considered Frau Materna to have the capacity to learn, and that was enough for him." Among his chosen singers, he told Hey, there were only four whom he regarded as possessing the desirable natural propensities for their tasks; these were Hill, Niemann, Lilli Lehmann and Franz von Reichenberg (Fafner). The rest would have to be trained.

Hey, looking at the company from the viewpoint of a vocal expert, was on the whole content with Wagner's choice, beginning with the three Rhinemaidens (Lilli and Marie Lehmann, Minna Lammert), who arrived in Bayreuth already perfect in their parts, and vocally well matched. In Hill he admired the passionate warmth he was able to put into his voice: he provided a fine contrast to Betz's noble Wotan, vocally so secure. Friederike Sadler-Grün had the powerful middle register so important to the role of Fricka. Marie Haupt's metallic high soprano was equally right for Freia. Of the two giants Hey was particularly impressed by Reichenberg's authentic bass timbre, whereas – at least in the preliminary rehearsals – Albert Eilers as Fasolt was hampered by poor enunciation. Vogl as Loge was in every way a happy choice, and Hey had praise too for Luise Jaïde as Erda.

The cheerful atmosphere prevailing throughout the rehearsals of *Das Rheingold*, which started on 11 July, was shattered when it came to *Die Walküre*, and the cause of the trouble was Niemann. He arrived in Bayreuth in a highly nervy state, and, experiencing difficulties in the rehearsal of the first act, he sought to relieve his feelings by advancing on Rubinstein, the accompanist, and shaking him violently. Wagner, normally so adroit in managing his singers, was this time at a loss what to do. "After a short pause," Hey wrote, "he broke the awful general silence with a word to the singer: 'Please continue,' and the latter resumed the interrupted scene in an agitated voice."

Worse was to follow after the rehearsal, when the singers escaped into the garden of Wahnfried to take refreshments. Seated there at a table with Liszt and Countess Dönhoff, Hey related, Cosima noticed Luise Jaïde offering Niemann a piece of ham from her own plate and with her own fork. Niemann, responding to a gesture which was no doubt meant to help soothe his uneasiness, accepted it and then proceeded to help himself to a few more morsels from Frau Jaïde's plate before taking his leave. After he had gone, Cosima called Frau Jaïde into the house, where she reproached her for her indelicate behaviour – so hurtfully, it seems, that after a meeting at a local inn, where the story was presumably told in full (but nowhere recorded), not only Frau Jaïde, but also Niemann declared they would leave Bayreuth straight away, and other singers (not named) threatened to do likewise.

Hey's anecdote is an intriguing one, and it would be a shame to cast too many doubts on it, though a close examination of accounts and dates in other sources does reveal certain discrepancies. However, it is safe to assume that there were temperamental clashes, and that Niemann was at the centre of most of them. It is equally certain that on 30 July Niemann threw up the role of Siegmund and left Bayreuth in dudgeon, but, as Richter calmly told Kietz (another eye witness): "Don't worry, he will be back in time for the performance."

By the beginning of August the orchestra had arrived, and activity was transferred from Wahnfried to the theatre, in which stage and orchestra pit had now been completed, though much work still remained to be done on the auditorium. The end of rehearsals was celebrated on 13 August with a party in the garden of Wahnfried, and Liszt played one of his *St Francis* pieces for the benefit of the orchestral players. "On the following day all depart, with great emotion," Cosima wrote in her diary, and, reflecting on the adulation her father received on all sides, added ruefully: "It is now I on whom abuse is loaded; it is said that I offend everybody, denounce to my husband all his friends, Prof. Hoffmann, Betz, Niemann, Richter, etc. – I have offended everyone, in fact, down to the costumier of the Munich theatre."

Given her fiercely protective attitude towards Wagner and her general distaste for members of the theatrical profession, it is not really surprising that such accusations were made against her. She took no active part in the rehearsals which were occupying Wagner all day, and she admitted to feeling isolated from him. It was at this very time, too, that Bülow came back into her life to arouse all the old pangs of guilt and remorse.

He wrote to her on 27 June from Hall in the Austrian Tyrol. As a result of the defection of his London agent, George Dolby, he told her, he had lost the sum of fifteen hundred pounds due to him from his English tour the previous year. On top of that his doctors in England – "absolute ignoramuses" – had treated him for gout when he had in fact had a slight apoplectic stroke which had affected his right hand. In consequence, "the capital designed for my three daughters" had been put in jeopardy, and he felt they ought to discuss arrangements for financing the children's education in the event of his disability or decease. Cosima, receiving this letter on 3 July, wrote in her diary: "Once more a sword twisted in my heart and all my wounds torn open again – how often will this continue to occur?" She begged him to give up his plan of going to America in his present state of health. In his reply of 3 July, Bülow said that he had not yet given up hope of recovering sufficiently to make the journey in September, but he felt it would be wise to make his will before leaving. He asked Cosima to send him the birth dates of Daniela, Blandine and Isolde, apologising for not knowing them: his stroke had affected his memory.

Cosima did not tell Wagner of her correspondence with Bülow. "We hardly manage to exchange a word between ourselves," she wrote in her diary on 6 July, "and I go around with my never-to-be-removed burden of pain, during the day as if in a hot, dry fever, during the night in tears."

His next letter, dated 11 July, contained a singular request: "Now, madame, may I venture to confide to you a delicate mission, very confidential, but simple enough, not likely to cause you more than a slight momentary vexation? It concerns the use of a sum of 5,000 francs (4,000 marks) for the purchase and despatch to a foreign country of a souvenir

– to a person who had been prepared to love me and whom my 'duties', complicated by my twin misfortune last winter, forced me to renounce – no great matter whether this resignation might have prevented further unhappiness or not. There is nobody else in this world whom I could approach to put this posthumous whim of mine into effect. If you should feel disposed, madame, to make this little sacrifice for me (I should wish you to condescend to make it personally – that is to say, by writing in my name), I should be infinitely obliged if you would answer me with a simple 'yes', so that I can insert this legacy among my other bequests, 'to Mme R.W. for a purpose known only to her'."

Cosima mentioned nothing of this in her diary, but simply noted on 13 July: "Letter from Hans, informing me of his last wishes!" She gave Bülow her 'yes', and on 14 July he revealed to her the identity of the lady: Sophie Alexeievna de Poltovatzki, of Kursk in Russia. He asked Cosima to choose the souvenir herself.

With that the correspondence ended, but the effects of it lingered, and it may have been some subconscious comparison with the man who now occupied the position which rightfully belonged to Bülow that turned Cosima's resentment against Richter. Having just taken over his new post in Vienna, Richter had had some difficulty in procuring leave of absence for the rehearsals in Bayreuth. He finally arrived, late, on 15 July, and in the following days seemed to Cosima to be identifying himself with Niemann and the other malcontents and somewhat ostentatiously keeping away from Wahnfried. In her letter to him, written on 25 August, a few days after the rehearsals had ended and Richter was back in Vienna, she told him that Wagner held him partly responsible for the "evil talk" regarding herself: "He has asked you to behave differently towards his family and to acknowledge your wrong, whereupon, he tells me, you declared that you were now experiencing the retribution which my long-nourished hatred had conjured up." Claiming to be writing more in sorrow than in anger, with the sole purpose of preventing a break between him and Wagner, she recalled to Richter her efforts to keep the peace between them during the period of rehearsals. As for her own feelings for him, Richter should surely have noticed during their long association "that I have no personal likes and dislikes, but love those my husband loves and give up those from whom he turns away. . . .

"Now I beg you, as earnestly as I can and in the name of those former hours in Tribschen, where you knew definitely and precisely what we meant to you and you to us, make up for your remissness, send a telegram to my husband immediately you receive the letter he wrote last night: say you heartily regret having listened to all the foolish chatter, and promise to come to us and be the Hans Richter of old. In advising you to do this I have *only* your good and your salvation in mind – over our cause and our fate there hovers a star that cannot be much affected, neither for better nor worse. . . . Recall the unusual circumstances attending my husband's union with me, and ask yourself whether he can continue to associate with you unless you make a sincere resolve to put an end to this nonsense. Make the effort to do this, my dear friend; for all you may have felt in your heart against me I forgive you with all my heart. And, if it gives you satisfaction to think ill of me, then you may have this satisfaction, may even speak ill of me if you wish, but do not let my husband know of it, for then not even I shall be able to do anything more with him on your behalf."

She read this letter to Wagner, and he was touched by it, telling her that it was far more conciliatory than his own had been. Both letters had their effect. On 26 August Richter despatched an express telegram: "Deeply revered master. Forgiveness for the penitent. Please write me all you wished to say, so I can acknowledge my wrong completely and repent. Regretting my absence, assure you never to have wavered in my loyalty. Your lifelong devoted Hans Richter." Cosima placed this telegram between the pages of her diary.

Wagner was silent about all these clashes in the account of the rehearsals he wrote on 22 August to King Ludwig. He gave the impression that they had gone splendidly, and he had a word of praise for every singer, even for Niemann, to whom, he said, he was thinking after all of giving the role of Siegfried as well as Siegmund, should Unger, in whom he still had confidence, fail in the end to come up to expectations. He came back then to the financial difficulties: money would be needed for the costumes, and for that and other expenses he would need all the proceeds from the certificates of patronage up to the 600th. So far, he said, they had sold 410. "If we have now to pay all the money coming in back to the royal treasury, we cannot of course continue our work, and the support granted us through your royal decision will have failed in its object."

This time the king yielded to his plea, if not quite in full. An amendment to the loan agreement of 20 February 1874 was made on 27 September 1875, and it provided that, after the sale of 425 certificates, the festival management should pay three-fifths of the money subsequently received to the royal treasury, and retain the other two-fifths for its own use.

CHAPTER XIII

The First Festival

RETURNING ON 19 September from a short family holiday in Bohemia, Wagner took Unger through the third act of *Siegfried* in the festival theatre, and decided that he should have the part. He stipulated, however, that Unger must continue to study the role with Hey in Munich and give up his engagement in Düsseldorf, a decision which involved Wagner in a dispute with the aggrieved theatre director in Düsseldorf, and cost him a substantial sum of money, since he undertook to pay Unger an allowance during all his months of study.

He then put the *Ring* out of his mind for the time being and occupied himself rereading Wolfram von Eschenbach's "Parzival" poem and books about the Parzival legend until the time came on 1 November to leave for Vienna. Franz Jauner, director of the opera house there, had invited him to produce both *Tannhäuser* and *Lohengrin*. Wagner's reason for accepting the invitation was, firstly, to keep on the right side of Jauner, who had command over several of the singers he wished to use in his festival, and, secondly, to earn money.

Though this was the first opportunity he had had to concern himself with the new version of *Tannhäuser* since the ill-fated first production in Paris (and he did make some modifications in it), Wagner found little satisfaction in the task, mainly because the singers were not of his own choosing. The first performance on 22 November, with Richter conducting, was a great success, but Wagner's exasperation with the singers and their vanities was such that Jauner had to use all his powers of persuasion to keep him in Vienna.

If, as Cosima recorded, he was in a profound state of depression and exhaustion during the rehearsals of *Lohengrin*, he did not allow it to show. A baritone singer, Angelo Neumann, who watched him at work, recorded in his book, *Personal Recollections of Wagner*: "What an inspiring director he was! How well he understood the art of spurring on his men, of getting his best work out of each one, of making every gesture, each expression tell! These rehearsals convinced me that Wagner was not only the greatest dramatist of all time, but also the greatest of managers, and a marvellous character actor as well."

Another onlooker was a nineteen-year-old musical student, Felix Mottl, who took the trouble to mark down in his score the tempi that Wagner imposed, and he later incorporated them in his piano arrangements of *Tannhäuser* and *Lohengrin*. Mottl, a protégé of Richter, impressed Wagner, who invited him to join his Nibelungen Kanzlei in Bayreuth.

This time Wagner and Cosima had more to do with musicians and musical life than was usual on their excursions abroad. They were present when on 2 November Richter conducted the first performance in Vienna of Verdi's *Requiem*, a work of which Cosima wrote in her diary that it would be better to say nothing. They saw Bizet's *Carmen* the following evening (its first production outside Paris): "There is talent," Cosima wrote to Marie von Schleinitz, "in this repulsive work." On 18 November they heard Brahms's Piano Quartet in C Minor at a *soirée* given by the Hellmesberger String Quartet. Cosima pronounced the work "very dry and stilted", and its composer (whom she was meeting for the first time) "a red, crude-looking man". Wagner already knew him from his years in Vienna, when Brahms had helped Cornelius, Tausig and Porges to copy Wagner's arrangements of pieces from *Die Meistersinger* for concert use. More recently, in July, they had been in correspondence about the score of the revised version of *Tannhäuser*, the only existing copy of which had been given to Brahms by Tausig. Wagner, needing it for the production in Vienna, requested its return, but Brahms refused at first to surrender it. However, in the end he did so, in exchange for a *de luxe* copy of the score of *Das Rheingold*.

Lohengrin was performed on 15 December, and they arrived back in Bayreuth two days later. Wagner's Christmas present to Ludwig that year consisted of the first three volumes of his autobiography, printed by Bonfantini in Basel. In January he yielded to Cosima's persuasions and resumed work on *My Life*, but then he abandoned it again on 9 February to begin work on a march, commissioned by Philadelphia to mark the centenary of the American Declaration of Independence. He wrote it reluctantly, the main spur being "the 5,000 dollars he has demanded and perhaps will not get", as Cosima noted on 14 February. One of his first "attempts to be American" turned out to be a gentle, rocking theme, but he did not use it in the march, having recognised it as the seductive melody the Flower Maidens would sing in the second act of *Parsifal* to the words (still unwritten) "*Komm, holder Knabe*".

By February the sale of certificates of patronage had reached only 490 – 810 short of the estimated number required in order to cover the expenses of the festival. King Ludwig's loan had not yet been used up, but money was urgently needed for purposes for which the loan was not available, and with Wagner's consent Marie von Schleinitz had begun at the end of 1875 to investigate the possibility of seeking an advance from the emperor. Wilhelm, it seemed, would have been willing to grant it, but Bismarck intervened, suggesting that instead a petition for a loan should be addressed to the Reichstag. This Wagner refused to do, declaring that his appeal had been to the emperor's grace, not to the "gentlemen of the Reichstag".

In his letter of 4 February to Heckel, Wagner admitted that it really was madness, in view of the financial position, to persist in staging the festival that summer: "The undertaking as originally projected has in fact virtually collapsed. Now we must take the risk of seeing what curiosity will do for us. Even Feustel believes we can risk it on that basis, though we are faced with a lack of funds for June, etc., when singers and musicians arrive and will need ready money. . . . Otherwise, we put a brave face on things. It will all get done (on credit!); the artistic details of the festival are being worked out to fine effect. Brandt magnificent as always – my main pillar of support!"

The only setback on the artistic side was a sudden demand by Scaria, just before Christmas, for a fee of 7,500 marks for his appearances as Hagen in the festival performances, plus 250 marks for each rehearsal. The reason, Wagner later found out, was that he urgently needed money for a lady who was dunning him. His demand placed Wagner in a dilemma: he could not pay that sort of money (even if he had it) without setting a precedent which other singers were bound to follow. His appeals to Scaria to modify his demands found no response, and he had in consequence to start looking around for a new Hagen. However, the loss of one important singer was to a certain extent counterbalanced by the return of another: the differences with Niemann were patched up, and Wagner undertook to supervise a production of *Tristan und Isolde* in Berlin, with Niemann in the leading role.

He finished the first draft of his *Grosser Festmarsch (Centennial March)* on 20 February and was still working on the orchestration when on 29 February the time came to set off for Berlin. Cosima's remarks that Niemann was increasingly unpleasant during rehearsals of *Tristan und Isolde* and sang badly at the first performance on 20 March can probably be taken as a reflection of her personal resentment against him. In any case it was a brilliant occasion: the emperor and empress, who headed the audience, received Wagner in the royal box during the first interval, and the emperor promised to attend the opening of the festival in Bayreuth. He also decreed that the full proceeds of the first performance should go to Bayreuth, and it brought in a welcome total of close on 13,000 marks. While in Berlin Wagner completed the orchestration of his *Grosser Festmarsch* and was immediately paid the fee of 5,000 dollars he had demanded for it – a sum he later augmented by selling the publishing rights to Schott for 9,000 marks.

They arrived back in Bayreuth on 27 March, having settled the problem of Hagen with the engagement of Josef Kögel, a bass singer from Hamburg, whom Wagner auditioned in Berlin. But in April a new problem arose: Vogl sent word that his wife was expecting a baby and would be unable to sing Sieglinde. Wagner at once offered the part to Vilma von Voggenhuber, his Berlin Isolde, who accepted with delight, only to withdraw a week later, when she discovered she was in the same condition as Therese Vogl. Wagner's next choice was Marianne Brandt (the Berlin Brangäne), but other members of the cast declared her to be too ugly, Niemann in particular fearing that her appearance would dampen his inspiration. To Lilli Lehmann, who conveyed the news, Wagner wrote a reproachful letter on 25 April: "The unappealing nature of her facial features is of significance only off the stage and for those in the closest proximity to her: on the stage, particularly in *my* theatre, such disadvantages disappear completely, and only her slim figure would make an effect – and that an advantageous one. Surely one can expect of an artist like Niemann that, in the excitement of the drama, all around him would seem transfigured, and he would not be conscious of vulgar reality: what matters for him is what it all – himself included – looks like, not what, stripped of dramatic magic, it really is. Garrick and Kean used to take a beer mug in their arms instead of a child, and roused even the nearest spectators to a frenzy of horror when they saw a father apparently throwing his child into the river." In view of Marianne Brandt's subsequent international career as one of the most celebrated of Wagnerian singers, Wagner was undoubtedly right in his view, but to avoid trouble he gave in on this occasion and, in what looks almost like panic, he sent off telegrams to two singers at once: Mathilde Mallinger, his Eva of the first *Meistersinger* in 1868, and Josephine Scheffsky, a soprano in Munich whom he had not heard, but who was said to be a favourite of the king.

Complications were avoided, however, when Mathilde Mallinger declined the invitation. Josephine Scheffsky arrived in Bayreuth on 8 May, and sang with Unger the Brünnhilde-Siegfried duet from *Götterdämmerung*. "The voice and personality good," Cosima noted in her diary, "he accepts her for Sieglinde." What particularly pleased him about her, he told Hey, was her excellent enunciation.

A smaller gap caused by the withdrawal of a Viennese singer was filled by calling in his niece Johanna Jachmann-Wagner to sing a Valkyrie and a Norn. Thus, when rehearsals started at the end of May, the cast was complete. All the same, there had been more difficulties to overcome before this happy state was reached. Jauner declared that he would allow Amalie Materna to participate only on condition that he was given permission to stage *Tristan* and *Die Walküre* in Vienna next winter; Wagner had, reluctantly, to consent. Munich then decided to open its autumn season on 15 August, before the Bayreuth festival ended, and in consequence several members of the chorus could not be made available. In Berlin, Hülsen decided to keep the opera open until 1 July, which meant that some singers, including Lilli Lehmann, would not be available for rehearsal in June; Wagner had to plead with him to release them.

There were other causes for alarm which persisted even after rehearsals began. Rumours of war impending between the Serbs and the Turks, and an outbreak of typhoid fever at the military barracks in Bayreuth were reported in the newspapers and led to a decrease in the demand for certificates of patronage. The theatre itself was not yet finally completed; in the middle of May the interior was still full of scaffolding. That was removed in time for rehearsals, but, when they began, rain was still leaking through the pasteboard roof, and the approaches to the theatre, in that cold and wet early summer, were a morass.

Above all, there were the financial worries. The daily running costs, consisting mainly of the participants' living expenses, amounted to 2,000 marks a day, and of each 900 marks which the sale of a certificate of patronage brought in, 540 marks had at once to be sent to the royal treasury to pay off the king's loan. A request to suspend these repayments for the time being was sent to Munich on 23 May, but it was not until 29 June that Düfflipp was able to authorise the suspension of all repayments up to the sale of the 800th certificate – and that only on the understanding that no further demands would be made on the original loan. The payment for certificates accelerated somewhat as the opening of the festival drew nearer, but it was clear that all would not be sold, and Wagner was forced to abandon his idea of "free" admittance and allow tickets to be sold at the box office in order to increase the takings. "A good day for the box office today," Cosima noted on 21 July, "5,200 marks come in – enough to keep us for 2 days."

Hopes that the publication of Cosima's diaries might throw an extra light on the events of that summer proved unfounded, for Cosima was kept so busy during the period of rehearsals and performances that she had little time for writing, and the entries in her diary were sketchy and sometimes at second hand, since she was not able to be present at all rehearsals in the theatre. She wrote nothing at all after 4 August for several weeks, completing her account of the festival only after it was over from hasty jottings in a notebook. However, there are other accounts on which one can rely, the two most important being Richard Fricke's *Bayreuth vor dreissig Jahren* (*Bayreuth Thirty Years Ago*) and Heinrich Porges's *Die Bühnenproben zu den Bayreuther Festspielen des Jahres 1876* (*Stage Rehearsals for the Bayreuth Festival of 1876*). These two books complement each other very usefully. Fricke, whose task it was to super-vise movement and gesture on the stage, left in his book, based on diary entries made at the time, a vivid picture of Wagner as a stage producer. Porges was invited by Wagner to attend all rehearsals and note in his score all that he had to say to his conductor, singers and orchestral players about the interpretation of the music. Both testified to Wagner's vigour and energy in pursuing his method of directing by example, demonstrating every movement to his cast, singing all their music, calling out instructions to Richter and the orchestra in the mystical chasm. "His stock of good ideas is inexhaustible," wrote another witness, Ludwig Strecker, who had taken over the firm of Schott following Betty Schott's death the previous year, in his diary. "How he manages to stand up to it all is a mystery to me."

Fricke too had anxieties about the effect of this strenuous activity on Wagner's health, and was not sure that it was all in a good cause. Describing a rehearsal of *Das Rheingold* on 8 June, he wrote: "He interrupts incessantly and demands highly comical things which thoroughly confuse the singers (who are after all not standing on the stage for the first time). He demands of the two giants, for instance, that they adopt a special way of walking when coming in over the rocky heights. He demonstrated it to them in so curiously comical a way that I intervened and said (quietly) to him: 'Master, it can't be done like that, it is unnatural, let me show it to them as I imagine it' (heavy tread in time to the music). 'Quite good, quite good,' Wagner said, 'my movements were no use.'" But it was not only bad ideas that were abandoned. Wagner often forgot what he had decided the day before, and it all had to be thought out afresh. "Again many things altered," Fricke wrote resignedly on 11 June. "Betz, Schlosser, Hill, Vogl take it calmly, since it is Wagner who is doing it. Later they will hardly bother their heads with it, but just do as they please."

Fricke's view was certainly affected to some degree by fears of his own function being usurped. But his conclusion that all this activity on Wagner's part was a psychological need, that he had "to sweat out what he has composed", was rather wide of the mark. Wagner had a definite purpose in his method of demonstrating actions and reactions to his singers, and that was to involve them in a complete understanding of their roles, thus enabling them to find their own natural form of expres-sion. Porges came nearer to the truth when he wrote in the introduction to his book: "The master's whole extraordinary activity during rehear-sals gave the impression of something directly *improvised*; one had the feeling that everything he demanded of his actors, and could so convin-cingly demonstrate to them by his own example, had only just come to him in a sudden lightning flash of revelation: his inner urge to com-

municate it with the utmost clarity and emphasis found expression in a
truly creative way. But to envisage fully what he was doing, we must
realise that the actual model of what he brought so vividly to life in his
demonstrations was the inner essence of life in all its sensual outward
reality. For the stylistic character of the *Ring* is determined by the fact
that it contains a hitherto unknown 'super-reality' of life and form, and
the efforts of its creator to reflect this were imbued in rehearsals with the
same spirit. . . . The aim in the production of the *Ring* was to combine a
realistic Shakespearean style with the idealism of Greek tragedy."

That this difficult goal demanded a great amount of initial
experimentation was hardly surprising. For Wagner himself it was the
first attempt to realise in practical stage terms the work that had existed
for so many years only in his imagination, and this called, on the
simplest level, for certain practical modifications: slight adjustments
here and there to the vocal line, a lightening of the orchestration at
moments when the volume of sound obscured vital words of the text.
"The relationship of the orchestral sound to the singer was often
discussed during rehearsals," Porges wrote, "and the master liked
repeatedly to declare that the orchestra should always bear the singer
along like a boat on a lively sea, but never run the risk of upsetting it, let
alone sinking it."

In matters of tempo too Wagner was constantly exhorting Richter to
be flexible, even at times to follow the singer's lead, but the singers were
never allowed to slacken the pace at emotional moments. Wagner
abhorred the stop and start of aria and recitative in the traditional
operatic form, and told his singers that the speed of the passages in
which dialogue predominated should be the pace at which the words
would naturally be spoken. False pathos must always be avoided. This
did not mean that, in highly emotional scenes, Wagner put a brake on
passionate expression: on the contrary, when the drama called for it, he
demanded it in full measure. Porges gave an account of a rehearsal of
the scene in the third act of *Die Walküre* in which Brünnhilde tells
Sieglinde that she is to bear Siegmund's child: "He laid the greatest
weight on the words '*Ein Wälsung wächst dir im Schoss*' ('A Wälsung lives
in your womb'). He himself sang them with truly shattering power. In
the tone of his voice there lay an expression of profound solemnity
combined with prophetic ardour, and they aroused in us emotions of
awe combined with joy, such as they must arouse in Sieglinde herself,
who, after her initial shock, starts up rejoicing."

During this intensive work nerves sometimes became strained: Unger
proved patchy at rehearsal, and Wagner's doubts about him were not
helped either by his persistent hoarseness or by the open criticism of
Niemann and others. He soon realised that he had been overhasty in

engaging Josephine Scheffsky, and he retained her only because it was too late to find a replacement. Even so respected and admired a singer as Amalie Materna was not proof against his ceaseless strivings for perfection. Fricke described a piano rehearsal of the second act of *Götterdämmerung* on 7 July: "At the very moment Frau Materna, in full flight, was sending shivers down our spines with her singing, Wagner springs up, drags her to another position, interrupts her singing. The passage is repeated. Frau Materna finds it impossible to regain her emotional mood, for it is as if she has had a bucket of cold water thrown over her. She makes mistakes. Hans Richter shouts that she should have learnt it all thoroughly before the rehearsal. The gigantic lady was completely shattered by this rehearsal and cried on her way home. It was almost impossible to comfort her." Kögel, the new Hagen, lost his nerve entirely under the strain and departed. Wagner appealed once more to Scaria, but in vain. When, at Hill's recommendation, Wagner invited Gustav Siehr of Wiesbaden to take over the role of Hagen, less than three weeks remained before the dress rehearsal.

Cosima found herself in difficulties with Doepler, whose sketches for the costumes she had initially liked, but the figurines disappointed her. "I should like everything to be much simpler, more primitive," she wrote on 13 July. At a costume rehearsal on 28 July she asked Doepler to make Siegfried's clothes a little less close-fitting and to dress Gutrune's ladies less brightly: "The poor man becomes so angry and rude that I realise for the first time what a hack one is having to deal with! The costumes are reminiscent throughout of Red Indian chiefs and still bear, along with their ethnographic absurdity, all the marks of provincial tastelessness. I am much dismayed by them and also rather shocked by the professor's manner. R. is having great trouble with Wotan's hat; it is a veritable musketeer's hat!"

Doepler was also at loggerheads with Brandt, who, Fricke remarked, was not the easiest of men to get along with. Fricke had difficulties with him too, for Brandt was inclined to regard his machinery and his technical effects as of prime importance, whereas Fricke preferred simpler solutions and occasionally tried to persuade Wagner to simplify the stage action. Wagner, however, had unbounded faith in Brandt. All the same, Fricke was generous in his praise for both Karl and his son Fritz, who was assisting him. "The finest stage managers I have ever seen," he wrote. "Such precision, such calm amid the most magnificent of transformations!"

Stagecraft was at that period at a high level of development, and Wagner, having witnessed the wonders of vaudeville theatres in Paris and London, had every confidence that all he had demanded in his written stage directions in the way of swimming Rhinemaidens, rainbow

bridges, sky-borne Valkyries, flames, collapsing buildings and rising
rivers was well within the compass of technicians such as Brandt and his
family. To achieve their effects they made ingenious use of painted
scenery on rollers and images projected through a magic lantern. Steam,
an essential element in their elaborate scene changes, was provided by
an old locomotive. Some of the contraptions the technicians used were
perhaps clumsy and extravagant in terms of manpower: each of the
swimming machines for the three Rhinemaidens, for example,
demanded one man to push it about and another, seated on it, to raise or
lower the arms on which the singers were strapped; in addition, each
machine had a musical assistant (Fischer, Seidl and Mottl) to direct the
matching of the movements to the music. Various props, among them a
serpent, Fricka's "car with a yoke of rams", a bear, a dragon and a pair
of ravens, had been ordered from Richard Keene, a maker of pan-
tomime gadgets in London, and Fricke was full of admiration for the
serpent into which Alberich turns himself in *Das Rheingold*, with its
movable jaw, revolving eyes and shining scales. The dragon for *Siegfried*
was still an unknown factor, since not all its parts had arrived by the time
the performances began. The only live animal to be brought on stage
was Brünnhilde's Grane, a nine-year-old black horse ("gentle as a
lamb", Fricke reported) supplied by King Ludwig. In rehearsal Wagner
decided to keep the horse out of sight during Brünnhilde's confronta-
tion with Siegmund, finding its presence too distracting, but it appeared
in both *Siegfried* and *Götterdämmerung*.

On 10 July two *de luxe* copies of Nietzsche's new book arrived at
Wahnfried. This, the fourth in the series *Thoughts out of Season*, was
entitled *Richard Wagner in Bayreuth*, and it paid tribute not only to the
significance of Bayreuth in the development of the German theatre, but
also to the man who had pursued his ideal with such tenacity and
personal self-sacrifice. The suggestion, later spread even by Nietzsche
himself, that this book was basically insincere hardly stands up to a
reading of it. There can be no doubting the deep veneration behind it,
and Nietzsche's act in putting it aside unfinished, completing it only
after his pupil Heinrich Köselitz (Peter Gast) praised it, was due to his
feeling that it was too private for general consumption. Having finally
decided to publish it on the eve of the festival, he did, however, feel some
anxiety about its reception by Wagner himself. "When I consider what I
have ventured to do, I feel like closing my eyes," he wrote in the draft of
a letter to Wagner. "The memory of it makes me shudder, and I do not
know what to ask of you, except that you should accept what is done
as done." In another draft he wrote: "My writing has for me the
unpleasant result that every time I publish a book something in my

personal relationships is placed in jeopardy and has then with the aid of generosity to be put right again."

In the end he decided to leave his misgivings unspoken, and he sent off the copies with a letter addressed to Cosima alone. In his book, he wrote, "you will see that I could not be content with preparing myself in solitude from afar for the great and momentous event of this summer, but had to communicate my joy. If only I may hope to have divined now and again a note of *your* joy and given expression to it! There is nothing finer that I could wish for myself."

Both Wagner and Cosima read the book at once. "A splendid piece," she wrote in her diary on 11 July, and she sent off a telegram to Nietzsche: "To you, dear friend, I now owe my sole refreshment of mind and elevation of spirit, apart from the powerful artistic impressions received here." Wagner's comment on 12 July was equally enthusiastic: "Friend, your book is simply tremendous! Where did you learn so much about me? Come soon and familiarise yourself with the impact at rehearsals."

Nietzsche arrived in Bayreuth on 24 July and attended all the rehearsals of *Götterdämmerung* on that and the two following days. But he was suffering severe headaches, and he spent most of his time with Malwida von Meysenbug, who had arrived a few days earlier, taking refuge from the sultry weather in the cool garden of her house. "I have to take great care of myself," he wrote to his sister on 28 July, "and refuse all invitations, even to the Ws. W. remarked how little they see of me." After attending on 31 July a rehearsal of *Die Walküre* at which he was unable on account of his painful eyes to look at the stage, he wrote to his sister that it was senseless to stay in Bayreuth any longer, and he went off to Klingenbrunn, a quiet village in the neighbourhood. There he began to draft those critical remarks on Wagner's works which first appeared two years later in *Human, All Too Human*, but these cannot be regarded as the direct result of his experiences in Bayreuth. His letters to his sister from Klingenbrunn contained no disparagement of the *Ring* (of which he had in any case seen only a fraction in rehearsal, and that without costumes) or of Wagner personally, and he certainly did not attempt to discourage Elisabeth from going to the dress rehearsals and the performances. His unhappiness during the rehearsal period can be attributed chiefly to the bad state of his health, and to that one can perhaps add the sense of inadequacy which the sight of this much older man, bursting with vigour and coping cheerfully with all the artistic difficulties and social obligations of the moment, always aroused in him.

The three private performances Wagner had promised King Ludwig were in the end reduced for practical reasons to one, and this was

officially designated as the final dress rehearsal. The king warned
Wagner in advance that he would make no public appearances during
his visit to Bayreuth. "I am coming," he wrote on 12 July, "to delight in
and renew my spirits with your great creation, to refresh my heart and
soul, not to display myself to inquisitive gapers and sacrifice myself to
ovations."

His arrival in the early hours of 6 August was in keeping with his
obsessive desire for secrecy. The royal train arrived just after midnight
and stopped on an open field outside the town. Wagner was waiting
close by with a carriage, into which the king quickly stepped, and they
drove together to the nearby Eremitage, where Ludwig was to spend his
visit in strict privacy. From there, where he resolutely refused to receive
any deputations from the town, he drove on the evening of 6 August in a
closed carriage to attend the dress rehearsal of *Das Rheingold*, ignoring
the cheers of the people lining the streets. He had insisted that there
should be no audience (though a few intimate friends were smuggled
into the theatre), and he watched the performance in solitude, with only
Wagner at his side. He did relax sufficiently afterwards to receive Cosima
and the children, but he declined an invitation to visit them at Wahnfried.

The process was repeated on the following three evenings, with the
difference that a carefully selected audience was admitted, the empty
seats during *Das Rheingold* having had an adverse effect on the acoustics
of the theatre, but all its members were under strict instructions to take
no notice of the king. Each of the four works was played without interruption and, except for the absence of the dragon, whose head had
not yet arrived from London, was complete in every detail. At midnight
on 9 August, after the performance of *Götterdämmerung*, King Ludwig left
by train as secretly as he had arrived. "R. professes to have detected a
certain ill feeling as he takes his departure," Cosima wrote. "The King
has forbidden any sort of ovation, yet he seems astonished when none
takes place."

In his letter of thanks, written at Hohenschwangau in the night of 12
August, Ludwig compared his joy with that of Tannhäuser on his return
to the world from the Venusberg: "You are a divine mortal, the true
God-given artist who brought to earth the sacred fire of heaven to
purify, inspire and redeem it! The divine mortal who in truth can
neither err nor go astray! Through hearing this ravishing, magnificent, profound poetry, so blissfully transfigured and consecrated by the
divinely inspired music in which it is clothed, I have been transported to
such a pitch of emotion, raised to such a state of happiness as never in my
life before." He implored Wagner to make it possible for him to see the
work again. "I beg you to shut me off from all the princes and nobles in

the royal box by an actual wall and prevent them, with policemen if necessary, from disturbing me even during the intervals. . . . Is there a single one among them who for thirteen years has been sighing as I have for these festival days, who has clung to you as I have from his earliest youth in unshakable friendship and loyalty and with a fervour that never cooled, and will never cool?"

Emperor Wilhelm arrived on 13 August and was met at the railway station by the complete company, singers and orchestra, with Wagner at their head. The emperor, now in his eightieth year, had little interest in the arts, but Wagner respected him, as he told Cosima, for his "decency and trustworthiness". The emperor, even if he cared little for Wagner's music, could nevertheless admire a man who fought his own cause so vigorously, and that feeling was reflected in the words he spoke to Wagner at the railway station, within sight of the festival theatre on the hill: "I never believed you would be able to do it, but now the sun is shining on your work." He had come to the opening, he added, because he regarded the festival as a national event. In a letter to King Ludwig written that same night Wagner observed ironically: "What has the 'nation' to do with my work and its realisation?"

There was another arrival at the railway station that day: the head of the serpent Fafner. If Wagner was pleased to see it, Fricke was not. "I whispered to Doepler: 'To the darkest lumber-room with the wretched beast!'," he wrote in his diary. "'Leave it out! This serpent will be the death of us!'" It had cost Wagner five hundred pounds, and, when it appeared on stage, it still lacked its proper neck, which in fact never arrived. Brandt had to patch it up as best he could.

The festival opened on Sunday, 13 August, and, during the following three weeks, the *Ring* cycle was performed three times, each cycle beginning on a Sunday. All performances were conducted by Richter, and the cast, except for a few minor changes, due mainly to indisposition, was the same throughout.

Wagner's final words of advice to his singers were written in a notice which was hung up at the back of the stage and in all the dressing-rooms: "!! Clarity!! The big notes will look after themselves, the small notes and their text are the main thing. *Never address the audience direct.* In monologues always look either up or down, never straight ahead. Last wish: stay kind to me, dear people!" The orchestra also received its final words: "No prelude-playing! Piano pianissimo – then all will be well!"

The first performance of *Das Rheingold*, Cosima reported, was ruled by a completely unlucky star: "Betz loses the ring, runs into the wings twice during the curse, a stagehand raises the backdrop too soon during the first scene change and one sees people standing around in shirt sleeves and the back wall of the theatre, all the singers embarrassed, etc.,

etc. . . . R. at first very upset, but gradually regains his spirits, and the sudden visit of the Emperor of Brazil restores the mood of ebullience."

Dom Pedro II, whose love of Wagner's music had led him in 1857 to invite the composer to stage his works in Rio de Janeiro, arrived in Bayreuth unannounced, and thus was not, like the other princely visitors, accorded accommodation in the royal palace. He went to a hotel where, asked to fill in a registration form, he wrote down his occupation as "emperor". Wagner, informed of his arrival, hastily invited him to a reception in Wahnfried.

As Wagner was well aware, Dom Pedro was probably the only princely personage beside King Ludwig who had been drawn to Bayreuth out of artistic interest: the remainder were there for social reasons, to which the presence of the German emperor naturally contributed. The main bulk of his audiences consisted of his professed admirers (among them Nietzsche, who returned to Bayreuth for the first cycle), who had, after all, been responsible, however inadequately, for the building of the theatre. Of the many fellow composers present – they included Bruckner, Grieg, Saint-Saëns and Tchaikovski – the attraction was the new work rather than the theatre itself; and the large body of critics, including Eduard Hanslick, was there for obvious professional reasons. All of these wrote their impressions of the occasion and, if it is possible at all to find a common note among them, it is on the mundane level of physical discomfort: the wretched train service, the profiteering of the Bayreuth citizens who provided the beds, the difficulties of obtaining meals in the town's few, overworked hotels and restaurants. From all these accounts it is well-nigh impossible to assess the artistic impact of Wagner's production. Ludwig Strecker wrote in his diary after the completion of the first cycle, which, after the technical accidents in *Das Rheingold*, went smoothly: "I had expected the audience's enthusiasm to be greater than it actually was after each act and at the end of the evening. Perhaps this was due to the placards which had been put up, saying that the artists as well as the author had agreed not to take curtain calls, however cordially invited. Just once, at the conclusion of *Das Rheingold* – before the placards appeared – there was strong applause at the end and calls for Wagner. Then only yesterday again, after the last act of *Götterdämmerung*."

The end of the first cycle saw the departure of the entire princely contingent (the emperor had in fact departed after *Die Walküre* to attend military manoeuvres). Wagner consequently invited King Ludwig to return to Bayreuth for the third cycle, a suggestion the king seized on eagerly. "I feel since the experience of those blissful days that I have been born anew," he wrote on 20 August, "and I can hardly wait to repeat them. . . . Led astray mainly by my historical studies, I for a time pursued other ideals, sacrificed at other altars. But now I feel more clearly than ever before that nothing on earth has succeeded in separating me from my original source, and I can with a good conscience apply to myself those words which in the prologue to *Faust* Goethe placed in the mouth of God: 'A good man in his dark, bewildered course will not forget the way of righteousness.'"

Now at last, as a birthday present for Ludwig, Wagner fulfilled his promise to set Brünnhilde's rejected address at the end of *Götter-dämmerung* to music, fitting the final words to the motive known as World Inheritance. He wrote a piano accompaniment, and made no attempt to incorporate the passage in the performance the king attended.

As before, Ludwig insisted that there should be no public ceremonies of any kind. He arrived in the night of 27 August and again took up his solitary residence at the Eremitage. Kietz wrote in his reminiscences: "The custodian told us that orders had been given for the whole park to be brilliantly illuminated and that the guards were to be stationed unseen behind the trees while the king made his nocturnal wanderings. I was very curious whether I should succeed in seeing him in the festival theatre. King Ludwig always came in with Wagner after the orchestra had begun to play and the whole house was in darkness. On the fourth evening, before the performance of *Götterdämmerung*, it was the same. But as soon as the king took his seat beside Wagner, the music suddenly stopped, the whole house was brilliantly illuminated and . . . Herr Feustel expressed his gratitude in an enthusiastic call for cheers for the king, in which the whole assembly joined heartily. After the third cheer all became dark again and the orchestra began anew. It was a wonderful performance, everyone full of the greatest enthusiasm, and, though people were not supposed to applaud, clapping broke out frequently during the action, as well as after every act and at the end, when it threatened never to cease. Until at last – a most unusual event – the king returned to his box with Wagner and stood beside him, applauding himself, while Wagner bowed to all sides."

Finally Wagner appeared on the stage, surrounded by all his artists in costume, including those who had appeared only in the earlier parts of the *Ring*. "And thus," Cosima wrote in her diary, "most astonishingly, the programme which nobody thought possible has been adhered to."

It was followed by a mixture of jubilation and depression: jubilation that it had been done at all, depression that it had not been better done. "He feels from day to day," Fricke wrote in his diary, "how differently his work might still be staged, he begins to feel the things that should be forbidden or rejected, sees that I was right in all I said. 'Next year we shall do it all differently,' he told me when we were alone."

Before Hey left, Wagner asked him to continue the training of Unger, whom he engaged for another year with an allowance of twelve thousand marks. He had, Wagner said, unbounded confidence in them both. Hey wrote to his wife that he found the parting very affecting: "This unique man occupies an immensely large place in my heart. He is undeniably a personality from whom one receives not just in passing but for *ever* new and vital nourishment for the modest needs of one's own work."

In the next few days Wagner wrote letters of praise to others of his singers, notably to Amalie Materna ("You were the best and closest to me of them all, living only for the one thing, never wavering"), to Lilli Lehmann ("You three were the finest of all. . . . My three Rhinemaidens gave the whole thing its magic"), to Siehr ("You are a born dramatic artist") and to Wilhelmj, who received a humorous poem. Wagner was sufficiently a man of the theatre to appreciate the value of praise, and he was lavish with it at the appropriate moment. Equally, he himself was vulnerable to slights, and the two singers whom in his "Retrospect of the Stage Festivals" (written in 1878) he called the soul of the enterprise, Niemann and Betz, incensed him at the time so greatly with their temperamental behaviour that he vowed to replace them when the festival was repeated next year.

Several of their most intimate friends stayed on for a few days after the final performance and joined in the post-mortem discussions. On 1 September, Cosima recorded, they dined with the Schleinitzes and Malwida, and Liszt played to them the first movement and the Adagio from Beethoven's "Hammerklavier" sonata. Judith Gautier, now divorced from Catulle Mendès, came from Paris to attend the second series of performances, but she remained for the third as well, finally leaving on 2 September. A note which Wagner addressed to her was probably written that day, though it was undated: "Dear one, I am sad! There is another reception this evening, but I shall not go down to it. I have been reading some pages from my life, dictated some time ago to Cosima. She is sacrificing herself to the habits of her father – alas! Was this morning's embrace my last? No, I shall see you again – I want to, because I love you! Adieu – think kindly of me! R."

The last visitor to depart was Mathilde Maier. She took home with her, as a present from him, one of the few printed copies of *My Life*. On that day, 9 September, Cosima wrote in her diary that she and Wagner continued to discuss the lessons learnt from the festival: "I mention the scene between Waltraute and Brünnhilde and observe that – wonderful as it is – it does prove tiring, because already too much music has been heard before it; R. agrees with me and decides to divide up the first act, to make a long pause after the introduction and begin the act with the orchestral 'Siegfried's Journey'. In this way *Götterdämmerung* would be a repetition of the whole, an introduction and 3 parts. – Costumes, scenery, everything must be done anew for the repeat performances. R. is very sad, says he wishes he could die!"

To recover from the strain of the festival Wagner decided to take his family to Italy for a prolonged holiday. While Cosima was busy preparing for the journey, Wagner sat down and outlined in a letter to King Ludwig his feelings about the festival and his plans for the future: "The indisputable outward success of the festival, even the praise of many enthusiastic friends, cannot conceal from me the truth from which the last veil has now been torn: I know now that I and my work have no place in these times of ours. . . . So it is now only for myself – and for you, my noble friend, that I shall strive to save my work. I shall continue to polish it until – as far as our badly managed and badly applied artistic means allow – it is brought to a state which is clear and understandable and at any rate correct, before handing it over to our fine fellow beings to be savaged. To start with, I intend to stage three more performances next summer: for these I shall try to achieve a better casting of some of the roles and, by giving it careful thought, to improve all the recognised deficiencies and incongruities of the production: the stage decorations also stand in need of considerable retouching and at some points indeed replacement. The means for this will come easily enough, since it will be possible this time significantly to reduce the admission charges, and the demand from all kinds of countries, now it is realised that there is every assurance of a great success, will presumably be very large, enabling me to devote the greater part of the proceeds to the payment of my artists. In the meantime therefore – just because I cannot yet consider it to have been well enough presented – I shall hold my work back from any wider distribution."

CHAPTER XIV

OCTOBER 1876 – JUNE 1877:

Sorrento and London

FROM SORRENTO IN the Bay of Naples, where they were living in a small cottage in the grounds of the Hotel Vittoria, Cosima wrote, probably on 15 October, a letter to Judith Gautier: "Shortly after you, everybody went away, and in our sudden solitude the hubbub you saw was succeeded by a fantastic stillness. Not a soul to introduce to my dear friend, no more acts of courtesy to perform – but above all, alas, nothing more to see and hear. On the first Sunday of this novel situation I began to tell my chambermaid to lay out my dress with the long train, since there would be no interval that evening – and she to laugh, and I to sigh. It had all vanished as if by magic, except for the distant shadow of our theatre speaking to us silently of what had been, and we looked at each other like sleepers awakened. My husband, however, was too exhausted to return to his work, and even less able to concern himself with the somewhat complicated business aspects of the performances. I had to promise him to settle all my domestic problems within a week, and on 15 September we set off with bag and baggage, that is to say with our four children [the four younger ones, Daniela being at her boarding school], their governess and all that that entailed in the matter of possessions. Our progress has so far been favoured by splendid weather, and you could hardly imagine the beauty of the spot in which we are now living. I have resumed my lessons with the children after a break of three months; we work from eight to midday, at midday we bathe in the sea, which is as gentle as a lamb, we have lunch at one, and after lunch we go for a walk, invariably in gangs of seven. . . . While I and the children are working in the morning, my husband is at his heavy task of gearing his chariot for next year. He is having to write to all and sundry in an effort to cover the deficit on this year, and then he has to reassemble the threads for next year's performances. It would make me deeply sad to see him using up all his physical, intellectual and moral energies in this way, were I not to tell myself that his task is an imprescriptible one, and that he is as much a man of action as of thought."

At the time of their leaving Bayreuth it had seemed as if the first festival might just about have paid for itself, but a letter from Feustel which reached Wagner on 23 September in Venice revealed that the out-standing debts amounted to some 120,000 marks (a sum which in-creased as time went on). According to a later balance sheet notified to Wagner by Feustel on 24 September 1878, the total cost of the festival, including the erection of the theatre, amounted to 1,272,876 marks, of which 177,824 marks represented payments to the singers and other participants. The sale of certificates of patronage yielded 724,775 marks, which, even allowing for the fact that a proportion of the total sum collected from this source had been deducted to repay King Ludwig's loan (of which only two-thirds was taken up), meant that the original target had not been reached. If it had not been for Wagner's own con-tributions to the funds and the last-minute sale of tickets at the box office, the deficit would have been even greater than it was.

Nevertheless, the size of it came as a severe shock, not least to Wagner's pride, and his sense of bitterness only increased when it gradually became clear that the task of paying off the debt was to be left to him alone. The town of Bayreuth, having promised its citizens that the festival would place no financial burden on them, was unwilling to advance the money, and the management committee was reluctant to sanction a general appeal to the festival patrons (Wagner's idea) for fear of the adverse publicity this might cause. A discreet private application to the more opulent patrons as well as to other well-wishers was another possible way, and indeed Heckel did manage by this means to secure 1,000 marks from Friedrich Schön, a factory owner in Worms, but Wagner was under no illusions that much could be obtained in this fashion. Inevitably he turned once more to Ludwig, whom Feustel and everybody else regarded as the natural saviour, but he chose a somewhat indirect way to do it. In his letter of 21 October he spoke first of his feelings of "superfluity" in finding that his fellow countrymen showed no desire, after the example he had set them, to continue along the path of theatrical reform, but he assured the king that, in spite of his dis-illusionment, he was determined to carry on. His plan was to invite the German state to take over the existing theatre, including all its assets and obligations, and to provide a yearly subsidy of 100,000 marks to help finance further performances of his works. In return, the state would be given five or six hundred seats at each performance to dis-tribute free to its poorer citizens, by which means "the whole under-taking would assume, outwardly as well, the character of a 'national' one".

This plan, Wagner observed, had only one defect: "that I should have to entrust its execution to the '*Reich*'. It would be greater, more worthy and altogether more apt if Bavaria and its King were to carry it out alone."

Ludwig took refuge from this appeal in silence, as did virtually all others to whom Wagner applied for help or advice. Only Heckel showed some sympathy with his personal distress, declaring in his letter of 30 October that it was the task of his supporters and not of Wagner himself to find ways of meeting the deficit. He suggested that this could be done by giving a fourth performance of the *Ring* the following year solely for that purpose, but Wagner felt it would be impossible to wait so long.

Cosima's diary reflects the conscious attempt they made during this holiday to put the children in the forefront of their concern, both as a refuge from their present worries and as a recompense to the children for past neglect. They saw nobody except Malwida, who came with Nietzsche and his philosopher friend Paul Rée to stay in Sorrento for a few days, and even then their meetings were infrequent (Cosima mentioned only two in her diary). This was partly because Wagner and she did not take to Rée, and partly because Nietzsche's wretched state of health made him a depressing companion.

Their usual pleasure in each other's company also threatened to fail them. "We admit to each other," Cosima wrote in her diary on 30 October, "that we frequently keep silent just in order not to have to impart to each other our gloomy thoughts concerning the present situation and all our past experiences."

There were other reasons as well for their temporary withdrawal from one another. The cause, on Wagner's side, was Judith Gautier. His note to her on her departure from Bayreuth had been followed by another, in which he told her that his first solitary walk after the festival had taken him past the house where she had been staying, and "I tasted your kisses". Then, from somewhere in Italy (neither place nor date is clear) he wrote: "Dear soul, sweet friend, I shall love you always! Always you will remain for me what you are, the sole ray of love in those days so diverting for some and so lacking in satisfaction for me. But for me you are filled with a gentle fire, soothing and intoxicating! Oh, how I should love to embrace you again, my dear sweet one! I pity you for your present life. But everyone is to be pitied – particularly myself if I were to follow your advice to forget you."

Judith did not reply to these letters, but she continued to write to Cosima. She was, it seems, rather embarrassed by Wagner's attentions, for, following her divorce from Catulle Mendès, she had found a very devoted companion in Ludwig Benedictus, the son of a Dutch diamond merchant and himself an amateur composer. Judith did not reveal in her own reminiscences how far her relationship with Wagner went, but she told her goddaughter, Suzanne Meyer-Zundel, that in 1876 Wagner arranged for a seat in the festival theatre between her and Benedictus to be kept empty for him, and, slipping into it when the lights went down, he held her tightly and whispered to her: "I should like to listen to all my works in your arms." On another occasion, visiting her at the house where she was staying, he asked her whether she would not like to bear him a son. For all this we have only Mlle Meyer-Zundel's word* – but there can be no denying the intensity of Wagner's feelings for the young and handsome Judith, which, though they found no further expression now for lack of opportunity, were shortly to break out again.

Cosima too had emotional worries about which she kept silent, and these were connected with both Bülow and Daniela, alone in her boarding school in Dresden while her sisters and brother were enjoying the delights of Italy. Cosima's strictness towards her eldest-born was closely connected with her feelings of guilt towards Bülow and her desire to make amends by presenting him with a well-trained daughter to take her place. She took every opportunity to remind Daniela of the father she had not seen since the age of nine. "The day on which I discover traces in you of your father's character," she wrote to her earlier that year (4 May), "of his loyalty, his veracity, his disinterestedness, his devotion to others and his disregard for himself, on that day, my child, I shall know a mother's happiness." Daniela, now in her sixteenth year, came home for the festival, and after her return to Dresden Cosima wrote to her on 11 September from Bayreuth: "Your behaviour here gave evidence of much good will and pleased me greatly. All that now remains is for you to realise or to learn that you must be tidy and diligent, able to take care of yourself. On this point you seem to be much mistaken, and that worries me for your own sake. The luxury of our home does not stem from me and will cease with your father Richard's life. . . . As a girl I never had servants, I made my bed and tidied my room myself, washed my own linen and did my own hair (even for balls)."

For Cosima, Bülow's absence during the festival was a painful reminder of her own responsibility for the course his life was now taking. He had written to her on 6 February 1876 from Chicago, telling her that he had decided to remain in America and had taken the first steps towards naturalisation. Ending his letter with a reference to the forthcoming festival, he wrote: "Do not doubt that I am praying fervently that Providence will grant you every satisfaction with the success of the greatest musical event of this century. Believe me, madame, it is the situation in which I am placed of finding it equally impossible *to be there or not to be there* that has led primarily to the irrevocable decision I have taken." A breakdown in health caused him to reverse his decision, and, on the eve of the festival he was in a nursing home in Bad Godesberg on the Rhine. From there he wrote at the beginning of July to Pohl: "I am

---

* Published in Léon Guichard: *Richard et Cosima Wagner: Lettres à Judith Gautier.*

finding it difficult to overcome a feeling of shame for having brought myself to such a sorry pass, and this had to happen just in anno Bayreuth, in the year I had resolved to remain in America because of the moral impossibility, applicable to a certain extent to both sides, that I, a Wagnerian of old, should not attend the festival. That is the bitterest thing about it. Yet to have remained in America in my totally ruined state of health would have been tantamount to slow suicide. Though perhaps I ought to have chosen that in preference."

Wagner left Sorrento with his family on 7 November, and two days later they reached Rome. There they spent three weeks, paying a couple of calls on Princess Wittgenstein, whom neither he nor Cosima had seen for several years. It was in Rome too that on 30 November they made the acquaintance of Count Joseph Arthur Gobineau, a French writer who had just retired from a diplomatic career. At that time they knew none of his works, but the man himself they found pleasant company. They concluded their holiday with a fortnight in Florence, where they paid a visit to Jessie Laussot, now the life companion (and later wife) of the German historian Karl Hillebrand. On 20 December they were back in Bayreuth.

On New Year's Day 1877, pursuing the thoughts expressed in his letter of 21 October to King Ludwig about the form the Reichstag's help might take, Wagner wrote a letter to the committees of the various Wagner Societies. He reminded them that, in order to fill the seats at the festival of the previous year, it had become necessary in the end to sell tickets to members of the ordinary public. This had been a betrayal of his original intention, which had been to provide a festival for the supporters of his ideas rather than to force those ideas on the general public. Though he was now being urged to repeat this process of selling tickets at the box office, he himself felt he owed it to his supporters and his artists to resist the temptation, and he proposed the formation of a Society of Patrons to finance an annual repetition of the festival through yearly subscriptions.

In this letter Wagner also mentioned the possibility of establishing a school for musical and dramatic art in Bayreuth. Both Feustel and the mayor were in favour of this, but their most immediate concern was to be allowed to announce at once a repeat of the *Ring* performances in the coming summer, confident of its ability to pay for itself. Wagner was unwilling to sanction it, declaring that he did not want to stage a festival "just on account of the deficit". Their hopes, however, of finding a solution to the deficit problem through King Ludwig were dashed when Düfflipp, coming to Bayreuth on 21 January to discuss the situation, had no proposal of any kind to make. On the contrary, he told Feustel and the mayor that the king had instructed him to demand the return of the money so far advanced by him, and he had no intention of providing more.

To Wagner there now seemed no way of paying off his debts other than by undertaking conducting engagements, and he began to consider a suggestion from Wilhelmj, now established in London, that he should conduct a series of concerts there. Suddenly, however, he found himself in the grip of another urge. Cosima wrote in her diary on 25 January: "He calls out to me: 'There is something I won't tell you.' 'Oh, please tell me!' 'I am going to begin *Parzival* and shan't let it out of my sight until it is finished' – whereupon I laugh aloud for joy."

The sketch Wagner wrote for King Ludwig in August 1865 was a prose narrative which had still to be cast in dramatic form. This was the task Wagner now began, and on 28 February he was able to put into Cosima's hands the complete drama, worked out in prose dialogue. He was completely absorbed by his work. "Three times as he was dressing he broke off to run upstairs and write additions to his sketch," she wrote on 10 February. "He also runs upstairs at lunch, to write down Klingsor to Kundry: '*Was frägst du mich, verworfenes Weib?*'" He was not yet concerning himself directly with the music, though he did allow the one melody that had come to him as he was composing the *Centennial March* ("*Komm, holder Knabe*") to influence his conception of the Flower Maidens, whom he decided to present as "languishing figures, not as demons".

Cosima's initial reaction to a visit to London had been one of dismay, for Britain was now one of Bülow's main fields of activity, and she felt it might be both embarrassing and damaging for his prospects if Wagner were to put in an appearance there. However, when she heard that Bülow was lying ill in Hanover and there was no likelihood of a clash, she withdrew her objections.

Wilhelmj had found in London a new firm of concert agents, Hodge and Essex, who were willing to promote a series of twenty concerts in May. Wagner wrote to three singers, Amalie Materna, Georg Unger and Karl Hill, asking them to accompany him to London. He seemed in his letters to them to take the whole affair rather lightly – "A lot of pieces, for the English gobble music" and "We shall do it the 'English way'" were two of the phrases with which he sought to tempt them, and he held out prospects of rich earnings, both for the singers and himself. His expectations might have been over-optimistic, but he had been told that the concerts would take place in the Albert Hall, and it was reasonable for him to assume that the promoters would not have hired it unless they were confident of selling all its huge number of seats. What he did not know was that Hodge and Essex had little experience of this kind of undertaking, and their estimates were as unrealistic as his own. By the time they realised that it would be impossible to fill the Albert Hall twenty times over, and reduced the number of concerts to six, Wagner had already made promises to his singers regarding their fees. Some adjustment was made, but by the standards of those days they were over-paid. Wagner then added to the difficulties by engaging more singers than he originally suggested, and the promoters, who had intended to import the best orchestral players from Germany, had to economise by assembling an orchestra in England.

Within a fortnight of his own departure, Wagner had received no money at all from Hodge and Essex. He wrote on 22 April to Wilhelmj: "The whole thing has so far cost me a lot of worry. I feel we are really doing something very senseless. Hodge and Essex may be excellent people, but they should not have made a contract with me, for by doing that they led me to assume certain things from which, when the first contractual obligations were not fulfilled, I had some difficulty in extricating myself. Well, in this matter I shall just have to rely on blind faith."

While engaged in these negotiations, Wagner worked on the text of *Parsifal*. This was now the spelling of the hero's name. Wagner decided that on 14 March, basing himself on an assertion of the German writer Johann Joseph Görres that "Parseh-fal" meant in Arabic "pure fool", a dubious piece of philology with, however, fruitful artistic results. He finished the first act on 29 March, at a time when Liszt was staying at Wahnfried. It was, according to Cosima's account, a singularly har-monious visit, during which Liszt worked too, correcting the proofs of his biography of Chopin, a revised version of the book first published in 1852. After Liszt's departure on 3 April Wagner made even swifter pro-gress, completing the second act on 13 April and the third six days later.

They arrived in London on 1 May. The writer Edward Dannreuther, who had been acting as go-between, took them to his home at 12 Orme Square, where they stayed throughout their visit. On the following day they crossed Kensington Gardens to view the Albert Hall. It was then a new building, having been opened by Queen Victoria in 1871, and it had been built mainly with monster choral concerts in view. By the terms of its charter, 1,300 of its 10,000 seats were in the permanent possession of "seatholders" who had paid £100 each towards the construction costs, and these seats could not be sold – a drawback of which Hodge and Essex seem initially to have been unaware, though it was of vital impor-tance in calculating their prospective financial returns from Wagner's concerts. The singers had already arrived, and Amalie Materna voiced her fears that she would be unable to make herself heard in so vast an arena. Wagner himself was undaunted. The orchestra Wilhelmj had assembled, and which he led, was a large one of 169 players, and, after a rehearsal on 4 May, Wagner expressed himself well satisfied with it.

The programmes had been arranged to show, in the first half of each concert, Wagner's development as a composer, covering the works from *Rienzi* to *Die Meistersinger*; the second part was devoted to excerpts from the *Ring*. Wagner, a relatively unknown figure in England when he first conducted there in 1855, was by this time famous. *Der Fliegende Holländer* had been performed at Drury Lane in 1870, *Lohengrin* at Covent Garden in 1875 and *Tannhäuser* in 1876 (all, incidentally, in Italian), and the Wagner Society in London, of which Dannreuther was the leading spirit, had since its inception in 1873 organised concerts which had attracted attention and in addition provided funds for the festival theatre.

His arrival, heavily advertised by Hodge and Essex in *The Times*, was regarded in London as an important social as well as an artistic occasion. Even before the first concert Wagner and Cosima found themselves dining, at the home of Maximilian Schlesinger, a Hungarian-born journalist who looked after the financial side of the tour, with such fellow guests as the poet Robert Browning and the painter Rudolf Lehmann, and on 6 May Cosima made the acquaintance of Mary Ann Evans, better known as the novelist George Eliot. Cosima had brought with her a letter of introduction from Liszt, who had met both Miss Evans and her life companion, the writer George Henry Lewes, in Weimar in 1852. This meeting opened still further doors: George Eliot wrote a note of introduction to the painter Edward Burne-Jones: "She is, I think, a rare person, worthy to see the best things, having her father's quickness and breadth of comprehension." Cosima, whose first visit to London this was, thoroughly enjoyed her social life, and Wagner's morning rehearsals turned into something like fashionable occasions, which Burne-Jones, the Leweses and other prominent people attended. Conversation with him had to be conducted through Cosima, whose English was fluent.

Despite the presence of Queen Victoria's youngest son, Prince Leopold, and two of the royal princesses, the first concert on 7 May revealed an alarming number of empty seats, due perhaps in part to the rather high prices: a stall in the amphitheatre cost one guinea. Cosima, sitting in her box with the Leweses, was horrified by the notorious Albert Hall echo. "No impression possible!" she wrote in her diary. "On top of that, our singers very feeble. Sad feelings, despite the brilliant reception for R." In its review of the event *The Times* praised both the orchestra and Amalie Materna, who sang the duet from the second act of *Tannhäuser* with Unger, but neither he nor the singers* in the excerpts

---

* In addition to Materna, Hill and Unger, these were Friederike Sadler-Grün, Schlosser, a bass named Chaudon from Vienna, and two ladies recruited by Hey in Munich (Fräulein Exter and Fräulein Waibel) as Rhinemaidens.

from *Das Rheingold* which occupied the second part were found worthy of mention. The second concert on 9 May, loyally described by Cosima as "an even greater success", and consisting of excerpts from *Der Fliegende Holländer* and the first act of *Die Walküre*, brought in only £600, a sum insufficient to cover the costs. And Wagner, who had already shown signs of fatigue in the first concert, found himself unable to bear the strain of conducting the whole programme: for the second part he handed the baton over to Richter, on leave from Vienna to assist him. The 20-year-old Bernard Shaw in one of his first pieces of music criticism, remarked in *The Hornet* that the orchestra only too plainly showed its relief when Richter took over, for Wagner's conducting technique was both abrupt and capricious.

For an event as much written about as these London concerts, it is remarkable how much uncertainty prevails about the amount of conducting done by Wagner himself. Some accounts claim that he conducted only the first item in each concert and then sat in an armchair on stage, watching Richter conduct the rest; others that he conducted the whole of the first half before handing over to Richter for the second. Cosima's diary fails completely to clear the matter up, since she did not mention the conducting arrangements at all. But in her letter of 10 May to her daughter Eva she wrote: "I can tell you that your father conducted only half of yesterday's concert, since he was too tired, and M. Richter replaced him for the second half." This suggests that Wagner did in fact conduct the whole of the first concert, and *The Times* review mentions that he conducted "a great part" of the third. This, which took place on a Saturday afternoon (12 May) in the presence of the Prince of Wales, attracted an audience twice as large as the first two concerts.

However, it was now clear to Wagner that the London venture would not wipe out the deficit on the Bayreuth festival by itself, and on the day following the third concert he wrote to Feustel, asking him to prepare a new appeal to his wealthy patrons, and to place his name at the top of the list with a personal subscription of three thousand marks. He added: "Should this also fail, I have made up my mind to effect an agreement . . . for America, and in that case to put my house in Bayreuth up for sale, go overseas with my family and never again return to Germany."

In the next days more difficulties arose. In the fourth concert Unger showed signs of hoarseness during the *Lohengrin* love duet and was unable to sing the "Forging Songs" from *Siegfried* in the second half; the Brünnhilde-Siegfried farewell scene from *Götterdämmerung* was substituted, but throughout Unger remained inaudible. On the following day Hill also became hoarse, so the fifth concert on 16 May had also to be rearranged. "The public," Cosima wrote in her diary, "already intimidated by the press and by Herr Joachim and consorts, will doubtless become even more timid, despite the brilliant reception given every time to both R. himself and all the pieces played. Requests are being made from all sides not to alter the programme, but how can it be adhered to?"

Wagner certainly had his opponents in London as in Germany, among whom the violinist Joseph Joachim, influential in both countries, occupied a prominent place, but the artistic impact of the London concerts was, for all their imperfections, sufficiently great to consider extending them; Wagner himself was in favour of doing so since, owing to the last-minute changes, nothing of *Siegfried* had yet been presented. Of the six concerts originally scheduled Queen Victoria had agreed to attend the last. Unable in the end to be there, she summoned Wagner to Windsor, where he went with Cosima on 17 May. Cosima herself was not received, but she sent Siegfried a picture of the queen. "She was very friendly towards Papa, and so were her children," she wrote. "I have seen nothing else as nice as the elephant, but other fine things, such as the Queen's castle in Windsor, which looks just like the olden times, when the men were entirely covered in iron. But it rains a lot here and it is rather cold."

That evening Lewes dined with the Dannreuthers and the Wagners at Orme Square, and he wrote in his diary: "No one else present until the evening, when a small party assembled to hear Wagner read his *Parsifal*, which he did with great spirit and like a fine actor."

The sixth concert, on Saturday afternoon, 19 May, consisted of excerpts from *Tristan und Isolde* and *Götterdämmerung*, together with the *Centennial March*. The two additional concerts could not be accommodated before the end of May, and in the meantime the singers had to be paid. The promoters had no money available for this purpose, and so Wagner asked Feustel to send him £1,200, a sum which appears to have been paid to him by the promoters as a guarantee before the concerts began. With this he paid his singers – virtually out of his own pocket.

With time to spare, Wagner joined in the social round. At a banquet on his birthday he presented to Amalie Materna, Richter and Wilhelmj medallions designed by Semper to commemorate the festival of 1876; on the following day he was guest of honour at a dinner arranged at the Athenaeum by William Siemens, the electrical engineer; on 23 May he went with Cosima to the fashionable photographers Elliott and Fry to have their portraits done; on 25 May they went to Greenwich and returned along the Thames by steamer. "This is Alberich's dream come true," he remarked to Cosima. "Nibelheim, world dominion, activity, work, everywhere the oppressive feeling of steam and fog." In the evening they saw *Tannhäuser* at Covent Garden, with Emma Albani and Fernando Carpi singing the main roles in Italian. They were not impressed. They visited the Tower of London on 26 May, on 27 May Wagner gave the painter Hubert Herkomer a sitting, and it was decided on a visit to the Leweses that Cosima's portrait should be done by Burne-Jones.

The two extra concerts, which included the *Kaisermarsch* and the *Huldigungsmarsch* as well as extracts from *Tristan, Die Meistersinger* and the *Ring*, took place on 28 and 29 May, and, if Unger, who had sung the "Forging Songs" and, with Amalie Materna, the third-act duet from *Siegfried* very well at rehearsal, had no voice left at the final concert, the audience was, to use Cosima's phrase, "very good-natured". On the following day Hodge and Essex gave Wagner a cheque for £700, which represented his total share of the proceeds of the eight concerts. "It was some relief to me," Cosima noted, "for I was expecting the worst, but R. is very depressed."

He sent the money off to Feustel on 3 June. "I shall one day tell you verbally all about it," he wrote, "into what confusion I have been thrown here by unparalleled recklessness, ignorance and fantastic assumptions based on a complete lack of experience. Enough: nobody has lost a single penny on or through me." He asked Feustel to raise his contribution to the subscription list for the deficit from 3,000 to 10,000 marks and to pay this sum at once to the most difficult of the creditors.

After a few more dinners, at one of which in the home of Dannreuther's father-in-law, Luke Ionides, they added William Morris to their list of distinguished acquaintances, they left London on 4 June. During the sittings Cosima had given Burne-Jones (the last on 31 May) he had done only a few drawings with which he was dissatisfied. "My fault, not yours," he wrote to her, "for you sat like Memnon." And so the portrait was never painted.

Arriving the following day at Bad Ems in Germany, where Wagner had arranged to take the cure, they were met by the children. The strain of the concerts had severely affected Wagner's health. He wrote to Dr Landgraf from Bad Ems, complaining of "sluggishness of the digestive functions, and in consequence distension of the abdomen, painful flatulence, etc.". On top of that, he was depressed by the knowledge of having exerted himself virtually in vain; indeed, of having aggravated the situation, for the creditors, put off with promises of riches from London, were now in a state of rebellion at receiving so little. It was at this stage that Cosima decided to sacrifice the 40,000 francs she had inherited from her mother, whose death in April of the previous year had left her virtually unmoved.

From King Ludwig, Wagner received a letter in the middle of June sympathising with him for the financial failure of the London venture.

"Oh, these tiresome pecuniary matters!" he wrote. Then, having heard from Düfflipp via Feustel of Wagner's threat to emigrate to America, he went on: "I implore you, by all the love and friendship that has bound us together for so many years, put this *appalling* thought right out of your mind. . . . In America, in that arid soil, your roses cannot flourish, in that land dominated by selfishness, uncharitableness and Mammon."

If, both here and in other books, Wagner's London concerts have been looked on mainly from the point of view of their financial significance and thus necessarily accounted a failure, it should not be forgotten that, from an artistic point of view, they played an important part in widening the appreciation of Wagner's works in Britain, and incidentally were the means of introducing to British audiences a man whose influence on musical development there eventually became very great: Hans Richter. On the human side too the visit had its rewards, as two letters to Cosima from London demonstrate. Since these have lain unobserved all these years in the depths of the Wahnfried archives, it is perhaps excusable to quote from them here at length.

One, from George Henry Lewes, was written from his Surrey home at The Heights, Witley, on 19 June: "First let me convey to the illustrious Meister the grateful acknowledgements of Madonna [George Eliot] for the prized photo, and autograph. Next let me assure you that 'Should we never meet again to Sense/Our souls will commune in intelligence'. You have established the secret vision of yourself too firmly in our souls for Time and Space (ideal entities as you know!) to dim, much less obliterate it. It was a complete case of conquest and 'love at first sight'. And, though you truly say *'on est autre dans chaque langue'* – when one is forced to appear not altogether as one *is* but as one *can*, and express oneself imperfectly – yet if the English photograph did not adequately represent the original, it presented something very exquisite and lovable; and I used to look in your clear eyes with a profound sense that we understood each other.

"Altogether the stirrings of the soul which the Meister's music and your personality excited in us will make the year of '77 ever memorable to us. We are at present deep in his Poems, and catching faint echoes of the music from the pianoforte. I have written for the volume of your mother's memoirs, but have not yet received it. When it comes we shall read it together, and think of you in this Paradise – for it is a Paradise we are in – firstly because of the divine love which would make a sunshine in the darkest place and a paradise of the ghetto – secondly because the country round about is indescribably lovely, our own grounds a picture, the weather transcendent, and the solitude complete. Nightingales, cuckoos, blackbirds, thrushes and finches make our wood and garden musical (by the way, thank the Meister for that delicious *mot* of his about the bird's interpretation of the thunder!), quiet work, fine books, and 'talking of lovely things that conquer death', fill up the long days. Nothing is wanting to complete happiness – except to see my Madonna out of pain, and with the bloom once more on her cheek."

The other letter, headed "The Grange, Northend, Fulham" and undated, came from Edward Burne-Jones, and began with lengthy apologies for his slowness in writing to thank Cosima for the plaster cast of Beethoven's death mask which she had sent him. She also sent him a photograph of herself which, he told her, "lives in dear company in my pocket, together with Margaret and Philip", his children.

"Indeed, I am glad of it," he went on, "for your friendship was a real gift of delight, and you left behind you a longing with many of us that some good fortune would presently bring you back, to renew and strengthen such a happy beginning of friendship. For my part I don't like even to pass that Albert Hall – for it all went by so quickly, and seems gone so utterly: all the music and the excitement – and the place looks as desolate as its haters could wish for it. But another year you will come back again – and we will make more fuss of you than before.

"As for what has happened since you left, it is little: I left my maiden [his daughter Margaret] in the country – where she rides a horse so big that she looks like a kitten on its back – the last I heard of her was that she had ridden by moonlight to Stonehenge – that is a great circle of stones set up, God knows when, by the Druids – and a funny sight it must have been to see that imp riding under the full moon on a wide heath, as if she were rehearsing for Brynhild.

"And of other friends all are well. Mr Grosvenor comes often, and sighs as only youth can sigh when that week is spoken of. At my age one sighs no more – groans begin instead – one day those will stop and then I shall grunt. And twice a week or oftener Morris comes, but of him I shall tell you in another letter. And wasn't he tiresome that night at Mr Ionides' and wouldn't talk, but sat as if, of all living men, an idea was most unusual with him – and do your friends ever behave so, when you want them to show off, and look their best, and when you have taken great pains to prepare the way for them, and have cleared the road for their march, and made an overture for them, do they ever nullify it all – till you could beat them with vexation? So that night I was vexed, for I wanted him to be bright and talk as no one else in England can, and he only sat and looked fat and sleepy. . . ."

Burne-Jones ended his very long letter with another apology for his delay in writing: "I don't know why a letter is so difficult to me – but it feels insufficient always – and this I hate in writing, that it never reads as

Villa d'Angri, Naples (at top of hill)

Malwida von Meysenbug

Paul Joukowsky

Auguste Renoir's portrait of Wagner, painted in Palermo in 1882

1882 (the year of *Parsifal*)

Above left: King Ludwig II of Bavaria

Above right: Carl Friedrich Glasenapp, Hans von Wolzogen and Heinrich von Stein (seated)

Below left: Hermann Levi

Below right: Count Arthur Gobineau

Wagner with family and friends outside the *salon* in Wahnfried:
from left (standing) Blandine, Heinrich von Stein, Cosima,
Daniela, Wagner, Siegfried; (seated) Isolde, Eva, Paul
Joukowsky

it feels when one writes: and one day an expert and wise man, having regard to this, will devise a musical notation for us – so that the very tone in which we think may be expressed – and this letter would sound very gentle if I could write a score for it."

CHAPTER XV

Judith Gautier and After

ON THEIR WAY home from Bad Ems, Wagner and his family paid a nostalgic visit to Lucerne. They saw Countess Bassenheim, Vreneli and her family, then, on 19 July, drove out to Tribschen. In the rain the house looked neglected, the garden overgrown, and they were told that a family of French Jews was living there. "Too much for one time," was Wagner's comment. From Weimar, where they visited Liszt, he returned to Bayreuth on 28 July, Cosima on 1 August.

On his return home he immediately set to work on the music of *Parsifal*, beginning with the theme "*Nehmet hin mein Blut*" ("Take ye this my blood"), which, he told Cosima, he had written down just before, his hat and coat already on, he left to meet her at the railway station. She wrote in her diary the following day: "He has had to alter the words to fit it, he says; this scene of Holy Communion will be the main scene, the core of the whole work."

The plan of forming a Society of Patrons, which he had mentioned in his letter to the Wagner Societies on 1 January 1877, had in the meantime developed to the extent that a meeting of delegates was arranged for September. In consequence, Wagner could not yet immerse himself in continuous composition, for he had to draw up the plans he intended to put before the delegates. The new society was to be concerned with the future of the festival, not its past, and the question of the deficit was a separate problem which for the moment he put aside. He was reminded of it, however, when on 12 August Dannreuther arrived from London, bringing with him a cheque for £561, the proceeds of a collection made among members of the Wagner Society there to recompense Wagner to some extent for the meagre personal rewards he had gained from his concerts. He refused to accept it, and Dannreuther left Bayreuth on 22 August with the cheque and a letter from Wagner thanking the donors for their sympathy, but declaring that "other and nearer ways to help me out of the difficulties arising from the deficit at Bayreuth have been found." This was not in fact true, and his rejection of the money can be attributed only to pride, a reluctance to accept what looked very much like alms.

Some twenty delegates from Germany's Wagner Societies attended the meeting in Bayreuth on 14 and 15 September. Wagner's proposal, afterwards published together with the statutes of the society, was for the setting up of a school in Bayreuth to educate singers, orchestral players and conductors who had already passed through a musical academy, or reached an equivalent standard, in performing musical-dramatic works – and not only his own – in a "true German style". Wagner undertook to take part personally in the lessons three times weekly. Beginning on 1 January 1878, the singers would study general principles of interpretation, and in particular the intellectual approach to dramatic roles. The second year would be devoted to a more detailed study of Wagner's own works and the methods of performing them, and 1880 would see the production on stage of *Der Fliegende Holländer*, *Tannhäuser* and *Lohengrin*. *Tristan* and *Die Meistersinger* would follow in 1881, the *Ring* in 1882, and in 1883 *Parsifal* would be given its first performance.

Chief among the assistants he intended to engage for his school were Klindworth and Hey. Another was Hans von Wolzogen, the son of the director of the opera in Schwerin. Now in his thirtieth year, Wolzogen had won Wagner's approval with some articles on his works, and in the previous year he had informed Wagner of his desire to found and edit a monthly periodical to propagate Wagnerian ideas. Wagner, still under the influence of his post-festival depression, was lukewarm in his reaction, but he ended his letter to Wolzogen, written in Rome on 23 November 1876, with an invitation to settle in Bayreuth. "If the *Bayreuther Blätter* then comes about – and God knows what else! – maybe there will be something in it for *somebody*." In time the idea of a periodical to propagate and support the activities of his proposed school began to appeal to him, and he invited Wolzogen to take a hand in the preparations for establishing a Society of Patrons to make it all possible. Wolzogen responded with alacrity, and the meeting of delegates in September owed much to his powers of persuasion.

Once the delegates had departed Wagner started his composing work in earnest, and on 26 September was able to play to Cosima, from the orchestral sketch, the complete Prelude to *Parsifal*. From this time until the end of January 1878 he worked virtually without interruption on the first act, writing composition sketch and orchestral sketch almost simultaneously. Cosima's diary provides occasional glimpses of its progress. On 10 October: "At breakfast R. says to me: . . . 'I wanted a somewhat drawn-out triple time for Amfortas's procession, so as to make the words of Gurnemanz fit. No artificial idea is of any help at such times, for it should all sound as if it must be like this and nothing else. But I have found it now.'" On 25 October: "He works, tells me afterwards that he is seizing every opportunity to conjure up a little

musical paradise, as, for example, when Amfortas is carried to the lake."
On 5 December: "R. tells me he has concocted a fine *mélange* for the
esquires as they remove the dead swan: Amfortas's theme, Herzeleide's
theme, and the swan motive from *Lohengrin*." On 20 December: "R.
does not feel very well, he tries to work but is not satisfied with what he
does . . . he laughs over it and says: 'If you know what is bothering me!
It is a rhythmical battle. This morning I suddenly understood none of
my things.'" On 21 December: "R. has survived his rhythmical battle
and tells me when he comes from his work, 'Today I have set a
philosophical precept to music: "Here space becomes time."'" On 28
December: "R. works on the Holy Grail March, he has cut out the
crystal bells: he looked again at my father's *Die Glocke von Strassburg* to
make sure he has not committed a *plagiarism*." On 13 January 1878: "In
the evening R. says he will have to rewrite everything he wrote during the
morning. He was looking for a certain key, and mechanical modulation
is something he finds impossible! 'I'm a fine musician,' he says with a
laugh." On 20 January: "In the evening R. improvises the Communion
service in the way he has now designed it: 'The percussion will accompany the singing, like a faint earth tremor.'" And on 26 January: "In the
evening he sings to me '*Selig in Liebe, selig im Glauben*' ['Blessed in love,
blessed in faith']. 'Oh, that's beautiful!' he cries, 'exactly as I wanted it.'

"And it *is* beautiful!" Cosima continued. "How can I describe these
feelings which send shivers through me? How express this wish to die,
this apprehension about his well-being, this blessing and trembling, this
pleading and thanking? Our life is now even more blissful, ecstatic, than
it was in Tribschen!"

Cosima was still unaware at this time of the nature of the secret correspondence that had been going on, during the composition of the first
act, between Wagner and Judith Gautier. She learned on 24 December
that they had been writing surreptitiously to each other about a Christmas present for her, and was delighted with the surprise gift, a Japanese
négligée. She herself had also been corresponding with Judith, for
Wagner wished Judith to translate the *Parsifal* text into French, and
Cosima made a literal prose translation to help her understand some of
the nuances of the original. Judith was rather shocked by the stiffness of
Cosima's prose, but, as she told Wagner, reluctant to comment on it to
Cosima for fear of offending her. It was to this Cosima was referring
when on 25 December she wrote to Judith in all innocence: "My
husband has acquainted me with your whole correspondence, and I
laughed heartily at the idea that I could be hurt by your remarks on my
translation. . . . If you knew me better you would know that I am
unhurtable . . . at any rate in this way."

Wagner, if he had in fact shown Cosima Judith's letters – he may only have told her about them – certainly did not reveal the whole of their correspondence, and particularly not his own letters, of which he would hardly have kept copies. While in London he had attempted to persuade Judith to visit him there. When she refused, he took the occasion of Daniela's approaching birthday to ask her to buy a present for him in Paris and to send it to him via Bernhard Schnappauf, a Bayreuth barber of whom he made occasional use as a general factotum.

Daniela's present, he wrote in his letter of 1 October, he left entirely to her choice, and with it she might send "half a dozen paper powder sachets such as I can put with my morning underwear: this will serve to remind me of you when I go to the piano to compose the music for *Parsifal*". Wagner's predilection for soft materials and perfumes, particularly when he was engaged in composition, was an effeminate trait in his character of which he was somewhat ashamed, and earlier that year he had been embarrassed by the publication in a Viennese newspaper of some letters he had written to a milliner, Bertha Goldwag, during his stay in Vienna in 1862–64, discussing materials he wished her to supply. To find him, so soon after this humiliation, taking Judith into his confidence on so delicate a matter can perhaps be seen as a measure of his intimate feelings towards her, though the tone of his letter of 1 October was otherwise not much more than mildly flirtatious: "When shall I see you again? You who were so naughty as not to accept my invitation to London? And for what reason? Good, I know it – but how naughty!"

After the present for Daniela had been delivered, he made Cosima's approaching birthday the excuse for prolonging the correspondence, and now the tone of his letters (all written in somewhat idiosyncratic French) became increasingly passionate. Judith's replies no longer exist, but it seems that his ardour distressed her, for he wrote on 18 November: "Do not go on weeping. I remember your embraces only as the most intoxicating and proudest event in my life: it was a final gift of the gods, who did not wish me to succumb to my vexation over the false glory of the *Ring* performances. But – why speak of miserable things? I do not weep, but – in my better moments – I preserve a wish, so sweet, so gracious – the desire to embrace you again and never to lose your divine love. You are mine! Is that not true?" And on 20 November (conjectural date) he wrote: "I see you always – there on the *chaise longue* to the right of my desk – regarding me (Heavens, with what eyes!). . . . You are the abundance of my poor life, so very calm and sheltered since I have had Cosima. You are my richness – my intoxicating excess!" He frequently passed by the house in Bayreuth where she had stayed, he told her on 28 November. "But everything has vanished, and the *Ring* along with you. I no longer think of it and retain no memory except of what happened there, there!"

Another outburst occurred on 11 or 12 December: "I dream of again treading the muddy streets of Paris as a refugee, abandoned by all. Suddenly I meet you again – you, Judith! You take me in your arms; you conduct me to your home; you cover me with kisses. Oh, it is all so touching, so touching! Oh, time and space – enemies! I should have found you at that time – but it is a long time since then!"

Judith – perhaps as a reminder that her heart was otherwise occupied – asked him to look through some of the compositions of her friend Benedictus. Wagner's undated reply, making it plain that he had no desire to see them, offended Judith. The letter in which she expressed her displeasure, he wrote to her on 24 December, had wounded him deeply: "How hasty people can be to wound someone and to imagine rigid 'principles'. I and principles! I who do nothing but suffer and produce a little, whose life is a perpetual hurricane, whose actions in connection with this world are nothing but convulsions! You will repent, I feel sure of that – and I shall immerse myself in your friend's 'audacities'!"

It was at this point that Cosima was told of the secret correspondence, and in her letter to Judith of 25 December she hastened to fulfil her usual role of pacifier. With regard to Benedictus's compositions, she wrote, "I imagine the very strong expressions he used led you astray about his feelings, for he did ask to see our 'cousin's' composition. In French he makes use of the first expressions which flow from his pen, and that can lead to misunderstandings. I should not be your friend, as I am (in spite of your inability to recognise it!*) if I did not tell you how much this incident has pained me, and how much suffering it has caused my husband. I know you appreciate his truthfulness and the grandeur of his character, which abhors empty phrases, but I understand your and your friend's feelings."

Though Cosima had now – at least partially – been let into the secret, Wagner continued to write love letters to Judith, seizing on the excuse that some of the materials she had sent from Paris had to be exchanged. He did in his letter of 4 January 1878 suggest that, while she should continue to address parcels to Schnappauf, she should now write to him direct, "perhaps giving a little thought that there are not things in your dear letters which I might have to hide. In case of absolute need – (oh!) – then – long live *Schnappauf*!"

Judith, in low spirits as the result of an attack of bronchitis, remained silent for a while, though Wagner continued to write to her and Cosima to send her pages of her *Parsifal* translation, the last of them just before Judith's letter to Wagner explaining her silence arrived. Cosima saw the letter which Judith wrote to Wagner, and replied to it herself on 27

* A reference to Judith's qualms about Cosima's translation of *Parsifal*.

January. "This whole dress correspondence is unique," she wrote, "and no one but my husband would go to such trouble, lovingly consecrating as much care and time to these trifles as to a work of his genius." Wagner wrote to Judith on the same day, again recalling "that humble house in Bayreuth from which you ejected me." Presumably he received another letter from her, for he wrote on 6 February: "Your dear letter was not calculated to reassure me about you! – When you were here for the *Festspiele* you seemed to me so radiant and of such robust health that this added to my delight in seeing you again. Try, try to put these attacks of indisposition behind you: there is nothing else you have to do in order to please me. . . . Cosima has continual feelings of admiration for and gratitude to you on account of the Japanese dress and all the other things you chose for her. God grant that these traditional disputes over poor Parsifal will at last come to an end. It is not worth the trouble, believe me. But – I love to see my address traced by your hand. Oh! What – what? – But – it is the way of the world. Why in the name of heaven did I not find you in the days following the failure of *Tannhäuser* in Paris? – Were you too young at that time? – Let us say nothing more, nothing more! – But let us still love one another!"

On 12 February Cosima wrote in her diary: "The grief I was fearing has not passed me by; it has come upon me from outside. May God help me! Oh, sorrow, my old companion, come back and dwell within me; we know each other well – how long wilt thou stay with me this time, most loyal and dependable of friends?"

Vague as these words are – no doubt deliberately, for Cosima was writing for her children – they almost certainly refer to her discovery of the nature of Wagner's letters to Judith. Exactly how she came to discover it cannot be known, but a later entry in her diary, written on 29 October 1879, provides a possible clue: "Gay memories of that daemonic night in January nearly two years ago; the sudden flaring of the flame which told me, as I sought him in concern about his rest, that paper had been burned here, his return to the *salon* after it had been put out, his surprise over my question whether something had been burning – how pleasant that one can speak gaily of dreadful memories!"

There is only one point in this which could raise doubts that Cosima was here recalling Wagner's correspondence with Judith: that she wrote of a night in January, rather than February. It could have been a simple mistake of memory, or it is possible that she did indeed come on Wagner burning letters sometime in January, and that her suspicions were aroused, though not yet confirmed. If her diary entry of 12 February 1878 ("The grief I was fearing") does hint at previous suspicions, her letter to Judith of 13 February suggests even more strongly that she had read Wagner's letter to Judith of 6 February and now knew what was confronting her. "We hope that you are better and that you can be 'radiant' even outside Bayreuth," she wrote. "Now that my husband's birthday is approaching, it is I who should have secrets, but I should like you to tell me first whether you are completely well. Many fond wishes on our side to you both – Cosima. P.S. I await your 'dispute' on the subject of Leconte de Lisle. Be quite frank, won't you?"

In her previous letter to Judith, Cosima had made a joking reference to the poet Leconte de Lisle. Her use now of the word "dispute" ("*querelle*"), and earlier in her letter the word "radiant" ("*radieuse*"), both of which had occurred in Wagner's letter to Judith, could hardly have been coincidental. Her whole letter was clearly a broad hint to Judith that she had discovered all, and a warning to confine her attentions to her lover Benedictus, whose name she managed to bring into her letter before offering many fond wishes ("*mille tendresses*") to them both together.

Wagner's last letter to Judith, written on 15 February, was a chastened one: "Dear soul, I have now asked Cosima to take over these commissions, or rather the final arrangements regarding these commissions with which I have been plaguing you so long. . . . Apart from that, I am at present so beset by business affairs – which are not at all agreeable – that I can no longer find the time to continue my composition of *Parsifal*. – Have pity on me! It will all be finished soon, and I shall recover those nice moments of leisure in which I love to talk to you about myself. But do not worry about me: the things that are wearying me will soon vanish. Be kind to Cosima: write to her nicely and at length. I shall understand everything."

Cosima's next letter, on 21 February, contained a dig about the "mysterious barber", but another dated 26 February shows that both she and Judith were trying hard to restore their old intimate relationship. From Cosima's letter it is clear that Judith had recalled the charades they had played together at Tribschen. "Do I remember them!" Cosima wrote. "For us things have hardly changed, since Wahnfried is like Tribschen, and here we also live cut off from the world: the children have grown, yet have remained the same, with the addition of Fidi, who dominates. In place of *Siegfried* it is *Parsifal* which is being composed; in place of the performances of *Tristan* and *Die Meistersinger*, it is that of the *Ring* on which we look back; everything is on a larger scale, but our life has remained the same."

After this their letters became less frequent, but more relaxed in tone. There were no more to Judith from Wagner. It seems clear that Cosima had not, as previous biographers have maintained, turned a blind eye on Wagner's pursuit of Judith, however serious or however illusory it might have been, but had fought back, and won.

Wagner was still at work on the first act of *Parsifal* when on 21 January Angelo Neumann came to Wahnfried to discuss with him a production of the *Ring* at Leipzig. Neumann had become co-director of the theatre there in May 1876 and, after attending the festival at Bayreuth, was fired with the ambition to present the four music dramas in his own theatre. Wagner was at first unwilling to release the works, but, when the deficit on his festival prevented further performances in Bayreuth, he found it impossible to resist the pressures applied on him by other theatres wishing to stage new productions of their own. In Vienna Jauner, who had wrung *Die Walküre* from him as a condition of allowing Amalie Materna to sing in the festival of 1876, insisted on securing the rights in the other three works before releasing Richter for the London concerts. Munich had contractual rights in the work which could not be ignored. In consequence, Wagner signed an agreement with Neumann's co-director, August Förster, in March 1877, granting Leipzig permission to stage a production. A few weeks later a dispute broke out between them regarding the interpretation of the financial arrangements, and the deal was abandoned. Neumann was greatly disappointed, and he decided that the only way of achieving his aim, in view of the acrimonious correspondence that had passed between Wagner and Förster, was to make a personal visit to Bayreuth. He described his meeting with Wagner and Cosima in the *salon* of Wahnfried in his lively book *Erinnerungen an Richard Wagner* (*Personal Recollections of Wagner*):

"For the first time I met him face to face – for I can hardly count the fleeting occasions of our previous meetings. He wore his famous skull-cap, a short dark house-jacket and grey trousers. Coming directly towards me with his most gracious manner, he said, 'I'm glad you've taken up the old plan again. I was keenly disappointed when that fell through. I can see that you're thoroughly in earnest too – you don't look like a man who would make that trip from Leipzig to Bayreuth in the dead of winter simply for amusement.' Then he picked up his little son Siegfried . . . took him on his knee, and turned to me, saying, 'Well, what have you to say to me?'"

Neumann put forward his plan to produce *Das Rheingold* and *Die Walküre* in the spring and *Siegfried* and *Götterdämmerung* in the autumn of that year, and could even quote the exact dates: 28 and 29 April, 21 and 22 September. Wagner was curious to know why he had chosen these dates.

"'It's very simple,' I answered. 'In Leipzig we have the Easter Passion music on 28 April and the St Michael's Mass on 21 September. I hardly think there could be better occasions than these for the first presentation of the *Ring*.'

"A Leipziger himself, Wagner was visibly impressed by my reasoning.

He scanned me keenly again for a while then, turning to his wife, asked: 'What would you say about it? Shall I trust this man?' After her affirmative answer and the few sympathetic words she spoke in my favour, the master turned again to me and began a series of questions with regard to our facilities for staging, the orchestra, and our singers."

Finally satisfied, Wagner suggested drawing up a contract then and there. "Beaming with benignity, [he] waved me to his seat at the desk . . . whereupon I remarked: 'I should rather you sat at the desk, master, and let me dictate to you!' He looked at me in blank surprise, yet did not seem offended. 'What!' he said. '*You* mean to do the dictating and I'm to take your orders down?' 'Yes, master, exactly. For in the first place I shall dictate such terms as will be to the best advantage of both sides, and furthermore I shall then have a document from your hand which will always be of inestimable value to me.'" Wagner did as he was asked.

Cosima's account of the meeting in her diary is briefer and considerably drier. "A curious interruption in our sublime life is provided by the visit of the opera director Angelo Neumann from Leipzig and Israel. He has come for the *Ring* but would also like to have *Parsifal*! Coaxes R. out of half the royalties for the subscription quota – in short, is just what such gentlemen always are. R. says he has nothing against his coming, in so far as it shows they still need him – and we need money, so agreement is reached!"

Wagner did not share Cosima's obvious distaste for Neumann; in fact, he was considerably impressed by this forthright man, then in his fortieth year, who made no apologies for being either a Jew or a theatre director. That meeting was the beginning of a relationship much more significant than either he or Cosima realised at the time.

Wagner had gloomy thoughts of what might happen to the *Ring* now that he had been forced for financial reasons to leave it to its own fate, and the pronounced success of *Das Rheingold* in Vienna, where it received its first performance on 24 January under Richter, took him by surprise. Yet each new production outside Bayreuth was for him a bitter reminder of his own failure to provide with his first attempt the model performance of the *Ring* for which his festival had been designed, and of the debt which still encumbered him as a result of his efforts. By skilful management Feustel had managed so far to keep the creditors at bay, but by the beginning of 1878 they were becoming restive, and there was talk of resorting to law.

Reluctant to worry Wagner during his work on *Parsifal*, Feustel confided his anxieties to Cosima. His suggestion was that, to avoid catastrophe, an appeal should be made to Ludwig to sanction the payment of royalties on performances of Wagner's works in Munich at the rate of 10,000 marks annually for ten years, thus enabling the still outstanding debt of around 100,000 marks to be paid off. Cosima took it on herself to put this suggestion to Ludwig, without telling Wagner about it. She wrote to the king on 16 January with some trepidation: "I hope I shall not bring on myself the disfavour of my gracious sovereign by this step."

She was much relieved by Ludwig's cordial response, which arrived on 2 February: "I was very glad to see from your letter that you did not mention these pecuniary affairs to my dearly beloved master and friend, whose genius is now engaged in preparing its greatest revelation; these fatal worldly cares would have been necessarily bound to wrench him away from his mood of inspiration and creation." He had, the king told her, instructed his new court secretary, Ludwig von Bürkel,* to discuss with Feustel and Perfall arrangements for making the royalty payments requested. Only then did Cosima tell Wagner what she had done. At the time they were engaged in reading Walter Scott's *The Heart of Midlothian*, and Wagner, recalling its heroine who went to London to plead with the queen for her condemned sister, called Cosima his Jeanie.

"I am now living the happiest days of my life," he wrote to Ludwig on 10 February, and went on to describe the *Bayreuther Blätter*, the monthly periodical which had just been launched, Wolzogen having by now taken up residence in Bayreuth. "I myself shall certainly have to write a small contribution now and again: but I have made it a condition that this must never stand in the way of *Parsifal*. . . . As far as my present attitude to the public is concerned, I feel, after all I have done and experienced as a result, so free and so liberated from the need to be considerate, that I could make it my basic principle either to keep entirely silent or else to speak only the bare truth. Neither the one nor the other will do any good, for German *décadence* has gone too far to be halted. My motto is to do all I can to stop the decline, though without hope. But probably very few people imagined that the dreary Prussian idea of a state would be forced on us as the model for the German Reich quite so swiftly!"

The first issue of the *Bayreuther Blätter* appeared in January 1878. Published by Nietzsche's publisher in Chemnitz, Ernst Schmeitzner, it contained an introductory article by Wagner and a long account by Wolzogen of the setting up of the Society of Patrons. Wagner himself indicated the change of function of the society, consequent on the failure of his school to attract any great interest among prospective pupils. He did not add, though he could have done, that neither Klindworth nor Hey had shown any desire to join him as teachers (mainly because the

---

* Düfflipp had resigned for health reasons in November 1877.

payment he offered them was too low), nor that he himself was glad to be relieved of it: that view he expressed only privately to Cosima. The society's main aim had now become the financing of a production of *Parsifal*, which Wagner promised for 1880. The festival management committee announced in the *Blätter* that persons joining the Society of Patrons would pay three annual subscriptions of fifteen marks, which would entitle them to a seat in the festival theatre in 1880 and free copies of the periodical during this period. The *Blätter*, the publisher declared, would not be on sale to the general public.

The second issue in February was again confined to pieces by Wagner and Wolzogen. Wagner took from his drawer the diary entries he had written in 1865 for King Ludwig and reviewed them in the light of after-events in an article entitled "What Is German?" His assurances to the king that the periodical would not interfere with his work on *Parsifal* were set at naught by Wolzogen's initial failure to attract any other writers of significance. The only outside contributor to the third issue in March was Heinrich Porges, and Wagner, who had begun work on the second act of *Parsifal* on 16 February, had to lay his music aside to write another piece to help fill the pages. This was "Modern", a short and un-remarkable protest on the familiar theme of the dire influence of the Jews on the German spirit.

The final agreement regarding royalty payments on performances of Wagner's works in Munich was signed on 31 March. This provided for royalties of ten per cent on gross takings until the deficit on the first festival was cleared, and as a *quid pro quo* it was agreed that Munich should have the unconditional right to produce *Parsifal* after its first staging in Bayreuth.

With its signing the main threat to their security was removed. While Wagner worked on his music, Cosima occupied herself with the children and assisted Wolzogen with the editorial work of the *Bayreuther Blätter*, in which she took a keen interest. Seidl, the only one of Wagner's musical assistants still in Bayreuth, was kept busy reconstructing the score of Wagner's youthful C Major Symphony from the orchestral parts, recently discovered, through Cosima's efforts, in a forgotten trunk in Dresden. The evenings were spent among themselves making music (mainly the symphonies of Haydn and Mozart as piano duets), reading (Walter Scott novels, a new biography of Schopenhauer) and playing whist, a pastime introduced by Liszt during his visit in April.

Another article written during the composition of the second act of *Parsifal* for the *Bayreuther Blätter* was "Publikum und Popularität" ("Public and Popularity"), which he began on 11 April. It was an attempt to deal with the problem of public taste, particularly in the theatre, how far it is genuine and how far influenced by the press or by the narrow outlook of theatre managers, and how far the creative artist should allow himself to be ruled by it. However, the first two parts, which appeared in April and June, hardly did more than present the problem without offering any real solutions.

Wagner was still working on this article when on 25 April a copy of Nietzsche's new book, *Menschliches, Allzumenschliches (Human, All Too Human)*, arrived at Wahnfried. They had not seen Nietzsche since their meeting in Sorrento, but there had been some correspondence between them. In October 1877 Nietzsche sent Cosima an essay on the *Ring* by Otto Eiser, an eye specialist in Frankfurt whom he had consulted about his persistent headaches, and she wrote a warm and friendly reply. On 1 January 1878 Wagner sent Nietzsche a copy of the *Parsifal* text. Nietzsche, now moving from one watering place to another in a vain attempt to regain his health and enjoined by Eiser and other doctors to read and write as little as possible, did not reply to him directly, but on 4 January he confided to a friend, Reinhart von Seydlitz, his feelings about *Parsifal*: "Impression on first reading: more Liszt than Wagner, spirit of the Counter-Reformation; for me, too accustomed as I am to things Greek, generally humanist, it is all too restricted by contemporary Christianity; nothing but psychological fantasy; no flesh and far too much blood (particularly in the holy communion too full-blooded for me), and then I have no time for hysterical females. . . . The language sounds like a translation from a foreign tongue. But the situations and the way they follow each other – is that not the purest poetry, a sublime challenge to music?"

By this time, using Köselitz as his amanuensis, Nietzsche had completed his new book, which was an elaboration of those reflections against the Wagnerian artistic outlook written down in 1876 in Klingenbrunn after his flight from the *Ring* rehearsals. *Human, All Too Human* was a wholesale rejection of what he later described to Mathilde Maier (in his letter of 15 July) as "that metaphysical obscuring of all that is true and simple, that battle *with* reason *against* reason which claims to discover miracles and monstrosities in all and everything – and on top of that a corresponding baroque art of exaggeration and exalted lack of restraint – I mean by this Wagner's art." He knew very well that his book, dedicated to the memory of Voltaire, would wound Wagner, and he considered publishing it anonymously, while confessing privately to Wagner who the author was. In January 1878 he drafted a letter to Wagner and Cosima: "In sending you – I place my secret trustingly in your and your noble wife's hands, and assume that it will now be your secret as well. This book is mine: in it I have revealed my innermost feelings about people and things and for the first time circled the periphery of my own thinking. In times full of paroxysm and torment this book was my consolation, which never failed me when all others did. Perhaps it is because I was capable of it that I am still alive." One of his reasons for publishing it under a pseudonym, he continued, was to facilitate an objective discussion in which all his friends could take part without feeling the need to be tactful. "I know of none who shares the views in this book, but am very curious about the counter-arguments which will be brought up."

However, on reflection he resolved to put his name to the book and to take the consequences. The letter to Wagner and Cosima was never sent.

The reaction in Bayreuth to *Human, All Too Human* fully confirmed his forebodings. 'Feelings of apprehension after a short glance through it," Cosima wrote in her diary on 25 April. "R. feels he would be doing the author a favour, for which the latter would one day thank him, if he did not read it. It seems to me to contain much inner rage and sullenness." Neither of them wrote to Nietzsche about the book, but disapproving letters from their friends, and even an attempt to deprive Schmeitzner of his contract to print the *Bayreuther Blätter*, revealed the extent of the anger against him. He wrote sadly to Köselitz on 31 May that he had been virtually excommunicated from Bayreuth, along with his book: "Wagner has failed to make use of a fine opportunity to show greatness of character. This must not deflect me, neither in my opinion of him, nor in my opinion of myself." To Seydlitz, who was president of the Munich Wagner Society, he wrote on 11 June: "I am both glad and desirous that one of my friends should be behaving in a friendly way towards Wagner, for I become less and less capable of giving him pleasure (as he now after all is – an *old* man beyond change). His aims and my aims point in entirely opposite directions. This I find distressing enough – but one must be prepared for all sacrifices in the interests of truth. If, incidentally, he knew all that I feel inside me *against* his art and his aims, he would consider me one of his bitterest foes – which, as you know, I am not."

He told Köselitz that attempts were going on in Bayreuth to retain his friends while rejecting him. Whether this suspicion was true or not (the published correspondence shows only Mathilde Maier breaking off relations with him entirely), he could certainly detect a certain coolness in such mutual friends as Erwin Rohde, Malwida von Meysenbug and even Otto Eiser, who told Cosima, in his capacity as physician, that he saw in Nietzsche's book the first signs of mental derangement. She herself wrote to Marie von Schleinitz that from the little she had read of the book she realised that the development she had foreseen in its author had now come to pass, and she blamed his downfall (as did others) on the influence of his friend Paul Rée: it was, she said, "the relationship in miniature between Judea and Germania".

Eventually both Wagner and Cosima read the book, and in the August issue of the *Bayreuther Blätter* Wagner attempted, in the concluding instalment of "Public and Popularity", to write a reply to it. He introduced a third type of "public" to add to the newspaper readers and theatregoers he had so far considered: the "academic public", and he launched into an attack on the prevailing educational system and its practitioners, who seemed to him to consider scientific learning of more importance than life: "Philologists, like philosophers, and particularly where they converge on the field of aesthetics, receive through physics in general quite specific impulses which encourage, not to say oblige them to venture out on the still unlimited territory of criticism of all things human and inhuman. It seems that from these scientific experiments they appropriate to themselves a basic right to a special kind of scepticism, which enables them to maintain themselves in a constant state of twisting and turning, abandoning previously held viewpoints and then in some confusion returning to them again, a process which appears to assure them a fitting share of progress in general. The less observed these scientific Saturnalia, the bolder and more pitiless the manner in which the noblest sacrificial victims are slaughtered and laid on the altar of scepticism. Every German professor must at some time write a book to bring him fame: but it is not accorded to everybody to discover something intrinsically new; so, in order to attract the necessary attention, a favourite device is to represent the views of a predecessor as fundamentally wrong, and the more significant and generally misunderstood the man now being held up to ridicule, the more effective the result." The third part of Wagner's essay had little to do with the original theme, and certainly did not add to its clarity, but the readers of the *Blätter* were well aware of the author's intention, even if Nietzsche's name was nowhere mentioned.

Nietzsche's own comment on Wagner's reply was contained in a postcard addressed to his friend Franz Overbeck on 3 September: "It hurt me, but *not in the place* W. intended." A week later he asked Schmeitzner to stop sending him the *Bayreuther Blätter* regularly as hitherto, telling him to save them up to the end of the year: "Why should I commit myself to taking monthly doses of Wagner's vexation-drivel? I want to go on keeping my feelings for his greatness pure and transparent, and for that I must keep his all-too-human side somewhat at arm's length."

These lofty rejoinders did not contain the whole truth. It was purely on the level of ideas that the friendship foundered, and on the human level that its loss continued to trouble them for the rest of their lives. The very bitterness of Wagner's frequent references to Nietzsche, noted by Cosima in her diaries after the break with him, revealed how hurt he was by the "betrayal", as he considered it, and on 17 January 1883 he told her they should be "downright ashamed of not having been able to keep a better grip" on him. In his biography of Nietzsche, Curt Paul Janz quotes from Lou Salomé's reminiscences an account of a visit Nietzsche paid to Tribschen on 8 May 1882 in her company: "For a long, long time he sat beside the lake, immersed in deep memories; then, drawing pictures in the damp sand with his stick, he spoke in a soft voice of those past times. And when he looked up, he was weeping."

CHAPTER XVI

APRIL 1878 – NOVEMBER 1880:

Religion and Art

PART OF THE reason for Wagner's slow progress on the second act of *Parsifal* was a succession of minor physical ailments such as colds, boils and lumbago, which, though they did not lay him up for long, had a debilitating effect. There were also compositional difficulties: the last music drama he had completed, *Götterdämmerung*, had been constructed almost entirely of material already clear in his mind from its use in the preceding parts of the *Ring*. *Parsifal* called for new inventions and inspirations, and it appears that in writing the text he had not been "immersed in the musical aroma" of his work, to quote the phrase in his letter of 1844 to Carl Gaillard about his working methods. Apart from the melody for the Flower Maidens' "*Komm, holder Knabe*", there is no evidence of a musical theme conceived before composition began, and in fact, as we have already seen in the first act, Wagner found it necessary at times to adapt the text to fit the musical idea when it came to him. It was only when he reached the Flower Maidens' scene in his composition sketch that he wrote the words the Maidens sing at their first sight of Parsifal. "No one in the audience will take any notice of the text," he told Cosima on 26 March, "but the singers sing differently and feel like individuals if they do not just have to sing senseless repetitions in chorus, and this adds to the general effect."

Yet, whatever his difficulties and however much scratching out and rewriting they caused him, there was clearly no lack of musical inspiration: in fact, he made his usual complaint that he had more ideas than he could find room for, and he showed Cosima the scraps of paper he kept in his waistcoat pocket to enable him to write down themes at the moment they occurred to him. The trouble was, he said, that when he had to compose Kundry, nothing came into his head but cheerful themes for symphonies. At this time he was producing not more than four lines of music a day.

In the personal sphere Nietzsche's defection, in the public sphere two assassination attempts on Emperor Wilhelm had the effect of increasing his feelings of isolation in a world which seemed to him to be going in a different direction from the one he wished for it, and to be paying less and less heed to his warnings. "All of this has a connection with my creative work," he wrote to King Ludwig on 15 July. "Up to this point I was able to hope I was helping my works towards a noble future life. This hope has now been finally crushed within me. I let everything go, and all I ask of the world is to allow me to see or hear no more of it."

This growing distaste for contact with outside events extended even to the performances of the *Ring* in Munich, Leipzig and Vienna. Beyond giving some coaching in the role of Siegfried to Ferdinand Jäger, who had come to settle in Bayreuth and could thus be considered part of the intimate circle of friends on whom he was coming increasingly to depend, he took no active interest in the productions beyond pushing the claims of Jäger at the expense of Unger, from whom he had withdrawn his favour entirely, and sending letters of complaint to Neumann and Jauner based on reports on the productions from Richter and Seidl. And his disenchantment with theatrical life influenced his feelings about *Parsifal*.

"As I work," he told King Ludwig in his letter of 15 July, "I have only it, and not the vision of its future performance, in mind. When during my work I think of various people, again (if only in their thoughts) taking delight in the possibility of a performance, perhaps quite soon, then I am assailed by feelings of indescribable bitterness. What misery, vexation, sorrow and – shame I see there once more awaiting me! For all the sublime, serious and noble things I am aiming at in such a performance – even the thought of the public to whom I shall one day have to expose my work for applause – all this will again and yet again be reduced to nothing, and once more everybody will know better than I what is good for my Parsifal! In this respect I have only one consolation: my work is described as a 'stage *dedication* festival play' ['*Bühnenweihfestspiel*']; I shall therefore strive to keep in mind the *sacredness* of the stage, and hope in this way to find the means of protecting my work and its sacred contents from desecration." He expressed the same emotions more wittily to Cosima on 23 September: "Having created the invisible orchestra, I now feel like inventing the invisible theatre! And the inaudible orchestra. . . ."

Visitors from outside the immediate circle of intimates became increasingly rare. Klindworth, Liszt and Malwida von Meysenbug, though none of them was as closely tied to him as he would have liked, were welcomed as old friends. For the rest, Wagner's time was spent mainly with much younger disciples, at their head the uncritically devoted Wolzogen. Another was his biographer, Carl Friedrich Glasenapp, who paid them a visit in July, and whom Wolzogen recruited to write articles for the *Blätter*. Rubinstein came to settle in Bayreuth and gradually made himself a position as Wagner's "house pianist", as well as an occasional contributor to the *Blätter*. Wagner's interest in Bayreuth and its citizens (except for Feustel, who was now a liberal member of the Reichstag) waned noticeably, and he appears to have ceased attending the Thursday meetings of the *Kränzchen*.

In the summer there was a further and more alarming deterioration in his health. Stabbing pains in his heart, which he felt on 12 August, returned on 4 September after a strenuous walk, when he also spat up a little blood. In spite of these signs, Dr Landgraf persisted in declaring that his heart was intact, and put all his ailments down to digestive troubles.

He completed the orchestral sketch of the second act of *Parsifal* on 13 October, having had to summon all his powers of self-persuasion to tackle the passionate scene between Parsifal and Kundry. He described his feelings about it in a letter to King Ludwig the following day: "Frequently I said to myself that, having so often lost myself in these spheres before, I could this time have spared myself the trouble. . . . However, I flung myself into my purgatory and have now emerged victorious. I know that this work too has turned out worthy of *us*."

He began the third act practically at once, though the first weeks were spent searching for themes rather than in continuous composition. He had difficulty with the orchestral prelude, and several sketches were made before he found the highly concentrated thirty-six bars with which the act now begins. He played it to Cosima on 31 October, observing: "My preludes must all be elemental, not dramatic like the '*Leonore*' overtures, for that makes the drama superfluous." He also did some preliminary work on the Good Friday music, but it was not until 12 November that he began to work in a continuous way on his orchestral sketch.

Shortly afterwards he suspended his composition work for a while to orchestrate the Prelude to the first act as a birthday surprise for Cosima. In the early hours of Christmas Day a complete orchestra of forty-five players from Meiningen was smuggled into the hall of Wahnfried, Siegfried was sent upstairs to awaken Cosima, and the *Parsifal* Prelude was played. "Then R. comes to my bed," Cosima wrote in her diary, "asks me not to weep or expire, jokes gaily, undresses and gets into bed, breakfasts again with me (he had already breakfasted with Lusch at 7 o'clock), and talks and talks."

In the evening a concert was given by the orchestra in the *salon* before an audience of their Bayreuth friends. The programme, apart from the *Siegfried Idyll*, was an all-Beethoven one: the overtures "Zur Weihe des Hauses" and "Egmont", the Eighth Symphony and, for Siegfried's benefit, the Andante and Presto movements of the Seventh Symphony. Wagner, though he had experienced chest pains during rehearsals which prompted Dr Landgraf to advise caution, insisted on conducting everything, including, after an interval for supper, a second perfor- mance of the *Parsifal* Prelude. "But the evening performance of the Prelude is not like the morning one, when I was all prayer and ecstasy," Cosima wrote. "This time I hear the Redeemer's call to salvation, addressed to an unheeding world, a call so sad, so sorrowful. . . . I recognise the wilderness across which this call resounds, and the awful recognition fills me with bliss! There stands he who has called forth these wonders, and he loves me. He loves me! . . ."

She, having voluntarily made him the centre of her world, was more than content to observe herself becoming more and more the centre of his. Anything that seemed to threaten her sense of complete possession could arouse emotions in her by which she herself was rather appalled. After reading Wagner's letter of 14 October to the king, which ended with the rather flowery expressions of undying devotion habitual to them both, she wrote in her diary the following day: "I am overcome by a very curious, indescribable feeling when at the end I read R.'s words that his soul belongs for all eternity to him (the King); it pierces my heart like a serpent's tooth, and I am uncertain what it is I want. I do not want it to be just a phrase, but also not a truth, and even if it were within my power, I should not wish it unwritten, for whatever he does is rightly done. But all the same I suffer, and I disappear, in order to hide my suffering."

Their reliance on each other was indeed such that when, in February 1879, she went to Munich by herself to have her portrait painted by Lenbach, the event assumed in the feelings of both the pro- portions almost of a catastrophe. From railway stations at which the train stopped on her journey she despatched anxious telegrams, and during the three days of her absence she received ten telegrams con- taining domestic news from Wahnfried, signed variously by Wagner, Wolzogen, Rubinstein and Wagner's servant Georg Lang. She herself wrote Wagner a letter from Munich. It is worth reproducing at length, for it is the only letter of real substance from Cosima to Wagner that has survived. It was dated 23 February 1879:

"Write! Yes, but who could describe yesterday's journey and all that went on in mind and heart? One thing I had to admit to myself with ever-increasing conviction: that I impose tasks on myself which I cannot really carry out, for which I lack the strength; such was my first marriage, my parting from Hans, and now this journey! I decided on it, hoping to achieve something that would give you pleasure, and for that reason ignored all feelings of consideration – God forgive me if I did wrong. And so I went off with your tears – like the Holy Child's, growing ever heavier – on my heart, and felt I was doing something I could not carry through. What is it that drives one on, yet does not give one strength, what is it that prevents one succumbing when all one's powers fail? Who can answer this riddle? Enough to say that, when I reached the first large station, I felt like getting out and returning home; what held me back was the thought that, after we had gone through the torment of parting, you would not think it very sensible to gain nothing by it, and so the journey continued in distress and anxiety. . . . Not being able to hear the sound of your voice made me feel dull and ghostlike; after a while I looked out of the window, on the world. Oh, this wilderness, resembling nothing but that picture of the moon landscape we saw the other day! If in *Tristan* you depicted the soul of this wilderness in all its terrifying sombre beauty, if in *Siegfried* its bliss, I saw it now in its meaningless ugliness as my gaze wandered across stubble fields, snow turned to mud and a grey sky that looked like an obdurate and brutal negation of all hope, or like a coarse, impenetrable cloth stretched tight over all joys. In this dead, silent, frozen world, only one warm hearth – your heart – only one light – your spirit ! . . . Then the lights were lit, 'twilight shrouded the meadows' [*Tannhäuser*] – I looked at them, and saw they were not gleaming, just dully staring; giving no illumination, just light in so far as night was growing darker inside me. Then I recalled the feelings I had so often had when joining large gatherings in lighted rooms, and I felt as if everything inside me had become quite black. And then I saw a brightly lit room where everything inside me was also bright, I saw Wahnfried, and greeted it with a greeting woven from the remotest threads of my soul. And now I was in Munich, in the city where the wilderness had turned to massive monuments, and felt myself as *myself*; I ordered this and purchased that – the whole redeeming work of love, the destruction of self, wiped out! In earlier times of unhappiness I would keep saying to myself: always do what you find most difficult, for I knew that was safe; but then came *St Richard's Day*, and everything changed: now I could also do what I enjoyed; how did I ever come that far? . . .

"Georg's telegram has just arrived, saying that you slept well, and with that I shall end, for that is happiness, genuine, lovely, golden happiness! But tell me if you can how it came about that I, wretched I, was permitted to live your life? Cosima."

On the following day (Sunday) she added a postscript: "Shall I tell you what it is on my writing desk that gives me joy? The faded bow I brought with me as a penwiper. It transports me back to my 'dream home', and I laugh to see it smiling at me! . . . Greetings to your children, who are dear to me because they are yours."

On Tuesday she was back in Wahnfried, having travelled through the night to take Wagner by surprise. In her diary, which she did not touch during her absence, since it was dedicated to his doings, not hers, she wrote: "I feel as if the heavens have reopened when I hear his sounds, the only music in the world for me! R. laughs and says he does not know what to make of it: when I went away, music abandoned him entirely, but now he has his head full of themes again!"

Wagner was at this time working on the Good Friday music, which he finished on 1 March. He wrote to King Ludwig on 27 March: "While I feel a restless urge to gain control over my somewhat rundown energies in order to reach the end of my composition sketch (in which of course the musical invention is fixed for all time), another feeling restrains my eagerness, telling me: 'Fool, are you in such a hurry to chase away again that deep satisfaction, which alone kept you during this work hovering above this world and its misery?' And it is true . . . with the final stroke of my pen I in effect consign my work to hell, which is well aware how to fashion with every bar an instrument of torture for me." But later in the same letter he wrote: "Solitude! Yes, if it were just an 'escape to the woods'. But escape from the world is no relief, for it can be won only by defiance and preserved only by sustained bitterness. It gives me no pleasure at all to cut myself off from the world; perhaps, if I were simply a philosopher, it would. But everything my mind thinks up to help it enjoy the busy silence of solitude, receives at the same time a thousand organs through which it demands to be imparted; and to be unable to satisfy this urge, it often seems to me, is equivalent to each act of conception ending in a painful miscarriage. That is not pleasant!"

At last, on 26 April, the orchestral sketch of *Parsifal* was finished. Wagner was satisfied with his work and, when they played through the final scene on the following evening, demonstrated what care he had taken to banish any suspicion of sentimentality from it. He had not, he observed to Cosima a few days earlier, been able to avoid "a certain restriction of feeling", but he felt affecting emotions such as those in *Tristan* or even the *Ring* would be entirely out of place. The orchestration would also be completely different from the *Ring*, free of figurations. She remarked on the "divine simplicity" of the work, comparable to the Gospels, she said, and he agreed: "It is all so *direct*!"

He put the orchestral sketch aside, and in the next few weeks wrote a succession of articles for the *Bayreuther Blätter*. The first of these, which appeared in June, was entitled "Shall We Hope?", and was little more than a rehash of his well-known views about the absence of the German spirit. The three following articles, which appeared in the issues of June, July and August, were of much greater substance, his first contributions to the *Blätter* that went beyond polemical journalism and dealt seriously with his aesthetic outlook. Wagner might complain, as he frequently did to Cosima, that in his previous books and essays he had already said everything he had to say, but, if the essays "On Poetry and Composition", "On Opera Poetry and Composition in Particular" and "On the Application of Music to the Drama" added little that was new, they did at least present it in a clearer and more concise form than the earlier writings.

The first essay was an attempt to define literary and musical art and its ethical purpose. The second turned to the practical aspects of the two arts in combination and examined the inability of various composers to set words to music in a way that allowed their meaning to emerge: it was largely their neglect of this vital aspect, Wagner declared, that had led to the artificiality he found so deplorable in traditional opera. In the third essay, the most personal, he dealt with symphonic and dramatic form, with a glance on the way at programme music (Berlioz, Liszt), which he saw as an attempt to widen the horizons of symphonic music, one doomed to failure, he observed, since programme music belonged to the dramatic category of music and was incompatible with symphonic form. But drama also demands a unity of form, and this need applies as much to the music as to the action. "This unity is derived from a web of basic themes permeating the whole work, contrasting, complementing, modifying, dividing and uniting each other, just like the movements of a symphony, but with the dramatic action controlling these laws of contrast and union, which in the symphony were derived originally from dance movements." This was of course a definition of his own form of music drama, and he proceeded to explain and justify it with examples from *Lohengrin* and the *Ring*.

Wagner's consciousness that in his essays in the *Bayreuther Blätter* he was addressing, not the world at large, but a small band of loyal supporters eager for enlightenment can be seen in the intimacy of their expression: he could, for instance, jibe at Brahms (as representative of the negligible modern school of symphonists) without mentioning his name, confident of being understood, and the by-no-means infrequent outbursts of anti-Semitism could be relied on to pass without protest, since most of the *Blätter*'s twelve hundred subscribers were certainly of the same mind – even the Jews among them. This was a phenomenon which surprised Wagner himself, and he remarked to Cosima that Bayreuth would soon be turning into a synagogue.

On 31 July a letter arrived in Wahnfried from an unknown woman in Wiesbaden appealing to Wagner to give his support to the movement against vivisection. With her letter she enclosed a copy of Ernst von Weber's book *Die Folterkammern der Wissenschaft (The Torture Chambers of Science)*. After reading it immediately, Wagner declared to Cosima that, if he were a younger man, "he would not rest until he had brought about a demonstration against such barbarism. . . . He says religion should be linked with compassion for animals. . . . 'We must preach a new religion, you and I.'" He invited Weber, a naturalist and founder of an international society against vivisection, to Bayreuth that summer, and afterwards he wrote an "Open Letter to Herr Ernst von Weber", which appeared in the *Bayreuther Blätter* of October.

This eloquent plea to human beings to show compassion towards animals was the first solid indication of the direction in which, under the influence of *Parsifal*, Wagner's thoughts were now turning: to the creation of a new idealistic society based on compassion, and one to be achieved, not by fulmination against the world's present evils, but by the gentler force of example.

He saw his own and Bülow's children as a vital part of this "new religion", for they represented the future, and must be brought up in the proper spirit, shielded from the world's corruption. The rigorous methods adopted by Cosima towards Daniela in order to curb her rebellious spirit had not proved necessary in the case of the more placid Blandine, and Cosima had removed her from the boarding school in Dresden after only one term. Since then Blandine had joined the younger children in their lessons with Cosima herself and a succession of (mainly English) governesses.

Siegfried, however, presented a problem, for Cosima doubted her ability to complete the education of a growing boy. In earlier years Wagner had looked on this task as one for Nietzsche, but now their thoughts turned in the direction of Wolzogen and Glasenapp. Eventually, however, they chose as tutor a stranger to them, Heinrich von Stein, a twenty-two-year-old student of philosophy from Halle who came to visit them on 20 October at Malwida's recommendation. Their only objection was that he was a disciple of the materialistic philosopher Karl Eugen Dühring and an opponent of Christianity, but these were matters with which both Wagner and Cosima felt confident of coping in time.

They were agreed that Siegfried was not to be pushed in any artistic direction, for which he anyway at this time showed no inclination (he was still only ten years old). Their ideal was that practised by the hero of Goethe's novel, Wilhelm Meister, who set out to make his son a useful servant of the community, both manually and intellectually. Lessons began immediately, and Siegfried's first day was spent learning the elements of geometry from his tutor and planing from a local cabinet-maker. "R. and I feel as if we are dreaming," Cosima wrote that day. ". . . God grant that the noble spirit of our young teacher and friend will now gradually begin to feel at home with us and abandon all this modern rubbish!"

Having, in the interests of *Parsifal*, spent two successive winters in the raw climate of Bayreuth, Wagner felt the need for milder surroundings, and they decided to leave after Christmas for a prolonged stay in Naples. There he would be able to work on the orchestration of *Parsifal*, the first performance of which had now necessarily been postponed for a year. He began with the preliminary work before leaving Bayreuth. This consisted of ruling the lines of his score and marking in the instruments, with such precision, he declared, that "another person could write the score by following it". He also made some alterations in his orchestral sketch, notably to the ending, which, he told Cosima, he had gone through thirty or forty times in his head before deciding on its final form.

They arrived in Naples on 4 January 1880, together with all five children, an English governess and their personal servants, and took possession of the Villa d'Angri, a large country house on the slopes of the Posillipo, set in its own grounds and from its windows and terraces commanding magnificent views over the bay. Before leaving Bayreuth Wagner had had a recurrence of his old complaint, erysipelas, and the exertions of the journey to Naples brought on another attack. For eleven days he was confined to the house, but his spirits rose when he was at last able, on 16 January, to go for a drive through the city with Cosima. "Naples is the city for me!" he exclaimed to her. "The D. . . . take all ruins, here everything is alive!"

Stein had arrived a few days earlier to resume his lessons with Siegfried, and on 18 January the visit of a young Russian painter, who had his studio not far from the Villa d'Angri, brought a new and important friend into their lives. Paul von Joukowsky, at that time in his thirty-fifth year, was the son of a Russian poet and a German mother. Having been introduced to Cosima in Munich on an earlier occasion, he visited her at Wahnfried in 1876, when he came to Bayreuth for the festival. Relying on that acquaintance, he presented himself at the Villa d'Angri. Wagner, meeting him for the first time, took to him at once, and from that time on he was a constant visitor.

Siegfried wrote later in his reminiscences that for the children their time in Naples was "the purest paradise", and their father was throughout in very cheerful spirits. Wagner's volatile nature and his constant pleasure in the children's company may indeed have given them this impression, but in fact he found it difficult to shake off his mood of depression. The weather was cold, his health continued to trouble him, and he found that, even away from Germany, he could not put it out of his mind. "Our rulers are not just stupid," he exclaimed to Cosima, "they are bad; they know it all, the Jewish problem and the rest, but that is how they want it, for they know that if something genuine and good were to come along, it would be all over with them." Cosima felt it necessary to ask him to talk less in this strain in the presence of the children, for fear of sapping their courage. "Again and again he keeps coming back to America," she wrote in her diary on 1 February, "says it is the only place on the whole map which he can gaze upon with any pleasure: 'What the Greeks were among the peoples of this earth, this continent is among its countries.'"

His interest in America began now to take a more practical shape in his mind, and on 8 February he wrote to his American dentist in Dresden, Newell Sill Jenkins: "I do not regard it as impossible that I may decide to emigrate permanently to America with my entire family and my latest work. Since I am no longer young, I would require for this a very considerable willingness to help from across the ocean. A society would have to be formed which, just for my domicile there and as a single payment for all my exertions, would place at my disposal a sum of one million dollars." This society, he continued, would have to find funds to mount a festival, in which he would stage in succession all his works, beginning with the first performance anywhere of *Parsifal*. "All ensuing contributions from me, whether as director of performances or as creative artist, would, in consideration of the payment already made me, belong free of charge and for all time to the American nation."

Dr Jenkins was somewhat alarmed by this proposal, as Klaus Liepmann has revealed in an article based on Jenkins's reminiscences.* However, he passed Wagner's letter on to various friends in America and Europe with a request for their opinion of its feasibility.

The activities of Wagner's supporters in Bayreuth served rather to strengthen his resolve to abandon Germany than diminish it. Above all, he was angered by a projected move of the committee of the Society of Patrons to persuade Emperor Wilhelm to take over the patronage of the festival. Knowing that such a move, though he himself had already suggested something like it, would greatly offend Ludwig, Wagner wrote to the king on 31 March, disowning it entirely: "My own deeds, creations and plans follow me everywhere like gnawing serpents, which twine around and crush me as if I were a Laocoön," he observed. "It was my misfortune to have thought up a Bayreuth ideal! . . . These useless efforts to gain the means for a permanent foundation, which the wretched state of the German 'nation' prevents it from giving, have aroused my fury, and I am firmly resolved to hear no more of it and to put a final stop to it. So I intend to make the performance of *Parsifal* dependent on nothing except the completion of my work and the discovery of two suitable singers." A production in Bayreuth, using the forces of the Munich opera house, could easily be financed with the money already collected by the Society of Patrons. The only considera-

* Klaus Liepmann: "Wagner's Proposal to America" (*High Fidelity Magazine*, December 1975).

tion that still made him hesitant to adopt this course, he added, was that it would have to be arranged with Perfall, with whom he was resolved to have no further contact. If the king could find a way of removing Perfall and replacing him, perhaps by Bürkel, then his feelings might change. Though he told the king of his thoughts of emigrating to America, he kept silent about his resolve to take *Parsifal* with him.

He had not done any work on *Parsifal* since his arrival in Naples, and, while the arguments were going on about its production, he felt in no mood to begin. Instead, he resumed work on *My Life*, dictating it to Cosima as before. Between 20 March and 23 April he took the story up to May 1864. It was still his intention to continue it up to the time of his union with Cosima at the end of 1868, from which point onwards her diaries would take over the task of recording his life, but, as it turned out, he did no further work on his autobiography, and the book ends with his summons to Munich by King Ludwig.

During the months in Naples Wagner avoided public engagements, and social activities were confined to their house, where their visitors were mainly established friends such as Malwida von Meysenbug and Prince Rudolf Liechtenstein, whom he had known since his Vienna years. Rubinstein joined them in April, and after his arrival Wagner's music was heard again in his home, though he himself took much greater delight in the Neapolitan folksongs which Joukowsky's man-servant Pepino sang to them. Joukowsky endeared himself to Wagner still further by embarking on a portrait of Cosima.

Wagner resumed his task of ruling the lines for the final score of *Parsifal* on 4 May, but he found the work tiring, and set it aside after three days. It was evident that Naples had not yet done for his health what it had been expected to do, and in consequence they decided to prolong their stay in the Villa d'Angri until the autumn. King Ludwig made this possible by undertaking to pay the rent for these extra months as a birthday present. Wagner, writing on 31 May to thank him, described an excursion the family had made, together with Stein and Joukowsky, to Ravello. "Here we discovered some magnificent motives for Klingsor's magic garden, and these were immediately sketched and earmarked for further development for the second act of *Parsifal*. And, since Joukowsky will be joining us permanently in Bayreuth, we have given him the task of making detailed sketches and pictures of both decorations and costumes, not only for *Parsifal*, but for all my stage works." In the visitor's book of the Palazzo Rufalo in Ravello, the home of an English-man, Neville Reed, Wagner wrote: "Klingsor's magic garden is found!"

On 1 June Wagner began work on the lengthy essay which had been oc-cupying his thoughts since his arrival in Naples, and in which he incorporated his new ideas concerning the regeneration of human society. "Religion und Kunst" ("Religion and Art") starts with a challenging statement: "One could say that at the point at which religion becomes artificial, it is the privilege of art to preserve the core of religion by treating those mythical symbols, which religion tries to present as actual truths worthy of belief, according to their allegorical value, in order thus, by depicting them ideally, to demonstrate the profound truth concealed within them." The profoundest truth of Christianity, Wagner maintained, lay in its appeal to the "poor in spirit", rather than (as in Brahmanism) to the "wise", and in the figure of Christ himself with his message of human compassion.

In conveying the essential message of Christianity, literature was severely restricted by words, he maintained, since they were also the vehicle of incomprehensible church dogma. "It was only through music that Christian poetry became a true art: church music was sung to words originating in dogma; but in effect music dissolved these words and the ideas contained in them to the point where they were no longer perceptible, and conveyed to the aroused feelings virtually nothing beyond the purely emotional content. Strictly speaking, music is the only art which fully conforms to Christian belief."

Wagner then embarked on a survey of the ills of mankind, going back to prehistory, and relying on his wide reading in Indian and classical literature, Darwin, Murchison, Schopenhauer, and "amateur writers" (his own words) such as the anti-vivisectionist Weber and the vegetarian Jean Antoine Gleizès to produce a picture of humanity as originally a plant-eating and pacific species, misled in their will to live by famine, greed and lust for power into becoming carnivores and exploiting the weak, whether human beings or animals.

It was Jesus Christ who attempted to bring mankind back to its proper path – by example, not teaching. But the church, in order to increase its hold over the nations of the world, resorted to the traditional methods of force, and thus undid his work. Learning from the disasters of history, Wagner went on, mankind should now make a new attempt to recover its lost innocence. He imagined a process of regeneration in which those who were fighting for their own particular interests – vegetarians, animal protection societies, temperance organisations and even socialists (who, though misguided in their methods, had the right ideas about property) – would combine, and thus provide the basis for a new religion.

"Let us acknowledge, with the Redeemer in our hearts, that it is not their deeds but their sufferings which bring the people of the past close to us and make them worthy of our remembrance, that our sympathies lie with the defeated, not with the conquering hero."

In the last pages of his essay Wagner, fully aware of the Utopian nature of his fantasy, returned to the original theme of his essay: religion and art. Looking back on his life, he declared, he was convinced that true art could flourish only on the basis of true morality. Horrified by mankind's conversion to incomprehensible aims, "it seemed to me a happy omen that I have been permitted a glimpse into a better and different future for mankind – not the ugly chaos which others see, but a future that is very well adjusted, since in it religion and art are not only preserved, but are even placed in a position to achieve for the first time their only true significance. From this direction violence is excluded completely, for all that is needed is a strengthening of the pacific elements which, though still poor and weak, have already taken root among us everywhere."

The foregoing is less an attempt to provide a complete summary of a powerful and often penetrating essay than to extract from it passages that throw a light on Wagner's outlook at a period of his life when youthful revolutionary ideas had mellowed into a vision of inward regeneration. The religious ideas are of course those which found expression in *Parsifal*. Wagner had not "turned pious", as Nietzsche alleged in commenting on that work. In his rejection of the "revengeful Jewish god" of the Old Testament and the power-hungry church, and in his veneration of Jesus Christ as a suffering human being, he was reiterating the metaphysical convictions he shared with (rather than took from) Schopenhauer. Cosima recorded in her diary his remark: "I do not believe in God, but in godliness, which is revealed in a Jesus *without sin*" (20 September 1879).

The addition of vegetarianism to his beliefs was a new one, and it arose from his emotional response to the anti-vivisection movement. In the Tribschen years he had laughed Nietzsche out of following a vegetarian diet, claiming that mankind was carnivorous by nature. Now, under the influence of Gleizès, whose book *Thalysia* he had read at the beginning of their stay in Naples, he had changed his view, and he did consider adopting vegetarianism himself as a cure for his physical ailments, a course in which his doctor in Naples, Otto von Schrön, encouraged him. However, he could never keep it up for long, just as he could not abandon alcohol and tobacco, though fully aware that they were bad for him.

To the catarrhal complaints which continued to plague him was added, as the weather grew hotter, an irritating heat rash. Shortly after finishing his essay on 25 July a severe attack of erysipelas confined him to bed for six days, and he resolved to seek a softer climate. On 8 August he and Cosima set off for the north, and on 21 August they found themselves standing in the cathedral in Siena. "R. moved to tears," Cosima noted; "the greatest impression he has ever received from a building. How I should love to hear the Prelude to *Parsifal* beneath this dome!" The cathedral of Siena did indeed become the model for the temple of the Holy Grail in the production at Bayreuth.

The children and Joukowsky joined them in Siena two days later, and they settled down in a rented house, the Villa della Torre Fiorentina. There, his heat rash having subsided in the cooler climate, Wagner resumed the task of ruling his score. During the quiet weeks that followed, the only visitor from the outside world was Liszt, and Wagner completed his work on 24 September. The 334 pages had still to be filled up with notes, but that, he told Cosima, was the pleasant part.

Beyond a telegram on 25 August thanking him for his birthday gift of the final volume of *My Life* (printed by T. Burger in Bayreuth), Wagner had heard nothing from King Ludwig since May, and he began to wonder whether he had offended the king by attempting to secure the dismissal of Perfall as a condition of presenting *Parsifal* with the Munich forces. In a letter from Siena, dated 28 September, Wagner voluntarily withdrew all demands on the Munich court theatre in connection with the production of *Parsifal*. He had now come to the conclusion, he said, that he could not possibly allow a work dealing with "the sublimest mysteries of the Christian faith" to be performed in a theatre which, on the day before and after, would be given over to frivolity. He had called his work a stage dedication play, "so I must now seek a stage to dedicate to it, and this can only be my isolated festival theatre in Bayreuth. There and only there shall *Parsifal* be performed, now and for all time; it shall never be offered for the amusement of the public in any other theatre whatsoever."

To raise money for the production, he told Ludwig, he intended in the autumn of the following year to make a six-month tour of the United States. In the meantime (though he did not tell the king this) he had heard from Jenkins that his plan to emigrate permanently to America had aroused no great eagerness there, and he had ceased to contemplate it seriously. The lesser project of a limited tour was still only an idea: no practical steps towards it had yet been taken, and Wagner's object in mentioning it to the king was perhaps nothing more than to spur Ludwig to some kind of action. In this he succeeded. A letter from Bürkel arrived on 16 October, informing him that Ludwig had given permission for the complete Munich orchestra and chorus to be put at his disposal for the Bayreuth production of *Parsifal* in 1882, and in this Wagner could discern the king's attempt to divert him from his American plans.

The news reached him in Venice, where he had taken his family after leaving Siena on 1 October. There they once more came into contact with Gobineau. Since their brief meeting in Rome, Wagner had given him no further thought, and had certainly read none of his works. Nor did Wagner warm to him now, since they had to converse in French, which, he told Cosima, he found horribly hard. It was Cosima rather than Wagner who was attracted to "this interesting and significant man", and it was no doubt she (though she did not say so) who gave him Gobineau's *La Renaissance* to read a few days later.

Wagner spent his working hours at the Villa Contarini in Venice writing a supplement to his essay "Religion and Art", which had been published in the October issue of the *Bayreuther Blätter*. In "Was nutzt diese Erkenntnis?" — somewhat unfortunately translated by W. Ashton Ellis as "What Boots this Knowledge?" ("What Use is this Knowledge?" would be more understandable) — he put forward the philosophy of Schopenhauer as the only practical way in which the Christian concept of love could be comprehended and acted upon: a recognition, as he put it, of the moral significance of the world. He saw no point in attempting to propagate his ideas by political means; what was required was a simple declaration by all who sympathised with them: "We recognise the reason for the decay of historical humanity and the need for its regeneration; we believe in the possibility of this regeneration and pledge ourselves in every way to the task of bringing it about."

Wagner was very conscious of the inadequacy of proclaiming such far-reaching ideas, which he now took so seriously that he vowed in future to write of nothing else, in a small periodical confined to his active supporters. Dissatisfied anyway with the *Blätter*, which, he told Cosima, contained "a lot of drivel", he began to consider ways of extending its scope and widening its circulation.

At Wagner's request Ludwig had allowed performances of his works to be given in Munich during the first two weeks of November for the benefit of the children. He himself attended a performance of *Lohengrin* on 10 November and invited Wagner to watch it with him from his box. Cosima, the children and a few of their friends (including Lenbach) sat in seats below in an otherwise empty theatre. Afterwards Wagner told Cosima that he found the king completely unchanged.

With that remark he must surely have been referring to Ludwig's conversation, for in appearance the king now bore little resemblance to the handsome youth at whose side Wagner had sat twelve years ago at the first performance of *Die Meistersinger*. Ludwig had now become rather stout, and his teeth had been ruined as the result of eating too many sweets. This disclosure comes from Bürkel, reminiscing in later years to Felix Philippi. But Bürkel had more favourable things to say about

Ludwig's mental state: "He often astounded me still with the precision of his thinking. In fact it was only when dealing with his building concerns that he seemed to me unmethodical and confused; then he lost all feeling for reality, and it was difficult to manage him. . . . At such times I was confronted with a self-willed, self-satisfied despot. But I also recall with great pleasure many conversations he had with me about art, about literature, theatre and people. Then it was a joy to listen to him, he could still seem charming."*

It was Wagner's last meeting with Ludwig. Two days later he was in the theatre again to conduct a performance of the *Parsifal* Prelude for the king, to whom he sent a written description of the piece. Ludwig, listening unseen in his box, sent down a request for the Prelude to be repeated. Wagner complied, but when the king then asked to hear the Prelude to *Lohengrin*, he lost patience, handed the baton to Levi and left. Cosima noted that Wagner was "very put out" by the king's request, and much has been made of the incident (particularly as a result of Lenbach's account of it) to suggest that it caused an estrangement between Wagner and the king. There is no evidence, however, that it had any lasting effect on their relationship, once Wagner had overcome his irritation at being asked to show off his compositions like samples in a warehouse. Ludwig was probably not even aware that there had been an "incident" at all. Certainly in the letters of mutual gratitude exchanged immediately afterwards there was no reference to it on either side.

On 17 November, after an absence of nearly a year, Wagner and his family re-entered Wahnfried. "A curious feeling," Cosima noted in her diary. "Have we been away? Are we back? – Neither seems real." Wagner too found difficulty in settling down among his loyal friends and supporters, to whom Joukowsky now belonged, for he and his servant Pepino had travelled with the family to Bayreuth. Wagner found them rather narrow-minded and boring. "Worst of all is probably the indifference one feels towards everything," he observed to Cosima. "When I hear people talking about a work like 'Religion and Art', it all seems to me utter nonsense."

Wolzogen, on his instructions, drew up a plan for reorganising the *Bayreuther Blätter* as a vehicle for the ideas expressed in that essay, but, after studying the plan with Cosima, Wagner decided to leave the periodical as it was. The only change he made was to make the *Blätter* available to the general public at the beginning of 1881, but the effect of that on its circulation was minimal.

---

* Published in *Ludwig II von Bayern in Augenzeugenberichten* by Rupert Hacker.

CHAPTER XVII

NOVEMBER 1880 – APRIL 1882:

Friendships and Reconciliations

WAGNER BEGAN WORK on the orchestration of *Parsifal* on 23 November, but his progress was slow at first, and he complained of making many writing mistakes. Italy had not restored his health as he had hoped, and back in Bayreuth he began to feel again what he called the "crab in his chest" – those spasmodic pains which neither he nor the doctors had yet identified as heart trouble.

These were usually the result of the rages into which he increasingly fell as things arose to distract him from his work. Neumann came on 28 November to seek his permission to stage the *Ring* in Berlin. Wagner was against his idea of presenting it at the court opera, for he wished to have nothing further to do with Hülsen, but he reluctantly yielded to Neumann's persuasions, supported by Cosima, and allowed him to negotiate with the Berlin director, a process that produced many vexations in the following weeks.

Then he became involved in a dispute with his agents Voltz and Batz, who had fallen out with each other. A file preserved in the Wahnfried archives shows that in the six years from 1875–1880 the agents collected on his behalf sums of between 18,000 and 22,000 marks annually, from which they deducted twenty-five per cent commission for themselves. Though glad of this substantial addition to his income, Wagner had become increasingly dissatisfied with his agents, above all because they interfered in matters which he felt were no concern of theirs and caused trouble with the theatres, which he then had to try to smooth over himself. The complicated nature of the agreement between them led to frequent differences. Voltz and Batz had been given full power to arrange terms for performances of *Rienzi*, *Der Fliegende Holländer*, *Tannhäuser*, *Lohengrin* and *Die Meistersinger* everywhere except in France, Italy and Berlin. In respect of *Die Meistersinger* the exceptions were further extended to Vienna, Dresden and Hanover. In the case of *Tristan* the agents were empowered only to collect royalties, not to sanction performances, and over the *Ring* they had no control at all. Wagner's attempt, on the occasion of Voltz's quarrel with Batz, to rid himself of his agents entirely foundered on their demand for 100,000 marks as compensation for giving up their rights. Though, after protracted negotiations in which Feustel played a mediating role, Voltz finally withdrew from active participation, Wagner found himself still saddled with Batz, in his opinion the more objectionable of the two.

Neumann's request to him, early in January 1881, to be given exclusive rights to present the *Ring* in Berlin, London, Paris, St Petersburg and America up to the end of 1883, came in contrast as a welcome relief. Since Neumann was offering him ten per cent of the gross proceeds of this transaction, he saw himself freed of the necessity of visiting America himself in order to make money, and so he willingly agreed.

With King Ludwig's undertaking to place the whole Munich orchestra at his disposal, Wagner now felt sufficiently secure to announce publicly the staging of *Parsifal* in the summer of 1882. Engelbert Humperdinck, a young musician who had visited him in Naples, was invited to act as copyist, and he arrived in Bayreuth on 9 January. On 13 January Karl Brandt came for technical discussions and gave Joukowsky, who was new to the work, instructions in the methods of preparing designs for scenery and costumes. On 19 January Levi was summoned to Wahnfried and told that the task of conducting the performances was to be given to him.

Cosima noted in her diary that day that Levi was astonished by the news, and responded with a "veiled expression" when Wagner added: "Beforehand, we shall go through a ceremonial act with you. I hope I shall succeed in finding a formula which will make you feel completely one of us." She herself had misgivings about the wisdom of allowing a Jew to conduct *Parsifal* in Bayreuth, and she expressed them to Wagner in private after Levi had left. "What an accursed subject you have brought up here," he told her.

As for Levi himself, his feelings towards Wagner were expressed in a letter written a little later (13 April 1882) to his father, the rabbi in Giessen. "If only I could be fair to Wagner!" the rabbi had written, and his son replied: "You can and you should. He is the best and noblest of men. That his contemporaries misunderstand and libel him is only natural; the world makes a habit of blackening all that shines; Goethe also fared no better. But posterity will one day realise that Wagner was as fine a human being as he was an artist, as those standing close to him already know. Even his fight against what he calls 'Judaism' in music and in modern literature springs from the noblest motives, and that he harbours no petty kink, like some country squire or Protestant bigot, can be seen in his behaviour to me, to Josef Rubinstein and in his former intimacy with Tausig, whom he loved tenderly. The finest thing that has happened to me in my life has been the opportunity given me to become close to such a man, and I thank God for it daily."

Possibly Wagner's decision to appoint Levi his conductor was responsible for bringing his thoughts back to the Jewish problem. On 2 February he broke off work on *Parsifal* to write a second supplement to "Religion and Art" for the *Bayreuther Blätter*. In this article, "Erkenne dich selbst" ("Know Thyself"), he pointed out that what he had once said about the position of Jews in art, popular feeling was now saying about their position in politics. He questioned the justice of this view, since basically the Jews had been encouraged by politicians, owing to their skill in manipulating money, and hence the Germans were themselves to blame for the power the Jews now wielded. They provided, he declared, a prime example of racial pride and consistency, and it was an example the Germans might have done well to follow.

In his new role of conciliator, Wagner refused to join actively in the anti-Semitic agitations that had been growing in intensity since the granting of full civic rights to German Jews in 1872. His failure to sign an anti-Jewish petition in June 1880 was one of the grudges held against him by Bülow, who had been persuaded by Wolzogen to support it.

Bülow's activities during the past months had continued alternately to touch and exasperate Cosima and Wagner. In 1877 he took over the musical directorship of Hanover and embarked on a series of new productions of Wagner's works. This had not progressed far before he quarrelled with the theatre director and left. In 1880, while Wagner was in Naples, he gave two piano recitals in Bayreuth in the course of a tour designed to raise money for the festival funds – an "egoistic act", he wrote to Klindworth, to facilitate his presence at the performances of *Parsifal*. The proceeds of his tour amounted to 40,000 marks and caused Wagner much uneasiness. He decided in the end to set the money aside for Bülow's children. Towards the end of 1880 Bülow took a new post as conductor in Meiningen, and Cosima thought the time had now come for a reunion with his daughter Daniela. However, her suggestion that Daniela should go to Meiningen to hear him conduct Beethoven's Ninth Symphony was abruptly rejected: Bülow told her in his letter of 9 December that he would have no time to attend to his paternal duties. As a result of this reply, which wounded Cosima and disappointed Daniela, Wagner decided to take steps to adopt Bülow's children legally. Feustel's son-in-law, Adolf von Gross, was despatched to Meiningen to broach the subject, and he was met with a flood of complaints against Bayreuth, among them Bülow's assertion that, through signing the petition against the Jews, he was now being hissed everywhere, whereas Wagner stood high in their estimation.

It was obvious that, with Bülow in this mood, it would be fruitless to pursue the question of adoption. Nevertheless, Cosima did not give up hope of one day persuading Bülow to accept Daniela into his home, and early in January she sent her eldest daughter to Berlin to learn something of the social graces. She wrote to Marie von Schleinitz, to whose home Daniela had gone: "If here in our home she can learn how to forget the world and never miss it, she will learn from you what in entering upon life is almost more important: how to stand up to and bear with it, how to combine truth with graciousness, enthusiasm with patience, and how to counter successfully the constant, demoralising effect of amusements by remaining eternally loyal to one's feelings and opinions."

She sought her father's aid in persuading Bülow to agree to a meeting with Daniela, and at last, at a time when both Liszt and Bülow were in Berlin, the opportunity came. Bülow wrote to Cosima from Meiningen two days after his meeting with Daniela in Berlin: "That day, 27 April, brought me a revelation. I thank Providence for having preserved for me this indescribable delight, this happiness whose sweetness is such that all the bitternesses, regrets, remorse mixed up with it cannot change it. Let me know, noblest and most generous of women, what paternal duties I should now fulfil towards this cherished being who has conquered my whole heart in a single instant. I should like to erect a chapel on the spot where your father brought her to me. . . . Thank you, thank you, thank you! I owe you an unparalleled felicity, however sorrowful it may be."

The reunion took place just before Wagner and Cosima arrived in Berlin to attend the opening of Neumann's production of the *Ring* at the Viktoria-Theater. Liszt as well as Bülow had thought it expedient to depart before their arrival, and Daniela herself was so overcome by the occasion that she failed to meet Wagner and Cosima at the station when they reached Berlin on 29 April. Wagner, hearing an account of the reunion the following day, was, Cosima noted, somewhat dejected, and "in his truthfulness" told Daniela his opinion of her father. Cosima had to play a conciliatory role between them, asking Wagner to show a little consideration towards Daniela, and writing a note to her daughter begging her to be kind to her stepfather: "For the past twelve years he has given you shelter and enabled me to do my task, finally he brought about the reunion. . . . To your Papa [Wagner] in particular I should like to see you affectionate, also in the presence of others." She replied to Bülow with the wish that he should allow his daughter a share in his life.

However, Bülow, once the first rapture was over, retired into his reserve and refused Daniela's request to be permitted to join him in Wiesbaden, where he was visiting his mother. "Perhaps you have not had the misfortune to inherit my nerviness," he wrote to her on 6 May. "All the same, living together with your grandmother demands a certain amount of self-denial which I find difficult to maintain, and would find it even more difficult if you had to share it." In the following months Daniela saw her father from time to time, when he would allow it, but her home continued to be with her mother and with Wagner, who was pleased that it should be so.

Wagner was now to see the *Ring* for the first time since his own production in 1876, and Neumann, understandably nervous, asked him not to attend rehearsals at the Viktoria-Theater. The conductor was Seidl, and among the singers were several who had appeared in Wagner's production: Amalie Materna as Brünnhilde, Vogl as Loge and Siegmund, Hedwig Reicher-Kindermann (who had sung Grimgerde and, for one performance, Erda in Bayreuth) as Fricka. The Siegfried was Jäger, whom Wagner had coached for the role but had not yet seen on stage. There was a perilous moment when Wagner learned on his arrival in Berlin that Scaria was to sing Wotan. Still angry with Scaria for the manner in which he had let him down in 1876, Wagner threatened to leave at once unless he were dismissed. With Cosima's help, Neumann persuaded him at least to hear Scaria sing the role at rehearsal. He began with the second act of *Die Walküre*. "As Scaria turned to leave the stage after his great scene in that act," Neumann wrote in his reminiscences, "Wagner sprang from his seat, flew down the steps, and tore on to the stage at such a frantic pace that I could scarcely follow, shouting: 'Where is he? Where is Scaria? That was glorious! Man alive, where did you get that voice?' and, catching the artist about the neck, he hugged him enthusiastically, kissing him and saying, 'But you did that well – that was well done.'"

After that Wagner not only attended rehearsals, but virtually took charge of them. "The fight between Hunding and Siegmund was not at all to his liking," Neumann wrote. "Scarcely had they begun their sword-play when we all had a fright that made our hearts stop beating! Suddenly, with the agility of an acrobat, Wagner swung himself up on to the railing and ran lightly along the high narrow ledge of the proscenium box, balancing skilfully, but too full of eager impatience to think of reaching the stage by the regular way. Here he snatched up Siegmund's sword, and finished the fight with Hunding on the heights at the back of the stage. Then, at the given signal, he fell with a crash close by the edge of a precipice; his head brought clearly into relief by the rise of the hill behind, and his arm hanging limp over the edge of the abyss in full view of the audience. All this with a certainty and a dashing agility that a man of twenty-five might have envied."

The major disappointment proved to be Jäger. Neumann, noticing at rehearsals that he was in poor voice, resolved to replace him with Vogl, but Wagner insisted on his remaining, and accused Neumann of prejudice against him. It was a demonstration of loyalty he later regretted, for in the first performance of *Siegfried* Jäger was a lamentable failure, and Wagner commanded Neumann to give the role to Vogl for *Götterdämmerung*. Now it was Neumann's turn to be obstinate: he declared that it was too late to make a change, and Jäger sang Siegfried in the final work too (rather better, Neumann reported).

Though, because of Wagner's hostility towards Hülsen, the *Ring* was being presented in a private theatre rather than at the court opera, it was still regarded in Berlin as a brilliant social occasion. Crown Prince Friedrich attended the first cycle together with his wife (Queen Victoria's daughter) and his son (the future Emperor Wilhelm II), and during the performance of *Götterdämmerung* the crown prince invited Wagner to visit his box in the interval. Wagner, who was unable to forgive the crown princess for having dissuaded her husband from taking out a certificate of patronage for the festival of 1876 (her exclamation – "Oh, no, Fritz!" – haunted Wagner for the rest of his life), begged to be excused on the grounds of tiredness. He did, however, make a speech of thanks from the stage, and left Berlin with Cosima on 10 May satisfied on the whole with the performance, and particularly with Scaria and with Seidl's conducting.

During their absence Gobineau arrived in Bayreuth, and they found him there when they returned to Wahnfried. Since last meeting him in Venice Wagner had read several of his books, including the work by which he is today best remembered, the four-volume *Essai sur l'inégalité des races humaines* (*The Inequality of the Human Races*), first published between 1853 and 1855. This Wagner read with mixed feelings, finding it overlong and immature. What he admired in the book were those passages which reflected his own views on the human composition, those views that he had already expressed in "Religion and Art" and the first two of its supplements. In the third supplement "Heldenthum und Christenthum" ("Heroism and Christianity"), which he wrote in August of that year – therefore after reading the *Essay on Inequality* – Wagner did indeed adopt Gobineau's racial theories and even his vocabulary (with suitable acknowledgements), but the basic theme of that essay – the hero as the embodiment of a superior intellect prepared to face suffering for a higher cause, and thus identifiable with the Christian saint – was conceived before he read Gobineau's book. It is consequently incorrect to claim, as is frequently done, that Gobineau was an influence on Wagner. It was a case, as with Schopenhauer in connection with the *Ring*, of respect based on the subsequent discovery of certain similarities of outlook.

During Gobineau's visit to Wahnfried, which lasted four weeks, Wagner spent long hours of discussion with him, and soon realised that their views on such basic matters as art and Christianity frequently diverged. He had in fact little in common with the much travelled French aristocrat and diplomat beyond the fact that they both saw themselves as prophets despised in their own lands, yet none the less Wagner was proud of the friendship, and this was certainly to some extent the result of his own sense of isolation. Surrounded by mainly young literary disciples, he had discovered in Gobineau at least one eminent man of letters of his own generation with whom he could converse on equal terms. "He is my only *contemporary*," he told Cosima.

That year's birthday celebrations included the performance by the children of farces by Lope de Vega and Hans Sachs, and, as a reward for their efforts, Wagner took the whole family, together with Gobineau and Joukowsky, to Berlin to see the fourth and final performance of the *Ring*. The impulsive expedition ended with an unfortunate incident. Reluctantly yielding to Neumann's persuasion to appear with the artists on stage at the end of *Götterdämmerung*, Wagner walked off just as Neumann was expressing thanks to the emperor, who was present. It looked like a deliberate rebuff, and so Neumann took it to be, refusing to accept Wagner's explanation that he had had one of his "chest spasms" and was afraid of collapsing on stage. He wrote Wagner an angry note stating that from now on all personal intercourse between them must cease, and on this sour note Wagner and his party returned to Bayreuth.

Cosima's account in her diary does not help to establish the real reason for Wagner's behaviour. If it had indeed been his desire to discomfit Neumann, the gesture failed in effect, for it was Wagner and not Neumann who was subsequently attacked in the Berlin press for his affront to the emperor (and previously to the crown prince). However, he continued to insist that he had left the stage for fear of a heart attack, and, when Neumann still refused to believe him, he wrote on 12 June to Förster, criticising the *Ring* production and suggesting the appointment of "a new and competent stage manager who shall be thoroughly conversant with my methods". Förster used his diplomatic skills to soothe ruffled feelings on both sides, and there was a reconciliation. When on 21 July Neumann visited Bayreuth to choose some stage properties for the travelling theatre he was organising, he was cordially received. As he left Wahnfried, Wagner once again assured him that illness had been responsible for his leaving the stage in Berlin: "He took my hand and laid it on his heart: 'If you only knew how it beats in here, how I suffer with it!' He looked at me with his deep, earnest eyes: 'Will you believe me now?' But even then I could not say 'I do.' Then he flung my hand away with an angry jerk, clasped his forehead in despair, and said in pained and bitter tones, 'Ah! Why should it be so impossible to find a trusting soul!' We went on in silence down the leafy path to the gate, stood there a while, and then, without another word, Wagner kissed me and put his arms around me. So we parted. It was some two years later, when the sad news came from Venice of the Master's sudden death from heart failure, that I was finally convinced of the tragic sincerity of his words."

Wagner had completed the orchestration of the first act of *Parsifal* on 25 April, shortly before his first visit to Berlin. He started work on the second act on 8 June, the day after Gobineau's departure. Preparations for the production were already under way. Brandt spent a few days in June inspecting the festival theatre for signs of decay during its five years of disuse and planning his new machinery. Levi came on 26 June to discuss matters of casting. While he was there, a letter arrived at Wahnfried, exhorting Wagner not to allow *Parsifal* to be conducted by a Jew; the anonymous writer also made hints about a scandalous relationship between Cosima and Levi. Wagner showed the letter to Cosima, and they laughed about it together, but he was then thoughtless enough to show it to Levi. The effect was catastrophic: Levi was quite unable to share their merriment. Though he said nothing then, he left Bayreuth the following day (30 June) and went to Bamberg, a town some thirty miles away, to consider his position. From there he wrote a letter asking to be released from his obligations.

Wagner replied to him immediately: "Dear and best of friends, with all respect to your feelings, you do not make things easy either for yourself or for us. It is precisely your habit of communing so gloomily with yourself that could perhaps embarrass us in our relations with you. We are completely at one in our resolve to tell everybody about this kind of sh . . [*sic*], and this means that you should not run away from us and in consequence allow silly suspicions to arise. For God's sake, come back at once and get to know us properly! Lose nothing of your faith, but find some courage and strength for it! Perhaps there will be a great turning in your life – but, in any case, you are my *Parsifal* conductor!" Levi returned to Wahnfried the next day (2 July), and the mood at lunch was (Cosima noted) "very relaxed, indeed even very cheerful".

At this time Daniela was visiting her father and Liszt in Weimar. It was a considerable shock, to Wagner as well as to Cosima, when at the end of June she received word from her daughter that Bülow wished to see her. The reason for his request was not clear, but Cosima felt that for the children's sake it would be better to comply. The meeting took place on 10 July at the Goldner Adler hotel in Nuremberg, Cosima travelling alone from Bayreuth, and Bülow with Daniela from Weimar. According to her account in her diary, Bülow was so overcome by emotion that he was unable to explain his wishes to Cosima, and she reluctantly agreed to remain in Nuremberg overnight so that they could talk again the following day. Even then he was still unable to control his feelings: "Hans tells me he does not know when white is white or black is black, he no longer has a guiding star. He is overcome by a nervous twitch, we take leave of each other. . . . Journey home in tears with Daniela."

She did not confide to her diary what it was that Bülow had wanted from her, if indeed she ever found out. She returned to Wahnfried and Wagner feeling "as if a new life were beginning for me, unconsoled and yet in peace, made happy entirely through his happiness". Wagner expressed that by playing to her, "joking, yet all the same moved", the finale from Weigl's comic opera *Die Schweizerfamilie*: "He's mine again!", and in the magnanimity induced by the sense of his victory, he held out the possibility of inviting Bülow to Bayreuth next summer to see *Parsifal*.

The meeting nevertheless continued for a while to cast a shadow over them. "I tell R. that this case makes me so clearly aware of the tragedy of life and the unatonable guilt of existence – that is to say, *my* guilt," Cosima wrote in her diary on 13 July, "for nobody had been better equipped than Hans to follow R., nobody more in need of guidance than he, and then I came between them – how can one ever close one's eyes to my sin? And when R. tells me, 'Your crime was a beneficial folly,' I may be enabled thereby to give him a look of serene contentment, but never to deceive myself about the misery of having ever been born!"

Another test of their emotions occurred in the early autumn of that year. Throughout the summer Cosima had been corresponding amicably with Judith about the prospects of finding a French publisher to reissue Gobineau's book on racial inequality, and no doubt she thought that enough time had passed since that secret exchange of letters with Wagner to allow a personal reunion to be lived through without embarrassment. On 26 September, at her invitation, Judith and Benedictus arrived at Wahnfried, where Liszt was also paying a visit. As on the first evening she watched Judith playing whist with her father in the *salon*, her feelings so overwhelmed her that she had to leave the room. She wrote in her diary the following day: "Yesterday I desisted from responding to R.'s remarks about Judith's character, which he finds embarrassing; instead, I kept bringing the conversation back to the children. He is sad today about that, weeps, and says that, if anything were to come between us, it would be all over with him; I seek to explain to him in all mildness the feeling which makes me so intensely aware of this strange woman in our house that yesterday I had to leave the room for a moment. We part in good spirits, I blissful that I have been able to account for something that could so easily have been presented in the wrong way. Even before I went to my bath, he appeared in my room: 'What shall we make our coffin of? Which do you want – lead or wood? For until death comes this nonsense will never cease – death is all that remains to us.'"

On the next day Cosima felt another twinge: "When I come downstairs, I discover R. at the piano and our friend Judith in rich, rather revealing finery: 'I was taken by surprise,' he tells me." The visit ended the following day, but neither Wagner nor Cosima was at the door to pay their farewells to Judith and Benedictus (their opinion of him, incidentally, summed up in Cosima's single dismissive word: "Israel"). Judith, equally aware that the visit had not been a success, sent a letter enquiring the reason for their apparently cool dismissal, and Cosima hastened to assure her that their absence had been due to a severe cough which kept Wagner to his room, and her with him. "I saw you from the gallery pass through with my father, saw M. Benedictus waiting, and I asked myself whether your intuition would direct you to look up. No, not at all! I sent you my silent farewell and went back to the bedroom I had left. . . . My dear, your friend did not arouse my husband's anger, not in the least: please tell him that, to put his mind at rest, for it is true. What is not true is that *nobody* wished to be embraced by you, and to prove it we now join together and press you to our massive Wahnfried heart, one and all, like God Almighty. Cosima."

A specialist in abdominal disorders, Wilhelm Leube, examined Wagner on 26 October in Bayreuth at Dr Landgraf's request, and came to the conclusion that there was nothing organically wrong with him. His chronic digestive troubles had been aggravated by his nervous energies, which had remained unimpaired by advancing age, and this was responsible for all his ailments, including the chest spasms and congestions and the cough.

All these could be cured, Wagner was told, by regular walks in the open air, and he was advised to seek a milder climate at once for that purpose. Having completed the orchestration of the second act of *Parsifal* on 20 October, he decided to leave at once and finish his work in Palermo in Sicily, which Rubinstein had recommended to Cosima as a quiet and idyllic refuge.

He had by this time already decided on the casting of the main roles in next summer's festival. Marianne Brandt was his first choice for Kundry (no other soprano he knew, he told King Ludwig in a letter, possessed the deep notes necessary to her "daemonic" character), and he decided to give the role of Parsifal to Hermann Winkelmann, a tenor from Vienna recommended to him by Richter. Since there were to be sixteen performances of *Parsifal*, he felt it necessary to have alternative castings for the main roles, and he told the king in his letter of 19 September that these would be Amalie Materna and Vogl, "and for emergencies poor Jäger and Frau Vogl". He also intended to give a few performances to Therese Malten and Heinrich Gudehus, whom he had seen in Dresden during a recent visit to Jenkins for dental treatment. Others on whom he had now decided were Siehr and Scaria (Gurnemanz), Hill (Klingsor) and Theodor Reichmann of Munich (Amfortas), while Lilli Lehmann had been invited to choose and lead the solo Flower Maidens. With Karl Brandt and Joukowsky now busy at work on the scenic arrangements, Wagner felt he could safely leave matters to them for a few months, and to Levi he gave full powers to look after the musical preparations, choosing singers for the lesser roles and so on. After the Bamberg incident there was now full accord between him and Levi, "whose remarkable diligence and almost passionate devotion", he wrote to Ludwig, "I feel able to trust completely, for which reason I gladly try to reassure him about his Jewishness."

The family (complete except for Daniela, who was paying an extended visit to Liszt) arrived in Palermo on 5 November and took up residence at the Hôtel des Palmes. In contrast to the dramatic splendour of Naples, the more modest beauties of Palermo proved much less distracting (if also a little disappointing), and Wagner began work on 8 November on the third act of *Parsifal*. The presence of Rubinstein, who was there to meet them, was useful, since he was making the piano arrangement of *Parsifal*, and thus could work closely under Wagner's supervision. Wagner was able to spend his mornings undisturbed on his orchestration work, make outings with the children in the afternoons and in the evenings refresh himself by reading to the family Shakespeare's *Henry the Sixth* (all three parts of which he greatly admired) and *Richard the Third*.

This quiet and contented life continued up to the end of November. Then, following an invitation by one of the local aristocrats, Count Almerita-Tasca, to lunch, at which he ate unwisely, Wagner's digestive troubles started up again, and with them the recurrence of those "chest spasms", which now began to afflict him with increasing frequency, indeed almost daily. A few days earlier he had reproached himself to Cosima for his "vulgar habit of guzzling", but he can hardly be accused of gourmandising, for he admitted to her that nothing tasted better to him than bread and butter, which he could not help eating in huge amounts with his coffee. The connection between his injudicious eating and drinking (though he was by no means a toper) and his heart condition was not fully appreciated by anybody until a post-mortem report revealed it.

His frequent indispositions slowed up his work on *Parsifal*, and he was unable to complete it in time for Cosima's birthday, as he had planned. As a gesture, he skipped several pages in his ruled score to orchestrate the final page, and placed the "finished score" in her hands on 25 December. After that a whole series of troubles began.

It started on 29 December with a telegram informing them of Karl Brandt's death from pneumonia. This was a severe blow, which sent their thoughts back to Schnorr von Carolsfeld. However, this time they had the consolation of knowing that the loss was not irreparable: Brandt's son Fritz could take over his work on *Parsifal*. Wagner wrote to him on 14 January, the day after he finished filling in the blank pages of his score and *Parsifal* was at last complete. "I stand now in the third generation of human life," he wrote, "and have already seen two generations of my contemporaries pass: with your father I lost the final member of that second generation still linked with my experiences. In you I now greet the third generation, to which I have entrusted the continuation of my mature life. Welcome to you!"

In this mood of melancholy the French painter Auguste Renoir found Wagner when he came on the following day with a request to paint his portrait. This mood, combined with Wagner's ill-health and exhaustion after the completion of *Parsifal*, may to some extent account for the great difference between Renoir's interpretation of him, so curiously withdrawn, and those of other painters. Neither Wagner nor Cosima had ever heard of Renoir before (she spelled his name "Renouard" in her diary), and it was Joukowsky (who had joined them at Christmas) who facilitated the thirty-five-minute sitting, during which Renoir worked directly in oil on canvas. Wagner, he related, was cheerful during the sitting, but ended it abruptly with the words: "I'm tired. That's enough." Examining the picture, he exclaimed to the artist: "I look like a Protestant priest." According to Cosima he had been amused by Renoir's excitement and his grimaces as he worked, and he gave her his private opinion that the picture made him look "like the embryo of an angel, an oyster swallowed by an epicure".

Tiring of hotel life, where he complained of feeling always under observation, Wagner accepted an invitation from a relative of Count Almerita-Tasca, Prince Gangi, to occupy a summer residence belonging to him in the Piazza dei Porazzi, a few miles outside Palermo, and there they moved on 2 February. It proved an unwise move, for the house was not equipped for winter occupation, and Wagner had to spend much money on stoves and carpets. Very soon he caught cold, and Siegfried also fell ill with typhoid fever, an illness which might have had something to do with his habit, while in Palermo, of sitting in the street sketching churches and other buildings, watched by crowds of curious onlookers. Siegfried's illness was a serious one, and it had the effect of confining Cosima and Wagner to the house and garden. Wagner became increasingly irritable, and tiffs with Cosima and the children were frequent. She, conscious that the secluded life she and Wagner preferred was unfair on her daughters, allowed them to go on outings and attend balls in aristocratic houses, but this upset Wagner, who felt his paternal authority was being usurped, and there was a family row when on one occasion he forbade the girls to attend a ball.

The sole creative work done in Palermo comprised a few jottings in the *Brown Book* under the general heading "Thoughts on the Regeneration of Mankind and Culture" and a short melody which was an offshoot of *Tristan und Isolde*. This, the so-called "Porazzi Melody", was written down on 2 March, but it remained a fragment.

When Siegfried was well enough to be moved, they decided to end their unhappy stay in Palermo. On 18 March, as an expression of gratitude to the Sicilian aristocrats who had befriended them and the children during their stay, they held a garden party at the villa, and Wagner conducted the local military band in performances of the *Huldigungsmarsch*, the *Kaisermarsch* and the *Siegfried Idyll*. The orchestra was horrible, Cosima recorded, and in the course of the concert Wagner suffered a "chest spasm".

The family, which now included Daniela, left the following day for Acireale, a spa on the east coast of Sicily, and there at the Grand Hôtel des Bains Wagner quickly threw off his depression and started on an essay, "On Male and Female in Culture and Art". He had not progressed beyond a page or so of notes in the *Brown Book* when, on 28 March, he suffered a major heart attack, certainly the most severe he had yet experienced. Cosima was summoned by the maid: "I hasten to him and am confronted with a sight which so affects me that I faint. I soon pull myself together again and return to R. from the bed on which I have been laid; his condition gradually becomes calmer, he is given electric treatment, starts joking again. . . . The doctors say attacks like this are not dangerous, but when I see him in such a condition, see him suffering, groaning, and there is nothing anyone can do, then, dear God, my strength deserts me!" But from her own reaction to the sight of his suffering she drew one consolation. It was always her cherished wish that, when his time arrived, she would be permitted like Isolde to die with him: "My fainting today has now given me hope."

For her the one positive gain of the visit to Sicily was Blandine's engagement to Count Biagio Gravina, whom Blandine, now aged nineteen, had met at those balls which Wagner so much despised. Gravina was gratifyingly well-connected, being the second son of the Prince of Ramacca, an ancient Sicilian family, and the only drawback to the marriage was that, at the age of thirty-two, he had no means of his own. However, he professed his willingness to apply himself to an active occupation, and, since Wagner also approved of him, Cosima gave her consent to the engagement.

As Blandine was Bülow's daughter, his formal consent was necessary. His short telegraphic reply to Cosima's request, addressed to Meiningen: "You have full powers, madame," she felt to be hardly sufficient, and still less satisfactory was his letter to Daniela of 3 April* in response to Cosima's request for a more practical interest on his side. Bülow wrote: "Fearing to compromise your sister's plans (I like to hope that she is playing an *active* role in them) by a reply in which I should not be able to conceal my *displeasure*, I shall follow the sage's advice that in matters of doubt it is better to abstain. . . . My dear Daniela, I appoint you my plenipotentiary in this affair. Justify my confidence in you."

It was probably this letter to which Cosima was referring when she wrote in her diary on 7 April of a letter from Bülow "which in offensiveness transcends everything so far experienced", and indeed it did contain some wounding phrases, among them the remark that Cosima's messages, "however rare and perfect in matter and form, fall on me exactly like bullets in the midst of my musical and social chaos." Wagner too was annoyed by it and wished Cosima to break off all relations with Bülow totally and at once.

Daniela managed in the end to avert the quarrel by a tactful reply, in which she told her father that Gravina had made a good impression on all of them, and it would be a pity to risk spoiling things for Blandine by making too much of his disapproval. Her diplomatic handling of the affair brought her an effusive letter of thanks from Bülow, who was evidently conscious that he had gone too far in his hostility. This (though he did not say so) could have arisen from his feelings of isolation in a matter concerning a daughter whom he had not seen since she was six years old and who seemed to have no interest in him. He told Daniela that he might come to Bayreuth for the wedding in the summer, and perhaps see *Parsifal* at the same time. "Pray to heaven for me, as I do for both of you. Yes, yes! Perhaps with its help all the main discords of our destinies will this summer be harmoniously resolved. Perhaps – if things are done, and above all thought, *visibus unitis*."

This letter, written in Hamburg on 14 April, reached Daniela on the day (17 April) the family arrived in Venice on their way back to Bayreuth, and it was greeted by Cosima with relief. A few days later she heard,

---

* Not included in the printed collections, but preserved in manuscript in the Wahnfried archives.

though she did not reveal from whom, that Bülow himself had become engaged in March to an actress, Marie Schanzer. "Is this perhaps the resolution of the discords Hans hinted at in his most recent letter?" she wrote in her diary on 22 April. Her question suggests that she did not recognise Bülow's hint for what it surely must have been: the hope of using his daughter's marriage as a means of achieving a reconciliation between himself and Wagner.

Parsifal *and* Venice

AT THE TIME of Wagner's return to Bayreuth with his family on 1 May, most of the singers he had chosen for *Parsifal* were in London, where Neumann was presenting the *Ring* under Seidl at Her Majesty's Theatre, and another group, got together by the London impresario Hermann Francke and the Hamburg opera director Bernhard Pollini, was simultaneously staging *Tannhäuser*, *Lohengrin*, *Tristan und Isolde* and *Die Meistersinger* at Drury Lane under Richter. Wagner refused to listen to Neumann's pleas that he should go to London for the occasion, and not even hints that he might at the same time have an honorary doctorate conferred on him by Oxford University could move him. Instead, he remained in Bayreuth complaining to Cosima that there was nothing for him to do.

There was in fact much requiring his attention, including final decisions to be made about the casting of the principal roles in *Parsifal*. He had once told Cosima that he would offer the role of Kundry to Amalie Materna only if all else failed, but he had since changed his mind. From Acireale he sent her in March a definite invitation, which she accepted. He now had four Parsifals – Vogl, Winkelmann, Gudehus and Jäger – and four Kundrys – Materna, Brandt, Malten and Therese Vogl – and he could see trouble ahead, particularly since he knew Vogl would insist on singing with his wife, to Wagner's mind the least promising of his Kundrys. In his letter of 20 May to Levi he attempted to extricate himself from his difficulties by granting Frau Vogl hardly more than a reserve position and threatening, if there were any resistance, to reduce the number of planned performances so drastically that he would be able to manage with a single singer for each role. The result was what he no doubt intended it to be: the Vogls withdrew.

Wagner further used these weeks before rehearsals began to work out with Heckel, Schön and Wolzogen a basis for the future of the Society of Patrons, and in a short article entitled "Open Letter to Herr Friedrich Schön in Worms", which he wrote in the middle of June for publication in the July issue of the *Bayreuther Blätter*, he finally laid the idea of a music school to rest, claiming in ironic phrases to have lost faith in his ability to change Germany's musical outlook. The most he could now hope to do, he declared, was to give a final demonstration with *Parsifal* of the way in which his works should be presented, and the task of the Society would be to find ways of ensuring that even the poorest could gain access to the festival. This was the origin of Bayreuth's scholarship fund, which was set up at once and is still in existence.

In the previous year King Ludwig had officially assumed the sponsorship of the Bayreuth Festival (a position involving no financial commitment) and, in order to enable him to watch performances undisturbed, a new royal box and adjoining ante-room had been added to the festival theatre. In his letter of 13 May Wagner assured Ludwig that, when he came to see *Parsifal*, everything would be done to guard his privacy.

Both Gobineau and Blandine's fiancé Gravina were in Bayreuth for Wagner's sixty-ninth birthday on 22 May. A "chest spasm" delayed the festivities in the morning, but otherwise Cosima's elaborate preparations, which included a performance by the children of a play, *Love's Distress*, written by herself, and the boys' chorus from *Parsifal*, sung by fifty local boys rehearsed by Humperdinck for the festival production, were rewarded with their usual success. King Ludwig's gift was a pair of black swans, to which Wagner gave the names Parsifal and Kundry.

Gobineau had intended to remain until the opening of the festival, but he was in very poor health and, shortly after having what Cosima took to be a slight stroke, he departed on 17 June. On the following day the costumes, made to Joukowsky's designs by the Frankfurt firm of Schwab und Plettung, arrived. They caused disappointment, particularly those for the Flower Maidens, since they lacked that "truthful simplicity" which, Wagner subsequently wrote in the *Bayreuther Blätter*, was the foremost aim of his production. Cosima and Isolde, who had a considerable talent for drawing, joined in the efforts to improve them.

Wagner was satisfied with the scenery, prepared from Joukowsky's designs by the Brückner brothers, but a difficult problem arose in connection with the transformation scenes. Gigantic rollers had been installed on which a moving backcloth would depict the changing scenery as, in the first act, Gurnemanz and Parsifal walk from lake to temple and, in the third act, from Gurnemanz's hut to the temple, the singers marking time in front of it. Karl Brandt had already pointed out to Wagner on first seeing the score that more music would be necessary for the transformation in the first act than he had provided for it, and in March 1881 Wagner, watch in hand, wrote an additional four minutes of music, which was pasted in the score. Now, when the machinery came to be tried out, it was discovered that the amount of music was still insufficient.

For the first act Humperdinck came to the rescue. He composed some extra connecting bars and presented them with some trepidation to Wagner, who was willing to accept them. All the same, the prolongation of the transformation scene offended his dramatic instinct, for its real purpose, as he pointed out later in his article about the *Parsifal* production in the *Bayreuther Blätter*, was not just to produce a picturesque effect, but to transport the onlooker unobtrusively along untracked paths to the temple of the Holy Grail "in a dreamlike trance".* The identical problem in the third act Wagner decided to solve by repeating the music of mourning for Titurel, but he disliked the effect, and before the opening performance adopted Scaria's suggestion of closing the curtain between the first and second scenes.

Difficulties such as these could not spoil Wagner's pleasure in being involved once more in active theatrical work. Oblivious of his troublesome heart, he climbed to the top of the rigging loft to try out the temple bells (in fact gongs): "What a fantastic place to be, a theatre like this!" he exclaimed to Cosima, and when at the beginning of July the singers arrived, he told Joukowsky and Stein: "They are real people!"

Full rehearsals began on 2 July. All the singers were bidden to be present throughout, and those who were to share the main roles were not told in which of the sixteen performances they would appear. Amalie Materna, who requested permission to arrive late, was firmly told that, if she did, she could not expect to be chosen for the first performance. She arrived in time. Winkelmann, hearing rumours on the second day of rehearsal that Gudehus would sing in the first performance, proclaimed his intention of leaving at once. Wagner cheerfully bade him goodbye, whereupon he changed his mind and stayed.

Of the singers Wagner had originally chosen to take part, only Lilli Lehmann withdrew against his wishes, but that was for personal reasons connected with Fritz Brandt, with whom she had once had an unhappy love affair. The control of the Flower Maidens was given to Heinrich Porges, while Fricke was brought in to devise their stage movements: "something completely unballetistic" was Wagner's instruction to him. The six soloists, mainly young singers at the beginning of their careers, had been visited and coached separately by Humperdinck in the opera houses at which they were engaged. The orchestra of one hundred and seven players included a few instrumentalists from Berlin, Darmstadt, Karlsruhe and Meiningen, but was otherwise the permanent orchestra of the Munich opera. Orchestra and chorus had been thoroughly trained in Munich by Levi and Fischer before coming to Bayreuth.

Thus the rehearsals progressed in a very much more settled atmosphere than had happened with the *Ring* in 1876. Wagner spent less

---

* In later years, when means were found of speeding up the machinery, Humperdinck's music was dropped.

time on the stage than he had done then, preferring to watch from the front row of the auditorium; from there he passed his instructions to the conductor through a little flap he had had inserted in the hood concealing the orchestra. A week was spent on each act, all the main singers taking over in turn.

On the very day that rehearsals began Cosima received a letter from Bürkel informing her that the king would not be coming to Bayreuth, but would command a performance in Munich next year. Wagner suspected political reasons for the decision: the king had neglected to open an important trade fair in Nuremberg two months previously, and consequently might have thought (or been advised) that it would be tactless to make a personal appearance in Bayreuth so soon afterwards. Wagner wrote to him on 8 July: "I could not have received a bitterer blow. . . . The best success, of which I am now assured, becomes for me the greatest failure of my life: what does anything matter when I cannot please *him* with it? And – it is the last thing I shall write. The tremendous over-exertion, which leaves me only enough strength for these few lines today, tells me how things stand with my powers. From me *nothing* more can be expected." The king, he went on, would certainly be given a private performance in Munich whenever he commanded it, "but it is quite impossible that these later performances in Munich could reveal my work to my King in the pure and transfiguring light that I can achieve only through my preparations in the festival theatre; *once* at least, for the *first* time, it ought to be presented to you, my beloved master, here and by me. But like this – I feel bereft of all hope! – Oh, why was this theatre not built at that time in Munich? Then everything would have been all right. But enough, and indeed already too much of what you will perhaps find hard to excuse."

It was a sharper letter than Wagner had ventured for some years to write to the king, and he told Cosima that in it he had done "what Luther did to the Lord in connection with Melancthon's illness – thrown his club at his feet". But Ludwig could no longer be stirred to passionate remorse, nor even to anger, by such outbursts. His reply, written in a mountain hut on the Krammelsberg on 17 July, was almost callous in its refusal to take Wagner's complaints seriously. He could well understand, he said, that Wagner should find his decision to stay away incomprehensible. "Unfortunately I have not been feeling well for some time, and it is certainly much better for my health to remain in the pure air of the mountains. It is regrettable that it has turned out thus, but it cannot be altered." For Wagner's argument about the importance of seeing *Parsifal* for the first time in the Bayreuth theatre he showed no understanding: "I have no doubt that the friendship you have so often proved towards me will enable you to ensure that the spirit of dedication will not be lacking in the performances I am looking forward to; if the participants should have lost their holy fire so relatively soon after the Bayreuth performances, I should consider that very regrettable." Finally, he commiserated with Wagner on his feelings of exhaustion, but "I can and will not doubt that, as after the *Ring*, you will recover completely from the exertions of *Parsifal* in the south, which you love so dearly; and then your cheerful spirits, your love of life and your joy in creation will return."

Rehearsals were still in progress as the loyal band of friends and patrons began to assemble in Bayreuth. Liszt arrived on 15 July, followed shortly by Strecker, Neumann, Malwida von Meysenbug, Glasenapp, Judith Gautier, the Schleinitzes, the Dannreuthers, Mathilde Wesendonck and Mathilde Maier, and they were allowed to attend the dress rehearsal on 24 July. "R. finds the tempi of the first act rather too long," Cosima noted in her diary. "He is also not satisfied with the lighting. The 2nd act goes better. . . . In the third act he is very touched. . . . Since there is applause at the end, he acknowledges it ironically from our gallery."

It was applause that marred for Wagner the first performance on 26 July, for which admittance was confined to members of the Society of Patrons. To curb their enthusiasm, he came forward at the end of the second act to inform them that there would be no curtain calls. The audience, interpreting this as a command to refrain from applause throughout, kept silent at the end, and Wagner had then to address them again, encouraging them to clap. At the second performance on 28 July, word having got around, the audience (also composed of members of the Society of Patrons) maintained a reverent silence at the conclusion of the first act, which (Cosima wrote) had a pleasant effect. A few people attempted to clap after the second act and were hissed into silence by the rest, so once again Wagner had to explain to them that applause was in order at this point. It was not until the third performance on 30 July (the first for the general public) that the audience got it right: silence after the first act, applause after the second, and curtain calls after the third. But the uncertainty Wagner created at the first performance has persisted to this day, when incautious clappers in Bayreuth are still liable to find themselves sternly hissed. The same fate overtook Wagner himself at a subsequent performance, when he was so delighted with his Flower Maidens that from his box he called out, "Bravo!" He was promptly hissed.

The fourteen public performances were given on three days each week, on Sunday, Tuesday and Friday. Winkelmann sang Parsifal at the first performance, since he had proved in rehearsal to be the most suitable partner for Amalie Materna, who was given the privilege of opening. Winkelmann sang the role in nine of the sixteen performances, Amalie Materna the role of Kundry in eight, but not necessarily together, for the partnerships (Gudehus and Marianne Brandt, Jäger and Therese Malten) were not rigid, and indeed the audience did not know in advance which of the singers they would be seeing in the main roles, since the single printed programme listed all the names together. Parsifal was sung five times by Gudehus and twice by Jäger; Kundry five times by Marianne Brandt and three times by Therese Malten. In the role of Gurnemanz Scaria appeared ten times, Siehr six; Hill sang Klingsor on twelve occasions, Anton Fuchs on four. The other singers were not called on to share: Theodor Reichmann sang Amfortas in all performances, August Kindermann Titurel, and the solo Flower Maidens included Luise Belce (at the beginning of a Bayreuth singing career which, under the name of Reuss-Belce, lasted thirty years) and Carrie Pringle, an English singer whose career seems early to have faded out.* There were in all 29 Flower Maidens, 31 Knights of the Grail, a backstage chorus of 29 and a boys' choir of 50. Assisting the two conductors (Levi and Fischer) in controlling these forces were Porges, Humperdinck, Ernst Hausburg, Oscar Merz and Julius Kniese.

Inevitably a few minor mishaps of a technical nature occurred at one performance or another, and equally inevitably there were occasional outbreaks of jealousy among the singers sharing the main roles, but on the whole the festival ran a smooth course. As in 1876, social duties kept Cosima so busy that she had to put her diary aside (on 26 July), and she did not take it up again until 18 September. The retrospective account she wrote then shows that Wagner left the task of entertaining their many visitors almost entirely to her and limited his personal contacts only to the closest of their friends. He complained of feeling unwell throughout, but Cosima recorded only one "chest spasm". He did, however, rouse himself to play a full part at the wedding of Blandine and Count Gravina. The civic ceremony took place on their own wedding day (25 August), and was followed next morning by a marriage service at the Catholic church.

Now, with only two performances of *Parsifal* still to come, Wagner had finally to abandon his hope that King Ludwig would change his mind and come to Bayreuth. His disappointment was expressed in the bitter quatrain he sent to the king on his birthday: "Though you have spurned the Grail's sweet comfort/This was all my gift to you;/Now may he not be despised,/Who can only offer, no longer give." Instead of Ludwig, it

---

* An article by Herbert Conrad in the *Nordbayerischer Kurier* (supplement *Fränkischer Heimatbote* No. 8, 1978) seeks to establish a possible love relationship between Wagner and Carrie Pringle. Though the article has attracted much attention, the evidence produced seems to me too tenuous for full acceptance.

was the Prussian crown prince who occupied the new royal box at the fifteenth performance on 27 August.

For the last performance on 29 August Winkelmann, Amalie Materna and Scaria were chosen to play the main roles. In the third act Wagner, who had spent most of the performance in the wings, went down into the mystical chasm during the transformation music and silently took over the baton from Levi. "I remained standing beside him," Levi wrote to his father, "because I was worried he might make some mistake, but my worry was quite needless – he conducted with as much assurance as if he had been nothing but a conductor all his life. At the conclusion of the work the audience broke out into a jubilation which defies all description. But the master did not reveal himself, continuing to sit down below with us musicians, making bad jokes, and when after ten minutes the noise in the auditorium still refused to die down, I shouted at the top of my lungs: 'Quiet, quiet!' That was heard up above, the people actually calmed down, and then the master (still at the desk) began to speak, first to me and the orchestra. Then the curtain was drawn up, all the singers and technical staff were assembled above, the master spoke with so much warmth that everyone began shedding tears. It was an unforgettable moment!"

His words were not audible in the auditorium, and owing to the invisibility of the orchestra, the audience could not have known that Wagner had conducted the final scene himself, but Cosima maintained that "almost all of us heard what was happening in the orchestra, even if we could not exactly explain it at the time". Wagner himself was amused by Levi's anxious concern that he might upset the performance, and told his friends that, when he put in an additional beat to help Reichmann over a difficult entry, Levi rewarded him with a "Bravo".

"And so these sixteen performances have come to an end," Cosima wrote in her diary under the date 30 August, "and never once did the spirit of eagerness and dedication desert the artists! And the audience, too, had the feeling of something out of the ordinary, indeed, in the highest sense of the word. I think we can be satisfied."

Wagner's own opinion of the performances was contained in his letter of 8 September to King Ludwig: "I was asked by theatre directors, astonished by the unusually smooth progress, who was in charge of all this, whereupon I replied jokingly that here in my theatre anarchy reigned, and everyone did as he wanted; however, since each of them wanted what I wanted, everything always went as intended. And truly, that is exactly how it was."

He complained that his poor health had prevented him from coaching his singers during the festival as much as he would have liked, "yet the few matters I did seriously undertake to correct, particularly in the decisive big scene between Kundry and Parsifal in the second act, bore the finest fruits: visitors to the first performance who returned to see the last were astonished by the improvements they noticed." He was full of praise for Amalie Materna, Therese Malten, Winkelmann and Gudehus, but maintained a discreet silence about Marianne Brandt and Jäger. As Gurnemanz, he declared, Siehr was perhaps the more correct in voice and delivery, but Scaria's performance was "sustained throughout by a certain naïve quality of genius which won him preference in the hearts of all." The Flower Maidens' scene was "quite surpassing, and perhaps the most masterly example of musical stage production I have ever encountered. . . . The engaging eagerness of these ladies defies description." Wagner ended his account by regretting that the transformation scenes had operated so slowly, dragging things out in a manner that was "wearisome and completely at odds with the magical character of my intentions".

Although the performances for the general public had been played to an auditorium only half filled, the festival ended with a healthy surplus of 143,140 marks, thus providing a sound basis for repeat performances in the following summer. As far as Wagner's personal finances were concerned, Strecker paid him one hundred thousand marks for the publication rights, an unheard-of sum at that time. Thus Wagner was able to depart with his family for Italy on 9 September in more tranquil spirits than after the festival of 1876.

Bülow married Marie Schanzer on 29 July 1882, just after the festival in Bayreuth had begun. From Daniela, who had kept him informed about the progress of rehearsals, he gained the impression that his presence in Bayreuth was not desired, and he told her to omit his name from the invitations to Blandine's wedding. That letter was written on 21 August from Klampenborg, a seaside resort in Denmark, from which nine days earlier he had written a much more explicit letter to a friend in Munich, Eugen Spitzweg:

"It is now nearly fifteen years since I began my convulsive struggle to blot out the past, to free my name, my individuality from the crust of fame to which it has been condemned on account of the 'contacts' with Weimar and Bayreuth. The hastening of my marriage – subjectively no time could have been less suitable – sprang from the same need – that of a soonest possible change of father-in-law. *I no longer want* to be reckoned among the Grail lot, to the music of *Parsifal* I prefer to adopt a negative, or shall we say a neutral attitude, without committing myself to an objective and artistic final judgment – something I should otherwise do, incidentally, if I were to consider it expedient or opportune. Wagner's greatest manifestations of genius are (a) *Tristan*, (b) *Meistersinger*.

All his later works fill me with various degrees of antipathy. False paths – madness (looked at from a musical point of view, and I am a *musician* and intend to function as one as long as I live, if I can). My nerves are strained to the utmost. For the past three days favourable weather has allowed me to take in a combination of woodland and sea air (and sea bathing), which, with the help of the touchingly selfless affection of my dear – and not exactly enviable – wife, may perhaps be of benefit to me. But all poison from outside – and almost everything affects me like poison – must be kept at a distance. I shall return to M[einingen] only after Bayreuth has ended, my newly-wed second daughter has departed for Sicily, etc."

Bülow hesitated a long time before committing himself to marriage again. He first saw Marie Schanzer on the stage in Karlsruhe in 1877, and it was at his recommendation that she gave a guest performance in Hanover, where he was then music director. There he came to know her personally, but, since her engagement at the theatre was not a permanent one, the friendship gradually faded after the exchange of a few letters. They met again in Hamburg in January 1882, and she joined him in Meiningen on a guest contract with the theatre there. His letters to her at this time suggest that he was genuinely in love with her, but, even after they became engaged in March, he continued to have misgivings about marriage, and Daniela was among those to whom he appealed for assurance. She in turn appealed to her mother for advice, and on 5 June Cosima wrote to her: "In your place I should deal with your father as I deal with you children, that is, try to see where the *true* inclination lies and strengthen this by understanding. . . . Do not let yourself be influenced by how things might look – for example, that people might say you prevented the marriage – if you feel your father's apprehension of marriage to be stronger than his desire for it. . . . But if he shied away from starting a new life with you, I cannot understand why he does not now tremble very much more at the prospect of another marriage. You would have had earnestness and courage enough to satisfy him!"

In fact, Bülow needed no warnings against rashness, for his own self-disgust made him doubt whether any other person could genuinely love him. He wrote to Marie on 16 July, only eleven days before their marriage, imploring her to consider carefully what she was doing: "Am I really lovable enough? Have you not told yourself that you must, that you wish to love me, hoodwinked yourself, decided to carry on with it through strength of character, as a *point d'honneur*, so to speak? Or are you just in love with love, loving an individual as unqualified for love as I am simply because I came on you bearing the standard of this all-conquering emotion at the right time?" He begged her to withdraw unless she was completely certain. Of his own feelings he had no doubt:

"You shall hold command over me completely, to the extent that I am in command of myself. I look forward with delight to all the manifestations of your will, and shall strive to behave as your complete property. You are so rich – a smile from you, an expression of satisfaction, that is so rewarding, so encouraging – one wants to do everything for your sake, invent new things, seek out what you have never known in order to win your approval. Oh, how I should like to be a different, a better man, to – serve you!"

It was not disappointment with marriage that was responsible for Bülow's nervous breakdown during their honeymoon in Klampenborg, but his utter inability to break with his past (he had once spent holidays in Klampenborg with Cosima). As usual, his illness had a psychosomatic cause, and his isolation from Bayreuth at the time of *Parsifal* – hurtful, however hard he strove to deny it – certainly provided a cause of this kind. On his return to Meiningen his condition became even worse, and he had to cancel all his public engagements. Marie found it impossible to continue with her own career as an actress. She longed, she wrote to her father on 24 September, to get him away from Germany and all his former associations.

In the Palazzo Vendramin, a large house on the Grand Canal in Venice, Wagner and his family occupied an apartment of some fifteen rooms on the mezzanine floor, overlooking the garden at the side. They arrived there on 16 September, bringing with them their personal servants, as well as a governess for the girls, Stein as Siegfried's tutor and Rubinstein. "His delight in Venice and our dwelling grows daily," Cosima wrote in her diary on 25 September, ". . . To watch the gondolas across the garden, 'flitting past like elves,' is for him the ultimate charm." They had a gondola for their exclusive use, the gondolier wore a livery of their own choosing, and sometimes Siegfried was allowed to propel the boat himself. Beside his architectural drawing, Siegfried had now developed a new interest: he had begun to write plays, mainly on historical subjects. Wagner was delighted. "In passing my father would peer into my notebook," Siegfried wrote in his reminiscences, "and would call out with a smile to my sisters: 'Quiet, children, don't disturb Fidi or he'll tumble from his Pegasus.'"

For the first time in his life Wagner had no major worries, real or imaginary, hanging over his head. The task of disseminating his works, both in Europe and abroad, had been taken over by Neumann, who, having now left Leipzig, was devoting all his attentions to that travelling production of the *Ring* which London had seen earlier in the year. At the beginning of September he embarked on a tour of Germany, transporting his company of 134 people (including an orchestra of 60 players) and all his scenery from town to town in a special train. His conductor was Seidl, and his leading singers included Heinrich and Therese Vogl, Georg Unger, Hedwig Reicher-Kindermann and Emil Scaria.

At the same time Neumann was considering the idea of building in Berlin a permanent theatre on the lines of the festival theatre in Bayreuth. Wagner was not averse to the plan, but he resisted all Neumann's efforts to acquire performing rights to *Parsifal*, with which he hoped to open the new theatre, if it ever came about (it did not). "*Parsifal* belongs exclusively to my Bayreuth theatre," Wagner wrote to him from Venice on 29 September. "It is of course true that this will fade out with my death; for who then will carry out my intentions is still a problem to me. Should my powers be exhausted before my life ends, and should I no longer be able to attend to these details, I should then have to think of some other plan for presenting my works to the world in as pure a form as possible. If by that time you have raised your Wagner opera company to a proper level and maintained it there by exclusive and better and better performances of my other works, I might then find it feasible to turn over to you my *Parsifal* for certain festival performances on stated occasions – and it is only to *you* and on these terms that I shall ever consign my *Parsifal*."

During the first tranquil days in Venice Wagner's health noticeably improved, though he could still become agitated and upset by any change in the prevailing pattern of his life. Stein's departure for family reasons on 15 October distressed him, not only because it meant that a new tutor must be found for Siegfried, but also because he had become deeply attached to the young man, and took a genuine interest in his writings. Rubinstein's departure on 22 October was less regretted than Stein's, but his ability to get on Wagner's nerves was inherited by Hausburg, who came to replace Stein temporarily as Siegfried's tutor until Glasenapp should be ready to take over.

Another cause of disturbance was a dispute with Batz, who, following a quarrel with Neumann over a production of *Tristan* in Leipzig the previous January, refused to hand over the royalties due to Wagner until the dispute was settled. Most distressing of all, however, was the news they received on 25 October: Gobineau, on his way to visit them, had died of a heart attack in Turin twelve days previously. "When one has at last encountered something," Wagner said to Cosima, "it slips like water through one's fingers."

His own heart began now to trouble him more severely, and "chest spasms" occurred with mounting frequency: no less than four on 10 November. The arrival of Liszt on 19 November brought a temporary raising of spirits. Liszt wrote to Marie Hohenlohe on 24 November: "Wagner lives in seclusion with his family in Venice; he abstains from either making calls or receiving callers. I shall try to copy him in this to the best of my ability, despite my lack of practice."

He did not altogether succeed, and before long the old jealousies that had previously marred his visits to them returned. They soon gave rise to an open quarrel between Wagner and Cosima. It began with a petty dispute whether or not Liszt was following his doctor's orders. "R. reproaches me for contradicting him," Cosima wrote in her diary on 30 November. "That arouses great annoyance in me, I angrily declare to R. that my entire efforts are always directed at not opposing him in anything, whereupon he jumps angrily out of bed with the remark that I obviously think I am virtue itself."

Her uncharacteristic display of anger towards him, for which she chided herself, was a sign of the strain she was under as she tried to maintain a fair balance between Wagner's desire for seclusion and Liszt's and Daniela's social inclinations. She eventually solved Daniela's difficulties by allowing her to spend most of her time at the Villa Malipiero, where Marie von Schleinitz was staying with her mother. Liszt, however, remained at the Palazzo Vendramin. Wagner strove to conceal his irritation by banter, but he frequently complained to Cosima of the unrest Liszt brought into his home. In addition, he disliked Liszt's latest piano compositions, finding in their dissonances evidence of "budding insanity". Cosima begged him to tell her father his opinion, "in the hope of preventing his going astray", but he decided to remain silent.

A friendly letter from King Ludwig, written on 26 October, had shown that his resentment over Wagner's reproach to him for "spurning" *Parsifal* was now forgotten. Wagner replied to the king in an equally amicable spirit on 18 November, accepting at last the explanation that it had been ill-health which prevented his attendance in Bayreuth. In his letter Wagner outlined his plan to present model performances of all his works from *Der Fliegende Holländer* onwards at the festival theatre, "for which I am allowing myself another ten years of good health, during which my son will come of age; he is the only person to whom I can entrust the spiritual and aesthetic preservation of my works, knowing no other to whom I could hand over my office." To make this possible, he said, he intended to present only *Parsifal* there for the next two years, believing this to be best fitted to provide the financial basis on which to extend the festival. As for the coming year, he begged Ludwig to tell him on which days he would be able to come to Bayreuth to see *Parsifal*: "How do I come to hope again? It almost seems to me that I am just persuading myself into hoping!"

Ludwig's letter of 26 November confirmed his feelings of scepticism. In the new tone of polite consideration they had adopted towards each other, he welcomed Wagner's future plans and assured him that the Munich opera would be at his disposal whenever he wanted it. As for *Parsifal*, he had been looking forward greatly to seeing it in Munich in the spring: "Now, however gently you allow it to show through, that no longer seems to be entirely to your liking. It is a great pity!"

Gross, who came to Venice with his wife on 6 December on a four-day visit to discuss the arrangements for next year's festival, brought the same message in a harsher form: the king, he had learnt in Munich, was insisting on seeing *Parsifal* there and not in Bayreuth. An angry outburst followed, but Cosima's suggestion that the king should be told the scenery was needed in Bayreuth in spring for repair and for rehearsals, and a performance in Munich would be possible only in the autumn of next year, calmed him down.

As a birthday gift for Cosima he had decided to conduct a perfor- mance of his Symphony in C Major, which had not been heard since its three original performances in Prague and Leipzig exactly fifty years ago. Though he was pleased with his youthful work (in style he placed it somewhere between Beethoven's first and second symphonies), he had decided, after the rediscovery of the lost parts and the reconstruction of the score by Seidl, not to publish it, and its performance in Venice was to be strictly private. It was intended as a surprise for Cosima, but he found it impossible to keep the secret from her, for she began to wonder why it was necessary for him to make daily visits to the music school, the Lyceo Marcello, whose orchestra had been put at his disposal for the perfor- mance. The activity of rehearsals restored his spirits: it did him good, he told Cosima on 17 December, to be conducting again. Though she had been let into the secret, Cosima was not allowed to attend rehearsals, but Wagner took Isolde and Siegfried with him, while Cosima remained at home with Eva, who was in bed with an undiagnosed illness.

For Siegfried, who had now begun his musical education in earnest under Hausburg's tuition, there were valuable lessons to be learnt from watching his father at work. "His method of conducting was dis- tinguished by its graphic simplicity and its great clarity," he wrote later in his reminiscences. "My father got his effects mainly through his eyes, which he repeatedly described as the most important means of imposing one's will. His emotional reactions were in consequence more restrained outwardly."

Joukowsky joined the family in Venice on 8 December, and on 18 December Humperdinck arrived to help with the rehearsals of the symphony, summoned by Wagner after Seidl, busy with Neumann's travelling theatre, had to decline his invitation. But on this very day, a Monday, just when a period of undisturbed contentment appeared to have been reached, the peace was abruptly shattered. A serious quarrel between Wagner and Cosima, certainly the most serious recorded in her diaries, began with Liszt, but chiefly concerned Bülow.

Liszt had gone out to dinner with a friend, taking Daniela with him. Their late return produced a jealous outburst from Wagner, who told Cosima that Liszt had already ruined his rehearsal, and his own influence over Daniela was being put in jeopardy. She wrote in her diary: "He says all this in the angriest of tones, pacing up and down! – Then he returns and loudly throws out the news which even now, after its harshness has been softened, I cannot bring myself to write down!" The news was that Bülow had had a relapse in Meiningen and had been sent to a mental institute. "I cannot stay with him any longer," Cosima wrote, "I flee to my room and see Hans before me, alone in that institution, and I feel like screaming, screaming to some god to help me!"

On the following evening Wagner, repenting his brutality, went to Eva's sickroom to apologise: "I have not the strength to respond to his expansive words, and I fear the effect his agitation may have on Eva; he goes off – in an ill humour, it seems to me. At table he says, and I feel only partly in fun, that I hate him; when I pick up his napkin, he says I do it only out of hate." The quarrel smouldered on all evening. His attempt to divert the conversation to Goethe's *Faust* failed to reconcile her. "We go to bed, after R. has made further complaints about the rehearsal. . . . I do not know why – I should have to ask life's daemons – but bitterness impelled me to say that no poet now means anything at all to me, that poetry seems to me like some wretched plaything. R. is very angry, accuses me of not understanding him; I immediately follow him into his room and beg his pardon, saying that perhaps, if he were to see inside my heart, he would excuse me. Very emotionally he tells me that I mean everything to him, that without me he is nothing. He says he came home from the rehearsal worn out, forced himself to read these two scenes [in Goethe's *Faust*] in order to shut out everything, all feeling, all suffering, and tell himself that the highest being is one transfigured through suffering, is myself! He asked himself, he says, whether he is a bad person, but he is not, and for several days he had kept this news to himself. I beg him for forgiveness and God for mercy! He calms down, goes to bed, falls asleep, while I lie and lie there with this dreadful picture which has haunted me ever since yesterday; at last sleep comes to me too!"

Better news of Bülow's condition helped the following day to relieve Cosima's distress. But their conflict remained for them both a deeply disturbing experience, centring as it did on the two men – Liszt and Bülow – who were always a threat to their emotional security. "At the start of the terrible night of Monday," Cosima wrote in her diary, "R. cried out from his bed, 'I hate all pianists – they are my Antichrist!'"

What in fact had happened to Bülow he himself described in a letter to a friend (Baroness D.) on 30 December: "It is only today that my poor brain – shattered like a 'shipwrecked' piano – has begun again to enjoy a few lucid moments since, a fortnight ago, I managed to injure my head rather severely – vertigo, fall on leaving a bath, etc. Do you know – and why should you not know – that it is almost a miracle that I have not been removed to a Bedlam of some kind? Still, what is so surprising about that? Did not my great deeds and gestures of the past summer provide the most characteristic signs of mental aberration? What then seemed acute has quite simply become chronic. . . . Music – impossible for months past. Fingers, eyes, memory, all play me false." He added a postscript: "Do not play *Parsifal*! My reading of it drove me 'insane' – or perhaps I was that already, ever since entering into this Capernaum of dissonance." However, by the end of January he was sufficiently restored to be able to conduct and play the piano at a concert in memory of Raff, whose death the previous July had greatly grieved him.

The performance of Wagner's symphony took place on Christmas Eve in the Teatro La Fenice. Two days earlier Cosima had been permitted to attend a rehearsal, on condition that she kept out of sight, and was touched by the thought that this "straightforward, courageous work", first performed in front of his mother fifty years previously, was now being played for her. Eva recovered from her illness in time for the performance, for which the audience was confined strictly to Cosima and the children (except for Blandine), Liszt, Joukowsky, Hausburg, the girls' reading companion (Mlle Corsani) and Count Contin, director of the Lyceo Marcello. Humperdinck was, as Wagner's assistant at the performance, also present. Following the symphony Wagner persuaded Liszt to play the piano for the benefit of the orchestra. "Towards 11 o'clock we ride home," Cosima wrote, "Venice transfigured in a blue light. The children enchanted with the evening, R. very content!"

Early in the new year Marie Dönhoff made her appearance in Venice and, though he was friendly towards her, all Wagner's dislike of society people burst out anew. He was particularly incensed when Makart's new portrait of her was put on display in his home, and people came at Liszt's invitation to inspect it. This was one more black mark against Liszt, who, Wagner remarked to Cosima, was like King Lear, "his acquaintances the 100 knights, and his arrangements the Learisms". Cosima's difficulties in maintaining the harmony of her home and dealing with Wagner's increasing irritability found expression in a letter to Marie von Schleinitz, ostensibly about Marie Dönhoff, who was seeking a divorce from her husband: "I hold the view that marriage is a monstrosity, unless husband and wife live for and in each other, whatever the sacrifices. A hell on earth, indeed one of the most terrible and vile of all inventions, as well as being the highest to which the human intellect can aspire amid life's inconstancies. It is so hard to imagine anybody, a man as well as a woman, who is capable or worthy of such absolute dedication, and a union to cope with the daily burdens of life demands such an expenditure of earnestness and gaiety, of emotion and prudence, that I find it awful to expect it from every couple. Certainly we cannot be too grateful to Luther for the possibility of dissolving a state which, if it is not with all its sufferings a noble one, is the most unworthy imaginable – for both partners. . . . I had some very painful experiences last month, and am regaining my balance only through the beseeching glances, the beseeching tones of my family – of all else I go in fear. Scarcely a day passes on which the old sorrow is not renewed and a new one comes to join it."

At this time Liszt composed his piano piece "La lugubre gondole", and later he came to look on it as a sort of premonition. There was, however, nothing in Wagner's condition to arouse thoughts of death: if his bouts of irritability and depression had become more frequent, they were as quickly replaced by outbreaks of gaiety. Siegfried related in his reminiscences an occasion on which he and his sisters saw their father, believing himself unobserved, dance "in the most expert and graceful way" the Scherzo movement of Beethoven's Seventh Symphony which Liszt was playing on the piano to Cosima and some friends. "One might have thought one was watching a youth of twenty," Siegfried commented. This, according to Cosima's diary, was on 10 January, the day on which she recorded Wagner's apology for having become such a burden on her with his rages, his depressions and his health problems. "He is also oppressed by the smallness of the rooms, he misses books and music, but when I suggest we return to Wahnfried, he cannot make up his mind to do so."

Part of his general vexation was connected with the difficulties Ludwig was causing through his obstinate refusal to come to Bayreuth to see *Parsifal*. Wagner made a final attempt to induce the king to change his mind by suggesting special performances for him alone in Bayreuth immediately after the public festival in the summer. In his letter to the king dated 10 January (but, according to Cosima, only completed the following day) he declared that only in his own theatre could he vouch for a performance worthy of *Parsifal* as he had conceived it. "Perhaps in saying this I am pronouncing a death sentence on myself and my whole artistic activity: for I must fear that all my suggestions and requests will be regarded as superfluous, even by him whom I call the master of my life. All the same, I know what I am asking: it is that for which this master took charge of my shattered life. So let him crown his work in the way he graciously raised me up: let him allow me to express my deepest reverence by laying the work that is my farewell to the world at his feet in the way I wish. I have suffered much to be in a position to do so."

Two days after that letter was sent off, Gross arrived in Venice, bringing a message from Munich: since an important exhibition was to be held there in August, could the festival performances in Bayreuth be confined to the month of July? To comply would mean that, instead of twenty performances spread over the two months as planned, only ten could be given, and there would be no time left to stage extra performances for the king. Wagner's immediate reaction was a threat to abandon the festival entirely, but in the end he agreed to the request: one ought, he told Cosima, to set the children an example of constancy.

On the day the decision to curtail the festival was made (13 January) Liszt at last left Venice. To some extent he had been aware of the tensions his presence had caused, but he felt no resentment against Wagner. "His bitter and ironic exclusiveness is related to his supremely absolute genius," he wrote to Marie Hohenlohe two days before his departure. "In such a most extraordinary case, to reproach him would be to make a mistake."

They parted on the best of terms, but it was with a sense of relief that Wagner and Cosima resumed their quiet life with the children, making local outings and spending their evenings reading or making music together. His German doctor in Venice, Friedrich Keppler, began a new treatment for his digestive troubles, involving daily massage and the use of a stomach tube, the last of which Wagner described humorously as an invasion of his personal rights. However, he endured it cheerfully, and maintained that the treatment was doing him good. On 21 January he set to work on his long-promised preface to Stein's forthcoming book *Helden und Welt (Heroes and the World)*, a series of imaginary dramatic dialogues which Stein had written since coming under Wagner's influence, and which had been read, mainly with approval, by both him and Cosima.

While Wagner was engaged in writing it, Cosima thought it wise, for fear of upsetting him, to withhold a letter in which Bürkel communicated King Ludwig's reply to his pleas about *Parsifal*: the king held to his decision to see it in Munich, but was willing to postpone the performance until 1884. When she did finally give the letter to him, his first feelings were of anger, then of relief that he would not have to trouble himself with special arrangements. "He copies out his article and then goes for a walk by himself, since I still have a cold," Cosima wrote in her diary on 30 January. "He returns home much delighted with the sight of the lively lanes, and observes that it is better for him to go out without me, however silly that sounds, but he is ashamed of his attacks when he is with me, the need to walk so slowly."

Levi came to Venice on 4 February to discuss the shortened summer festival, and he went with the family on Shrove Tuesday (6 February) to watch the carnival celebrations on St Mark's Square. Wagner, he wrote to his father, strode along with Isolde "with the sturdiness of a youth", and they did not return home until one in the morning. But the strain told on Wagner, and he spent a large part of the following two days in bed. During this time he went through his musical papers and discovered among them a neatly written melody which he had composed to be attached to *Parsifal* as a dedication page, but had then forgotten. "He declares, incidentally, that he will never make any use of these musical scraps," Cosima wrote in her diary on 9 February, but then immediately added: "In the gondola he tells me that he will still do his article about masculine and feminine, then write symphonies, but nothing more on the literary side, though he still intends to finish the biography."

On 12 February he and Cosima spent the evening reading Friedrich de la Motte-Fouqué's novel *Undine* together. "When I am already lying in bed," she wrote in her diary, "I hear him talking volubly and loudly; I get up and go into his room. 'I was talking to you,' he says, and embraces me tenderly and long. 'Once in 5,000 years it succeeds!' 'I was talking about Undine, the being who longed for a soul.' He goes to the piano, plays the mournful theme '*Rheingold, Rheingold*', continues with 'False and base all those who dwell above'. 'Extraordinary that I saw this so clearly at that time!' – And, as he is lying in bed, he says, 'I feel loving towards them, these subservient creatures of the deep, with all their yearning.'"

On the following morning, while Cosima was writing these lines, Wagner did some work on his essay "On the Womanly in the Human", which he had begun two days earlier.

Cosima came down to lunch at two o'clock, saying that Wagner was feeling unwell, and the family and Joukowsky began their meal without him. In the middle of their cheerful conversation Cosima's maid came in to say that Wagner was asking for her. "I shall never forget how my mother rushed out through the door," Siegfried wrote in his reminiscences. "It expressed all the force of emotional pain at its most violent, and she collided so heavily with the half-open door that it almost broke." While writing at his desk Wagner had suffered a heart attack, and this time there was no recovery. He died in Cosima's arms some time after three o'clock.

She stayed there holding him for the rest of the day and throughout the night. She had always hoped and believed that like Isolde she would be granted the blessing of dying with him, and only on the following afternoon was Dr Keppler able to persuade her to leave him and lie down in the adjoining room. She was still there, refusing to eat or to see anybody but her children, when Gross and his wife arrived, hastily summoned from Bayreuth. She consented to receive them, but all she said was: "I entrust the children to you." Otherwise she remained silent.

Gross attended to the funeral arrangements, and Dr Keppler conducted an autopsy, in which he established that both heart and stomach were enlarged, and that "massive accumulation of gases from stomach and intestines" had had a restrictive effect on the heart, leading finally to a rupture of the right ventricle. "It cannot be doubted," he added, "that the innumerable psychical agitations to which Wagner was daily exposed on account of his particular mental outlook . . . contributed much to his unfortunate end."

On 17 February the coffin was conveyed by gondola to the railway station. Before it was closed, Cosima cut off her hair and laid it on Wagner's body. Then, with her children and Gross and his wife, she boarded the train that was to bear him to Bayreuth. Liszt, who received the news of Wagner's death in Budapest, offered to return to Venice to accompany her, but she declined. She gave no attention to the many people who were assembled at the station to pay their last respects, nor, when the train arrived at the German border, did she receive Bürkel, who came bearing a letter from the king, though she accepted the letter from Daniela's hands. She remained speechless and out of sight during the mourning ceremony at the railway station in Munich and, when the train arrived at midnight in Bayreuth, entered the waiting carriage with her children, oblivious of the surrounding crowds. She did not even attend the funeral ceremony at Wahnfried as the coffin was carried by Muncker, Feustel, Gross, Wolzogen, Seidl, Joukowsky, Wilhelmj, Porges, Levi, Richter, Standhartner and Niemann to the grave at the bottom of the garden. Only after they had left did she emerge from the house with Daniela, Isolde, Eva and Siegfried (Blandine, expecting her first child, had been unable to come) to watch silently as the tomb was sealed.

In his letter of condolence to her King Ludwig wrote: "May the Almighty grant you strength to bear this terrible trial and *preserve* you for your children, who so greatly need their mother." And Bülow, on whom the news of Wagner's death had a shattering effect, sent Cosima a telegram when he heard of her desire to follow him: "*Soeur, il faut vivre*." These were the truths she now at last acknowledged. Abandoning the romantic dream of a *Liebestod*, she accepted the task of living, not only for the children, but for the memory of the man to whom, for the past fourteen years, she had dedicated her whole existence. He had not known, up to the end of his life, to whom he could entrust the heritage of Bayreuth. Yet all the time that person had been standing at his side.

Bibliography

(Author's note: This bibliography is confined to books, articles and letters of which direct use has been made in the preparation of my book.)

Barth, Herbert, Dietrich Mack and Egon Voss (Eds.): *Wagner, sein Leben und seine Welt in zeitgenössischen Bildern und Texten* (Universal Edition, Vienna, 1975). English edition: *Wagner: A Documentary Study*, trans. P. R. J. Ford and Mary Whittall (Thames & Hudson, London, 1975)

Bülow, Marie von: *Hans von Bülow in Leben und Wort* (Engelhorn Verlag, Stuttgart, 1925)

Bülow, Marie von (Ed.): *Hans von Bülow: Briefe und Schriften*, 8 vols (Breitkopf & Härtel, Leipzig, 1895–1908)

Burne-Jones, G.: *Memorials of Edward Burne-Jones* (Macmillan, London, 1904)

Clark, Ronald W.: *The Royal Albert Hall* (Hamish Hamilton, London, 1958)

Cornelius, Carl Maria (Ed.): *Peter Cornelius: Ausgewählte Briefe*, 2 vols (Breitkopf & Härtel, Leipzig, 1904)

Du Moulin Eckart, Graf Richard: *Cosima Wagner: Ein Lebens- und Charakterbild*, 2 vols (Drei Masken Verlag, Munich, 1929–31)

Du Moulin Eckart, Richard Graf (Ed.): *Hans von Bülow: Neue Briefe* (Drei Masken Verlag, Munich, 1927)

Eger, Manfred: *Der Briefwechsel Richard und Cosima Wagner* (The Letters of Richard and Cosima Wagner) (Programmes of the Bayreuth Festival 1979, *Das Rheingold* and *Die Walküre*)

Ellis, W. Ashton (Ed.): *Letters of Richard Wagner to Emil Heckel* (Grant Richards, London, 1899)

Fehr, Max: *Richard Wagners Schweizer Zeit*, 2 vols (Verlag H. R. Sauerländer, Aarau, 1953)

Förster-Nietzsche, E. (Ed.): *The Nietzsche-Wagner Correspondence*, trans. Caroline V. Kerr (Duckworth, London, 1922)

Fricke, Richard: *Bayreuth vor dreissig Jahren* (Bertling, Dresden, 1906)

Gautier, Judith: *Le troisième rang du collier* (Paris, 1909)

Geck, Martin: *Die Bildnisse Richard Wagners* (Prestel Verlag, Munich, 1970)

Glasenapp, Carl Friedrich: *Das Leben Richard Wagners*, 6 vols (Leipzig, 1905–11)

Gregor-Dellin, Martin: *Wagner Chronik* (Carl Hanser Verlag, Munich, 1972)

Guichard, Léon (Ed.): *Richard et Cosima Wagner: Lettres à Judith Gautier* (Gallimard, Paris, 1964)

Hacker, Rupert (Ed.): *Ludwig II von Bayern in Augenzeugenberichten* (Karl Rauch Verlag, Düsseldorf, 1966)

Haight, Gordon S.: *George Eliot* (Clarendon Press, Oxford, 1968)

Hey, Julius: *Richard Wagner als Vortragsmeister* (Breitkopf & Härtel, Leipzig, 1911)

Hueffer, Francis: *Half a Century of Music in England* (Chapman & Hall, London, 1889)

Janz, Curt Paul: *Friedrich Nietzsche*, 3 vols (Carl Hanser Verlag, Munich, 1978–79)

Jerger, Wilhelm (Ed.): *Wagner-Nietzsches Briefwechsel während des Tribschener Idylls* (Alfred Scherz Verlag, Bern, 1951)

Kaiser, Hermann: *Der Bühnenmeister Carl Brandt und Richard Wagner* (Eduard Roether Verlag, Darmstadt, 1968)

Kapp, Julius: *Richard Wagner und Franz Liszt: Eine Freundschaft* (Schuster & Loeffler, Berlin, 1908)

Karpath, Ludwig (Ed.): *Richard Wagner: Briefe an Hans Richter* (Zsolnay Verlag, Berlin, 1924)

Kietz, Gustav Adolph: *Richard Wagner in den Jahren 1842–1849 und 1873–1875* (Reissner Verlag, Dresden, 1905)

Kloss, Erich (Ed.): *Richard Wagner an seine Künstler* (Schuster & Loeffler, Berlin, 1908)

La Mara (Ed.): *Briefwechsel zwischen Franz Liszt und Hans von Bülow* (Breitkopf & Härtel, Leipzig, 1898)

La Mara (Ed.): *Marie von Mouchanoff-Kalergis in Briefen an ihre Tochter* (Leipzig, 1907)

Levi, Hermann: *An seinen Vater: unveröffentlichte Briefe aus Bayreuth von 1875–1889* (Letters to his father) (Programme of Bayreuth Festival 1959, *Parsifal*)

Liepmann, Klaus: *Wagner's Proposal to America* (High Fidelity Magazine, Great Barrington, Mass., December 1975)

Meysenbug, Malwida von: *Memoiren einer Idealistin*, 3 vols (Schuster & Loeffler, Berlin, 1904)

Millenkovich-Morold, Max: *Cosima Wagner* (Reclam, Leipzig, 1937)

Neumann, Angelo: *Erinnerungen an Richard Wagner* (Leipzig, 1907). English edition: *Personal Recollections of Wagner*, trans. Edith Livermore (Constable, London, 1909)

Newman, Ernest: *The Life of Richard Wagner*, 4 vols (Knopf, New York, 1960)

Nietzsche, Friedrich: *Nietzsche Briefwechsel: Kritische Ausgabe*, ed. Giorgio Colli and Mazzino Montinari, vol. 2 (Walter du Gruyter, Berlin, 1977)

Porges, Heinrich: *Die Bühnenproben zu den Bayreuther Festspielen des Jahres 1876* (Schmeitzner, Chemnitz, 1881). English edition: *Wagner Rehearsing the Ring*, trans. Robert L. Jacobs (Cambridge University Press, 1982)

Schemann, Ludwig: *Hans von Bülow im Lichte der Wahrheit* (Bosse Verlag, Regensburg, 1935)

Scholz, Hans (Ed.): *Richard Wagner an Mathilde Maier* (Verlag Theodor Weicher, Leipzig, 1930)

Semper, Manfred: *Das Münchener Festspielhaus: Gottfried Semper und Richard Wagner* (Kloss Verlag, Hamburg, 1906)

Shaw, Bernard: *How to Become a Musical Critic*, ed. Dan H. Laurence (Hart-Davis, London, 1960)

Sitwell, Sacheverell: *Liszt* (Cassell, London, 1955)

Strecker, Ludwig: *Richard Wagner als Verlagsgefährte* (Schott, Mainz, 1951)

Strobel, Otto: *Wie Wagner nach Bayreuth kam und dort Bürger wurde* (Bayreuther Festspielführer 1939)

Strobel, Otto (Ed.): *König Ludwig II und Richard Wagner: Briefwechsel*, 5 vols (G. Braun Verlag, Karlsruhe, 1936–39)

Thierbach, Erhart (Ed.): *Die Briefe Cosima Wagners an Friedrich Nietzsche* (Nietzsche-Archiv, Weimar, 1938)

Wagner, Cosima: *Die Tagebücher*, ed. Martin Gregor-Dellin and Dietrich Mack, 2 vols (Piper, Munich, 1976–77). English edition: *Cosima Wagner's Diaries*, trans. Geoffrey Skelton, 2 vols (Harcourt Brace, New York, and Collins, London, 1978 and 1980)

Wagner, Richard: *Bayreuther Briefe, 1871–83* (Schuster & Loeffler, Berlin, 1907)

Wagner, Richard: *Das braune Buch*, ed. Joachim Bergfeld (Atlantis Verlag, Zurich, 1975). English edition: *The Diary of Richard Wagner: The Brown Book*, trans. George Bird (Gollancz, London, 1980, and Cambridge University Press, New York, 1981)

Wagner, Richard: *Briefe an Hans von Bülow* (Diederichs, Jena, 1916)

Wagner, Richard: *Gesammelte Schriften und Dichtungen*, 10 vols (Fritzsch, Leipzig, 1888)

Wagner, Richard: *Mein Leben*, ed. Martin Gregor-Dellin, 2 vols (List Verlag, Munich, 1969)

Wagner, Siegfried: *Erinnerungen* (Engelhorn Verlag, Stuttgart, 1923)

Waldberg, Max Freiherr von (Ed.): *Cosima Wagners Briefe an ihre Tochter Daniela* (J. G. Cotta'sche Buchhandlung Nachfolger, Stuttgart, 1933)

Westernhagen, Curt von: *Die Entstehung des "Ring"* (Atlantis Verlag, Zurich, 1973). English edition: *The Forging of the "Ring"*, trans.

Arnold and Mary Whittall (Cambridge University Press, Cambridge, 1976)

Wille, Eliza: *Fünfzehn Briefe Richard Wagners mit Erinnerungen und Erläuterungen* (Verlag der Corona, Zurich, 1935)

Das Bayreuther Festspielbuch 1951 (Niehrenheim, Bayreuth)

Documents in manuscript

Bülow, Daniela von: letter to Hans von Bülow from Acireale, 7 April 1882

Bülow, Hans von: letter to Cosima von Bülow from Munich, 17 June 1869

Bülow, Hans von: letter to Cosima Wagner from Baden, 4 August 1878

Bülow, Hans von: letter to his daughter Daniela from Meiningen, 3 April 1882

Burne-Jones, Edward: letter to Cosima Wagner from London, undated (1877)

Lewes, George Henry: letter to Cosima Wagner from Witley, 19 June 1877

Rubinstein, Josef: letter to unknown correspondent (with biographical details), July 1876

Stocker, Verena: letter to Cosima Wagner with reminiscences of Wagner (undated)

Voltz, Karl, and Batz, Karl: financial statements, 1872–83

Wagner, Cosima: letter to Hans Richter from Bayreuth, 25 August 1875

Wagner, Cosima: letter to her children from London, 18 May 1877

Wagner, Cosima: account of Wagner's dealings with Voltz and Batz, 1882

Wagner, Richard: letter to Dr Landgraf from Bad Ems, 16 June 1877

All above in Wagner Archives in Bayreuth

Wagner, Richard: extracts from letters to Cosima concerning their daughter Eva, 1867–68 (copied by Eva Chamberlain-Wagner)

Above in Richard Wagner Museum, Lucerne (Tribschen)

INDEX

Unless otherwise stated, all literary and musical works listed by title are by Richard Wagner